What is Madness?

DARIAN LEADER

First published by Hamish Hamilton 2011
Published in Penguin Books 2012

Copyright © Darian Leader, 2011
All rights reserved

The moral right of the author has been asserted

Typeset by [illegible], Falkirk, Stirlingshire
Printed in England by Clays Ltd, St Ives plc

Except in the United States of America, this book is sold
subject to the condition that it shall not, by way of trade or otherwise,
be lent, re-sold, hired out, or otherwise circulated without the publisher's
prior consent in any form of binding or cover other than that in
which it is published and without a similar condition including this
condition being imposed on the subsequent purchaser.

PENGUIN BOOKS

Published by the Penguin Group
Penguin Books Ltd, 80 Strand, London WC2R ORL, England
Penguin Group (USA) Inc., 375 Hudson Street, New York, New York 10014, USA
Penguin Group (Canada), 90 Eglinton Avenue East, Suite 700, Toronto, Ontario, Canada M4P 2Y3
(a division of Pearson Penguin Canada Inc.)
Penguin Ireland, 25 St Stephen's Green, Dublin 2, Ireland
(a division of Penguin Books Ltd)
Penguin Group (Australia), 707 Collins Street, Melbourne, Victoria 3008, Australia
(a division of Pearson Australia Group Pty Ltd)
Penguin Books India Pvt Ltd, 11 Community Centre,
Panchsheel Park, New Delhi – 110 017, India
Penguin Group (NZ), 67 Apollo Drive, Rosedale, Auckland 0632, New Zealand
(a division of Pearson New Zealand Ltd)
Penguin Books (South Africa) (Pty) Ltd, Block D, Rosebank Office Park,
181 Jan Smuts Avenue, Parktown North, Gauteng 2193, South Africa

Penguin Books Ltd, Registered Offices: 80 Strand, London WC2R ORL, England

www.penguin.com

ISBN: 978-0-141-04735-5

www.greenpenguin.co.uk

MIX
Paper from
responsible sources
FSC   FSC™ C018179

Penguin Books is committed to a sustainable
future for our business, our readers and our planet.
This book is made from Forest Stewardship
Council™ certified paper.

ALWAYS LEARNING   **PEARSON**

PENGUIN BOOKS

WHAT IS MADNESS?

Darian Leader is a psychoanalyst practising in London. He is a member of the Centre for Freudian Analysis and Research and of The College of Psychoanalysts – UK. He is the author of *Why do women write more letters than they post?*, *Promises lovers make when it gets late*, *Freud's Footnotes*, *Stealing the Mona Lisa* and *The New Black: Mourning, Melancholia and Depression*, and co-author, with David Corfield, of *Why Do People Get Ill?* He is an honorary visiting professor at the School of Human and Life Sciences at Roehampton University.

For M again

Contents

Introduction

Many years ago, when I was still a student, I started weekly voluntary work in a therapeutic community. I had my head full of psychoanalysis, and wanted to understand more about the strange phenomena of psychosis: the hallucinations, delusions and language disturbances that I had read about yet never experienced at first hand. Most of the people I met were rather calm and showed few signs of being 'crazy'. Long-term medication had worn them down, and they had settled into their own quiet routines. One man, however, was eager to talk, and we would spend many hours discussing philosophy, politics and current affairs. He was articulate, lucid and extremely intelligent, and it mystified me to learn that he had spent the last few years in psychiatric hospitals. Chatting with him, he seemed no more or less disturbed than the student friends I would meet with after work at the community.

As our conversations continued, I asked a couple of the staff members why he was living in a therapeutic community and why he was medicated. The wry smiles I received in reply suggested that there was something obvious I had missed, some glaring fact that had not registered on my youthful radar. And indeed, it was true. Several months later, during the course of one of our chats, he referred to a country I had not heard of. His surprise at my ignorance was followed by enlightenment: he explained that he lived not in England but in Xamara, a place populated by wild animals and a legion of exotic gods. He described its geography, its history and its infrastructure. Everything had been named and classified, like the kingdoms of Angria and Gondal invented by the Brontë sisters during their childhood.

For him, there was no incompatibility between his role as a protagonist in the saga of Xamara and his everyday life and chores at the community. Describing it, there was no excitement in his voice, no accent of emotion, no change of tone, as if it were simply one further fact of his existence. It was this continuity in his voice that really struck me: there was no sign or marker in his speech that we were leaving the territory of some shared reality to enter a private world. It was as if everything were the same, and our subsequent conversations bore no trace of a secret initiation or inclusion into his confidence. Life just continued as before.

How could it be, I wondered, that delusion and everyday life could be so seamlessly woven together? How could one inhabit two apparently different places at the same time as if there were no barrier between them? And even if living in Xamara seemed crazy, why should it require a medical regime or a hospitalization? It hurt no one, and caused no turbulence in that person's life. These are questions that I still ask, and in this book I have tried to explore some of the links between madness and normal life. Are delusion and sanity to be rigidly separated or, on the contrary, could the former be not only consistent with but even a condition of the latter?

These are not abstract, intellectual questions, and they have a real bearing on the way in which psychosis is treated in society today. Our attitudes to madness will shape our response to it, in terms of both our everyday interactions and in the choice of therapies that are available. Yet there has been a marked absence of dialogue between traditions here. There are theories and therapies of madness that have been developed around the world for at least half a century, yet which are more or less unknown outside a very narrow professional field. They provide fascinating and powerful tools for understanding the experience of madness and explaining why and how it can come about. They also offer a rich set of possibilities for therapy and for thinking about how a psychosis can stabilize. Although we may like to think that knowledge is cumulative and unified, especially in the age of the Internet, this is far from the case. There is a superficial and troubling confidence in what advertises itself as 'up to date' research, as if an article published in a fancy journal in 2010 were more valuable than one written in a now-forgotten medical review a hundred years earlier that we can access only in some dusty archive.

The work that I am going to focus on comes out of the Continental tradition in psychiatry. Late-nineteenth- and early-twentieth-century psychiatrists have been much maligned for their prejudices on issues such as hereditary, constitution and mental degeneracy, yet many of them took the time to listen to their patients and developed theories of madness that were faithful to what they learned from their clinic. The absence of long-term drug treatments made it possible to study how a person whose life had been torn apart by psychosis could find a new equilibrium over time. Exploring what psychiatrists called these 'restitution mechanisms', the pathways back into life, formed a central part of this research, and we have much to learn from it today.

When the young medical student Jacques Lacan began his psychiatric training in the Paris of the 1920s, this is the culture in which his own ideas began to grow. Today, Lacanian clinical work with psychosis takes place around the world, especially in France, Belgium, Spain, Italy and the Latin American countries, and, increasingly, in the UK. There is a flourishing culture of journals, books, newsletters, conferences, courses and lectures all devoted to exploring different aspects of madness. To date, several thousand case histories of work with psychotic subjects have been published by Lacanian clinicians. Yet sadly, outside of the field itself, most psychiatrists, psychologists and mental health workers will never have come across any of this research.

There are many reasons for this. It is often assumed that psychoanalytic work with madness means classical psychoanalysis: the patient lies on the couch and free associates and the analyst makes interpretations about their childhood. Aside from the fact that most psychoanalysis isn't like that anyway, the real confusion is about the difference between theories and techniques. A psychoanalytic theory of psychosis doesn't mean that psychoanalysis will – or even should – take place. Rather, it means that analytic ideas can be used to inspire other kinds of work, other treatments that are tailored to the singularity of each individual patient. This fact has been clear to clinicians for the last hundred years, yet it continues to generate misunderstandings and confusions, perhaps due to the deep-rooted prejudices against – and within – psychoanalysis itself.

The attention to the uniqueness of each patient that the psychoanalytic approach involves is all the more important now, as we live in a society that has less and less space for the detail and value of individual lives. Despite the ubiquitous lip service to respecting difference and diversity, people today are coerced more than ever to think in uniform ways, from the nursery to the corridors of professional life. We see this reflected in the mental health world, where treatment is often considered an almost mechanized technique to be applied to a passive patient, rather than as a joint collaborative work, where each party has responsibilities. There is increasing pressure today to see mental health services as a kind of garage, where people are rehabilitated and sent back to their jobs – and perhaps to their families – as soon as possible.

The psychotic subject has become less a person to be listened to than an object to be treated. The patient's specificity and life story are often just airbrushed away. Where old psychiatry books were once filled with the reported speech of patients, today all one sees are statistics and pseudo-mathematical diagrams. Studies hardly ever mention what happens in unique cases, but present figures where the cases have been aggregated together. We never find out, for example, why one individual responded to some treatment and what exactly their response was; instead we get the statistics of what percentage of participants responded or failed to respond. The individual has vanished.

These are facts of contemporary discourse, and not just of psychiatry, yet one might have hoped that it would be precisely psychiatry that would have offered something different here. Despite the warnings of progressive psychiatrists over the years and the anti-psychiatry movements of the 1960s and 1970s, psychosis is still too often equated with the ways in which some people fail to fit the norms of society. As the pioneering clinician Marguerite Sechehaye pointed out many years ago, 'When we try to build a bridge between the schizophrenic and ourselves, it is often with the idea of leading him back to reality – our own – and to our own norm. He feels it and naturally turns away from this intrusion.' Today's premium is set on conventional adjustment to social norms, even if this means that things will not go well in the long run for the individual.

We can see this at the most basic level of our culture, in primary- and secondary-school education, where the formula of multiple choice has been replacing that of the child's original response. Rather than encouraging children to think for themselves and elaborate an answer, multiple choice simply proposes two or three answers that the child must then choose between. This means, of course, that children learn that there is a 'right answer' that someone else knows, and that their own constructions are discouraged. The key to success is figuring out what someone else wants to hear, rather than attempting an authentic solution oneself. No wonder that social commentators describe our times as an era of the 'false self'.

We have moved so far away in the last fifty or sixty years from a culture of inquiry, open-mindedness and tolerance that comparing the texts of the clinicians who worked with psychosis in the 1950s and 1960s with those of today is astonishing. Many contemporary authors write as if the problems of madness have just been solved by genetic or neurological research: psychosis is a brain disease and drugs will cure it. There are of course notable exceptions – and in particular the work of many psychiatrists and mental health workers in the Scandinavian countries – yet the general situation is quite miserable. A pseudo-scientific emphasis on measurable outcomes and visible 'results' has replaced careful, long-term work that gives a dignity to each individual patient.

Two American psychologists who have continued the old tradition of psychotherapy of psychosis compare their efforts with Dr Seuss's Horton. This sympathetic elephant can hear the inhabitants of a microscopic world contained on a speck of dust, yet no one else in the jungle believes him. He knows about their plight and the impending disaster that they face, yet cannot make anyone else listen. Horton's endeavour to save them is solitary and made even more difficult by the lack of support from his macroscopic friends, who do their best to hamper his efforts. Anyone working in the mental health field who favours the psychotherapeutic approach will recognize the analogy immediately: the obsession with predetermined outcomes, surface behaviour and 'normalization' makes alternative views seem far-fetched and implausible.

I hope that the ideas set out in this book will generate some dialogue around a set of questions that, after all, concern all of us. Different traditions need to listen to each other, in the same way that

Phillippe Pinel, often praised with humanizing psychiatry in the eighteenth and early nineteenth century, listened not only to his patients and his Continental colleagues, but also to William Tuke and his co-workers at the York Retreat in England. These Quakers favoured humane treatment, with small institutions and an emphasis on relations between people as opposed to medicalizing interventions. They urged a tempering of the passion to 'cure' and a critique of the 'cult of curability'. Tuke was opposed to the use of restraints and punishments, and his work, taken up by Pinel and others, would lead eventually to the demise of the most barbarous techniques in psychiatry in many countries.

Although this cruelty perhaps seems absent today, violence towards psychotic subjects has taken a different form. Later historians of psychiatry have been critical of Pinel and Tuke, arguing that restraint simply moved from the outside to the inside, in the form of techniques of moral management and suggestion. If the use of external force and restraint was diminished, violence was still present in the imposition of a worldview. The clinician who attempts to graft his own value system and view of normality on to the patient becomes like the colonizer who seeks to educate the natives, no doubt for their own good. Whether the system is secular and educative or religious, it still bulldozes away the culture and history of the person it purports to help.

Not long ago one of my patients was hospitalized during a manic episode. When I arrived at the ward, a large security guard was sitting on top of her, while a nurse attempted to administer an injection. Since being forcibly restrained was one of the most devastating aspects of her childhood history, this situation was not a happy one for her and she resisted most vigorously. This led to even greater physical pressure, yet the brutality of the scene continued after her sedation in a distinct but no less significant way.

The checklist and interviews she had to go through after sedation gave her little room to speak about what had happened. There was no interest in the detail of what had precipitated her episode. Instead, she described how she was forced into a set of concepts and categories that were alien to her, like the protagonist in Sarah Kane's *4:48*

Psychosis, whose fury grows as her doctor refuses to go beyond the question of whether her act of self-harm provided relief or not. My patient was told how her behaviour was incorrect, and how she needed to learn to think differently and to see herself as a person with an illness requiring chemical treatment so she could be 'normal' again. And she had to have a diagnostic label, a stamp on her that would remain inscribed not only in her medical records but also in her mind for the rest of her life.

However valid we might believe such conceptions of illness and health to be, we must surely take seriously the inner life and beliefs of each person, and avoid imposing our worldview on them. This is the difference between mental hygiene – in which we know what is best in advance for the patient – and psychotherapy – in which we don't. It is easy to miss the violence at play here, yet it is present each time we try to crush a patient's belief system by imposing a new system of values and policies on them. We could contrast this with an approach that looks not for the errors but for the truth in each person's relation to the world, and the effort to mobilize what is particular to each person's story to help them to engage once again with life: not to adapt them to our reality, but to learn what their own reality consists of, and how this can be of use to them.

A word on vocabulary and concepts. I refer to 'madness' and 'psychosis' throughout this book, using the terms interchangeably. I don't hold a relativist view – that madness is just what doesn't fit social norms – for reasons that will become clear in later chapters. Recognizing that there is such a thing as psychosis, however, does not mean that we need to buy into the discourse of mental health and illness. Although many people experience unbearable levels of suffering, this does not make them 'mentally ill', as there is simply no such thing as mental health. The more we explore each individual case, the more we find that the seemingly 'healthy' person may have delusional beliefs or symptoms that generate no conflict in their lives and hence attract no attention. Each of us faces problems that we tackle in our own unique ways, and what is labelled mental illness may in fact, as we shall see, be an effort to respond to and elaborate these difficulties. Using such labels not only entrenches the false dichotomy of health and illness, but also eclipses the creative, positive aspect of psychotic phenomena.

I would like to thank several friends and colleagues for their kind and various contributions to this book: Josh Appignanesi, Chloe Aridjis, Devorah Baum, Sadie Coles, John Forrester, Anouchka Grose, Andrew Hodgkiss, Richard House, Ruiz Karu, Peter Owen, Colette Sepel, Christos Tombras and Lindsay Watson. In Paris, I learned about psychosis from Éric Laurent and Colette Soler, and their psychoanalytic approaches have informed much of this book. As ever, Geneviève Morel's work has inspired me to question received wisdom and to link theoretical and clinical questions as closely as possible. Jay Watts was indefatigable in her endeavours to balance and critique my Lacanian views, and to broaden my horizons. Astrid Gessert, Sophie Pathan and Pat Blackett gave me invaluable help with research, and everyone at Hamish Hamilton has made the publication process a smooth one: thanks especially to Sarah Coward, Anna Kelly and Anna Ridley. Simon Prosser was once again a perfect editor, both critical and supportive, and I am especially grateful to him for his insights and suggestions. My agent, Tracy Bohan at Wylie, has also helped me consistently with her encouragement and advice. Last but never least, thanks to my psychotic patients for everything they have taught me. I hope that the book remains faithful to their experience, and that they can hear their voices within it.

1.   Quiet Madness

Whether it's *One Flew Over the Cuckoo's Nest*, *Girl Interrupted* or *A Beautiful Mind*, why is madness always made so visible, so tangible, so audible? People talk to imaginary companions, they foam at the mouth, they have terrifying hallucinations, they blabber incessantly, they rant and rave about a plot against them. Generally, they are depicted either as incredibly clever or incredibly stupid, as genius or brute, yet with little in between. There is no doubt that madness is sometimes accompanied by striking symptomology, but what about the case of the man who calmly goes about his business and family life, one day goes to work, does his job impeccably, then goes to a public place, pulls out a gun and shoots some public figure? There is nothing noticeably abnormal about their behaviour until that moment. They may in fact have been a model citizen, responsible, respectable and even-tempered. But, in the time preceding their homicidal act, could we really say that they were not mad? Surely it invites us to think about those instances of madness that are compatible with normal life. This is a quiet, contained madness, until the moment it erupts in the act of violence.

But what if the act of violence never came? What if, in our example, the man just carried on with his daily life? If there was madness before the act, what if it just continued in its quiet way, bothering no one, drawing no attention to itself. If madness and normality are indeed compatible, would that person be any more mad whether they had pulled the trigger or not? What if nothing of any note had occurred, and they had just pursued their daily routines and activities. Perhaps they might have taken up some hobby at retirement – a piece of historical research, a genealogical investigation, the study of a science – or started writing – letters, notebooks, a novel. This would be a normal life by all accounts, yet would it be any less mad than its more visible, spectacular shadow?

The fact that newspaper reports of 'mental illness' so often associate it with violent crime mean that dramatic outbursts become almost
what we expect madness to be about. Mental health campaigners
have worked long and hard to challenge such associations, yet they
continue to shape popular perceptions of psychosis. Although the
chances of being randomly attacked by a so-called 'paranoid schizophrenic' are infinitely less than those of being set upon by a gang of
young white males at pub closing time, it is the former stories and
not the latter that make the news. Perhaps, at some level, we not only
expect this from madness but actually want it, as if to externalize the
latent feelings of violence we all harbour within ourselves.

When the great nineteenth- and early-twentieth-century psychiatrists began their explorations of madness, they focused first of all on
the visible, attention-grabbing symptoms. They studied the acts of
violence, the hallucinations, the delusions, mood swings and extreme,
acute passions that could convulse a human life. They tried to classify
these phenomena, dividing up disorders, creating new diagnostic
entities, searching for the details that would allow a taxonomy. But
soon enough, they found that the most obvious, socially disruptive
symptoms could not be used exclusively to define the forms that madness could take.

Almost every major author in this period who made claims about
the defining course of their favourite diagnoses – dementia praecox,
schizophrenia, chronic hallucinatory psychosis – would then gradually admit that they had been hasty and that not all cases fitted the
pattern. Progressively, they found that the initial features used to
make the diagnosis and which attracted attention could mutate,
transform or even disappear. A bizarre thought disorder, for example,
might settle into a picture of social integration and cohesion. Terrifying hallucinations might, over time, fade away, and a rhythm of
normality be established. Someone might complain of persecutors,
yet later on would barely mention them. An acute feeling of internal
deadness could coexist with an uneventful working life and a position of social responsibility within one's community.

An even greater number of cases would simply never come to the attention of psychiatrists. These were the discreet psychoses that had always managed to fit in well with society, never exploding into spectacular symptomology, never disintegrating into breakdown or crisis. Being psychotic would not mean that one's psychosis would actually trigger, in the sense of a sudden detonation apparent to both the person and those around them. A popular pre-war psychiatric textbook could state categorically that: 'Most paranoiacs will go through life without ever developing psychosis.' And Eugen Bleuler, often credited with first theorizing and popularizing the diagnostic category of schizophrenia, could conclude after many years of research that the most common form of schizophrenia was in fact the latent variety, the kind that never became visible as madness. He added that there was ultimately no clinical sign that could exclude the diagnosis of schizophrenia, a suggestion that shocked many of his readers and would no doubt shock many today.

Bleuler's view, as one psychiatrist put it, broke 'the equilibrium and harmony of psychiatric concepts'. It meant that there was no test that could prove that someone was not schizophrenic: not the kind of schizophrenic whose actions and speech attract attention, but the quiet, discreet kind that Bleuler and many of his colleagues would study. As the schizophrenia researcher Silvano Arieti could conclude, reviewing studies in his field after more than three decades, 'Typical psychotics who are not under treatment do not seem to know that there is anything wrong with them.' This subtle, reserved madness has been called 'white psychosis', 'normal psychosis', 'lucid psychosis', 'everyday psychosis', 'private psychosis' and 'ordinary psychosis'.

Recognizing the prevalence of this kind of psychosis and studying its structure is especially important today, for a number of reasons. It can not only help in the effort to destigmatize madness, by weakening the equation with extravagant and dangerous behaviour, but, once we realize that people can *be* mad without *going* mad, and live perfectly normal lives, this will have significant consequences when it comes to helping those whose madness has indeed detonated. If we can understand what has allowed someone to remain stable and avoid the most shattering and painful symptoms of psychosis, we can use what we learn to think about directions for work with those whose madness has, in fact, triggered.

—

Early in the twentieth century, the French psychiatrists Paul Sérieux and Joseph Capgras reviewed the massive literature on quiet madness. The psychotic subject could be well adapted to their milieu, showing no confusion or intellectual impairment, no hallucinations, no euphorias, no depressions. Their emotional lives could seem normal and their language clear, precise and logical. These cases showed 'the strange association of reason and madness', with a central delusional idea that might not seem extravagant or even unrealistic. The person would not display any manifest oddities, yet certain categories of thought would be ruled out. There would be blank spots in that person's consciousness, areas where information could not be assimilated.

Such psychotic subjects were like 'specialists', who saw the world in terms of their primary preoccupation. They could function perfectly well in everyday life, and those around them might never suspect that anything were remotely out of the ordinary. Indeed, Sérieux and Capgras even ask, at one point in their study, if the kind of delusions they were studying should be classified as 'mental illness'. The person might complain of some injustice from their superiors, someone of humble birth might try to prove their connection to a titled family, or one partner might accuse their spouse of immoral behaviour. Generally, everything could be made to fit one fixed idea, based on a false premise. But, after this, the person's reasoning was watertight. There would never be any appeal to supernatural powers, just good arguments using what was not inherently impossible.

The psychoanalyst Piera Aulagnier discusses the case of a patient who was by all accounts a 'normal' member of society, married with children, keeping a shop, conversing with her customers and who sought help only when a phobia intruded into her life. Before long, Aulagnier learned that she had a peculiar theory of how children were born: the man's sperm played no part, except to excite the woman's 'procreative apparatus', and the vagina would be forced to insert the male substance into that apparatus. Hence men died younger and lost their hair. These delusional ideas had never attracted any attention, since no one had ever asked her to expound her view of conception, and when other people did raise such themes, 'Either I go out, or I don't hear,' she said.

To take another example, one of my patients complained of a diffuse feeling of anxiety, and spent many months telling me about his history and his childhood. He had never seen an analyst or therapist before, and was troubled by the recent encroachment of anxiety into his life. His career in the legal profession had been successful, never hampered by any manifest symptoms or inhibitions. After some time, the cause of his apprehension became clear, and he was able to find what seemed like a workable solution to attenuate it. With this, he left the treatment. In one of the last sessions, however, he mentioned something peculiar: the belief that anyone who shared his first name must also share some common quality with him. The name itself was not unusual, and it meant that whenever he encountered a namesake, he would gravitate towards them, inquisitive to learn more.

When I probed further, he was uneasy, understanding that his belief would seem odd. Yet beyond it was an absolute certainty: the name was only applied if the people in question possessed an inner essence, immutable and invariant. He took care not to broadcast this delusional thought, and it had never caused him any problems. Indeed, we could suspect that it helped him maintain an identity, as he believed also that those sharing the name must have had a common ancestor. As with Aulagnier's patient, there was no reason for the belief to become problematic or cause conflict, and it could remain hidden in the course of his everyday life.

If Aulagnier's patient had not developed her phobia and had not visited an analyst, the delusional ideas would perhaps never have become apparent. She might have continued with her life and kept quiet about her beliefs. If there were no major frictions with her environment, there would have been no suspicion of a psychosis, as was the case with my patient, whose delusional thought was highly encapsulated. Yet it is exactly these forms of psychosis that we can learn from: through studying them, we can try to understand the mechanisms that have allowed the person to be mad – quietly – without going mad. Since today mental health is so often defined as a lack of conflict with the world around us, this kind of psychosis simply goes off radar: it vanishes.

This disappearance of what earlier clinicians took to be the most common form of psychosis is reinforced by the fact that delusional thoughts are generally kept secret. As one of Manfred Bleuler's patients put it, 'In my world I am omnipotent, in yours I practise diplomacy.' Today, few clinicians will have studied the old psychiatric category of 'reticence', which described the ways in which topics may be avoided and kept silent. Yet long-term work with a psychotic subject always shows that there is a lot that does not get revealed immediately, if at all. De Clérambault could speak of 'those silences that are the hallmark of delusion', and the psychiatrists of the early twentieth century warned against confusing remission and reticence. Bleuler spoke of the psychotic subject's 'double book-keeping': he knows that most people won't understand his thoughts and beliefs so hides them carefully, even when in a confidential and benevolent setting.

In the case we will discuss in Chapter 9, it took more than 300 sessions for the patient to reveal to her curious and dedicated young psychiatrist what was really on her mind. Imagine how little one could find with a questionnaire-style interview for an hour with a patient today. Indeed, the success of many contemporary treatments is measured in terms of how well a psychotic subject can hide their psychosis, how well they can conform and comply with the expectations of others. We lose out here on what can be learned from long-term conversations: not an hour every month but, often, a conversation that runs over years, and, indeed, decades. It is telling that since the end of the nineteenth century, the psychiatric literature on reticence has been almost non-existent, as if we want to know less and less about what matters to our patients.

Historically, the movement to follow visible madness to quiet, invisible madness began through critiques of the principal diagnostic entities. Emil Kraepelin and many other late-nineteenth- and early-twentieth-century psychiatrists gave a special place to the evolution of psychosis: the course of the illness would determine how it was classified. Dementia praecox, for example, would move towards cognitive and affective impoverishment. The term 'dementia' implied a decomposition, the morbid intrusion of an organic process into the psyche that followed its own irreversible laws. If it didn't, then it wasn't dementia praecox.

This progressive movement towards dementia was the defining characteristic, which differentiated it from manic-depressive psychosis. The idea that it was thus more or less incurable and doomed to a bleak outcome played its part in forming popular conceptions of madness. It meant despair for both patients and their families. This emphasis on poor prognosis and breakdown worked powerfully to shape expectations: if the patient seemed to be doing well, they couldn't be psychotic. As one psychiatrist told the American anthropologist Tanya Luhrmann about a patient diagnosed with schizophrenia: 'She's had a partner, she's actually got this guy interested in marrying her and he's apparently perfectly reasonable, she's managed without meds. I just don't think the label makes sense.' She couldn't be psychotic because her life wasn't falling apart in the expected way. The diagnostic preconception was thus a vehicle of prejudice: to be schizophrenic one would have to be visibly disintegrating and unable to attract a mate.

Such rigid ideas about psychosis are present also within the world of psychoanalysis. The Russian aristocrat Sergei Pankejeff first visited Freud in 1910, and, after a four-year treatment, Freud wrote up the case of this patient who became known as the 'Wolf Man' after a key dream in which a group of wolves gazes terrifyingly at him. He returned to see Freud for another brief period of analysis, and then continued with Ruth Mack Brunswick, who diagnosed him as paranoiac. Despite good clinical evidence, this diagnosis was unpalatable to future generations. The American analyst Muriel Gardiner, who knew Pankejeff well, contested it on the grounds that 'He made a most orderly and reliable impression, was always appropriately and carefully dressed, was very polite and considerate of others.' This attitude is just as prejudiced as that of Luhrmann's interviewee, as if psychotic people have to stay psychotic in a visible, noisy way, and ultimately don't have the right to live fruitful, bearable and orderly lives, or even dress carefully.

If these prejudices seem to stem from an adoption of the Kraepelinian view of a chronic, downward spiral in psychosis, defined by its terminal state, we should remember that both Kraepelin himself and his contemporaries would question these very views. Some Anglophone psychiatrists did not read Kraepelin's original German texts, and assumed that dementia praecox was what the name implied: a disorder starting in adolescence (the *praecox*) that got worse (the *dementia*). Yet Kraepelin would acknowledge in the 8th edition of his textbook that the term was ill chosen, and both he and Bleuler would relativize their initial prognostic pessimism, admitting the possibility of positive evolution and change.

Kraepelin acknowledged that the 'disease' could be arrested or, indeed, in some cases, 'cured', with 'a complete and lasting recovery'. Emmanuel Régis spoke of a 'dementia praecox without dementia', adding that the pessimism attributed to Kraepelin may have been due to its hospital-based framework rather than the city practices of other physicians. Many of Kraepelin's colleagues, likewise, criticized the use of the term 'dementia', with its implications of long-term destruction of mental faculties and psychical decay.

In France, Philippe Chaslin wrote a brilliant and neglected critique of the notion of dementia praecox, proposing instead the concept of 'discordant madness', with an emphasis on the curability or improvement that was clinically possible. The term 'dementia' suggested a morbid organic process, yet he pointed out that if some cases were triggered in the teens or early adulthood and worsened rapidly, others didn't, despite the same initial symptom picture. Like many other psychiatrists, Chaslin insisted on how the psychotic subject may retain all their mental faculties, again questioning the implications of Kraepelin's initial formulation. The problem was less in the faculties – like memory or will – than in the relation between them: in other words, in their discordance.

Symptoms of discordancy could of course get worse, but they

could just as well improve or vanish entirely. Perhaps surprisingly, despite the hundreds of critiques of the simplistic understanding of Kraepelin's concept, and the efforts of epidemiologists and of 'survivor' organizations to emphasize positive outcomes, a diagnostic pessimism is still with us today in both consulting rooms and hospital wards. Although we ought to know better, today's risk society reinforces these prejudices. In both public and private health services, the possibility of litigation looms so large that clinicians are often obliged to present worst-case-scenario pictures to patients and their families. Their alibi is the language of 'science', the clinical trials and studies that generate the statistics that we set so much store by today. Bleak outcomes are conveyed as humane candour, without the realization that the very fact of making the prognosis may have significant effects for the sufferer. What impact might it have on the manic-depressive patient who, stable for two years, is told that the statistics indicate that they are likely to relapse within the next six to twelve months?

—

In contrast to the image of decay suggested by the term 'dementia', many of the early-twentieth-century psychiatrists developed their observations of a kind of madness in which all the psychotic subject's faculties were intact. Thought disorders would only become apparent, if at all, when areas of particular sensitivity were approached. Thus Daniel Paul Schreber, a German judge whose memoirs of his 'nervous illness' were first published in 1903, and who believed he was being transformed into the begetter of a new race, inhabiting a bizarre universe of divine rays and filaments, could still deliver acute legal arguments and expertise, not least concerning his own tutelage. He was able to convince the courts, using both legal argument and personal narrative, that he was fit to be released from his incarceration in an asylum and to take charge of his affairs.

Discussing the Schreber case, Freud observed that what we take to be the defining features of madness – delusions, hallucinations, etc. – are in fact not primary but secondary symptoms. They are less constitutive of madness than responses *to* madness, attempts at self-cure, as Bleuler, Jung, Lacan and Winnicott would also argue. What would happen, for example, if people around you started to whisper, spreading malicious gossip about your lack of morals and sexual behaviour, for no apparent reason? You would have to invent a reason. As one woman explained, how could one make sense of all the horrible gossip about her if not by realizing that a double with loose morals was dressing in her clothes and pretending to be her. This was less a bizarre efflorescence of madness than a hypothesis with explanatory power, less insanity than a response of reason to insanity. It was, perhaps, good thinking. Madness and reason were thus not opposed but identical, as Erasmus and Pascal had famously argued

But why the whispering and gossip in the first place? As this process of logical reasoning continues, a delusional system can be constructed. The double was put there to damage one's reputation, to then ensure one missed out on an inheritance, for example. If the TV or radio started to speak, it was to alert one to something, or perhaps to antagonize. The engineers responsible, in turn, may be mere agents for some other power. Thinking here is not really disordered, just more ordered than everyday thinking: if someone else heard a voice, they might just dismiss it as an effect of fatigue and continue with their life. But the psychotic person takes things seriously. For psychiatrists like Charles Lasègue and De Clérambault, the psychotic can be a master of rational deduction. First he hears voices, and then he makes sense of them, using powers of reasoning that are absolutely intact.

A delusion can thus be a way of trying to understand one's experiences, drawing on all the faculties of inference and deduction at one's disposal to find an answer. In the words of G. K. Chesterton, the madman has lost everything except his reason. Such thought processes are usually pursued with some privacy, and would only rarely be broadcast. Many other cases discussed by the early psychiatrists showed highly capable, intelligent and articulate subjects who discreetly held to mystical, sexual, religious or persecutory belief systems. These 'contained' cases challenged the view of madness as an organic and psychological decomposition, yet over the course of the twentieth century they received less and less attention. Their study moved from mainstream psychiatry to Existential, Phenomenological and

Lacanian psychoanalysis and psychiatry. Given the early focus on such forms of psychosis, how could one explain this gravitation of interest?

There are three main answers to this question: first of all, the fate of the diagnostic category of paranoia, which is the clearest example of quiet madness; secondly, the effect of pharmacology on the landscape of mental health; and thirdly, the radical revision in diagnostic procedures that characterized the biological psychiatry of the 1980s, which effectively removed the problem of meaning from the study of psychosis. These three factors would lead to the eclipse of the study of the everyday psychoses that had once seemed so evident to early-twentieth-century psychiatry. Although recent studies that examine psychotic phenomena – such as hearing voices – in the general population have helped to counter this trend, their statistics, which hover anywhere between a prevalence rate of 2 per cent and 30 per cent, underestimate both the frequency and the discretion of quiet madness.

The question of paranoia had once polarized this debate on the coexistence of madness and normality. When Kraepelin described 'true paranoia', the two defining characteristics were delusional thought and a striking conservation of all mental capacities and intelligence. Delusions, often with ideas of grandeur or persecution, would be combined with an unimpaired clarity of thought and action. Although he at one time believed it to be chronic and irreversible, he would admit, after many critiques, that there were other forms of paranoia, and, indeed, in one of his later texts, he described paranoia as less a 'disease process' than a 'mental torsion' or 'malformation'. But how could it be that one's faculties were so preserved?

The answers to this question were progressively clouded by the assimilation of paranoia into the heterogeneous group of schizophrenias. Where paranoia had once accounted for a large part of hospital diagnoses, the popularization of the diagnosis of schizophrenia would quite swiftly absorb it. Psychiatrists like Henri Claude had warned against the confusion of paranoia and paranoid states, yet the distinction would become weakened and often lost sight of. We can see this reflected in translations of the title of Lacan's thesis *De la psychose paranoïaque dans ses rapports avec la personnalité*: the first phrase is usually rendered as 'paranoid psychosis', although, at the time of writing, there was already a psychiatric distinction between 'paranoid psychosis' and 'paranoiac psychosis' that Lacan was well aware of. Paranoid states can occur in almost any type of mental disturbance, yet paranoia as such was a distinct diagnostic category involving the construction of a stable system of beliefs with a named persecutor. Yet, all too swiftly, paranoia lost its diagnostic dignity.

The case of Ernst Wagner, studied by the psychiatrist Robert Gaupp and his students at Tübingen, was of particular significance here. Wagner was a highly respected schoolteacher, an educated, intelligent man who led an orderly life and had never attracted medical or psychiatric attention. But, on the night of 4 September 1913, he calmly slit the carotid arteries of his wife and four children, then travelled by train from Stuttgart to the village of Mülhausen where, after starting a series of fires, he shot all the men he could see, killing nine and wounding twelve others with the guns he had strapped to his hands.

This spectacular outbreak of violence naturally made the front pages, fuelling a litany of hatred against the 'mentally unwell'. Wagner, it was said, carried out his killing spree during an acute attack of insanity, yet, as Gaupp bravely and persistently demonstrated, the murders had in fact been planned years previously by a man who felt unbearably persecuted, as his notebooks and diaries confirmed. The wealth of written evidence that Gaupp now examined was an invaluable resource, tracing the mental development over several years of a man who would eventually feel compelled to realize his homicidal projects. The psychiatrist did his best to challenge the demonization of Wagner, and bring out the fact that he was, like his detractors, a human being whose actions could be explained without appeal to notions like 'evil'.

For Gaupp, the conceptual interest of the case lay in the light it shed on paranoia, which was clearly compatible with a normal life in the community. Wagner, after all, had delusions for at least twenty years, yet could function as a good citizen and family man with no visible signs of madness. This ran against the simple Kraepelinian view that paranoia followed an insidious course, unaffected by life events. Until 4 September 1913, no one had guessed that anything was wrong. He killed his whole family that night, yet the evening before he was his usual polite self, exchanging pleasantries with another teacher's wife and her daughter, and fulfilling his duties with commitment and competence.

The written texts, together with his interviews with Gaupp, brought out the logic of the homicides. At eighteen Wagner had started to masturbate, which heralded a catastrophe of self-torment. He was certain that others could tell his guilty secret from his appearance, and interpreted the remarks of those around him as allusions to it. In 1901 he obtained a teaching post in Mülhausen, where, despite various heterosexual relationships, he continued to masturbate. One evening, on the way home from a local inn, he had some kind of sexual contact with animals: no details of what exactly he did were ever fully explained, despite years of questioning by Gaupp. No one had seen Wagner's act, but he felt he had sinned against the whole of mankind. After that night, he wandered about in an agony of persecution, interpreting conversations he overheard as alluding to his act and sensing the laughter and jeering of the local population. He had become an object of mirth.

Wagner knew that if he retaliated he would lose his job, less because of any aggression than because his crime would become known. He began to carry a loaded gun in case the police came for him, even concealing it under his jacket at his own wedding. His marriage was not enough to temper his despair, and Wagner realized that he would have to kill his family as his children might carry the germ of his sexual anomalies. As his feeling that he was an object of scorn and mockery for the men of Mülhausen spread to encompass the neighbouring villages, he bought more guns, practised and planned his revenge. As his sense of persecution increased, Wagner eventually asked for a transfer and was moved to Stuttgart, yet even there he came to believe that his sin was known and laughed at. He had to kill the men of Mülhausen, he said, to stop the gossip.

First of all, however, he had to kill his family, out of compassion and to block the stain of bad hereditary transmission. The thought of his children having to live with the shame of their father was unbearable to him, so killing them would save them this pain and simultaneously eradicate any trace of his sin from the world. Then he would set fire to Mülhausen and kill his enemies there. The murders were thus divided into two groups: first of all, the altruistic homicide of his family, and then the retaliatory elimination of his persecutors. What they shared was the task of erasing a fault.

Gaupp's careful reconstruction of the case showed how a paranoia could develop over a period of many years, responding to events in the life of a patient rather than simply following a predetermined course, and how it could operate seemingly independently of surface behaviour. Wagner was a respected man, a fine teacher and a functioning member of society. He showed none of the disturbances one might have associated with a 'mental illness', and Gaupp's students, such as Ernst Kretschmer, would develop these ideas, emphasizing the role of lived experience as affecting the course of paranoia and contesting the outright biological determinism of many of their contemporaries. When Lacan published his doctoral thesis on paranoia in 1932, it was this tradition that he developed and refined.

Yet paranoia as a diagnostic category would fade rapidly in Western psychiatry after the Second World War. By 1973, the *British Journal of Psychiatry* could refer to it as 'an obsolete category', its substantive form weakening into adjectival qualifier: there was 'paranoid schizophrenia' or 'paranoid personality disorder' or 'paranoid reaction', but no 'paranoia' as such. The old distinction between 'paranoia' and 'paranoid' had been lost, and the term was dropped from the most influential textbook, the *Diagnostic and Statistical Manual of Mental Disorders* (or *DSM*), in 1994, and, despite a few defenders, is no longer considered a discrete category in mainstream psychiatry. Was this because the new emphasis on surface behaviour led precisely to a blindness to what was invisible, the quiet form of madness that Gaupp had documented with such care?

Developments in pharmacology were certainly a significant factor in the eclipse of paranoia. New drug treatments seemed to offer amazing hope, and antipsychotic medication would redefine the tasks of psychiatry. The key moment is usually identified as the introduction of chlorpromazine in the early 1950s, which allowed a new calm and distance from the world: a 'hibernation therapy', as it was at first called. Agitated, troublesome patients would become mute and immobile. The emphasis here was on changing surface behaviour rather than on identifying deep-rooted underlying problems, although initially many of these drugs were seen as tools to allow psychotherapy to get under way, not as concrete alternatives.

There have been many eloquent critiques of psychiatric medication, and I don't want to go over these arguments in detail here. We could just note the serious and permanent side effects of many neuroleptics: docility, passivity, diabetes, Parkinson-type symptoms, dental pathology, weight gain, salivation and elocution problems, to name only a few. The drugs have also been shown not to work for a high percentage of patients – up to two thirds – and if you take them there is a higher rate of relapse and readmission to hospital than if you don't. Some critics argue that those who regularly take antipsychotic medication risk reducing their lifespan by twenty-five years, not through suicide but mainly through death due to cardiovascular and metabolic problems.

It is worth remembering here how these side effects of antipsychotic drugs, when they are admitted, are usually deemed negative. Docility, passivity and a general blunting of one's cognitive processes are seen as a price to be paid for a greater good. Yet it was these very features that, earlier in the century, were seen as the *goals* of medication. The long line of earlier medical interventions, from insulin coma therapy to metrazol injection to electroshock, had aimed to destroy or severely damage the so-called 'higher functions' of the brain. It was these higher functions, after all, which caused the symptoms of psychosis. Treatment should aim to 'knock out the brain' and 'impair the memory', as one psychiatrist put it in the early 1940s.

Indeed, the eureka moment in the development of electroshock came when Ugo Cerletti saw how electricity could be used to stun animals in a slaughterhouse, running current not through the whole body, as he had been doing, but just through the head. Dulling the brain was the aim rather than the side effect: shock treatment was like the 'kicking of a Swiss watch'. This would temper the symptoms as well as making patients easier to deal with, quieter and more compliant. Metrazol, for example, apparently produced a lack of emotional depth, a tendency to withdraw from personal contacts and a decrease in the capacity for self-observation: qualities that, as Kurt Eissler pointed out, would make the patient a more socially accepted individual.

Many psychiatrists writing in the era of drugs expansion also made an observation that seems just as sharp today as it did then. Psychotherapy with psychotic subjects is generally long, difficult, gruelling, and lacking in the kinds of gratification we might associate with more conventional medical treatments. It must be nicer to have a patient who will perceptibly change for the better via a medical act than one with whom change may be traced only retroactively after many years of work. And surely, they argued, the fact that many patients diagnosed with schizophrenia failed to improve might generate some antipathy from their doctors? The brain-numbing drug regimes – just like their predecessors, the insulin coma and shock treatments – could then be seen as an unconscious form of retaliation: beyond the conscious care and concern for the patient was a feeling of impotence and frustration. These treatments, at one level, were a punishment for not getting better. As Gérard Pommier observes, is it an accident that today's drugs are not labelled 'anti-psychosis' but, precisely, 'anti-psychotic', as if it is the psychotic person themself that needs to be eliminated?

This dimension could of course add to their efficacy. A woman started to feel that 'the whole world was against her': people in the street were spying on her and plotting, and the radio and TV were talking about her. Two years before this she had married a much older man, a wealthy antique dealer, in whose family she had been a governess for the previous twenty-five years. The new husband's family and children had apparently approved warmly of the marriage, which had promoted her in social and economic terms. The psychosis triggered at the precise moment that she received a cheque, sent to her in her name, which had been arranged by her husband.

She had the feeling that she was profiting from her new situation, and depriving the children of what was theirs, however generous and understanding they had been. This guilt was immediately transformed, it seems, via projection, into a feeling of persecution. A course of electroshock treatment brought about a remarkable improvement, and an affectionate and 'normal' family life ensued. It is difficult not to link the happy outcome to the nature of the treatment: weren't the electroshocks experienced by her as a sufficient punishment for her crime?

Many of the early studies of physical treatments such as electroshock and metrazol would find that there were powerful links between their efficacy and the psychological meaning ascribed to them, by both patient and doctor. Although the methods used would vary enormously, the 'results' were surprisingly similar, and were correlated to whether they were conducted with the therapist's intense expectations or merely as routine procedure. One of the most significant lessons of the early research is all too often forgotten here: the effects in the body of the various shock treatments were more or less identical to those subsequent to *emotional* shock. This suggested that it was not the detail of the physical procedure but its impact on the patient – what it meant to them – that was significant. As Manfred Bleuler pointed out, one study even showed that the amputation of a limb could have as 'good' an effect as a leucotomy.

Today, there is little reason to doubt that the same principle operates. Drugs are not taken in a vacuum, but form part of interactions that will have effects on the patient. To say that the drugs work doesn't tell us much, since what exactly they do varies a great deal. The success story here is perhaps more to do with public relations than it is with scientific advancement. Curiously, the first generations of antipsychotic drugs were never the result of targeted research. They had all resulted from chance discoveries: chlorpromazine was used as a tranquillizer in anaesthesia; reserpine was used to treat hypertension; iproniazid was used as a euphoriant in treating TB; and the urate salt of lithium was used to sedate guinea pigs prior to experimentation.

Clinicians noticed the pacifying, blunting effects of the drugs and began to think about their use as 'antipsychotics'. These numbing qualities would then become marketed into a rhetoric of 'cure' and 'treatment'. Historians have shown how the public relations wings of the drugs companies crafted the drugs from chemical restraints into precision cures. The message was clear: here at last were the remedies that psychiatrists had been waiting for during all those years in the wilderness.

This involved a convenient amnesia about earlier treatments. There have always been 'cures' for mental illness presented to the public and the profession with scientific backing. Doctors did not wonder if they were doing the right thing until the drugs of the 1950s came along and let them see the light. Many psychiatrists were absolutely sure from the late 1930s onwards that insulin coma therapy worked and, later, that metrazol was a certain route to recovery. Chlorpromazine was so miraculous not because it was so much better than earlier treatments, but because the public relations companies were now so much more professional themselves. Spinning narrative was now big business, and with plenty of staff to do it.

Public relations has also tried to rewrite the history of the social changes the drugs apparently introduced. Psychotic people, we are told, were now able to continue their lives outside hospital, and the deinstitutionalization of psychosis that has taken place over the last four decades has relied on the medical backup of the new drugs. As one commentator put it, the new drugs 'made it possible for most of the mentally ill to be successfully and quickly treated in their own communities and returned to a useful place in society'. However, historians have shown that the move towards deinstitutionalization was not merely a consequence of the new drug therapies. Changes in social and community psychiatry, such as open-door policies, began an emptying of the asylum beds well before the arrival of chlorpromazine in 1954.

In the States, asylums began sending patients to nursing homes after the new Medicaid and Medicare laws of the 1960s provided subsidies for alternative care. Welfare legislation would also provide disability benefits, so that hospitals discharged yet more patients to boarding houses and welfare hostels. All this happened some ten years after the arrival of chlorpromazine and the first neuroleptics, weakening the cause–effect link that is usually posited between them. If it is true that from the mid to late 1960s, more and more patients moved to the community, it was also observed that ever-increasing numbers of psychotic subjects started to turn up in prison or on the streets. Compared to hospitals, was this really a better alternative? And today, despite the discovery of the effects of chlorpromazine and its successor drugs, the number of those diagnosed with psychosis has jumped fivefold.

The 1960s also saw significant changes to drug legislation, which now required that each new chemical agent specify its active ingredients, the outcomes sought and the delivery period for attaining them. This meant a new kind of surface precision. Drugs would have to pass expensive trials proving they were more effective than a placebo and would work better than other drugs used for the same group of target patients. Likewise, the illnesses they claimed to treat would have to possess well-defined contours. In such a landscape, historians of psychiatry agree that it was the drug industry that largely created the new diagnostic categories. With each new category came a new medication, creating market niches.

This shift had a remarkable consequence, predicted with uncanny prescience by the historians. The drugs acted on the visible, disruptive symptoms of psychosis, and over time the actual 'illness' that they were supposed to treat became redefined in terms of the effects of the drugs. Rather than seeing the drug as the key to the lock of the illness, the illness was defined as whatever would fit that key, rather like Cinderella's slipper. One of my patients recently had to see a psychiatrist, and at the end of the consultation he asked about his diagnosis. The psychiatrist replied that he'd have to wait to see how he would respond to the drugs. This was exactly what historians predicted was going to happen. As the anthropologist Andrew Lakoff observes, rather than asking 'Is this a case of bipolar disorder or schizophrenia?' the question would be 'Is it a lithium or an olanzapine response profile?' The drugs had now come to define the illness: it was less about finding a drug to fit an illness than an illness that would fit the drug.

The new focus on drugs, and their power to actually shape what was seen as the illness, shifted the direction of research on to exactly those symptoms that the drugs could be seen to act on. This meant a neglect of the quiet forms of madness that so interested the early psychiatrists, since most of these cases did not display noisy symptoms and did not require medication. It is certain that most clinicians today would not diagnose as psychotic the cases that the early psychiatrists – and today's Lacanians – took to be untriggered psychosis, for the simple reason that they have been taught to see psychosis as something else: a limited set of phenomena linked to visible responses.

The discreet paranoias that had so fascinated Gaupp and other Continental psychiatrists have been largely forgotten in this redrafting of diagnostic categories as a set of biologically based problems of brain chemistry. Through the apparent success of the drugs, psychiatry lost interest in the changes and developments a psychosis could undergo without medication and the restitution mechanisms that it could construct. Short-term studies replaced the twenty- and thirty-year studies of the older clinicians, allowing less opportunity to see how people might create their own solutions and stabilizations of psychosis over time, and introducing new dangers.

By dulling the person's mental abilities, the drug treatments threatened the ability of the psychotic subject to build self-generated defences against their experience of madness. Once we see psychosis as involving a work of construction and creation, there is a real and serious risk that long-term use of drugs will irreparably compromise this. And, indeed, some studies have noted a gradual decline in patient improvement over the last forty or so years, as if the numbing of the patient's psyche blocked the production of genuine and long-lasting stabilization processes. Ironically, public perceptions of psychosis tend to equate the actual side effects of antipsychotic medication – excessive salivation, jerky movements, extreme lethargy – with the primary symptoms of psychosis itself.

The apparent success of the drugs helped to move the emphasis away from the processes by which someone could get better without medication. There have been fewer and fewer studies of the ways in which people could find an equilibrium over time. The medicalization of madness and the development of national health services along managerial and bureaucratic lines meant that madness became seen as nothing other than a medical problem to be treated pharmaceutically. Gradually, funding was withdrawn from many open-minded and progressive projects to create therapeutic environments for psychotic subjects. The contact hours between psychiatrist and patient were also radically reduced, a fact that would have catastrophic consequences for both the theory and the therapy of psychosis. Many countries now have an embarrassingly low level of contact hours per patient, in some cases averaging between an hour and an hour and a half per year.

The dominance of the medicalized view of psychosis is shown nicely on the website of the American Psychiatric Association, where, until 2008, you could see images of psychiatrists studying CT images of a patient's brain, most of them wearing white coats or surgical scrubs. This was the supreme scientific psychiatry that many had dreamed of, with the patient reduced to a brain and the object of the professional gaze of the psychiatrists. Yet as Richard Bentall points out, besides the fact that white coats can have little obvious function for a doctor with no physical contact with patients, the only psychiatrists who wore scrubs were those who carried out prefrontal leucotomies, 'a procedure which the profession has been in a hurry to forget'.

—

By the late 1970s, madness had become increasingly equated with its visible symptoms, those that the drugs took as their targets. Naturally enough, the emphasis on visibility meant that a whole host of prejudices and value judgements could come into play. Pierre Janet had pointed out in the early twentieth century how a wealthy patient would receive a less 'serious' diagnosis than an apparently impoverished one, and now, in a series of well-known experiments, it was found that well-dressed, articulate people who complained of bizarre thoughts and ideas would be more likely to be described as 'eccentric' than their shabby, poorly spoken counterparts who complained of exactly the same symptoms. The latter were more likely to receive the diagnosis of schizophrenia, be detained in hospital and medicated.

In his famous study, David Rosenhan arranged for eight 'sane' people – three psychologists, a paediatrician, a psychiatrist, a painter, a housewife and psychology professor Rosenhan himself – to seek admission to twelve different American hospitals. None of them had any reported symptoms, yet they were instructed to complain, when seeking admission, of hearing voices that said the words 'Empty', 'Hollow' and 'Thud'. After this, if admitted, they were to simply conduct themselves as usual and report no further occurrence of the voices. This all proved even easier than expected. All but one were admitted with the diagnosis 'schizophrenia', and all of them were discharged with the diagnosis 'schizophrenia in remission' after stays of between a week and nearly two months. They were prescribed nearly 2,100 pills, from a wide variety of different drugs. Remarkably, staff seemed to have no awareness that these were 'pseudo-patients', but inmates were often suspicious: 'You're not crazy. You're a journalist,' as one patient said.

After reporting these initial findings, Rosenhan then told the staff at an important research and teaching hospital that he would be conducting the experiment again at some point during the next three months. Staff were asked to rate admissions according to a scale of probability that they were pseudo-patients. Eighty-three patients were deemed pseudo by one or more members of staff, when, in fact, Rosenhan, in a double bluff, had not dispatched a single one of his recruits to the hospital. Yet, despite this, all these diagnoses had been made. Without wishing to deny the gravity of mental distress, his study had challenged the assumption that the sane and the insane could be distinguished so clearly.

This variability was reflected not only in terms of economic status, as Janet had observed, but also cross-culturally. Film footage of a patient shown to American and British psychiatrists produced radically different diagnoses. Americans were more than twice as likely to diagnose schizophrenia than their British colleagues. A series of studies in the 1960s and early 1970s produced similar results. A film of a young woman complaining of mild symptoms of anxiety and depression and of the frustration of her ambition to be an actress received a diagnosis of schizophrenia from a third of the American psychiatrists, and none from the British, who preferred terms like 'emotionally unstable'. The British were generally less likely to diagnose pathology than their American counterparts, with one exception: they tended to diagnose manic depression with far greater frequency. One can imagine the unfazed pipe-smoking British psychiatrists applying the one diagnosis of people who make fervent efforts to communicate, breaching the cultural decorum of distance and understatement that the 'nation of hermits' described by Stendhal so valued.

It was clear that different cultures and traditions made diagnoses in different ways. The globalization of psychiatric categories had not yet taken place. As these differences were publicized, the search for a fully 'objective' system of mental health diagnosis grew stronger, given momentum by the new drug legislation. The new clinical categories had to work internationally, so that markets would not be limited to particular geographical regions, with the same symptoms producing the same diagnosis in different parts of the world. The emphasis on surface symptoms – externally classifiable features of behaviour and even dress, which would, supposedly, transcend the prejudices of the investigator – would now redefine much of the work of psychiatry. Focusing on external symptoms meant effectively that the individual's own experience was devalued: what mattered was what symptoms they had rather than how they processed these symptoms, what they made of them, how they bestowed meaning – or not – on their experience.

The *DSM* classification system that grew out of this consolidated the emphasis on surface and visibility. This textbook sells hundreds of thousands of copies of each edition and has a massive impact on psychiatric practice and medical education around the world. Seen by many as a gold standard, it lists mental disorders and explains how to diagnose them. Disorder is mostly defined in terms of behaviour, so that visible, external aspects of our lives are used to define clinical categories. If you're nervous and shy, rather than seeing this as the symptom of an underlying clinical category to be discovered, it becomes a clinical category in itself: social phobia.

For each so-called 'mental illness', *DSM* lists a number of visible symptoms, and if you have, say, five or six out of ten, then you get the diagnosis. One of the symptoms in the list of defining features of schizoid personality disorder, for example, is 'wearing ink-stained clothes'. The absurdity of this behavioural, external definition becomes troubling when we realize that it forms part of a diagnostic system that, if it can grant access to treatment and insurance payments for some, it can restrain and section others, and have significant effects on their lives. As we will see later on, it is even possible that this very emphasis on using external features of behaviour to define human beings may itself be a symptom of psychosis.

Gone is the idea of complex psychical causality or even of an interior life. For *DSM*, only two kinds of causes exist: biological and stress-related. The new diagnoses are made on surface symptoms that an observer could swiftly classify rather than invisible structures that can only be diagnosed responsibly after considerable time. As one American psychiatrist put it, using the ever-expanding diagnostic system of *DSM* was like trying to carve the Thanksgiving turkey according to its feathers rather than its bone structure.

There was a strange irony in this reversal. Popular conceptions of madness privileged behaviour, after all, that didn't make sense: bizarre remarks in the middle of a conversation, delusional ideas, sudden changes of emotional tone. What characterized madness here was the fact that it broke with conventionally expected behaviour: in other words, it broke away from what could be made sense of. Surely, one might have thought, this would imply that the study of madness should start off from the problem of meaning. Yet meaning and the inner experience of the psychotic subject would matter less and less in the new symptom-based paradigm. A recent survey of MEDLINE publications on schizophrenia showed that a mere 0.17 per cent of articles were related to the subjective experience of the patient.

The effect of *DSM* has been massive, and perhaps the most significant erosion to earlier values in psychiatry has been the collapse of the distinction between symptom and structure. Anyone can have a tic, an insomnia, a phobia or an eating disorder, but the place it occupies in their life will need to be explored carefully. If a teenager stops eating, for example, we may find out that it is because they are having romantic daydreams about a classmate: they might imagine, perhaps, that the thinner they are, the more loveable they become. But, in another case, they may refuse food because they believe it to be poisoned, or because they experience their body as a hole that cannot be filled. Treating these cases in the same way would be ill-advised, and a diagnosis of, say, anorexia, would be profoundly unhelpful, as it would equate the surface symptoms – the refusal of food – with the disorder itself, rather than seeing the one as a symptom of the other. The pre-*DSM* system would see anorexia as a symptom of an underlying diagnostic category rather than in itself constitutive of one.

Identifying surface behaviour with disorders thus obliterates the distinction between surface and depth, and naturally generates more and more clinical categories: every aspect of the human condition can now become a disorder. Conversely, conformist surface behaviour can hide a serious underlying problem. Think, for example, of the case of Harold Shipman. He murdered more than 250 people, yet worked for years as a respected GP, earning the admiration of the community he served. He joined local societies and followed every possible Continuing Professional Development event organized in his area. He kept up to date on the latest medical research and maintained a popular and busy practice. He was kind, considerate and an excellent listener. Yet at the same time he was carefully killing off many of his patients. When psychiatrists examined him, they could find no clear indication of 'mental illness'.

It is the very absurdity of this result that should make us realize that the *DSM* system of mental health diagnosis is totally off the rails. Just because Shipman did not have any of the visible symptoms of madness we see depicted in movies and listed in the mainstream psychiatric manuals does not mean that he wasn't mad. And, in fact, it is precisely the madness focused on by the earlier psychiatric tradition, which explores its discretion, that is helpful here in allowing us to pinpoint Shipman's psychosis and to suggest what may have triggered it and led to his homicides. What matters, as we shall see, is to unearth the logic in what psychotic subjects say about their experience.

Diagnosis here cannot be based on external behaviour and surface features but, on the contrary, on their articulation in language.

A teenager brought up in a Catholic culture may see an apparition of the Virgin in church one morning, but in itself this tells us nothing. Whether it is a genuine hallucination or not depends, as Esquirol pointed out, on how this vision is interpreted, what meaning it is accorded by that person in their discourse: will it be understood as a sign directed to them or as the unintended effect of a late night or state of confusion?

If we recognize this fact, madness is never reducible to external, attention-grabbing symptoms. Thought here is not seen as dis-ordered, but follows a rigour that may indeed be absent in the 'sane'. Diagnosis cannot be made from an external classification of behav-iour, but only through listening to what the person has to say about what has happened in their lives, taking seriously the position they have in their own speech, the logic they have developed themselves. In this tradition, normality and madness are less contrasted than assimilated. But what, then, is madness? What concepts do we need to define it? And if madness cannot be opposed to normality, what could be its counterpoint?

2.　The Basics

To go further, we need to introduce some basic psychoanalytic ideas. These will allow us to move on to explore the particularity of psychosis: what it is, where it comes from and what forms it can take. The simplest place to start is with the notion of defence. Freud argued in his early work of the 1890s that most aspects of human suffering were linked to how we defend ourselves against disturbing thoughts or images. If we have experienced a traumatic situation or had an unpalatable thought, we tend to do something about it. We can't just keep it in consciousness, where it would continue to affect us, so we try to transform it. The most obvious way of doing this is simply to forget that it ever happened. We apply an amnesia to what is too unbearable for us to remember. Everyone is familiar with this on an everyday level, where an upset or argument can be swiftly obliterated from memory.

Although it is usually possible to remember an everyday tiff with some prompting, Freud believed that more fundamental traumas and disturbing trains of thought cannot be accessed so readily. They have been buried so deeply that they won't obligingly appear when we search for them. To find them, however, there are clues: in place of the forgotten memory, a symptom appears, like a ghost that keeps on coming back. This could be a phobia, a tic, a headache, an obsessive thought, a paralysis or any other form of mental or physical intrusion into our lives. Usually unexplainable medically, the symptom troubles us, yet we have no conscious knowledge of its cause.

In one of Freud's examples, his patient Emma developed a phobia of going into shops alone. She linked this with a memory from when she was twelve: she had gone into a shop and seen two shop assistants laughing together. She had rushed out in a fright, with the idea that the men had been laughing at her clothes and that one of them had attracted her sexually. A second memory soon inflected the first.

Aged eight, she had twice gone into a sweetshop and the shopkeeper had touched her genitals through her clothes. Although it had happened on her first visit, she had still returned to the shop the second time. Linking the two scenes together, she realized that the shop assistants' laughter in the most recent memory had evoked for her the shopkeeper's grin in the earlier memory. None of this, however, was in her mind when she experienced the fear of being in shops alone, but only after the work of eliciting and then linking the memories. All she was conscious of was a problem with her clothes.

The symptom – her phobia – thus acted as a memorial for the traumatic scenes, which had not been remembered until the analytic work with Freud. This form of defence – what Freud called 'repression' – characterized neurosis, and it was why, he believed, many of us have little memory of our infancy and childhood. The tragic facts of being distanced from our mothers and having our infantile demands for love frustrated mean that we cast a net of amnesia over our earliest years. The few memories we do have, which often seem trivial and innocuous, are like screens, beyond which are important and painful experiences that we cannot remember directly.

Amnesia, for Freud, was not the only form of defence. There was also a repression that operated by displacement, moving the emotional charge of an event on to some small and contingent detail. To take the example of the sweetshop, it would be as if the person could in fact remember perfectly everything that happened: the shopkeeper, the sexual assault and fleeing the shop would all be described, yet with no sense of the importance of what had taken place. And yet the person may have a horror of doors not being closed properly, spending hours each day carefully checking to see that every door in their home was tightly shut. The symptom – their obsessive ritual of door-checking – seems to have no immediate link to the memory, which is itself described like any other. But the emotional and traumatic charge of the scene has been displaced on to the detail of the door, perhaps echoing the door that the person used to enter or leave the shop.

Clinically, it is often difficult to locate the significant memories here since they may be described flatly, as if nothing of any importance had occurred. The threads that link the symptom back to the memories have to be retraced, and in this process it is sometimes possible for the person to realize what these events meant to them at the time. Doctors encounter this on a daily basis, when they ask their patients if anything significant might have happened around the time of the emergence of some physical symptom. After a negative response, it might take detailed questioning for it to become clear that there had been a bereavement, a break-up or some obviously relevant event at that time, which the person has simply distanced from their thoughts.

These two forms of repression – repression via amnesia and repression via displacement – characterize the two main forms of neurosis: hysteria and obsession. They are ubiquitous in everyday life, although the obsessional form of defence may attract less attention as the person will often not complain about it. Hysterical symptoms, on the contrary, can be noisier and they appeal to a witness, be it a doctor, a partner, family or friends. The symptoms of hysteria and obsessional neurosis tend to be ways of asking a question, a question about one's sexuality or existence. Beyond Emma's phobia of entering shops alone, there was perhaps a question about what it means to be a sexual object for a man.

One of my patients complained of the symptom of always becoming involved with men who were ambivalent to her: with them, she said, 'I never know where I am.' And yet she would flee those men who clearly did like her. Her symptom, she realized, was a way of perpetually asking the question 'What am I for you?', which could not be posed if her partner's affection was unequivocal. If there is no ready solution in our lives to the dilemmas of sexuality or existence, we can spend a great deal of our time posing these questions in different ways. My patient's move from one relationship to another was a way of pursuing an inquiry about her femininity, and we often find problems in the transmission of femininity or masculinity from one generation to the next here: the mother is accused of not bestowing a feminine identity on the daughter or of not being feminine enough herself, the father of not initiating the son into adult life, of contradicting his own ideals, and so on.

But what would happen if someone's symptoms turned out to be less a way of asking a question than the imposition of a solution? This is one of the most fundamental differences between neurosis and psychosis. In the case of Helene Renner, described by Ernst Kretschmer, a young woman felt attracted to one of her male colleagues. She had a strict moral code and struggled with these sexual impulses. Doing her best to suppress her thoughts, she was very reserved with him but sensed that at some level he returned her interest. She would be hurt whenever he talked to the other office girls and realized that she could no longer bear his gaze, as they sat opposite each other, and she struggled with this mixture of attraction and repulsion for a considerable time. She then began to think of an earlier experience, when the uncle in whose house she was now living had entered her bed against her will when she was twelve. Nothing had happened, yet she had worried that she might get pregnant and reproached herself with this unbearable thought. With her current erotic desires, she convinced herself that she must be an evil creature.

She began to think that people could notice her lustful appearance, and again the thought that she might be pregnant forced itself upon her. Confiding in her aunt did not help, and, indeed, the aunt became impatient with her, speaking to her by an open window. Now, she felt, all was lost. She began to think that people in the street were looking at her, and would hear remarks alluding to her pregnancy. Although she knew that a pregnancy would break every law of nature, she wondered whether someone had not injected her with semen as she slept. Now the conversations at work began to refer to her: 'She is bad', 'What a pig', she heard.

She started to fear that the police were on their way to the house to arrest her and her uncle. Newspapers seemed to contain allusions to her sins, each day disclosing more about her. 'After a while,' she said, 'everything seemed to be referring to myself to the extent that I could hear nothing in any conversation, or read nothing in the paper, other than accusations directed against me.' Returning to her old job and home town marked an improvement for her, yet things worsened when she was forced to work closely with other people. When she saw a brick one day with '1906' engraved on it, she took it as a reference to the date of her infatuation with the young man. She deduced from other signs that a machine had been set up by the police to read her thoughts, and later that the sexual impulses she had were being imposed by other people.

This case seems very different from that of Emma. The sexual content of the thoughts is not repressed but rather attributed to others. It's as if the whole world knows something about her, and is reproaching her for a wicked sexuality. If the symptom of being unable to enter a shop alone was opaque for Emma, it was transparent for Helene: she would avoid a public place because everyone there knew she was pregnant and a woman of low morals. If Emma had the unconscious idea of a pregnancy linked to the sexual assault, perhaps she would have developed a swollen stomach or back pain, or some other symptom she associated with being pregnant. The actual idea of pregnancy, however, might not enter consciousness, but remain repressed. With Kretschmer's psychotic patient, on the contrary, the idea of being pregnant was right there on the surface, plain as day.

—

How could we explain this difference between neurosis and psychosis? Freud believed that there is a much stronger defence mechanism in psychosis, as if the unpalatable thought is split off from consciousness so powerfully that it returns from the outside. Repression, after all, is always partial: it leaves symptoms in its wake, which can then be used to track the repressed material. But psychosis, for Freud, involved a more radical process. Disturbing ideas or experiences would not just be forgotten or have their emotional charge displaced: rather, they would be totally abolished. The person would act as if these ideas did not exist, as if they had been cast out of the psyche. As Freud put it in 1894, 'The ego rejects the incompatible idea together with its affect and behaves as if the idea had never occurred to the ego at all. But from the moment at which this has been successfully done the subject is in a psychosis.'

The key for Freud lay not in the content of the disturbing idea, but in the mechanism of its rejection – 'Verwerfung', a term translated by Lacan as 'foreclosure'. In one of Freud's examples, a woman developed paranoid ideas that her neighbours were making allusions to her relations with a man who had boarded in her home. There had indeed been a sexual scene with him, which she later denied, insisting instead on the reproach coming from those around her. For Freud, she had spared herself the initial reproach of being 'a bad woman' by imputing it to what was external to her: what had been an internal criticism was now heard coming from the outside. Whereas she would have had to accept the judgement coming from within, now she could reject it as it was coming from without.

There is something absolute about this process. Indeed, the thoughts that the person rejects can't really be described as disturbing or unpalatable, since this would imply some kind of cogitation. Freud's idea is that they are actually unthinkable, as if they had never been properly registered in our minds. This would imply that the person can take no responsibility for them: they simply return from the outside, attributed to others. In a case described by Henri Flournoy, a woman in her sixties became convinced that a certain Dr C was plotting against her. He sent emissaries to follow her and acted on her body itself, via 'shocks to her senses', which she would feel when he was close. These physical sensations were due to his external influence, as he had 'cast a spell' on her. He had in fact treated her a year previously for her varicose veins, and she reported feeling a 'heat', as if there were 'flames all around her', 'a heat that would rise up to my head, as if someone was squeezing my chest and back. It was the first time in my life I'd ever felt anything like it.' Each time he visited, she'd feel this physical sensation, this 'jolt': 'in feeling this, I thought that a young woman might fall in love like that from one moment to the next'. From then on, she had ideas that he was following her, watching her, and she would also have the thought that her son suspected that she was the doctor's mistress.

The descriptions of the 'heat' and the physical sensations clearly evoke an erotic response, yet, unable to assume these subjectively, they were systematically ascribed outside herself: the feelings were the results of the doctor's spell rather than aspects of her own sexuality. The neurotic's slip of the tongue and the psychotic's hallucination could be contrasted here. When the neurotic makes a slip, they feel embarrassed and responsible, because they recognize that the slip comes from them. But in the psychotic hallucination, the disturbing element comes from outside: it's not us, it's the Other. It comes not from 'inside' but from 'outside': not us speaking despite ourselves, as in the neurotic slip of the tongue, but the Other speaking to us directly.

An idea is projected outwards, for Freud, or split off in a radical, uncompromising way, so that the person is totally unable to recognize that they may be its source. There is a kind of impossibility to assimilate the rejected idea. Or, the person can recognize that they are the source, but only through positing a splitting of their own self: it's not me, it's an alien biological process inside me. Charles Melman describes the case of a young man experiencing auditory hallucinations, voices that commented on his thoughts and his actions, before actually anticipating them and engaging him in a strange dialogue. The voices, he said, spoke in a very sophisticated way, using terms that he didn't even know. He had to consult a dictionary to find the meaning of words like 'psychomotor', 'existential', 'hallucinosis' and 'grey matter'. But who, Melman asked, was speaking? The young man's response was categorical: 'It's my neurones,' he said. 'It's my brain, I know that it's me,' and then he asked, 'Can the brain be divided?' Even though admitting his self as the locus of the phenomena which had invaded his life, they were still designated as external, as coming from the outside, in the form of a split brain.

Repression operates on things that are already symbolized and structured, that have already been thought, but this more extreme mechanism of foreclosure doesn't admit the first stage of integration. The rejected element has never been admitted into the person's mental universe, as if there were no possibility of symbolization. It is like an unassimilable signification, something that cannot be thought. With no place in the unconscious, it will remain as a blank spot in the person's thought processes, or, in some cases, it will return from the outside as a hallucination, with a detachment from any sense that it belongs to them. Hence it is no surprise that the person will use any available knowledge to explain it: brain neurones, radio waves, a machine set up by the police, and so on.

A clinical example can illustrate this process. A woman developed the delusional thought that she was being poisoned by a work colleague. He had sat next to her during a long meeting, coughing and wheezing, and, when she began to feel unwell a few days later, she assumed that he had deliberately infected her. Now, she said, 'there is something growing inside me', something that 'has been put there by him'. She imagined the virus expanding uncontrollably inside her body, and eventually bursting her belly. In her childhood and adolescence, her mother had never said a word to her about the female reproductive apparatus: menstruation simply did not exist, and it was as if her body had no sexed interior. Her mother would even remove the seeds from grapes, as if to deny that they had an inside capable of reproduction. Unable to think the idea of pregnancy, it would return in delusional form: a man was introducing a toxic element into her that would grow inside and burst out of her.

The psychotic process here can consist not only in the rejection of an idea, which then returns from outside, but also in a transformation of this, some inflection that makes the defence even more effective. In the case of the woman described by Flournoy, her initial delusional thoughts would change form: soon, it was her daughter-in-law who had erotic feelings for the doctor, her own physical sensations being those the daughter-in-law experienced when he approached. Thus what were clearly her own erotic feelings towards the doctor were rejected, and attributed first to him, then to the daughter-in-law, with no responsibility ascribed to herself. Instead of recognizing that she wanted to follow him, she was certain that he was following her. Her feelings could not be assimilated, yet rather than being repressed, they were violently pushed out of her mind, to return in delusional form. The second form of the delusion distanced her involvement even further: she was not implicated at all now, only the daughter-in-law, and it was because she knew the truth about the latter that she was being followed and spied on.

If a patient's experience of reality can change so suddenly and so radically, we have to ask the question of what the world must be if it can become so totally transformed. If Emma could simply avoid a portion of her reality by not entering shops alone, Kretschmer and

Flournoy's patients were convinced that the world was talking about them, that newspapers and even bricks were sending messages to them. What kind of world could undergo such a terrifying and strange metamorphosis?

As reality decomposes in certain moments of psychosis, we find clues as to how it has been built up and constructed in the first place. The neighbour's gossip, the allusions in the street, the remarks in the newspapers, the talking neurones and the brick that sends a message all show that the world has started to speak. Everything in that person's reality has become a sign, communicating to them, whispering to them, addressing them: if reality was once silent, now it can't stop talking. And for reality to be able to do this, doesn't it suggest that it is made, in part, from language?

In what psychiatry calls 'mental automatism', a person may feel that every action or thought they have is commented on by an internal or external voice, a kind of running commentary on their existence. 'Now he's gone to the shops, now he's buying a newspaper . . .' Sometimes, this language has no direct content: the person is aware of being spoken to continuously, yet has no idea of what exactly is being said. There is just an endless murmuring or whispering, which may later become interpreted as a threat or menace. This shows language working on its own, as if separated from our everyday experience of the world. It has started to function autonomously.

In some cases, the hold of words on reality dissolves. This is described poignantly by Renée, the teenage patient of Marguerite Sechehaye who had been diagnosed with schizophrenia, yet after a long therapy was able to leave hospital, pursue a career that interested her and write an account of her experiences. This remarkable text records how meaning became undone for her: 'My eyes met a chair, then a table; they were alive too, asserting their presence. I attempted to escape their hold by calling out their names. I said, "Chair, jug, table, it is a chair." But the word echoed hollowly, deprived of all meaning: it had left the object, was divorced from it, so much so that on the one hand it was a living, mocking thing, on the other, a name, robbed of sense, an envelope emptied of content. Nor was I able to bring the two together, but stood rooted there before them, filled with fear and impotence.' The language of reality breaks down, and we are confronted with the gap that separates signifier – Renée's words – and object.

These examples show how language can split off from our conscious control, or literally come apart, as it did for Renée. They suggest that what we tend to take for granted as reality is actually made up of different levels: bricks, newspapers, tables and chairs can all lose their everyday meaning and become enigmatic and threatening. To lose their everyday meaning implies that meaning is not intrinsic to them: they are what we call 'signifiers', and they can become disconnected from their usual meanings, called 'signifieds'. Reality involves a soldering together of signifier and signified, so that we don't perpetually ask what things mean. But in psychosis, at certain moments, these dimensions come apart, for reasons we will examine later on.

Language, of course, is not everything, and psychosis also illuminates another thread of how our world is constructed. There are cases where visual images seem to have a life of their own, and a total dissociation is experienced between one's image and oneself. A schizophrenic woman described how, after her marriage, she had installed a mirror in her dining room and, when she gazed at it, felt that she had become a part of it. Her image, she said, had become trapped by the metal in the back of the mirror. When the mirror was moved from her home, she could feel this in her body, as if the mirror contained her.

In cartoons, we sometimes see characters continue running after they've left the edge of a cliff, and one could also think of the gruesome farmyard scene of a chicken still moving about after it has been decapitated. This is how some psychotic people describe their everyday existence, as if they are already dead, but their body just hasn't realized this yet. They walk around and function socially yet feel a million miles away from anyone else. The image of the body has become prised apart from any idea of conscious possession or control. These examples show how our bodies need to be unified and held together in an image. When this process is compromised, the image separates off, as if the visual form of our bodies were not really a part of us.

The body itself is not a given either. A patient complained repetitively that she didn't have a body, and had to touch the interior of her mouth with her tongue all day to reassure herself of her existence. Another spoke of how his body was in pieces and how he could see its parts attached to other people. This disintegration of the body is common in psychosis, as the following quotations show: 'My legs don't belong to me, they're someone else's. They're being moved to see if they work'; 'I feel as if I'm going to shatter into thousands of pieces at any moment'; 'My stomach has been replaced with someone else's.' In schizophrenia, the subject can feel that their body does not belong to them, or that they are in fact someone else, or that their physical sensations belong to another person, as we saw in the case described by Flournoy.

They may experience bizarre and invasive sensations, not localized to any one part of their body. Schreber observed that wheareas most people experience excitation localized to their sexual organs, for him it was spread over the whole of his body, 'from the top of my head to the soles of my feet'. Feelings of excitation intrude into the body, and may be felt as either pleasure or pain, or a mixture of both. These experiences are often continuous, a kind of non-stop assault: there is no let-up, no pause, no safe space where the person can find refuge. They naturally search for an escape, some way to master or temper the sensations that besiege them.

Lacan thought that these three dimensions – language, the visual image and the body – are bound together to give our lives a sense of stability and, indeed, establish our basic sense of reality. When they become undone, each dimension can disrupt and ravage the person's life. He called these registers the 'symbolic', the 'imaginary' and the 'real'. The symbolic is the world of language and law, the imaginary is the body image, and the real is the libidinal life of the body, the states of morbid excitation and arousal that assail us. So how are they connected together? And what link does this have to psychosis itself?

—

Lacan first developed the idea of the imaginary in the 1930s, taking as his point of departure material from psychology and ethology.

Many animals will undergo physiological changes when confronted with their mirror image, as if the reflection had direct effects on their bodies. Just as a pigeon, for example, might start to ovulate on seeing her image in a mirror, so human infants undergo a strange and compulsive capture in their own reflections or in the images of other children. Humans, unlike most other animals, are born prematurely: the brain and nervous system are still developing and mastery of motor functions takes several years to acquire. A newborn is unable to fend for itself, and a necessary dependency on adults must occur if the infant is to survive. But how, Lacan wondered, did the process of mastery of the motor functions of the body come about?

Psychologists like Henri Wallon had noticed a fascination with the mirror image at a certain phase of infancy, and this had been linked to a phenomenon known as 'transitivism': if child B is hit, child A will cry, showing that A has identified with B. The one child has put him or herself in the other's place. Lacan's idea was that, in our infantile situation of uncoordination and helplessness, we identify with images that seem to hold the promise of wholeness and completeness: we see ourselves as more powerful or capable than we are in visual images outside ourselves. This image could be our own mirror reflection or the image of another child. Parents know that a child will learn to walk faster if in the company of an older child who can walk already. There is thus a difference between the body schema – not yet completed – and the body image – which captures us in the very place of this incompleteness.

For Lacan, this 'imaginary identification', as he called it, came at a price: if we occupied the place of someone else, we would want what they wanted, establishing a basic function of human jealousy, especially around the possession of objects. Here we find many of the phenomena of jealousy, competition and sympathy that fill the nursery. And at the most fundamental level, imaginary identification meant that to get a sense of our own unity, we had to find this first outside ourselves. We become aware of ourselves through copying others. As the psychologist James Baldwin had argued earlier, the constitution of the human ego is simultaneously the constitution of the alter ego. We are both lost and found in the mirror image.

The idea of a mirror phase suggested that there was a discordance between registers of our experience: the incomplete body schema and the false unity of the mirror image. Indeed, Wallon's student René Zazzo had noted how the interest in reflecting surfaces seems to follow a phase of unrest and disquiet in the infant. We appeal to one register to resolve problems in another. Our capture in images would thus both help and hinder us. It would allow us to gain mastery of our body, through the identification with the virtual image provided by our reflection or the image of the other, yet at the same time would alienate us and give an aggressive form to our relations with our counterparts. Identifying with the image promises to unify us, yet never entirely delivers, as the very thing that gives us unity takes it away. We grasp our unity through something that is not us, that is outside us.

Remaining in this state is hardly possible. If our world is limited to us and our reflection, we will be caught in an endless battle, with no option but to annul the other or ourselves. We will want what the other wants and they will want what we want, to create a mortal tension. As the ethological work of Konrad Lorenz showed, destruction will ensue if no third party is at hand. To take one of his examples, at the time of mating for sticklebacks, without a rival there is no one else to target with aggressive tension and the two creatures end up destroying each other. With only two players, the expression of conflicting and ambivalent feelings is equivalent to destruction.

Think of all the Westerns where the rookie gunslinger tries to challenge the seasoned professional, who embodies the image of wholeness and completeness, the person they want to be. After being turned down, they burst into the saloon later on, intent on an obviously suicidal dual. The famous scene in *The Magnificent Seven* where the young Horst Buchholz challenges Yul Brynner is a typical example. In that blinkered, drink-fuelled moment, all that exists is himself and his rival, and the only thing that can happen is that one of them will have to die. This is the pure imaginary, and it's why a mediation is necessary, an intervention from the outside to move beyond this destructive, lethal space where there is only the subject and their mirror image, the image of completeness that they aspire to.

An image, after all, needs to have a place. When children contemplate or play with their image in a mirror, it is often in their mother's presence. The adult sanctions the image, binding it to the child through speaking, and through a loving and approving gaze. The child's reflection is invested through these channels with maternal libido, and the detail of these interactions will be decisive in determining how the child is able to inhabit its body image. The parent might use the child's name, teaching them to link word and image, as well as making associations: 'You've got your grandfather's eyes, your grandmother's ears,' etc. These words have a determinant power, and may shape lives, even if we remain unaware of their effects. A woman for whom kissing had a massive importance and who chose a career as a singer would remember, with surprise, that all she knew about her birth was the fact that her emergence into the world had been greeted with four words from her father: 'What a beautiful mouth.'

Words situate us in the symbolic world, and children understand very early on that they are not just biological accidents, but have a place in family history. They search avidly to find what meaning their existence has: where were they before being born, were they expected, wanted, desired? Thinking about who we are and where we are from is made possible thanks to the symbolic coordinates that situate us in the world. They allow us to go beyond the imaginary, as they give us a place that is not defined by our reflection or the image of our counterparts. To take the example of the young gunslinger caught in a face-to-face deadlock with his master, it is only when a third party intervenes, calming him down and eventually giving him a place as one of the 'Magnificent Seven', that the destructive whirlpool of the imaginary is overcome. He leaves a dual relation to become a member of a symbolic set, taking on a mantle that gives him a place in a structure. Now, he is 'one of them': no longer Yul Brynner's double, he becomes part of a group. It shows how the imaginary must be structured, tempered by a symbolic relation.

Without this, we remain in a lethal and potentially murderous space. Think of the Cumbrian gunman Derrick Bird. He killed twelve people and wounded more than twenty others in a homicidal rampage that shocked Britain in the summer of 2010. After the shoot-ings, everyone searched for a motive, focusing on the pressure he had apparently been under from the Inland Revenue and his suspicion that his twin brother – whom he had killed – was cheating him out of money from their late father's inheritance and their mother's will. Although it would be unwise to do more than guess here, it is diffi-cult to ignore a small but striking detail: the family at one point announced that the two brothers would share a funeral. Imagine how shocking this must have been, the idea of burying together both vic-tim and murderer. Yet as the family were quoted as saying: 'They came into the world together, they'll go out of the world together.'

This is the clearest illustration we could have of the imaginary, as if the twins were just mirror images of each other, and that this sym-metry would override the actual facts of their lives and the murders. Given this equation, the asymmetry opened up around the question of the legacy and the will makes more sense: as a sign of favouring the brother, the mirror relation was put in question. They were no longer equal. And hence all that was left, perhaps, was the murderous space between them. Bird's twin brother, indeed, was his first victim.

—

The symbolic refers to the pre-existing discourse in a family, and to the system of laws that anthropologists have discovered in their stud-ies of kinship and social organization. The symbolic is what gives us a place in the world, establishing coordinates and boundaries, and it is transmitted primarily through speech. Although often equated with language, it is in fact much more than this: not just language, but language plus law. This law is first and foremost the prohibition of incest, understood as not simply the internalized limit that separ-ates mother and child, child and mother, but also the system of reciprocal renunciations that organizes each society. In Lévi-Strauss's formulation, this collapses any monopolization of women in the family group: the fact that a man gives up his sister and daughter means that they can then circulate, giving others the chance to marry them, assuming that the same law is obeyed by the other men in that society. Rules of marriage and inheritance are highly structured, regulating the scope of human behaviour, determining which marriages could and could not take place and how the family and social group would be reorganized by these changes. Like the grammar of a language, such rules would not generally be found written down anywhere, or, at least, not before they had become the object of scientific study. People obeyed these laws without conscious knowledge, suggesting that the symbolic was a set of systems governing human relations yet usually outside our awareness.

The elements of the symbolic order are not isolated but depend on each other. Anthropologists have studied the ways in which what seemed to be unique behaviours or traits would take on their meaning in terms of the global context in which they occurred. Pretending to be an animal, for example, may have a different meaning in the context of a hunt, of a ritual ceremony or of a magical incantation. In itself, animal mimicry does not have a fixed and immutable meaning, but is an element of a structure: the whole organizes and confers meaning on the parts. What seems to be the same piece of behaviour can have different origins, different social meanings and, in consequence, different relations with other behaviours. Inversely, two radically different behaviours could, in principle, have identical functions in different cultural contexts.

Anthropologists have also shown how elements of the natural world are always caught up in complex symbolic systems. Animals, colours, planets and plants all have different meanings in different cultures and contexts: the sun could be a cruel monster for one social group and a benevolent protector for another, just as black could be associated with grief in one culture – or even for separate generations in the same culture – and with joy in another. These ideas from anthropology were echoed in the work of the linguist Ferdinand de Saussure, who saw language itself as a system of differential elements whose meaning depended on their relations to each other. Words do not have any intrinsic meaning, but signify by virtue of their place in a network, just as the ten o'clock train may have different carriages each day, yet is still the ten o'clock train because it is different from the nine o'clock and the eleven o'clock trains. Each element in the symbolic takes on its value in its relations to other parts, and the system works due to its introduction of divisions and contrasts between elements.

These ideas were disappointing to the early generation of anthropologists who wanted to believe that 'primitive' societies lived in harmony with nature, in a kind of continuity with their habitat. The study of the complex symbolic systems that made up the world of these societies showed the work of language in organizing reality, and also how language introduced a certain negativity, building our worlds at the same time as creating a distance from them. A system of divisions and contrasts, after all, requires what Lévi-Strauss called 'an impoverishment' of empirical reality, in the sense that the reality was broken down into units and sets of units that could be conceived as distinct. Complex systems could be built up from the initial contrast of two elements – such as 'red–green' or 'black–white' – instantiations of the elementary symbolic matrix of +/-. We introduce discontinuities into the world where no such contrasts may necessarily exist, and through this process, our reality becomes meaningful and differentiated. High/Low, Earth/Sky or Bear/Eagle could all act as parts of a code in different cultures to convey an identical message. Apologizing for the triviality of the image, he compares it to the kitchen utensil used to cut potatoes into chips: a preconceived grid which can be applied to all empirical situations, so that the resulting elements will all preserve certain general properties.

A defining feature of the symbolic order is this negativity it introduces, this distance from the supposed immediacy of experience. Entering the symbolic means accepting the rules and conventions of society, together with the prohibitions and limits necessary for it to function, which will have effects on the body itself. Freud called the sexual energy of the body 'libido', and part of growing up involves the draining and restructuring of bodily excitation. We are told what and when to eat; when to excrete and when not to; when we can and when we can't look or listen; that we have to wear clothes to cover our bodies; that we can't touch ourselves in front of other people, and so on. The reason that parents are always so exhausted is because they are constantly setting limits to their children's libidos, transmitting the symbolic 'no's that will allow their kids to become properly social beings. The symbolic clips the body, removing libido.

The more that the body is drained in this way, the more the world becomes liveable. Children become interested in their surroundings through equating these with bodily functions: a dripping tap can be fascinating for a child as it evokes the penis, a hole in a wall captivating because it seems like a mouth. Interest in the world can also mean terror, if the equations the child makes do not become progressively spread out and symbolized: without this, the world would just be one immense body and the hole in the wall might threaten to swallow up the child. As the symbolic does its work, the elements of reality become transformed into systems of signs, whose value depends on the other parts of the system, rather than on bodily equations. If too much of the body is present, we cannot enter a shared, social space. Reality, if the symbolic operates, becomes an out-of-body experience.

If it doesn't, the world and the body remain in a continuum. As Renée put it, 'When I urinated and it was raining torrents outside, I was not at all certain whether it was not my own urine bedewing the world, and I was gripped by fear.' In another case a patient thought that when other employees in her office said 'water' they were referring to her. In the office there was a water cooler that had to be hit for the water to flow. When people hit it, she thought they were hitting her. Why? As she explained, 'I never walk, I run, like water, and I deserve to be hit.'

Through language, the symbolic enters the real of our bodies and organizes them for us. It inscribes the law within us, providing a principle of mediation. Lacan thought that the symbolic order contained a privileged representative of this principle, what he called the 'Name-of-the-Father'. Early-twentieth-century anthropologists at times showed bafflement at how 'primitives' attributed pregnancy to a woman's encounter with a spirit at some sacred rock or spring rather than to the facts of coitus. If they had been having sex and babies for centuries, they asked, how could they have failed to notice the connection? Yet this 'primitive' lack of understanding in fact reveals for Lacan the true structure of paternity: that there is a difference between the real progenitor and the symbolic function of paternity that must frame reproduction. The spirit and the sacred space form part of the symbolic context of reproduction, necessary to symbolize it, to make it part of that person's world. Without such a context, it is hardly possible for a human being to understand that they are at the origin of a biological process.

Whenever a man and a woman have babies, a third term is present, whether in the form of the spirit, sacred space, ritual or medical and social discourse that will organize and make sense of the reproductive process. When we read myths and legends in which a woman gives birth after, say, a magic fish swims into her mouth, rather than interpreting this as a crude form of symbolism, we can understand it as an appeal to a network of mythic representations beyond the flesh-and-blood characters. The magic fish entering the mouth is less a disguised symbol of a penis entering a vagina, as it might well be in a dream, than an evocation of an order beyond the mother and father necessary to sanction and give meaning to the act of reproduction. This texture of myths, stories and meanings allows us to situate the changes taking place, at both the level of the biological body and of social relations.

Lacan was especially interested in the place of the father in this configuration, not the real flesh-and-blood progenitor but the symbolic place appealed to at moments such as pregnancy and parenthood. He drew attention to the more abstract nature of paternity, in contrast to the certainty of motherhood. The old saying 'pater semper incertus est' – 'the father is always uncertain' – highlighted the way in which paternity required less a biological than a symbolic recognition. The fact that many cultures acknowledge that the legal father may not have begotten his children echoes this non-biological, artificial function. This symbolic place would often be occupied, indeed, by a non-human figure, anyone or anything that was heterogeneous to the biological beings involved, represented in myths and folklore by divinities or supernatural beings.

The study of childhood phobia was significant here, and it allowed Lacan to develop his ideas about the place of the father's function. Phobias tend to fall into two groups: transitory fears that quickly pass, and sustained processes that involve creation and construction, as in the case of Little Hans discussed by Freud. Hans was three and a half when his horse phobia began, and it went through a remarkable number of transformations. Starting with a single element – the horse – he created a grammar that included all the aspects of his everyday life. The horse could bite or not bite, fall down or remain upright, be attached to carriages or not, and so on. Hans was creating a system to reorder his world, creating prohibitions as to what he could do or not do, where he could go or not go, through the phobic object – the horse – that he was using as his instrument. When the phobia subsided, he was much less anxious.

Now, where had this phobia sprung from? Hans had two big surprises at that moment in his life. He experienced his first erections, and a little sister was born. What sense could he make of these unexpected and traumatic impingements into his world? They had a powerful effect on the seductive relations he had with his mother. Now her delightful and satisfying little boy had a penis, which she didn't really take too seriously, mocking it tenderly. And the new sibling meant that her attentions were no longer so centred on her son. These events meant that Hans had to reassess his relations with his mother and find a new place for himself. To do this he needed his father's help, yet this father was not so effective, and showed an inability to exert much influence over his wife. In fact, they were to divorce not long after the resolution of the phobia.

So what was the function of Hans's symptom? For Lacan, it was a way of appealing to the symbolic function of the father where the real father had let him down. It was the horse and not the father that became the mythical, frightening, powerful figure that was to literally reorder his world. The phobia was a properly creative process, which we can follow day by day in Freud's published account. It showed Hans busy appealing to the Name-of-the-Father, accessing the latter's function in order to move through the Oedipal involvement with the mother and to situate the new and disturbing bodily changes present in the erections. The result of this process would be a new symbolic configuration, a new place for him in the world.

This appeal to an external, heterogeneous element is beautifully illustrated in Marcel Pagnol's memoir *My Father's Glory*. Young Marcel is a great admirer of his schoolteacher father, yet when his Aunt Rose takes up with the wealthier and more polished gentleman Jules, the paternal image is undermined. The two families rent a holiday villa and the men go off shooting. Whereas Marcel's father has never killed beast or bird before, Jules is an expert. His gun is magnificent, whereas the father's is out of date and rather absurd. As Marcel watches the sizing-up of the two guns, he feels humiliated and a strange malaise sets in, a dissatisfaction the cause of which he does not understand. When he realizes what is going on, the problem is still there: his father, the great teacher, has now become a schoolboy, instructed by Uncle Jules, the specialist. For the first time, Marcel says, he doubts the 'omnipotence' of his father.

As the two men continue to hunt, the field of their trophies is divided neatly into two parts, the animals that they can and do hit, like the ordinary partridge, rabbit or hare, and one special animal that is distinguished from all the others: the rock partridge. This is the ultimate prize of the hunter, yet its value is matched by its rarity. As Marcel assists the adults on their hunt, he does his best to restore the crippled image of his father: at one moment, he produces some feathers to suggest that his father had hit something. Banned from trailing along, he follows in secret, abject at his father's poor show, until suddenly the latter strikes lucky. He shoots not one – which would have been miracle enough – but two rock partridges, one of which lands on Marcel's head. While Jules mistakenly admonishes Marcel's father for missing the rare birds, Marcel emerges from the undergrowth carrying the trophies.

Returning to town, the locals are struck dumb by this unheard-of feat, and the father is photographed with the dead birds. Later, he will send a copy of the photograph to his own father, thus giving the rock partridges a value in the link between generations. Now Marcel feels a new love for his father. This story brings out the difference in the registers of paternity. The father is idealized, until the arrival of

Uncle Jules, whose gun is better. The father is progressively humiliated, until the hunting episode, where he takes on his crest in the form of the rock partridges. They function like a coat of arms, fixing not only transgenerational identity – the photo sent to the grandfather – but also conferring a status on their bearer. The birds, after all, had a special value since the start of the narrative, distinguished from other animals as a mythic bounty: they are less real birds than symbols. The symbolic elements crown both son and father, bolstering the latter's weakened image.

We could think here of the countless films and TV series where the true salvation of a family takes the form of some animal (Lassie) or even extraterrestrial (ET). The rescue mission is carried out not by the real father but by a non-human protagonist, as if to emphasize the disparity between the biological progenitor and the symbolic function of paternity. It was this symbolic texture of the father that made Lacan use the expression 'Name-of-the-Father', as if the outside force necessary to introduce order into human relations was beyond flesh and blood and situated rather in the register of symbols.

We can see a stagnation of this process in the case of Joey, a nine-year-old boy who would spend several years at the University of Chicago's Sonia Shankman Orthogenic School, a centre for disturbed children. It was there that he would meet Bruno Bettelheim, who published a striking account of their work together in his book *The Empty Fortress*. When Joey had first been treated in a special nursery at the age of four, he would pay no attention to anyone around him but run to and fro gyrating his arms like a propeller. When he discovered an electric fan, nothing else could distract him, and when separated from it, he would return to running around, moving his arms and making a noise like a fan or aeroplane propeller. He would imitate these sounds with almost mechanical precision, and other objects, such as spades, sticks or spoons, would only become interesting to him if they could be used as propellers.

What was the source of this strange fascination? It turned out that his interest in fans had first been aroused at an airport where he would meet his father departing or returning from assignments. Beyond this was the fact that the mother had been in love with a man who had died in air combat shortly before she married Joey's father. Bettelheim recognizes that this link to the father was what accorded such an exclusive value to the propellers, yet notes that 'despite the propellers and the airport's direct link with the father, we cannot believe it was the father as a person who caused Joey's obsession'. His intuition is precise: it is not the father as a person but as a function that matters here, yet the appeal to this symbolic dimension fails for Joey.

In contrast to Hans's horse, Joey's propellers would not mediate and reorganize his world. They were less a tool that he used than an element that, on the contrary, possessed him. Although clearly linked to some term beyond the mother, indexing the father and perhaps the lost lover, they produced no psychological movement or dialectic, but rather a stagnation, as if he were caught at the moment that a symbolization might have started but never did. The propellers were not a symbol he could use but in fact froze him in one isolated repetition. Rather than opening up his reality, they contracted it.

—

It is often through the real father that the symbolic father's function is transmitted. Parents become curious when, at a certain moment, their child elevates the father into some kind of hero. However ineffectual or feeble he may be in reality, he suddenly becomes a champion, capable of the most amazing feats of prowess and accomplishment. What logic might there be behind this transformation? If the child is faced with the problem of separating from the mother – which will include within it the problem for the mother of separating from her child – what better strategy than to suppose that the mother is herself powerless, enthralled to another, more powerful figure. The child has essentially constructed a fiction to show that the mother does not have absolute power but is herself lacking, subject to the paternal law.

In this process, the child is appealing to the symbolic father, through transforming the real father into an imaginary figure of might. Myth and folklore often articulate this effort to transform the image of the mother by an appeal to the father. A huge monster turns out to be controlled by a tiny dwarf, or the Wizard of Oz turns out to be controlled by a humble and cowardly figure. These fictions show how an apparently all-powerful presence is in fact subject to a law — a puppet rather than a puppeteer — exactly as the mother's status as an omnipotent being is challenged by the idea that she is herself subject to a law beyond her. This is surely one of the attractions of the Russian dolls that so fascinate both children and adults. This clearly maternal representation of one figure enveloping another shows, by its very structure, that the enveloping figure is always enveloped itself, and we could speculate that a Russian doll with only a central figure and one containing shell would be far less intriguing. What matters is that the second, containing figure is herself contained, exactly as the child must find a way to show that the mother is herself subject to a force beyond her. Otherwise the child is left entirely at the mercy of her power.

This process of weakening the mother's power is how Lacan reformulated Freud's theory of the Oedipus complex. For Freud, the first sexual object for both the boy and the girl is the mother. Their demands for physical closeness and love are directed at her. The father, for the boy, is seen as a rival for her love, and when he recognizes the difference between the sexes, the possibility dawns on him that he might lose his penis, and so he backs down: he gives up his demands on the mother due to the threat of castration, which he attributes to the father. His longing for the mother now becomes unconscious, and he may search later in life for women who evoke her in some way.

For the girl, sexual difference is also decisive in this early period of childhood. She reproaches the mother for not providing her with a penis, and now turns to the father not as a rival but as a saviour. He will be able to give her a penis, not as an anatomical organ but in the form of a child. So where the Oedipal love for the mother is blocked for the boy by the idea of castration, the girl's love for the father is established by it.

Freud's theory is more complicated than this summary, but it gives us the basic idea of the Oedipal journey for the child. Lacan's version is very different. He sees the initial relation with the mother as problematic and uneasy. Closeness to her may be valued, but it is also a source of anxiety. She has the power to dispense love and care at her will. This gives her a real dominion, echoed in her delivery of nourishment. As provider of food, she is not simply the one who gives, but the one who is felt *to decide* to give. Everything, in a sense, depends on her: she can give or withhold milk, and this confers on food its role as a sign of maternal love.

Anticipating her responses, a basic trust may be established between mother and child, which involves repressing the very idea that her actions depend on her will. This is a faith in the symbolic order as such, a fundamental foothold that makes the mother–child relation subordinate to the symbolic law that we care for our offspring. Yet, in some cases, this basic trust does not register. The symbolic order comes without a guarantee. In her memoir of schizophrenia, Renée remembers how her mother would say, 'I have an absolute power over you; if I wanted to, I could kill you'; 'I know everything you are thinking; it is my right to know, even what you dream. And at night in your room, I know if you are moving in your bed; your body, your mind, your soul are mine.'

This mortgage upon the child is brought out in another example, described by the American psychoanalyst Harold Searles, in which a woman slept in the basement of the family home, with strings attached to her wrist that ran up to her mother's wrist, sleeping on the floor above, so she could respond immediately to the mother's needs. Although these examples may seem extreme, they bring out aspects of the psychological situation of many infants. As we will see later on, it is difficult not to link the experience of things being 'up to' someone else to the kind of thinking we find in psychosis where things happen *because of* someone else's will. The plane is flying overhead or the wind is blowing due to some plot or conspiracy, as if the basic situation with the caregiver had become generalized to the whole of one's reality. There is no mediation to show that the mother is herself subject to laws and constraints.

A child will naturally want to find a safe space to exist in this atmosphere of dependency and relative helplessness, and will question its own place in relation to the mother. What value do they have for her? Why is she present at one moment and absent at another? What is it that she wants? Lacan saw the Oedipus complex as a way of answering these questions, creating an order in an initial situation fused with both love and terror. There are three phases now in the Oedipal process. First of all, the child recognizes that the mother is interested in something that isn't him or herself: her desire is directed beyond her baby. This presupposes a registration of the mother's absences, which indicate that she is not saturated by her child, and hence can go away from them.

To be able to formulate the question of her comings and goings involves a basic symbolization of the mother's behaviour, the ability to think about her absences and the way she is perceived to dispense or withhold affection. Lacan calls this initial enigma the 'desire' of the mother, and the central task for the child is now an interpretative one. Where Lacan referred to desire, the anthropologist and social scientist Gregory Bateson spoke of the mother's 'moodsigns', coining this expression to show that the mother's presence requires decoding. This process is often accompanied by games in which an object is clasped and then thrown away, together with verbalizations opposing distinct sounds for each of these states: in Freud's famous example, his grandson pulled a cotton reel towards him saying 'Da' ('There') and then threw it away with 'Fort' ('Gone').

This is not an automatic process, as we see from those cases in which the child is unable to ask a question about the mother's absences. Her disappearance can be experienced as an unbearable hole, or as a betrayal or abandonment that admits no explanation. But if this first symbolization does take place, the child seeks an answer to the question of the mother's desire. Her absences show that there is something that draws her away. And this means that she is not omnipotent, that she is lacking: otherwise, why would she be so pulled?

In a second phase, the child may try to explore this 'beyond', testing it in games of seduction and prestige. The child becomes like a little lover here, trying to 'be' something for the mother, to satisfy and complete her. Just as in the mirror phase there was a movement towards a false image of wholeness, so these new efforts follow the same imaginary template: the child aims to become an image it is not.

In a third phase, there is a recognition of the fact that this is doomed to failure. The child now understands that the magnet beyond the mother cannot be him or herself, but is linked in some way to the father.

Children will often protest this connection, doing their best to separate the parents, but beyond the drama and turbulence of their thwarted ambition lies a basic question of what other pathways are open to them. Will they remain in the world of the mother or choose another direction? The father's function here does not just signify to the child that it is not the unique object of the mother but will equally affect her, situating a limit to her own propensities to cling on to her child. It establishes a barrier between both child and mother and mother and child, an active negation of the wish to reintegrate her offspring.

Both the boy and the girl must now learn to give up their efforts to seduce her, to be the object of her desire, and reorganize their world around certain insignia of the father, which they identify with. These provide a new compass point, a way out, as it were, of an ill-starred situation. In analytic terms, the child must renounce trying to *be* the phallus for the mother – at the imaginary level – and accept *having* or *receiving* it – at a symbolic one: for the boy, as a promise for future virility, for the girl as a hope for future maternity, with her baby unconsciously equated with a phallus.

For both the girl and the boy, this transforms the relation to the mother, as it establishes a horizon for her, a meaning that her actions are now linked to. First, the child registers that the mother is not all-powerful but lacking, and second, this lack is named. The father's function here is to make sense of things: it allows an interpretation of the mother's desire. It gathers the thoughts about her into a set that is constructed around the father and, specifically, the phallus. The phallus here is not the real penis, but a signification, an indicator of what is lacking, an index of the impossibility of completion or fulfilment. As such, it has no visual image, it can't be caught or clearly defined. If it signifies potency or plenitude in the first moment of the Oedipal process, it now takes on a more fundamental value of loss, what we cannot be and cannot have in the present. Always out of reach, it is a way of symbolizing incompleteness and it thus introduces a sadness into the child's life, but also an order, a symbolic framework that will allow the child to progressively move beyond the world of the mother.

The child's experiences of physical and mental excitation are transformed through this framework into desire, which implies a minus rather than a plus: the mother is lost for ever. The libido is now channelled outside the body, towards those elements of the world around us that remind us unconsciously of her. Since the mother is forbidden, later evocations of an inaccessible or prohibited person or object will excite our interest. The mother is thus emptied out: she becomes less a real, physical presence than the pole of unconscious desire. The eroticized memories of her succumb to repression. We can see this in the way that children sometimes cry 'I want my mummy' even after they have found embrace in the latter's arms. The word 'Mummy' refers to something out of reach, something that is now beyond the flesh-and-blood creature in front of them. This is reflected equally in the fact that the most common choice of computer or bank password is the mother's name or telephone number, as if the most secret thing in life is still her.

Lacan calls this process the 'paternal metaphor': the father is substituted for the aspiration to complete the mother, who now takes up her place at the vanishing point of unconscious desire. The father, as we've seen, is not just a real, empirical figure, but a function, a third party present in the symbolic world of the child. This substitution is evoked in the term 'Name-of-the-Father' itself, since the transmission of the paternal name to a child means that it replaces that of the mother. Lacan would modify his views over time, arguing that the symbolic function that the child invoked was not necessarily linked to paternity. The father was simply one example of many things that could all contribute to providing the mediating principle to the world of the child, some third term that would temper the relations with the mother. Anything could count as a Name-of-the-Father as long as it worked to introduce limits and to bind together the registers of the symbolic, the imaginary and the real. It could be a professional endeavour, a lifestyle, an activity: what mattered was less what it was than what it did.

The Name-of-the-Father, likewise, is not a single point but a process. It cannot be reduced to any one tangible element, but is transmitted through complex family relations. What would matter for the child is the availability of what one of my patients called 'rivets', strong points in the surrounding symbolic network that they can draw on. This could take the form of family members, adjuncts or myths about moments in the family history. Many years ago, a group of patients at a French hospital asked their psychiatrist if he could arrange for a surgical implantation of the Name-of-the-Father after they had heard that it was absent in psychosis. To see the Name-of-the-Father as a single, isolated element, like the missing piece of a jigsaw puzzle, can in itself be delusional.

—

This account of the Oedipus complex may seem rather idealized. In the modern family, one might object, the father is either totally absent or present when the mother is absent, so her disappearances can hardly be correlated with her desire to be with him. Seeing his children so rarely, he is more likely to be a playmate than an authority figure. These critiques are interesting, and shed light on changes in family structure, but they miss the dimension of the Oedipus complex less as a reflection of the real power relations in a family than as a construction, a fiction produced by the child to bring an order to its world. If the focus on the signification of the phallus as the key to the mother's desire appears comic, well, it is: that's why post-Oedipal life is like a comedy, as we see clearly from the *Carry On* films.

This once interminable series of British films put the same cast in a variety of different situations: there was *Carry on Nurse*, *Carry on Doctor*, *Carry on Camping*, *Carry on up the Khyber*, *Carry on Constable* and, indeed, every aspect of life was sent up, from family dynamics to the health service to British imperialism and the trade unions. The series showed that the whole of reality could be reduced to a phallic joke, as essentially all the humour in these films consisted of sexual double entendres.

This was post-Oedipal life, where the child now saw things – unconsciously – through a phallic lens, with few other possibilities.

Interestingly, this suggests that as we grow up we become less aware of the world, more restricted in our perceptions and sensitivities. It is as if a filter is introduced into our minds which only allows us to grasp certain aspects of reality. The earliest relation with the mother may involve an extraordinary degree of attunement: babies can pick up on the mother's moods incredibly quickly. The meanings ascribed to her – and others' – behaviour may be wide, yet with the establishment of phallic signification this is reduced. Life becomes a *Carry On* film where all we understand is a limited range of meanings.

In psychosis, however, where, as we will see, the paternal metaphor has not operated and the phallic lens is not set into place, the result will often be a kind of super-attunement, where the person can sense uncannily the therapist's moods and thoughts. As one of my psychotic patients put it, 'The difference between me and a neurotic is that a neurotic would project their own stuff on to you, but I actually know what you are feeling.' Although madness is often defined as a failure to be in touch with reality, it is in fact, as the psychiatrist Eugène Minkowski observed, about being too in touch with reality.

Kurt Eissler noted how a schizophrenic patient of his, although unable to see him as he was lying on the couch, would ask his analyst to repeat what he had just said at exactly those moments when Eissler had stopped listening. 'At moments when I actually was unable to repeat the patient's last words, he demanded categorically that I should repeat what he had said.' Amazingly, this demand would occur only when Eissler could not meet it. Likewise, he describes how an interpretation of a dream linking it to childhood sexuality was greeted with the comment 'You don't prove that to me, you prove that to yourself' at the precise moment when Eissler was concerned with proving a related point to his colleagues. The patient was super-attuned to his analyst's unconscious.

—

The Oedipal process introduces a negativity into our lives, establishing both a meaning and a limitation to meaning. At the same time, it has effects on our libido, the excitation in our bodies and the strength and direction of our attachments. The most important part of this process is the establishment of lack. We have given up the mother, to create a zone of emptiness that later objects can eventually occupy. Our libido has been exiled from our bodies, more or less, and linked now to the sign of absence.

Giving up the mother also means giving up who we imagined we were for her. As the symbolic process operates, we have to abdicate from our aspirations to complete or fulfil her. We register the fact that we cannot be everything for her, and that she is interested in something beyond us. Recognizing that her behaviour has a cause which is not linked to ourselves is both tragic and liberating. Without this, everything would be interpreted as referring to oneself: the mother is happy or sad because of us, a position that a child might aspire to but which is ultimately unliveable. Being the unique cause of another person's emotions places a terrible weight upon us, as if we were always responsible. We would remain in a world with no mediation between ourselves and the mother, and what we imagine she wants.

These ideas about the Oedipus complex always involve two levels: a recognition of some process – like the mother's desire – and then the naming of this process – the father. It is not just a question of sensing the mother's lack, but of naming it, registering it. Lacan's ideas here echo and inflect those of Bateson, who saw the key process in childhood as the establishment of what he called 'communication about communication'. The child is confronted with many signals and messages, and must learn how to categorize these. If, for example, someone asks 'What would you like to do today?' the message could be understood as a literal question or as a condemnation of what was done yesterday. Presumably the context and the tone of voice will determine which interpretation is more likely, and so the message can be labelled, assigned to one of many different sets that will allow its meaning to be grasped.

Lacan's theory focuses on the same question: how the child interprets the mother's speech and behaviour, and how this interpretation will assign the latter elements to a set. This Oedipal process gathers up the various representations of the desire of the mother through the act of naming, and generates an unconscious categorization. For both Bateson and Lacan, problems in this process are indicative of psychosis. As we will see later on, these problems will allow us not only to distinguish different kinds of psychoses, but also, if the paternal function fails to operate in psychosis, it will show us how other forms of set construction can help the individual create a less invasive, more bearable world.

The Oedipus complex thus does three things. Firstly, it introduces meaning, by tying the question of the mother's desire to an answer: the father and the phallus. Secondly, it localizes the libido, the strength of our sexual attachments and interests, making of the prohibited image of the mother – or parts of her – the horizon of sexual desire. There is thus a localization of libido, an anchoring that locates the objects of our desires outside the body. Thirdly, it allows us to situate ourselves in relation to the Other, to find a safe distance, and move into another space where it is not simply us and her.

But what would happen if these processes failed to take place? If something were to block or hinder this passage through the Oedipus complex?

3. Psychosis

We have seen how the Oedipus complex has three basic results. First of all, it establishes a new meaning; secondly, it localizes the body's libido; and thirdly, it establishes a distance, moving the child away from being the exclusive object of the mother. Once we recognize these processes, many of the clinical phenomena of psychosis suddenly come into perspective. Rather than seeing them as indications of disorder, chaos or collapse, they can be understood as attempts to solve these three fundamental problems: how can a meaning be given to one's reality, how can the body's libido be anchored, and how can a safe distance from the Other be created?

When Schreber became unwell during the summer of 1893, the world began to seem strange to him. Everyday events seemed odd, not quite right, as if they harboured meanings that were opaque to him. The thought – 'so foreign to my whole nature' – that it would be pleasant to be a woman 'succumbing to intercourse' troubled him: conflicting with his sense of manhood, he could not accept it. Soon, his body began to undergo peculiar transformations: he would ejaculate repeatedly at night and his nerves gave him feelings of what he called 'voluptuousness'.

His hallucinations and bodily sensations became unrelenting and torturous. Voices would jabber endlessly and he felt caught in a physical and mental web with a God who was not well disposed to him. At the end of the long process of constructing a delusion, meaning and his sense of a body were to some extent restored. He knew that he had been chosen as an exceptional being, and that his mission would be to beget a new race. The terrible pain of his physical symptoms and the intensity of the voices he heard would lessen: what had been 'terrifying and threatening' was now 'increasingly harmless'. And his voluptuous sensations were now focused on a scenario in which he would adorn himself with 'female trinkets' and contemplate himself in a mirror.

The disturbing thought that implied his feminization had now become an idea that he submitted to, one which would be for the 'greatest good of mankind': he had 'reconciled himself' to the idea of being transformed into a woman, not, as he had initially believed, to be used as a base sexual object – 'a female harlot' – but as one who would create the new race. The feelings of female enjoyment he felt in his body were not to be rejected now, but seen as both his 'right' and his 'duty' to cultivate. It was a way of trying to restore what he called the 'Order of the World', a harmonious system that his voices had described to him and that he felt had been broken.

The delusion had thus given a meaning to Schreber's experience of his world and had succeeded in assigning his diffuse feelings of bodily libido to a more structured, localized point. This had been achieved through his allocation to a special place, the one human chosen to become the begetter of a new race. Although he had been plagued by a lack of understanding regarding the changes that were taking place both within and around him, now these took on a signification. If, in the first years of his delusional construction, his distance from God was always problematic – either too close or too far away – it was now more solid: he even pitied this God who grasped so little of human affairs.

The delusion had thus accomplished the three crucial Oedipal tasks: treating the problems of meaning, libido and one's place in relation to a more powerful Other. Although for Schreber the delusion was not as robust as he might have wished, and he was forced to return to hospital after his mother's death and his wife Sabine's stroke in 1907, it shows us nonetheless the aims of delusional constructions: less as primary symptoms of psychosis than efforts to repair. What may appear to be signs of deterioration can in fact be parts of a larger restructuring process.

Another example can illustrate this restorative function of delusion. Brought up by an invasive mother who watched her continuously and whose mood swings were terrifying and unpredictable, a young girl developed the conviction that she was the only human left in the world. All her surroundings, her family and her acquaintances were illusory, created by aliens to study her reactions. Her life was simply part of an immense and highly complicated experiment to observe and document human life. Isolated in her bathroom, she would experience a state of bodily excitation, with the idea that here she was being scrutinized by alien medics. This delusion, which was tightly structured, allowed her to survive. It made sense of her world, explained the bizarre behaviour of her mother, and gave her a position in the scheme of things. Without it, we might wonder how she could have understood the mood swings and the intense, perpetual gaze she was subjected to.

As with Schreber, the delusion assigned a place to her in a meaningful design. Although less elaborate than his system of rays and nerves, it brought a solution to the three Oedipal problems: establishing a meaning, localizing the libido and situating a place. Rather than being the prey of her unpredictable mother, she was the one human chosen for the experiment, moving her away from the place of a purely passive victim. Delusion here gives a new inflection to the experience of *being an object*: for Schreber, the movement from being a degraded 'harlot' to being the vehicle of mankind's future, for my patient from being the 'butt' of her mother to being the subject of scientific research. In bot' cases, through giving a place to the subject, the delusion distanced them from being simply something to which brutal things were done, as now these had a purpose and a meaning. Both Schreber's delusional system and that of my patient would not prove entirely successful over time, yet they show how these primary concerns are central to the work of psychosis.

We can see this movement from object to agent in the work of the American schizophrenic Louis Wolfson. In the 1970 book that he published about his experiences, he described a key childhood scene in which his mother looked on while a nurse forced a rectal thermometer inside him. This traumatic insult was to leave traces in many psychotic phenomena for Wolfson, including the compulsion to cry out the word 'Enema!' in the street. In the 1980s, however, it seemed that a new idea had emerged. After his mother's death, he became preoccupied with the idea of cleaning up the planet. A transformation had thus taken place: instead of being in the passive position of a pure object given over to the cruel will of the Other, he was the orchestrator of a mission of salvation. As Serge André pointed out, the intrusive attempt to clean his body became a wish to clean the planet, just as Schreber's degrading experience of being feminized would become his glorious mission of embodying God's chosen begetter of a new race. Wolfson's idea involved a shift from being the site of an invasive libidinal intrusion to the project of draining libido from the whole planet.

These examples show us how delusion is less a problem than a solution. For over 150 years, psychiatrists from Lasègue and Bleuler to Lacan had observed that what are generally taken to be the symptoms *of* madness are in fact responses *to* madness. The most 'striking and noisy' of the phenomena of psychosis, Freud observed, are 'attempts at restitution or recovery'. Delusion, for Freud, is not a primary symptom of psychosis but an attempt at self-cure: it is 'found applied like a patch over the place where originally a rent had appeared in the ego's relation to the external world'. What we take to be the 'pathological product is in reality an attempt at recovery, a process of reconstruction'. When a hole opens up in a person's world, a delusion offers repair through the provision of meaning: the cars going by are there to spy on me, the curtains are moving because of a listening device, the friend who greeted me differently today is in league with my persecutors. Delusion is thus a positive rather than a negative phenomenon, an attempt at healing rather than a pathology in itself, even if it can often fail in its tasks.

For Freud, much of psychosis is about restitution, the effort to recreate reality or re-establish contact with it. The oddness of delusional thought often makes it appear quite the opposite, yet its curative function can be singularly clear. In one case, a woman with erotomania – the delusional certainty of being loved by someone else – wrote to the man in question to request that he send her a formal letter denying that he was trying to influence her and confirming that he was simply a stranger. She gave him a formula, which he had merely to copy out, sign and return to her. This was not the advice of the psychiatrist but a product of the delusional movement itself. She even sent a stamp, showing how the therapeutic procedure was contained in the very gesture of madness.

—

Delusions are almost always preceded by a period in which the person feels that there is some kind of meaning in the world, although it remains imprecise and elusive. A poster on the tube, an article in the paper or a TV advertisement seem to concern them, but they aren't sure in what way. They just know that it is something to do with them. Either swiftly or little by little, the whole of reality starts to harbour a meaning: it speaks, even if its message is opaque. This period of perplexity confronts the person with meaning as such, meaning before it is fixed and pinned down. And the task of a delusion is to remedy this situation, to inject a fixed and determinate meaning into the place of perplexity.

Writing under the pseudonym John Custance, a British economist, banker and wartime intelligence analyst described his psychosis and the crystallization of delusion. Attending a war memorial service, 'Suddenly I seemed to see in a flash that the sacrifice of those millions of lives had not been in vain, that it was part of a great pattern, the pattern of Divine Purpose. I felt, too, an inner conviction that I had something to do with that purpose; it seemed that some sort of revelation was being made to me, though at the time I had no clear ideas about what it was.' There was no doubt that the 'Divine Purpose' concerned him, even if the definite meaning of his involvement was suspended. Soon after this, he would hallucinate the male and female sex organs hovering above him and pulsating, a sign, he knew, of the 'Power of Love', a name that imposed itself also at that instant.

Later, he could conclude his extraordinary account of madness with a chapter entitled 'The Theory of Actuality', in which he puts forward a basic explanation of the universe and his place within it, similar in this way to Schreber's idea of an 'Order of the World'. It was so named after a hospital nurse asked him one day why he used the word 'actually' so often and what he meant by it. He tried to explain yet was unable to, until he suddenly realized that this was 'the ideal name' with which to christen the theological 'will-o'-the-wisp which haunts me'. It could now be 'tied down and labelled'. The theory is both compact and versatile: it makes sense of the whole of human history, current world events, good and evil, and the relation between opposites.

Delusions tend to fall into two groups: the transitory attempts to find meaning, which don't endure for too long, and the more methodical systems, built up over time, which are often more solid. These latter may become interconnected into elaborate belief systems, which confer a single or limited set of meanings on most things in that person's world. Although we are all confronted with the question of how to make sense of our lives, it is usually only psychotic subjects who really take this seriously. Anyone can reflect on such questions, yet the system builders are invariably those for whom such a task has a real, existential urgency.

As we saw in the last chapter, the problem of meaning is to some extent solved for the neurotic as he passes through the Oedipus complex: his horizons are narrowed when he enters the tragicomedy of the phallic world of the parents. Prior to this, meaning is a burning question. The presences and absences of the mother must be made sense of: her comings and goings are experienced as signifying something, yet this meaning takes time to set, and may become linked, later on, to the father and phallic signification.

This process will create the grid that we call the Oedipus complex, soldering signifiers and signifieds together to organize the world. But what would happen if there were problems in connecting the two registers, if meanings were not available to help the person construct their reality? In one case, a man became unsure about the meaning of words after his father's death, and had to carry a huge dictionary everywhere with him in his backpack. He had to be certain that he had understood everything. In another example, a man explained that 'The other day one of the older farmers was addressed as "father"; immediately it went through my mind that I was his son. I always experience such meanings with words like that; they come at me directly.' He was compelled to give words a 'second meaning', especially if they were spoken by other people.

In the one case, words became disconnected from meanings, in the other they were too connected. These strange vicissitudes of the relation of signifier to signified are common in psychosis. The American critic Van Wyck Brooks describes how, in his psychosis, every knife became something with which to cut his throat, every building something to jump off, every belt a garrotte, the top of every door a bracket for a rope to hang from, every bottle something to be swallowed in splinters. This terrifying transformation of everyday life made these elements take on a new and indissoluble meaning. The semantics of the world around him had irrevocably changed. Rather than each signifier – a knife, a door, a bottle, etc. – taking on different meanings according to their context, they just meant one thing: a means to take his own life.

This metamorphosis is evoked in films such as *Final Destination*, where we know that the protagonists are going to die horribly in freak domestic accidents. In every scene we search for the potential culprit: a fridge, a washing machine, a clothes line, a polished floor all take on lethal resonances. Imagine how frightening and impossible life would be for someone for whom this were not an isolated terror but a constant experience. A signification – in this instance, not just of mortality but of some Other's wish to kill – is not repressed, but instead attaches itself to every aspect of that person's reality.

Where in some moments of psychosis we see the subject working hard to make meaning, at deciphering or uncovering not only the signification of words but also the secret relation between things, in others there is an effort to escape from a meaning that has become too fixed, too intrusive. If in neurosis the paternal function establishes and limits meaning, in psychosis this has not happened. Hence there is a search for an alternative, something like a code or a formula or even a gadget that would bring order and meaning to the world. As Lewis Hill pointed out, 'schizophrenics, as compared with other people, are extremely serious and are interested in meaning. They are trying to find some unifying principle, trying to find some sort of peace, symmetry or harmony in the world. Since it is not in the real world, they look for it elsewhere.'

—

So what forms can a psychosis take? In contrast to the ever-expanding number of diagnoses that flood the marketplace today, Lacanians tend to favour a parsimony: rather than the 360 labels of *DSM*, they recognize just three mutually exclusive mental structures – neurosis, psychosis and perversion – and within the psychoses, a further three – paranoia, schizophrenia and melancholia, with debates about how to situate autism and manic depression. These diagnoses derive from classical and not contemporary psychiatry, and they may mean something quite different from what the professional reader today is familiar with. Their meanings should become clear as we continue, but it is perhaps important first of all to say something about the use of the term 'schizophrenia', as this is so often subject to misinterpretation, and calls for abandoning the category altogether are widespread.

There have been more than forty definitions of schizophrenia now in psychiatry, not to speak of psychoanalysis and related fields. Kraepelin stressed problems with affect and volition, yet his contemporaries complained that he never gave a unique diagnostic criterion. Bleuler, on the contrary, did give a diagnostic criterion, yet argued at the same time that schizophrenia was a group of disorders rather than a single, unified category. Critiques of both Kraepelin and Bleuler were common in the first decades of the twentieth century, and yet despite many warnings, the term 'schizophrenic' was employed so indiscriminately that it was often synonymous with 'psychotic' or simply used to label any particularly difficult patient, in the same way that the category of 'personality disorder' functions today.

Anxious to restore some kind of precision, psychiatrists made new differentiations: there was schizomania, schizonoia and schizothymia, to name only a few. As these novel categories continued to ramify from the concept of schizophrenia, the German psychiatrist Karl Jaspers could comment: 'Just as the rings made on the water by raindrops are first small and distinct and then grow larger and larger, swallow each other and vanish, so from time to time in psychiatry there emerge diseases which constantly enlarge themselves until they perish with their own magnitude.' Later critics made sense of the classificatory confusion bemoaned by Jaspers by arguing that the asylums grouped together those suffering from psychosis with those suffering from syphilitic infections of the brain. Hence the vagueness and therapeutic pessimism of Kraepelin's clinic, which had mistaken a specific form of organic disintegration for psychosis.

Since the presence of syphilitic spirochetes in the brain was discovered only in 1912, it seemed likely that many of those diagnosed with schizophrenia would have simply been undiagnosed cases of organic infection. Yet in fact the same idea had occurred to Kraepelin and his students, and it seemed even further proof that psychosis had a strictly organic aetiology. As for syphilitic infections, the meticulously recorded case notes were studied after 1912 to see to what extent they might have been responsible for the patients' conditions. In the majority of cases, they were not, yet this research was unfortunately missed by Kraepelin's critics.

Today, the *DSM IV-R* defines schizophrenia via a selection process: you need to exhibit at least two from a list of five main types of symptom, including delusions, hallucinations, disorganized speech, disorganized or catatonic behaviour and so-called 'negative symptoms', such as lack of affect or volition. Some disturbance must have been present for more than six months, and if the delusions are bizarre or the hallucinations involve a running commentary or dialogue with each other, then only one of the symptoms is necessary to make the diagnosis. Critics of *DSM* have often pointed out how the diagnostic criteria here are hopelessly vague, as they entail that two people can have schizophrenia without sharing any symptoms. Similarly, they leave aside the problem of untriggered psychosis that we have discussed earlier.

Not least thanks to *DSM*, the diagnosis of schizophrenia today still generates confusions and prejudice. Patients are often taught to see it as an incurable disease that requires continuous chemical restraint. Refutations of naive views and paradigm shifts in the field have also been sadly forgotten. In a massive review of schizophrenia research, Manfred Bleuler could write in 1951 that 'Most investigators no longer consider schizophrenia *a* disease entity, an inherited disorder, an expression of a somatic disease, or a disorder susceptible to a "specific" somatic treatment.' And yet since then, the appetite for simplistic models of illness combined with the ever-present prejudices against the 'mentally ill' mean that this is exactly how most people today do see schizophrenia.

Also often forgotten were the observations of many psychiatrists in the 1970s, who claimed that the most common form of schizophrenia was one that would not require hospitalization. Gone was the biological finality of Kraepelin's initial pessimism, and clinical descriptions often reversed the prevalent image of a withdrawn, catatonic person: instead, the 'new' schizophrenics were in search of society. They would seek out relationships, marry, look for jobs, travel, explore their sexuality, and experiment with drugs. Schizophrenia was equated less with a disease entity than with the very attempts to use social networks to counter disintegration. It was no longer catatonia that gave the visual image of a schizophrenic, but an outgoing, talkative personality, greedy for social links. This conception was sadly not as influential as it might have been, and yet it showed how lifestyle could be used to find equilibrium, a fact we cannot afford to ignore today and which we will return to later.

Given the problems with contemporary uses of the term, why continue to refer to 'schizophrenia'? Lacan was reserved here, hardly ever using the word, and at times qualifying it with the prefix 'so-called'. Yet the idea of a group of schizophrenias has a certain clinical and conceptual validity, to indicate the variety of cases in which there is no solid unification of the body image, in which the libido returns primarily in the body, and in which the robust construction of delusions is abridged or absent. As Jay Watts puts it, 'what binds this group together is a problem in binding'. It is through comparing and contrasting the schizophrenias with paranoia and melancholia that their contours become sharper.

We have seen already how delusional thought can be transitory and undeveloped, or systematized and expansive. To distinguish the different forms of psychosis here, and to shed light on the kinds of delusional construction that follow, we can turn back to the three basic problems that the Oedipus complex treats. Rather than try to base a classification on surface features, such as the themes of a psychosis – for example, religious, spiritual, fantastical – the underlying questions of meaning, localization of libido and one's distance from the Other enable a real clarification of the diagnostic question. If the paternal metaphor regulates these in neurosis, in psychosis this process does not take place. It is left to each psychotic subject to invent their own solution to these problems, and the styles of response can allow us to differentiate and define the different forms that psychosis can take.

In paranoia, a meaning crystallizes: the person knows what is wrong with the world. There is a plot against them, they have a mission to accomplish, a message to disseminate. Whatever the actual content of the delusion, there is a solidity to the meaning ascribed to their situation. Libido is localized outside: in the persecutor or in a fault in society or the order of the world. The FBI or the Catholic Church or BP is evil and must be denounced. There is a 'badness' out there that has been situated and named. The content of the paranoiac delusion here may be absolutely true: BP might be blamed for destroying nature. The paranoia lies less in the idea itself than in the certainty and the rigidity with which it is held and broadcast, and the place it occupies in that person's life.

Paranoia here does not mean paranoid, and the two are often confused. Anyone can be paranoid, and certain situations can induce paranoid thoughts in all of us. But this is very different from paranoia as such, in which the person will construct something, build a system of ideas as a response to their experience of collapse. Paranoia involves creating a knowledge, a belief system centred around a fault or a persecutor, which has a high yield of explanatory power and which goes beyond simply assuming that one is being targeted or maligned by others. There are also many cases of paranoia where the emphasis is not on a persecutor but on a problem in the world that has to be solved.

There is a proper work here, the building up of a knowledge which structures that person's relation to the world. This should be distinguished from the paranoid thoughts and ideas that we can often find in the group of schizophrenias, as Henri Claude pointed out.

The absence of the inscription of a third term will make this an ever-present possibility: the person may feel threatened or persecuted or that some other is too close. In schizophrenia, paranoid ideas are often a form of defence against the terror of disintegration. One of my patients could track with great precision the movement from his first feelings of anxiety and loss of control of his thoughts to the marshalling of diverse targets of his hatred: the tax inspector, his neighbour, an old teacher. The hatred, he said, 'lets me stay more in control of my thoughts, I know where they're going'. As another psychotic subject put it, 'hatred is a way to form'.

Paranoiac delusions are different from paranoid ideas in another way as well. In paranoia, self and Other are strictly separated, but the schizophrenic's paranoid thoughts may well blur this boundary. The Other is present within themselves, as if a total separation is not possible. A schizophrenic may believe that their thoughts and even feelings are not their own but somehow put there from the outside, or are even the experiences of someone else. The paranoiac, on the contrary, sees external forces as acting outside them, not inside them, and there is never the idea that their thoughts have been stolen from their mind or inserted. The split between self and Other is thus maintained, which means that the paranoiac is fundamentally innocent: it's always the fault of others, be it the neighbour, the CIA or the State.

In melancholia, on the contrary, it is always the subject's fault. Despite counterargument and even legal exoneration, the person believes with delusional conviction that they have done something wrong. This tort can be identified with a misdemeanour or neglect in their conduct, but ultimately concerns their very being, the core of their existence, which is judged harshly and mercilessly. The self is irredeemably guilty, and nothing can be done about this: the meaning is fixed. They may besiege their entourage with a litany of self-reproach, and if a therapist tries to persuade them that things are not their fault, or if they are found innocent of some charge by a court, they may endanger themselves and at times others to prove their sin.

Some clinicians see melancholia as a mirror image of paranoia, although there are cases where the melancholic subject has not yet convicted themselves: they remain in a terrifying limbo, constantly in the dock of a court which has not yet passed judgment. The self-accusation can also often be quite discreet, perhaps hiding beneath some practice of self-poisoning through alcohol or drugs. The melancholia may never take the form of overt self-reproach that is broadcast to the person's milieu, although when it does, it tends to be clamorous and repetitive.

The fault in melancholia is fundamentally with the subject and not the Other. As Jules Séglas pointed out, the melancholic is never attacked from the outside, and hence does not appeal to civil or legal authorities for defence: he is already lost or condemned. In paranoia, the fault does lie with the Other, and if it often takes a persecutory form – the Other is attacking me, undermining me, accusing me – it can take less invasive tones when the Other is identified with nature or some abstract quality of the world. The key is that the person wants to bring an order to it, to strike out some badness, whether this is understood to be engineered by humans or by some natural process. This could be compatible with any kind of scientific research. If the badness is identified, for example, with an illness, the person might devote their life to valuable medical research.

As Piera Aulagnier observes, the paranoiac may insist that the world must be 'made to conform to an order, a law, a knowledge which the group has forgotten or betrayed'. He often presents himself as the sole interpreter or legitimate heir to a law or knowledge, be it a religious dogma, a social or educational theory, or some form of scientific truth. As well as creating a new order, the idea of restoring a lost order or system to the world is also very frequent. The person may search in the Bible or ancient texts for some hidden knowledge that must be disseminated once again to bring reason, peace or order to the world. These efforts can attract a wide audience, as we see in the popular appetite for both secular and religious movements that claim to access a secret wisdom.

The paranoiac aims to denounce or strike the bad libido in the Other, whether this is embodied by an individual, an agency, an illness or even by a race. The target here often represents a corruption of morals, of purity, politeness or decency. In some cases, the paranoiac's efforts are sanctioned by society as worthy, in others con-demned as homicidal. Hitler's equation of the Jews with a malign stain to racial purity was – and still is – accepted by many people, just as the assassination in 1986 of the Swedish president Olof Palme was seen by some as a legitimate act supported by a moral system and by others as an unacceptable outburst of murderous violence.

The misdiagnosis of paranoia is no accident in today's society. In paranoia, the libido is assigned to the Other, which means that the subject is innocent. It's always someone else's fault. It's not me that's got a problem, it's the aliens in the spaceship that's following me. The paranoiac is in the position of a complainant, pointing to the fault in the Other, and this is often compatible with normality. The person will not complain of any symptoms themselves, and if they keep relatively quiet they might build up a knowledge about their perse-cutor, construct defences or pursue some research linked to what they believe is wrong with the world.

The paranoia may become more visible when a real event, often an accident or an inheritance issue, is followed by legal action, a quest for justice, with the subject feeling wronged. Letters to authorities and newspapers follow. Society encourages us today to see ourselves as victims, and almost all human activities are legal only if we are able to make a complaint about them. Social forces thus create a landscape in which complaint is not an ultimate recourse for citizens but a basic feature defining all transactions. Children today can even make for-mal complaints about their parents and take legal action against them. There is thus a concord between modern subjectivity and paranoia, between normality and madness.

What old psychiatry took to be the defining features of paranoia – an innocence and a sense of injustice – have now become those of the modern individual. Of course, this is not to deny that sometimes people are persecuted and mistreated by external agencies. Yet what matters will be how they interpret this, how they process it, how they make sense of it. A strong sense of right and wrong is often a sign of an underlying psychosis. The more fixed and inelastic the attribution of blame to the outside world, the more likely is the diag-nosis of paranoia. Sometimes we meet paranoiacs who describe to us in the greatest detail all the injustices they have suffered: their friends turning against them, a victimization at work, some terrible accident or calamity that has befallen them. Although each of the examples seems unimpeachable, the litany of complaint betrays the rigidity that is the hallmark of paranoia. The individual examples really do seem to have been bad luck, the other people really do seem to have been at fault . . . but all the same, it is the very innocence of the complainant that should alert us to the diagnosis.

Although some paranoiacs seem resigned or calm, others keep busy and are often agents of important social change. Neurotic people don't fight for very much, living rather with the fantasy that someone else will sort out their lives for them. They avoid risk, yet paranoiacs devote their energy to the causes they believe in and we owe both the best and the worst transformations in our society to them. Because it is their mission to convey a truth and denounce some form of wrongdoing or badness, they may well do a lot of good, and, as we noted earlier, a paranoiac delusion can be perfectly compatible with a truth. The Hungarian physician Ignaz Semmelweiss saved millions of lives with his observation that poor hygiene at childbirth results in infant mortality, yet his delusional conviction as to the truth of his idea meant incarceration in an asylum.

Often, clinicians misunderstand this, and assume that if something terrible has happened to a patient, this rules out the presence of delusion. Yet a real event and a delusion are absolutely compatible. One can have been abused as a child and also have a delusion about being abused: the key lies in how the person constructs meaning around an event, the place that they ascribe to it in their lives. Severe trauma in childhood or adult life often diverts attention from this. The therapist may feel so sorry for the hardships endured by the patient that they fail to listen to how traumatic events have been processed. Indeed, we sometimes find that the traumatic events which seem to push someone into psychosis have actually been precipitated by an initial change in the person's relation to their environment: suspiciousness and distrust, for example, can lead to friction with those around the patient. The effects of such frictions are then incorrectly seen as the causes of the psychosis.

We could contrast the effect of broadcasting a traumatic history with its opposite, an emphasis on physical or mental health. A person who is given the all-clear after a medical and then insists on telling everyone around them that they are in excellent health may be just as delusional as the melancholic subject who complains incessantly that they are doomed to perdition. The content of the thoughts may be absolutely correct – the medical results prove it – but the place they occupy in the person's discourse can indicate psychosis, suggested by the litany of self-esteem, which takes no account of the speakers to whom it is addressed. The clinician may have far less hesitation in recognizing the diagnosis here than in cases where the complaint focuses on traumatic events.

Whether the content of a delusional idea is correct or not, it is the person's relation to it that matters. In paranoia, it is often treated as a message that has to be conveyed, and this passion for truth may be accompanied by a rejection of what is false, inauthentic or socially conventional. This could take the form of a dismissal of modern technology, medical care or common dietary habits, and may be linked to a project to return to nature, as if nature were in itself a form of unadulterated 'truth'.

The fact that everyone on the planet today is encouraged to do their best to save the world is useful here. The world reformer or saviour can now coexist with others without attracting too much attention. We are all invited to save the planet in small ways. The idea of restoring the world to a former state, likewise, ties in nicely with much of today's concern for ecology. There may be an image of an organic order, like that popularized by the film *Avatar*, in which everything is connected and joined in a kind of seamless biology.

The idea of a mission is interesting, and it nuances a popular view about psychosis. Work in the late 1950s and 1960s increasingly drew attention to the communication networks in the families of psychotic subjects. How did people speak to each other? What latent communications were being made beyond the manifest ones? What messages was the psychotic subject receiving?

Gregory Bateson and his colleagues argued that in many cases the messages were contradictory or mixed: the child is told to do one thing while understanding that they are also being told not to do it. Loving behaviour from the parent may conceal hostility or anxiety, yet this cannot be openly acknowledged. In one example, a hospital-ized patient seemed pleased to see his mother and reached out to hug her. She stiffened, yet when he then withdrew his arms, she said, 'Don't you love me any more?' When he blushed, she added, 'Dear, you must not be so easily embarrassed and afraid of your feelings.' He stayed with her for only a few more minutes, and after her depart-ure he assaulted a hospital aide.

Schizophrenic subjects, Bateson argued, find themselves in this kind of 'double-bind' situation, paralysed between conflicting mes-sages. Indeed, there is a difficulty here in knowing what kind of message a message is. Is it a direct command? Is it a joke? Is it a genu-ine inquiry? From this point of impasse, there may be a variety of responses: to always assume that a message is hidden behind the message received; to act as if all messages were equal, with no weight attached to them, laughing them off; or to simply ignore them, seeing and hearing less and less of what is going on and detach-ing oneself from one's environment. For Bateson, these positions mapped respectively on to the paranoid, hebephrenic and catatonic forms of schizophrenia.

We could contrast this notion of mixed messages in schizophrenia with the position of the paranoiac: the subject's predicament may be precisely the fact that they do not receive contradictory messages. We could compare Freud's discussion of Little Hans – where it is clear the boy receives one message from his mother and another from his father, not to mention internal contradictions in these messages – with that of a child who is told exactly what his or her role is: for example, to be a replacement for a dead child or an ancestor. It is this very stagnation and impossibility of a dialectical tension between messages that may contribute to the choice of a paranoiac position.

This idea resonates with an observation sometimes made about the childhood of schizophrenic subjects. Even if they are cared for and loved, there may be a certain 'anonymity' in how they are valued. A woman once explained to me how she loved all of her five children equally, and added, 'When you have a child, it's your duty to love it.' Or, to take another example, when questioned about Joey's birth and infancy, his mother described him like 'some vague acquaintance, some person or event she had heard about and noted without interest'. This lack of a particularity may be felt by the child, and it could be contrasted, as Pierre Bruno suggests, with the designation experienced by the future paranoiac, as if he is named for some role, place or mission. Later, in contrast to the schizophrenic, they will designate their persecutor rigidly, fixing them, in turn, with a name.

Old psychiatry gave a special importance to the moment when the paranoiac names their persecutor or whatever is in the place of the Other for them, and this can give us an important clue as to the underlying dynamic. We saw earlier in our discussion of the Oedipus complex that a key moment involves a symbolization of the mother's comings and goings, a realization that there is a space beyond her that pulls her away from her child. This will later become linked to the father, and, specifically, to phallic signification. In paranoia, where this operation has not taken place, the person still tries to come up with their own interpretation of the mother's desire. They succeed in naming it, and this brings us to a major difference with the schizophrenias: in this latter group, there is a difficulty in the actual symbolization of the mother's desire.

The problem here is that the registration of a space beyond her proves problematic: hence the person may try desperately to introduce or create some form of lack in their surroundings. We see this clearly working with childhood schizophrenia, where there is so often an attempt to remove something from the therapist's body: a hairband, a pair of glasses, a pen. This may also take the form of trying to find a place where they can't be seen: if the Other is too present, too close, too invasive, the subject must make a space where they can subtract themselves from this proximity. With no initial registration of an empty space, the schizophrenic endeavours to find one. Persecutors, likewise, don't take on the same consistency and longevity that they do in paranoia: they tend to be more transitory and may even be referred to as 'they' rather than by a single name which would pin them down.

In paranoia, then, there is a naming of the desire of the Other (the CIA, the FBI, etc.), whereas in schizophrenia the subject remains at the level of trying to make sense of this desire. Where paranoia involves an interpretation of the desire of the Other, schizophrenia leaves it open. Meaning is thus more or less fixed in paranoia, but unstable in schizophrenia. This is exactly what we see clinically: the paranoiac's complaints are refractory to advice or intervention, while the schizophrenic may describe their openness, their lack of defence against everything that is happening to them, as if there isn't a central, unifying signification that could provide them with a protection and an orientation. This may be apparent in speech itself, which moves from one topic to another without a focal, guiding meaning.

We can see this difference clearly in the contrast between Sergei Pankejeff and Harold Shipman. Whereas Pankejeff spent more or less his whole life asking analysts, psychiatrists and psychologists to tell him what to do, to order and make sense of his experience and his body for him, Shipman had little to say. He was taciturn and uncommunicative, yet certain of his grasp of medical knowledge and his mission to dispense it. Shipman made no appeal to psychiatrists, police or forensic investigators, and refused any dialogue. For him, there was no question, no suspension of meaning, as we find in schizophrenia.

A young psychotic subject I worked with would wander around all day repeating the word 'Wassup?' – a contraction of 'What's up?' – as if afflicted with Tourette's syndrome. The expression would echo in his head as well as pass through his lips continually, and he linked it to the rapper Jay-Z. Although the refrain was common enough, he had been struck by a video in which all Jay-Z seemed to do was repeat this again and again. We could interpret this mimicry as an effect of awe or fascination with the rapper, but it seems to also show the basic position of the subject: 'Wassup?' indexes a suspension at the level of meaning, as if he were stuck asking this basic question, in contrast to the paranoiac, who, in fact, does know what is up.

This instability of meaning is echoed in some of the physical feelings that schizophrenics describe. They may complain about bodily pains or bizarre sensations, perhaps seeking medical advice to name them and make sense of them. Interestingly, what we often find beyond these appeals is the wish to communicate that *something has changed*. This change uses the body as its idiom: the person tries to get the message across that things are no longer as they were, that they are now different. As with the problem in symbolizing the mother's desire, it can't be made sense of. Where in paranoia the subject may feel compelled to deliver a message about the world or religion or science, some schizophrenics just want to say that there has been a change. And, usually, they want this change to be somehow represented, registered and named.

If in the neurotic's Oedipus complex the function of the father names the desire of the mother, pinning it down and providing a meaning, in psychosis new ways of naming have to be invented. It is fascinating to see how efforts to name can actually be encrypted in delusions themselves. We could think here of James Tilly Matthews's famous 'Air Loom'. Matthews was a London tea broker who was interned in Bedlam in 1797, after disrupting a debate in the House of Commons. He came to believe that his body and mind were being influenced by a gruesome machine called an 'Air Loom', positioned near the hospital and which acted on him by 'pneumatic chemistry'. The tortures it could inflict were so real to him that he had to coin new words to designate them. Controlling the machine were a gang whom he named 'The Glove Woman', 'Sir Archy', 'Jack the School-master' and 'The Middleman'. This ruthless team was not simply concerned with tormenting him but was obliged to make a record of its activity: it included a 'Recorder' whose task it was to make short-hand notes. A naming function was thus present within the delusion that Matthews constructed.

Judge Schreber described a similar function in his *Memoirs*. Books or other notes, he tells us, were being kept which recorded all his thoughts and sayings, as well as the articles in his possession and those he came into contact with. Unsure as to who exactly was doing the writing down, he guessed that it must be 'creatures given human shape on distant celestial bodies'. With no intelligence, their hands were led 'automatically': their sole function was to keep a written record.

Recognizing the importance of the naming function allows a sensitivity to the efforts of the psychotic subject to structure their world. Rather than dismissing their productions as worthless or fantastical, the effort to name requires respect and encouragement. Neurosis and psychosis, in turn, can be seen as different modalities of nomination. Where, in neurosis, the Oedipus complex succeeds in naming the desire of the mother, through an appeal to a normative fiction, in the psychoses the subject has to invent: for the paranoiac, in naming what is wrong with the world; for the melancholic, in naming what is wrong with themselves; and for the schizophrenic, as a perpetual and unresolved activity.

—

If we now move from the question of meaning to the problem of localizing the libido, further contrasts appear. For the neurotic, the libido is always linked to a sense of loss. Enjoyment is never enough: it is fleeting, out of reach. This is an effect of the symbolic separation from the mother: she is always inaccessible, and we may be drawn to details that remind us of the mythic, lost enjoyment we associate with her. But in psychosis, as we've seen, the libido is not linked to a minus sign but to a plus sign. It is too present. And where in paranoia it is localized outside in the Other (the persecutor or the fault in the world), in schizophrenia it invades the person's body.

Schreber noted how, although what he called 'nerves of voluptuousness' were localized around the sexual organs for men, in his own case they were spread out across his whole body, 'from the top of my head to the soles of my feet'. Hence he would have feelings of 'female sensuous pleasure'. Excitation was not limited to the erogenous zones, as it might be for the neurotic, but penetrated his whole body. One of my patients felt that her sex organs stretched up to her head and that her brain would habitually 'puff up' like a vagina.

Invaded by this excess, the schizophrenic subject may try to negate it, appealing to doctors, surgical procedures or practices of self-harm to try to turn the plus sign into a minus. The libido here deprives the person of any sense of bodily unity, and they may try desperately to re-establish the limits of their body, through exercise, gym visits or a particular attention to clothes. Another patient felt that her body was dissolving, with no barrier between inside and outside. She was terrified that her internal organs would quite literally fall out of her. To save herself, she purchased an expensive handbag, small and compact, and this allowed her to create the sense of a bounded as opposed to an open space. Whereas she had never looked out for traffic when crossing the road, with the idea that being run over would be a relief, she now crossed carefully: not, she said, to protect herself, but to make sure that the bag did not get damaged.

In another case, a schizophrenic subject explained that she had not cleaned her flat for several years: blood, urine and faeces were everywhere, amidst piles of rubbish, washing-up and detritus. Concerned for her well-being, I encouraged her when she had the idea of hiring a cleaner, as if a cosmetic treatment of her personal space would have an impact on her mental state. She knew that she should do something about her living conditions, yet at the same time was worried, as, for her, the flat was her body: not 'like' her body, but simply her body, and that was why she had to keep the effluvia around her, to reassure her that she knew where the inside of her body actually was. When the cleaner entered her flat, her psychosis flared up. The introduction of a third party into what was quite literally her body was catastrophic: now, she said, she no longer knew where her internal organs were. The division between inside and outside collapsed, and she felt that her body had been dismembered.

This concern about bodily limits is crucial in schizophrenia. 'My body hasn't been boundaried off,' one patient explained, 'there is no separation substance like skin as others have. Anything can and does come in at any point. I am constantly under attack.' 'The organs that are supposed to be inside my body,' he continued, 'they are outside my body.' Sometimes the person feels that parts of their body have been exchanged with those of other people, and vice versa. 'There's been a change in my body,' a woman reported: a part of her wrist had been replaced by that of another woman and now she feared the same fate for her arm. 'My hand,' she said, 'doesn't belong to me.' 'It's as if [the other woman's] disgusting body parts had replaced my own.' She had to make violent efforts to retain the rest of her body, safeguarding it from appropriation.

Bodily changes in schizophrenia can take many different forms: sensations of movement inside the body, of pulling or pushing, of heat or cold, of shrinking or enlargement of organs or body parts, of disappearance of organs, of an excess of vital energy or total depletion, burning sensations, scratching or itching localized to one point or the whole surface of the body. The patient may complain that the body part affected is narrowed, widened, flattened, swollen, dried, knotted or displaced. They may feel held down and compressed by strings or tongs, or that foreign bodies are being inserted into them, and have sensations of cracking, tugging, compression or dislocation.

This inclusion of the libido in the body means that the schizophrenic person is often preoccupied with health issues, and explains why so often the psychosis first manifests itself in the form of hypochondria. The person may consult a GP with odd pains or sensations, even if no delusional thought is apparent. They will usually be dispatched to a consultant for checks, and medical scrutiny may continue without ever recognizing what is really at stake. The physical sensation may be localized to a definite area yet not linked to any known diagnosis. Diagnostic clues can be found, however, in the way the person describes their experience: they may use the same word or expression, which the patient repeats to several doctors, or their speech may become filled with curious similes and imagery to try to pin down the sensations.

The influx of libido to the body makes it too present, too material, yet in some cases we see exactly the reverse. The body is experienced as a two-dimensional image rather than as an unbearable, torturous mass. Bleuler quotes patients who felt 'merely a reflection' of themselves, of being 'a drawing in a book' or of 'feeling like a moving picture projected on to the wall'. The two-dimensional quality of a virtual image becomes the subject's actual bodily experience. After her psychosis triggered, one woman described how she could not recognize herself in the mirror: 'I just saw emptiness. I was nothing more than an illusion. I wanted to break the mirror to kill the illusion and see reality.' She had to sit in front of the mirror for hours repeating her name to feel reconnected to her image.

All of the above examples show a problem in the construction of the body image, as if the unification of the mirror phase had not operated. 'My body isn't held together . . . my neck and my head aren't connected,' complained one man. 'There's nothing beyond my chest. My stomach and the top of my skull are open.' This instability of their bodily boundary can incite bodily regimes such as dieting, gym visits or a pattern of self-harm. Cutting or burning part of the body can be a way, as a patient put it, 'to make my body my own'. All these practices may be attempts to find a way of inhabiting the body, and it is obviously dangerous to try to remove them before some alternative pathway has been found.

The lack of a bodily consistency in schizophrenia suggests that the imaginary and real dimensions have not been connected securely to the symbolic. There is nothing to pin down the body image, no internal framework that would provide a structure. Hence, in some cases, the visual image can just float away or the body is felt as an external surface which the person has no solid attachment to. James Joyce described an experience in his youth when he was attacked by a group of boys, yet he felt no real pain: it was as if, he said, his body image just peeled away from him. Where the mirror phase solders our image to us and designates it as our own, in schizophrenia this is problematic: the person can be quite literally confused with someone else, not recognizing their body as their own, or suffering the intrusion of another person's body into theirs.

When the integrity of the body is compromised in schizophrenia, suicide can seem a solution, a way of recreating a boundary to the body. As the woman quoted earlier explained, 'my organs and innards are outside, which is so intolerable that the overwhelming pull to get some relief was to go out the window for then hopefully a body would be found at the bottom and all the innards could be put back in and then sewn up and then I could be buried rightfully'. The idea of suicide here is less about dying than about re-situating the organs back inside the body, and then, with the idea of a 'rightful' burial, indexing it symbolically. Another patient, desperate to restore order to her body, said that 'if I hang myself or fall at least that way my body will be whole'. She was fascinated by the chalk contours that marked out the space where a body had been found in TV crime dramas, as if this were the 'ultimate solution' for her: contained and bounded, they offered the 'perfect image' of what a body should be.

The invasion of the body by libido in schizophrenia and its localization in the persecutor in paranoia can be contrasted with melancholia. Here, the libido is neither situated in the Other nor in the body as such but in the person's self-image, their ego: they are worthless, a waste of space, trash, and they insist on this with a never-ending monologue of self-denigration. It is not the Other that is at fault, as in paranoia, but the person themself: they are the cause of the world's calamities. In contrast to neurotic doubt – 'Am I to blame?' – the melancholic is certain that something – or everything – is their fault: 'I am to blame.' Living with the impossible burden of this guilt may lead to suicide. It is as if the melancholic subject harbours a primary, ontological fault within themself, and they may even have to sacrifice themself to ensure that the world is saved.

We should note here that not every case of psychosis in which the person insists on their sins is a melancholia. Persistent self-blame may in fact be a form of megalomaniacal paranoia, as Karl Abraham pointed out. The declarations of guilt can disguise a paranoia, in the sense of being 'the greatest sinner'. The Wagner case is a good example. He condemned himself for the unspeakable crime of sexual relations with animals, and would kill his family in order to wipe out the bad genes that risked transmission, yet he was not melancholic. We see this in the outward direction of his reproach to those supposedly persecuting him, and in the act of naming his persecutors: the men of Mülhausen.

It is interesting to note that both before and after the murders, Wagner wrote poems and plays that he imagined would get published or performed. He would be recognized, he believed, as Germany's greatest dramatist. It is difficult not to link this to the motif of the paranoia: where the world around him judged him a sinner, with his literary production he could be judged a great writer, as if this latter glorification formed the counterpoint to his equally delusional condemnation. As he would write later, 'Leaving aside the field of sex, I was the best man out of everyone I have ever known' – a man who just wanted to be judged from the perspective of art, as in this field he was no longer a prisoner of what he had lived through and suffered.

—

Why the ubiquity of this motif of being the exception in psychosis? Whether it's as hero or scapegoat, the subject occupies a special, unique place. It is important not to interpret this too hastily as a delusion of grandeur. As Bleuler noted, the kings and emperors, popes and redeemers of his wards were all quite happy to do menial work. The Bride of Christ would do the laundry without complaining, and the King would be pleased to do farm work. Despite their elevated status, the Son of God or Pope could speak of their situation with perfect indifference. How could this apparent contradiction be explained?

Although delusions of grandeur do certainly exist, they are a subclass of all those delusions that aim to give the subject the place of an exception. As Arthur Burton pointed out many years ago, the narcissism the person may appear to display here is more existential than selfish. They are not so much interested in inflating their ego as they are in simply surviving. And to survive entails creating a singular, individual space, which is not part of some pre-existing set or group. We could think here of all the fantasies children have of making a home within their home, a special cubbyhole or hideaway which is linked to but not part of some family house or garden. In psychosis, this is not a childish whim but a necessity.

Why would the creation of such a space have such an important function in psychosis? The common-sense idea is that it is merely a transformation of delusions of persecution: 'Since they are all attacking me, I must have some special secret, gift or power.' Schreber explains that 'Since God entered into nerve-contact with me exclusively, I became in a way for God the only human being, or simply the human being around whom everything turns, to whom everything that happens must be related and who therefore, from his own point of view, must also relate all things to himself.' The subject's idea of themself thus seems to follow from the place they occupy for the Other.

This was essentially the view of Theodor Meynert, Carl Wernicke and some of the late-nineteenth-century French psychiatrists, who saw delusions of grandeur as rationalizations of delusions of persecution. Yet, clinically, such a sequence is uncommon. And, indeed, if it were a deductive process, one might expect most ideas of persecution to become ideas of grandeur. The explanation must lie elsewhere. Doesn't the place of an exception give the person a solution to the childhood question of what they are for the Other, a way of situating their existence as involved in yet also *outside* the world they inhabit? Too much inclusion will be felt as unbearable, and so a safe space must be built elsewhere, in the place of the third term that was never there for them.

Schreber's idea of being the unique begetter of a new race was both a solution to his terrible experiences of persecution and the creation of such a space: he now occupied a position that was meaningful and, for him, logical. The place of an exception was the place of providing what the Other lacked: the Order of the World had been broken, and so someone would have to go into the space required to restore equilibrium. He went into that logically necessary space, or, more precisely, he imagined this as his future.

We find this frequently in the project of psychotic subjects who invent things. Whether it is a new idea in business or some gadget, the person has understood what is lacking in the world and now endeavours to supply it. Beyond what may seem on the surface to be mere pursuit of financial reward, there is often this underlying logic of calculating what the Other lacks and then producing something to fill it. It is one way of interpreting the desire of the Other, not in terms of persecution but of lack. Where the paranoiac may have the aspiration to complete the Other him or herself, the schizophrenic is often more cautious: the project is situated in the future, so there is still an empty space that separates them from the Other.

In contrast to these cases, there are true delusions of grandeur, and we often find a childhood history of a mother who valorizes the child and then drops them. This rhythm is echoed in the swift alternation of ideas of being of great worth and then of being empty and despicable. As we explore these thoughts, we find that the person often attaches themself to someone else with whom they identify in a kind of magic way, as if they literally were the other person. A patient told me that she had no need to go to a reception because a certain celebrity would be there. When I asked what she meant, she explained that his presence meant that she was there. Separation from or loss of such a figure may result not in melancholic depression but in suicide. Clinically, it is extremely difficult to work with this aspect of psychosis, since the Other is so vital yet at the same time so destructive for the patient. Often, the person does nothing in life since the Other stands in for them, a situation that can become unbearable in both the manic and the depressive phases.

In manic elation, everything seems possible, and the person has a sense of communion with the world, of being a part of another person or process. In *The Sound of Music*, Sister Maria explains why she is late for her convent duties in the opening scene: out there on the mountain, she says, she felt that she truly was a part of nature. We could contrast this infectious gaiety with the ideas of grandeur sometimes found in schizophrenia, where the person doesn't need the world and may well withdraw from it. In paranoia, things are very different, since truly paranoid ideas will rarely appear as moods: that's why the person can be calm and quiet and then, as we saw with the Wagner case, go and kill someone. Until the paranoid area is touched on, everything seems normal.

4. Language and Logic

How could we explain some of these differences between the psychoses? If in both paranoia and schizophrenia there is the idea of being acted on from the outside, why is it that this influence can literally enter the person in schizophrenia, robbing them of both thought and body? A depressed person can tell you that they walk and eat as if someone else were doing it, and that they feel disconnected from their actions, but in schizophrenia there can be the idea that one is actually being *made* to do those things. This is a crucial difference. Actions as well as feelings and thoughts can be produced from the outside, rather than just experienced as distant.

What is it, first of all, that acts on us from the outside? As infants, it is our caregivers, whose discourse we are born into. We depend almost totally on them, and our own subjectivity tends to be asserted and formed through acts of refusal. When we say no to being fed, for example, we show that we are different from them, that we are not simply their puppets. If we can do this through action, we can also do it through speech, but this is complicated by the fact that speech, initially, comes from them. We learn words through them, and if we accept that thinking relies on verbal structures, our thought, at a certain level, derives from them too.

As Freud argued in a discussion after Viktor Tausk gave his paper on the idea of external influence in schizophrenia, 'the infant's conception that others knew its thoughts has its source in the process of learning to speak. Having obtained its language from others, the infant has also received thoughts from them; and the child's feeling that others know his thoughts as well as that others have "made" his language for him, and along with it his thoughts, has, therefore, some basis in reality.' As a schizophrenic woman said, when she was younger her father could hear her thoughts and, quite rightly, took them away from her.

Jean Piaget had also noted that as adults seem to children to know so much more than they do and to have so much more verbal skill, they might assume too that adults know their thoughts. This will be reinforced by the fact that adults will also try to understand them and to anticipate their thoughts and desires. The key moment, then, will be when the child realizes that the adult does not know its thoughts, and this is reflected in children's relation to truth. If they can tell a lie, it means that they are not in the control of the parents: they have created a space which is theirs alone, and hence the way in which most children go through a phase of playing with the truth. They may withhold it, delay it or plainly contradict it. Through this process, the dominion of the caregivers over the child's thoughts is weakened, if not simply impeached.

In schizophrenia, however, this dominion is not always broken, and it can affect both the body and the mind. The person may feel as if they are being duped, hypnotized, invaded, manipulated and deprived of their will. Where the paranoiac has a boundary to their body and to their thoughts, the schizophrenic may feel subject to some outside power that controls them and can drop them at any time. They are in the position of an object, used by a powerful Other, perhaps with the idea of being their passive plaything, a motif that we rarely find in paranoia. As Kraepelin observed, in paranoia there isn't the idea of an abolition of the will.

This apparent absence of will, however, is linked to the question of language. In schizophrenia, there is a permeability to language, as if words and images had a direct effect. Some schizophrenic subjects will obey any command or suggestion coming from the outside, and this is one reason why it so often seems that their childhoods were happy and uneventful. Doing everything that they are told in a continuous and passive obedience removes the dramas that tend to punctuate other childhoods. A patient of Arieti's would stop, when walking, whenever he saw a red light, and if he saw an arrow he would go in the direction indicated. If he saw no signs, he was immobilized.

Obedience here does not have any of the conflicts that we might expect: resentment, protest or embarrassment. Instead, words are followed like instructions: the person may take up yoga because a magazine advised it, get married because friends recommended it, or see a therapist because someone suggested it. As Serge Leclaire noted, it is as if the indicator lights on a car told the driver where to go rather than indicating what they were going to do. A young man told me how he had stabbed a teacher at school simply because another boy asked him to. He had no particular hostility to this teacher, yet when he heard the command of the other boy, he felt he had no choice but to obey. As he struck his victim, he felt like a machine, with no emotion, no feeling.

This permeability can operate at a number of levels. Andy Warhol would explain his peculiar complexion as a loss of pigment: 'I saw a girl walking down the street and she was two-toned and I was so fascinated I kept following her. Within two months I was two-toned myself. And I hadn't even known the girl – she was just somebody I saw on the street. I asked a medical student if he thought I caught it just by looking at her.' There is a directness here, as if one thing can just cause another, which is perhaps echoed in popular conceptions of illness: the person has this problem because of this cause. The complex web of predisposing factors, conditions and precipitating causes had been wiped out.

We can also see this permeability in cases of *folie à deux*, where it seems as if two people share the same delusional system. Psychiatrists were once intrigued with this phenomenon, and would separate the two subjects to see whether the delusion persisted. It was often found that, once apart, one of them would see the 'error' that they had been led into by the dominant partner. But, just as frequently, we can observe that the recognition of the error has replaced the 'mistaken' delusion with a suspicious rapidity: in effect, the permeability of the person hasn't changed, even if the delusion has. They now believe someone else, who tells them that they were deluded. The cure – recognizing the absurdity of the delusion and dropping it – may thus be the very sign of madness.

But why this permeability to language? Although everyone is shaped and directed, to an extent, by the discourses they were born into, the lack of mediation in schizophrenia is striking. An external force is described as entering directly into the subject. If this comes first of all from the parent, it suggests that the child has remained soldered to the latter's ideas and words, without being able to separate from them. This appropriation occurs also at the level of the body. Anna Freud noted how a child's body is first of all the object of another person. The caregiver has absolute power over that body, attending to it and administering care. Both external and internal processes will be linked to this Other. The sensation of hunger, for example, is inseparable from the caregiver's will: if we are hungry, it is not just because we don't have food, but because the Other hasn't fed us. Most internal feelings will be linked in a similar way to the caregiver, as if they had the power to respond. The Other is thus intimately linked to our actual body, both inner and outer, so that what happens inside depends on them. This fact must be of special importance in schizophrenia, due not only to the bizarre bodily sensations we find there but also to the ascription of such feelings to external influence. It is only in schizophrenia, after all, that we find disturbances of volition, as if our interior lives – our thoughts and our flesh – did not belong to us, something that is absent in paranoia.

If the symbolic hasn't separated child from mother, they will remain included in her. As one patient expressed it, 'I look at my arms and they aren't mine. They move without my direction. Somebody else moves them. All my limbs and my thoughts are attached to strings and these strings are pulled by others.' The Other is present within the subject here, and they may do their best to force the Other out, through self-mutilation or, in some cases, suicide. As Gisela Pankow observed, these suicides show less an attempt to kill oneself than to kill something within oneself.

Such cases show us that the subject remains too connected to the Other, unable to establish proper boundaries. The symbiosis here is not simply with someone else's body, but also, as Lacan pointed out, with the signifiers coming from the Other, with their ideas, their discourse, their speech. That's why we are often struck by the identical narratives in a family: both parent and child describe the family history or some event in exactly the same way, as if a single discourse has been swallowed whole. There is a kind of ventriloquism from one generation to the next.

Piera Aulagnier describes the case of Jeanine, a schizophrenic woman who was catatonic when she began working with her in a hospital setting. Gradually, Jeanine was able to speak about her life, yet her words seemed to mirror almost exactly those of her mother. Her version of her upbringing matched her mother's account perfectly, with the same signification attributed to events that her mother had given them. The mother had been very kind, working selflessly for her children, Jeanine had been a good girl, happy, with no major problems until her hospitalization many years later.

As Jeanine began to remember more details of her childhood, she described how her mother would shut her and her sister away in a cupboard, in order to shield them from the possibility of an encounter with their father, who was banned from the house. She also remembered that for years she and her sister had been tied to the dining-room table for several hours at a time by their mother, in order to protect them from the pins that she used in her work as a dressmaker. She described this scene with no emotion, and when Aulagnier suggested to her that it must have been painful, Jeanine replied with conviction that it had been necessary to protect them.

Of course, at one level this was true. Tying her daughters to the legs of a table would indeed have prevented them from being injured by the many needles that lay around them. Yet the idea that the mother might, over the years, have found another solution did not occur to her. She could not question the meaning of these scenes in her childhood, yet in her psychosis she would give her persecutors the intention of killing her after tying her to her bed. The TV spoke to Jeanine, and especially scenes of violence that involved someone being immobilized. Seeing the image of an explorer bound to a tree and about to be scalped, she interpreted this as a message that she would also undergo the same fate. Her doctors, she said, wanted to 'immobilize my body and my thoughts to be able to impose this punishment on me'.

Linking this to the childhood scenes produced an instantaneous relief for Jeanine, but this would last for strictly the length of the session only. It showed how the signification that Aulagnier tried to convey to her could not be integrated into her psyche, returning instead in the form of her delusional ideas. The signature of psychosis here is not only this inassimilable thought, but the accord with her mother's discourse. The fact that she was unable to even think of questioning her mother's version of the events of her childhood shows a symbiosis, not with the physical body of the mother but with her speech, her ideas.

—

The relation to language has often been studied in psychosis, and we can again contrast paranoia and schizophrenia. The frozen condensation of meaning found in paranoia is very different from the polysemy, the wealth of meaning, found in schizophrenias. Schizophrenic subjects certainly make connections to produce meaning, to try to explain what is happening to their body or to make sense of the voices they might hear, but these efforts are often inadequate. Where the signification established by the Oedipus complex is absent, the person is left at the mercy of too many meanings: this can at times result in literary and poetic dexterity, but often the person feels overwhelmed and invaded by meaning. It is as if the rivets connecting signifier to signified have come apart, and the person hasn't been able to pin them back together again through the construction of a delusion.

Sadly, much of the research on language and psychosis in mainstream psychiatry has involved experiments that both infantilize their subjects and misconstrue the key questions. People with a diagnosis of psychosis are asked to define terms like 'table' or 'chair', or to arrange words into groups or define proverbs. Perhaps unsurprisingly, such tests showed some lack or deficiency in the psychotic subject, yet the inherent absurdity of the task seems to have escaped most investigators. What would it mean, after all, for a subject to be asked by an experimenter to define a word?

This crucial question is not factored into the material. When Silvano Arieti asked a patient, 'What is life?' she replied, 'I have to know what "life" you happen to be referring to. *Life Magazine*, or to the sweetheart who can make another individual happy?' He saw this response first as an example of 'schizophrenic thinking', but later understood it in a different way: 'You ask me, a high-school graduate, to define what even Linnaeus and Darwin would not be able to do?'

When Arieti asked the same patient to define a fool, she said, 'A fool is a fool when a fool calls a fool a fool.' He saw this as a psychotic iteration of the same word, yet later realized that she was alluding to the fact that he was a fool if he thought she was a fool because she was a mental patient. It took him many years to grasp this, yet such experiments continue today with no acknowledgement of what Arieti eventually understood. The negative results of these tests are reminiscent of Richard Neuhaus's conclusion that people in the South Sea Islands had worse vision than Europeans, since they didn't do well when he tested them with the Western ophthalmological letter charts he brought with him.

As well as treating the subject of the experiment like a child, these tests ignore the question of who one is speaking to. As Gregory Bateson pointed out, the psychotic subject is especially aware of metalinguistic processes: if someone says something, there is not only a consideration of the 'content' of what is said but also, significantly, there will be a question, 'You are saying this to me now, but why are you saying it?' When Louis Wolfson's mother asked him, 'Can I please have a sheet of paper?' he devoted no less than twelve pages of his memoir to an analysis of what her words could have meant. Given this sensitivity, what would be more natural than to ask this question in the test situation: 'You have taken me to a special room and are sitting there with a notepad or tape recorder and are asking me what a table is or what life is. What do you really want?'

It is interesting to see how an awareness of who one is speaking to is nuanced in different forms of psychosis. Early researchers thought that in so-called 'schizophrenic speech' words are joined to other words through sound, rather than through a direction of meaning, a message that is being conveyed. As Louis Sass puts it, 'Instead of being guided by an overall sense of intended meaning, the flow and sense of the message is determined largely by intrinsic and normally irrelevant features of the linguistic system.' It is as if the needs of the listener were being neglected. This has sometimes been explained in terms of an excess of possibilities for the speaker, so that the person can't talk or act, paralysed, as it were, by the multiplicity of options.

Patients, we often hear, flit from one idea to another. There can be oddities in the tempo of speech, sudden shifts, unexpected by the listener, and allusive references. Bleuler stressed interruptions in speech, which he believed indicated a suspension of thinking. As one of my patients put it, 'It's not that I decide to stop thinking or that I want to block anything out: it's just that there is a splice. Like a movie splice, first there's one thing and then there's something else.' The splice can be understood as an effect of foreclosure: when the speaker approaches a meaning that cannot be assimilated, a hole opens up. Hence the sudden shift to another theme or idea.

The allusive references suggest a further underlying difficulty. Speaking involves adjusting our words and our understanding to the person we are speaking to. We include our interlocutor in what we say, through the tone we adopt, the way we speak and the message we intend to convey. That's why we might be nervous sometimes: our words come out badly, as we are too aware of how they might be judged by their addressee. But, whatever the situation, the other is always there when we speak, and we need this to be able to say anything. Beyond the flesh-and-blood listener, this other also evokes a more abstract function, a place in speech from which we can be heard: the Other with a capital 'O'. When a friend said to me 'I've got a new job, don't I?', this function was included in his sentence in the 'don't I?'. It indexed less the specificity of the listener than a place inscribed in speech, necessary for us to define our own position. As the communications theorists put it, words not only define the world but define the person who employs them.

Lacan drew attention to this Other present in speech and its effects on the direction of meaning. There was a problem with this process in psychosis, and the difficulty or impossibility of including the Other had as one of its consequences that the listener was not encrypted in the subject's speech. The man I used to chat with at the therapeutic community never said, 'I live in Xamara, don't I?' This might make it seem as if the speaker were oblivious of who he was talking to. Meaning would not be constructed as one spoke, relying on the Other to guide it and shape it, but could arrive preformed, as it were. This might at times take the form of a hallucination. The speaker would either be caught up in empty, meaningless everyday chatter, with no symbolic centre, or they would perhaps be the target of divine communication. Being in the former position might make them all the more open to suggestion and the permeability that we discussed above. Similarly, the addressee would either be in the position of an empty husk, a kind of puppet, or of a radically alien and potentially menacing presence.

This difficulty in situating the Other can affect not only the place of the listener but also, quite radically, the place of the speaker him or herself. It is through the Other, after all, that we find our own position in speech. When this is compromised, the very reference of the personal pronoun may be put in question. In a celebrated example discussed by Lacan, the patient was unsure who the 'I' referred to in her sentence 'I've just come from the pork butcher's'. We find this quite frequently with auditory hallucinations, where a pronoun is experienced as allusive: when asked who it designates, the subject hesitates, even though they know that the hallucinated sentence or phrase containing the pronoun concerns them. The vacillation here was evoked beautifully by a patient when she said that she was unable to dispatch a letter as 'there wasn't anyone to send it from'. Rather than being a slip of the tongue – with 'from' replacing 'to' – this was exactly what she intended to say: there was simply no place from which she could speak. The 'I' for her was a hole.

It is important to recognize that the language problems we have been discussing are not by any means continually present for the schizophrenic. Most of the time, a schizophrenic subject will talk like everyone else, and it is only at certain moments that this will change. The many generalizations made about psychotic language are really just applicable to certain cases at certain moments. We often hear it said, for example, that for the schizophrenic words are treated as real things, but once again this applies only to certain words in certain circumstances.

In a famous vignette reported by Tausk, a young woman believed that her eyes were twisted. She explained this via a series of reproaches to her lover: she couldn't understand him, he looked different all the time, he was a hypocrite, he was an 'eye twister' ('Augenverdreher'). This latter term means 'deceiver', and she had moved from this phrase to the idea that he had twisted her eyes: hence now she had twisted eyes. The expression had become literal for her, as the words had directly shaped the experience of her body. This kind of transformation was seen as an example of concrete thinking: as Bleuler observed, if a secret love burns within them, the schizophrenic subject may believe that someone is burning them with real fire.

In another example, a boy was sent to his family doctor because of his nervousness at the time of parental divorce. The doctor explained to the boy that he had 'bad nerves' and that nerves are like worms under the skin. The boy began soaking his hands and face in water twenty to thirty times a day, and it turned out that he knew from fishing that worms would burst if they dried up. Hence he had to keep his nerves perpetually wet. The boy had taken the doctor's metaphor literally, and this kind of process is not infrequent in psychosis. A letter is received with a stain on it and the recipient interprets it to mean that there's a stain on his character. Sérieux and Capgras discuss the case of a woman who would scrutinize all her correspondence, interpreting the punctuation in a literal way. When her brother wrote to her 'We hope that you get better' ('Nous désirons ta guérison'), she noticed that the full stop (the 'point') at the end of the sentence was inordinately large, which allowed her to reread the sentence as 'Nous ne désirons point ta guérison' ('We don't want you to get better'). Words and even punctuation are thus read literally, rather than as conventional or figurative tropes.

How could we make sense of this way of reading? Arieti speaks of active concretization: the patient who feels that his wife is making his life miserable starts to experience a strange taste in his mouth when he eats the food she has prepared. The thought that she is poisoning his life is transformed into the perception, the strange taste, that indicates she is giving him poison in his food. Another patient sees himself as a rotten person, and hallucinates a disgusting odour coming from his body. This is not a metaphorical process, as the bad smell doesn't symbolize anything: it is just equivalent to his very being. As Arieti observes, the smell may be a symbol for us about the way he feels about himself, but not for him.

It is at this point that theorists usually invoke the distinction between abstract and concrete, as if the abstract idea of being rotten is turned into the concrete idea of the odour. What can't be sustained at an abstract level becomes a concrete representation. Kurt Goldstein thought that 'schizophrenic language' involved a weakening of abstract thought. The schizophrenic, it was argued, could not think generally of an abstraction such as 'the table' but only of a specific table. The concept could not be abstracted from its real incarnations. This rather absurd idea is refuted by the example we quoted above, as Maria Lorenz pointed out: the reply of Arieti's patient shows a perfect grasp of the distinction between the concrete – *Life Magazine* – and the conceptual – one's emotional life.

We could also think here of Joey, who at a certain moment gave up naming foods 'correctly', to create new groupings. Sugar would become 'sand', butter 'grease', water 'liquid', and so on. He deprived food of taste and smell and abstracted these physical qualities from their nutritive sources. Bettelheim saw this not as a sign of some deficit but as a successful achievement, to make language reflect his experience of an impoverished world.

Yet the distinction between concrete and abstract itself is ultimately unhelpful, as what qualifies as abstract and concrete will depend on speakers, contexts, cultures and many other factors. There may be nothing abstract about the expression 'one's emotional life', just as *Life Magazine* may be concrete at one moment and abstract at another, indicative of a certain worldview or social status, for example. When a patient who feels intruded upon by sounds and noises describes them as 'fingers going into my head', to call this abstract or concrete is beside the point. What matters is how the person uses these words, what place they have in their discourse. And this, indeed, was what interested old psychiatry.

—

Late-nineteenth-century psychiatrists paid a great deal of attention to how psychotic subjects used words. They were especially interested in neologisms, the created words that would so frequently punctuate their speech. 'I've been satanized,' says one patient. 'I'm intolerated,' says another. Where meanings always refer to other meanings, the neologism is discordant, fixed, rather than open to changes and shifts in signification. These words are isolated, and carry a special weight, different from the rest of the person's speech. Jules Séglas noted that although new words are often minted in psychosis, a neologism could just as well be an everyday word that has taken on a special, personal meaning for the subject. A patient explained that he had been abused as a child and now wanted to be 'disabused' via therapy. We could see this as simply a learning error, an incorrect use of a word, but the key always lies in how the person uses it, at what points it returns in their speech.

Rather than seeing neologisms as primary symptoms of psychosis, Jung argued that they were in fact attempts at restitution. They aimed to circumscribe an experience for the subject, and the Italian psychiatrist Eduardo Tanzi's categorization of psychotic neologisms demonstrated this clearly. He divided neologisms into a number of groups: those that designated persons or symbolic beings in a delusional world; the forces or machines they had at their disposal; the means of action and procedures they could appeal to; the mental states of the subject him or herself; those designating the subject; and the qualities that they ascribed themselves. This classification is telling, as it shows that the points where the psychotic has to invent, to create new signifiers that can have a limiting, naming function, are precisely those points where they are at the mercy of the Other.

The classification shows how the words cluster around the relation of the Other to the subject, the ways that the Other can act on, influence, persecute or invade them. These special words thus come into being at the exact point of being an object for the Other. In a case discussed by Yrjö Alanen, the patient described how he was receiving messages from people around him, in an ambiguous language he called 'second-degree language'. He felt like a 'robot' whose life was being controlled by others, their 'second-degree language' generating 'pressure variations' in his body. These expressions formed part of a private language, one invented by Eric to name the feelings of invasion and threat to his integrity. He added other expressions, such as 'pressure regulation' for the action produced on him by fellow workers, and 'hole makers' for those who would not understand him. Such languages can at times be remarkably similar to those of conventional psychology, or even use existing categories. Alanen's patient did not require hospitalization and functioned very well in his social environment, and we could guess that it was the minting of his new words that helped him to do this. As one of Jung's patients said, her neologisms were 'power words'.

If meaning is sliding and unanchored in schizophrenia, neologisms can function to block the drift of signifiers and to bind the libido. It is for that reason that they seem to carry such a charge. As the psychiatrist Karl Kleist saw, it is the use of the word that matters, its function to seal associative pathways, which is why he called such neologisms 'stock words'. This means that rather than trying to 'correct' the person's neologisms, it is more beneficial to accord them a dignity, learning more about them and valorizing them. New words must be created to designate what our language cannot refer to, in exactly the same way that scientists and scholars often coin new terms to designate some novel fact or phenomenon: the psychotic's neologisms must be given the same value. Indeed, we often find that there is a correlation between the creation of neologistic terms and a reduction in the subject's hallucinations.

In one case, a woman repeated the word 'Eseamarrider' endlessly, a corruption of 'He's a married man', which referred in turn to an unfortunate liaison she had been involved in. The word here takes the place of an unsymbolizable situation, like a highly individual seal or stamp within speech. We can find another example in the work of the chemist Ludwig Staudenmaier, who was asked by a colleague to investigate the fluorescent forms believed to appear during spiritualist seances. He began to study the literature on this field and to experiment with automatic writing. His initial scepticism would change as he found that his writing was subject to the influence of ghosts, who soon started speaking to him. He documented these forces and his other hallucinations with great precision, and these external agents would later take up residence inside him. He believed that living entities controlled his body, internal 'poltergeists' who gave orders from each of his organs. 'Roundhead' would control the movements of his tongue, and in the act of peristalsis, every single moment was the work of one of the demons located in his intestines: 'Cloven Foot' in his colon, 'Horse Foot' in his rectum and 'His Highness' in the small intestine. Thanks to these acts of naming, the invasion of his body could be linked to a structure, and thereby tempered.

Recognizing this function of certain words in psychosis allows us to avoid a common confusion. We often read that the schizophrenic uses words to denote rather than connote, as if the word was linked to its initial context of use rather than its more general meaning. To use the example dear to researchers, the word 'table' would designate the specific table it had once been used to refer to rather than the concept 'table'. Although this is nonsense if taken as a generalization about the speech of schizophrenic subjects, we could understand it as an oblique recognition of the fact that the function of certain words is precisely to stop the sliding of meaning. That's why it seems as if the word just pins down one single thing, one original table. To make a word do this is less a mistake than an achievement, and it works to name the invasive presence of the Other, as Staudenmaier's example suggests.

The coinage of new words is one example among many of how a psychotic subject may try to deal with the problem of the Other's proximity. Since, in schizophrenia, the desire of the Other is not interpreted in a consistent way, the problem of meaning is more present for the person, as we have seen. Neologisms can help the person deal with this question, but so also can stereotype phrases, obsessive rituals and certain hallucinations. Auditory hallucinations often involve threats and curses, as if to name the subject at the point where a hole is experienced. When they are involved in some situation that cannot be made sense of, a word may suddenly impose itself, usually an insult: 'Bitch!', 'Faggot!', etc. Their place is nailed down here with violence, the insult being the one part of human speech that refers directly, without equivocation, thus solving the problem experienced at the level of meaning.

We see this clearly in Wolfson's memoir. On every page, the author refers to himself in the third person: he is 'the schizophrenic student of languages', 'the mentally ill person', 'the alienated subject', 'the psychotic', 'the schizophrenic young man', 'the demented subject'. The first-person pronoun appears only a handful of times, as if the multiplication of psychiatric-like designations is necessary for him to situate himself within the narrative. Rather than words pinning him down in the register of hallucinations, they are used in the process of writing itself, as points where his existence can be fixed. Like proper names, these words are more about designating than about creating meaning.

The less meaning is emphasized here, the more prominent the formal, material aspect of the word will become. A distinction made by Saussure can help us to delineate the role of neologisms here. While recognizing that language was made up of an arbitrary system of signs, he also distinguished a category of expressions within language that were what he termed 'relatively motivated'. The French 'dix-neuf' is motivated, being a combination of the elements 'dix' and 'neuf', which are already part of the code, while the term 'vingt' is not. For Saussure, the human mind contrives to limit the arbitrariness of language, in the sense of its lack of limitation and restriction, by introducing a principle of order into the mass of signs: and that is the role of relative motivation. Although the linguist associated arbitrariness more with lexical elements and motivation with grammatical structures, the example of psychosis shows how it can be both: a single word or expression, as well as a grammatical sequence, can serve to provide the principle of order that Saussure describes.

Leclaire gives the example of a psychotic man who explained to him with the utmost seriousness that the new raincoat he was wearing was called 'Beaujolais'. When he had bought it with his wife, she had remarked that it was 'joli' ('pretty'). He then wondered why she hadn't said the same thing about him, and guessed that her remark was in fact alluding to one of the friends from her youth whose name was 'Jo'. But Jo could only be ugly ('laid') in comparison to him, so the new name 'Beaujolais' signified 'I am beau and Jo is ugly'. This might seem to be a mere verbal game yet it was absolutely vital for the patient. In Saussurian terms, it was a case of relative motivation, which fixed meaning for him and blocked its sliding into delusional jealousy.

Let's move now from the language of psychosis to its logic. A patient became panicky when she saw a man who happened to have red hair near her home. He had done nothing to her and she had no idea who he was, yet he immediately became an invasive presence for her: she was utterly terrified. She felt as if he were intruding into her, even though he was by no means close to her spatially. As a child, this patient had been the object of a traumatic sexual encounter with a red-headed adult, and the sight of the man now acted as a conduit to her feelings from the past, but without the repression one would find in neurosis. It was as if her thoughts followed the equation: red-headed man = abuser = any red-headed man.

Because the abuser had red hair, any man with red hair was an abuser. Where a neurotic subject who had been abused by a red-headed man might have become anxious but without knowing why, or felt anxious around that particular man because he reminded them of the abuser, my patient would soon insist that it was the same man, even though his age and location would have made this impossible. Nothing I said could persuade her that it was a different person. What kind of logic could explain the tenacity of this equation?

The German psychiatrist and philosopher Eilhard von Domarus discussed the case of a schizophrenic man who stated that Christ and a cigar were the same thing. Explaining this, he pointed out that both a cigar and Christ had a gold band around them. Rather than assume that two subjects (Christ and the cigar) could share the same predicate (to have a gold halo), he identified the subjects on the basis of the predicate: they were the same because they had the gold band. Outside the psychotic process, an identical predicate does not mean that two things are the same, and even if they have many shared predicates, we might consider them different. Think of Groucho Marx's quip: 'He may look like an idiot, and behave like an idiot, but don't let that fool you: he is an idiot.'

This form of logical equation occurs in psychosis, but only at certain points. A schizophrenic mother described by Arieti wanted her child to become an angel. Since angels live on spiritual as opposed to terrestrial food, she did not feed the baby. The predicate 'to live on spiritual food' would thus make her baby and the angel identical. Advertising and marketing tend to rely on the opposite logic. Consumers are told to buy certain products to become like a celebrity – 'Buy these trainers and become like Beckham' – with the knowledge that the predicate (to have the trainers) will never confer identity on the subjects. Hence the consumer will be open to buy the next product, and so on. We could contrast this with a psychotic version: 'I've bought these trainers so now I am Beckham.'

This peculiarity of predication is common in other schizophrenic phenomena, where, just as identity of predicates can confer identity of subjects (Christ = Cigar) so difference in predicates can confer difference of subjects. After several years of marriage, a woman realized that she had two husbands rather than one. This was the result of a sustained observation over a period of a few months. She noticed that her morning husband had blue eyes and was enthusiastic about his conjugal duties, whereas her evening husband had greenish eyes and was more indifferent to her charms. She concluded that the evening husband was her real husband, and that the morning husband was a lover. Both had blond moustaches, but the husband's had a different tint. 'Amazing,' she told her psychiatrist, 'they are so alike: they are both saddlers; they're both called Adolphe and have the same height; and the same tone of voice.'

It is these logical processes that illuminate what psychiatry calls 'misidentification' phenomena. Paul Courbon and Gabrield Fail discussed in 1927 the case of a patient who believed that the people around her were at times other people in disguise, sent to torture her. Her persecutors could take on their appearance and impose on others the transformations they desired, like the Italian actor Leopoldo Frégoli, famous for being able to play all the parts in the same production himself. Her persecutors, she said, had the power to 'fregolify' the world, and this 'fregolification' affected both the world around her and her own body. As well as showing us the function of neologisms, created here to index the effect of the Other on her, the difference in predicates did not entail an identity of subjects but, on the contrary, their equation. One persecutor could be many people all at once.

—

These logical processes will obviously impact on the psychotic subject's emotions and affective life. Equating the red-headed man with her abuser created terror in my patient, and precipitated an intense emotional outburst. Interestingly, it was not acute emotion but its absence that Bleuler saw as a defining feature of psychosis. The more withdrawn the person appeared, the less able to show emotion, the more cut off, the more likely the diagnosis. Yet such so-called 'negative' symptoms were not as clear as they first seemed. Bleuler recognized that behind the facade of indifference and mutism there could be a turbulent emotional life.

Even if the subject seemed to show no feeling, they might later describe a heightened awareness of their emotions. As Harry Stack Sullivan and his colleagues pointed out, a catatonic patient, coming out of his spell, is often able to describe with great detail a wealth of feeling and information that he ostensibly did not react to at the time. Likewise, the movement into apparent indifference may have clear defensive purposes. As one woman explained, 'I had to die to keep from dying. I know that sounds crazy but one time a boy hurt my feelings very much and I wanted to jump in front of a subway. Instead I went a little catatonic so I wouldn't feel anything – I guess you had to die emotionally or your feelings would have killed you.'

This mechanism has often been described. One of Kurt Eissler's patients would at times feel elated – like on a fine spring day – and hence free for a moment from her sense of deadness, but this was unbearable for her: she couldn't bear 'these feelings of life', or she would have to kill herself. The 'onrush' of the emotions was agonizing and would bring destruction to her. The sense of mortification that this can produce is common in psychosis, with the paradox that although the person feels dead, this state is often accompanied by an increased sensitivity to the world around them. Dead means distant and cut off yet at the same time incredibly open and unprotected.

Such states can be precipitated by the loss of an essential reference point or support: a position at work, a benevolent look, a form of representation, such as a title. 'I am like a zombie living behind a glass wall,' one patient said, 'I can see all that goes on in the world but I can't touch it. I can't reach it. I can't be in contact with it. I am outside.' Or, to take some examples collected by Jaspers: 'Everything appears as if through a veil; as if I heard everything through a wall'; 'The voices of people seem to come from far away'; 'I am only an automaton, a machine; it is not I who senses, speaks, eats, suffers, sleeps; I exist no longer; I do not exist, I am dead.' Although the person exists biologically, as Jaspers says, he can no longer feel he exists.

In such states, which can continue for years, there is no organizing lack, no object to pull one towards it and nothing to look forward to.

'When I'm walking, I don't know where I'm going,' a patient explained. 'I don't feel I'm touching the ground. I'm like a ghost. I'm not part of the human world. Sometimes I have to hold on to things in the street to stop floating away.' Nothing interests the subject: no element in the world around them captures them, as the libido cannot be localized anywhere outside. Another patient described his existence as 'dead', as if he were a space suit floating around in outer space and not tethered to anything: 'It's unclear if inside the space suit is a dead person, nothing or anxiety,' he said.

He linked this to his fascination with werewolves, vampires and mummies. These horrific creatures, he explained, 'at least have a topography'. They gave him, he said, a sense of concreteness: 'they had a purpose, a physical direction, like zombies, they are moving towards something'. He remembered a zombie film he had seen as a teenager in which the robotic creatures moved mechanically towards a shopping mall. These monsters 'at least have a delineated body, as if they are just one absolute function, just one, with no ambiguity or choice'. 'A human being would sit on a park bench and wonder "should I do X or Y?" but a zombie would just have a magnetic force pulling them.' This, in fact, was what he aspired to.

Several psychotic subjects have described another aspect of this strange kind of living death. One of my patients was haunted by stories of a person being cut in half by a pane of glass, and knowing for a millisecond that they would die. This, for her, was an everyday experience, as if the horror of that millisecond was her regular time. Another patient described the moment in vampire movies when the stake is pushed into the heart and the vampire starts to turn to dust. 'In vampire films, they are about to turn to dust but there's a second when they know what's going to happen, a second before the body catches up with the knowledge.' This, she said, was her experience of time all day every day, as if that second had become her reality.

Sometimes, this feeling is linked to being dropped, as if the person could simply be cast off, a process even more primordial than a rejection. They feel as if they could just be replaced by someone or something else, yet rather than protesting this usurpation they simply disappear, at all levels of their existence. The absence of link to the body image here suggests that the mirror phase has not been structured by the symbolic, and this in itself can evoke a mortality. Think of the fact that when someone sees themself in an out-of-body experience – for example, lying in a hospital bed, or giving birth – this often makes them think that they are dead. When we have a separation from our image, a kind of death is experienced, showing how the motif of mortality is connected to the specular relation.

—

We will turn to the question of how diagnosis can be made in the next chapter, but we should by now have an idea of some of the central preoccupations in psychosis. As we have seen, it is important to separate primary and secondary phenomena: once a hole opens up in the person's life, the ways in which they respond to it and try to defend against it may be mistaken for the initial dilemma. Distinguishing these allows us to recognize how the person is struggling with the questions of meaning, localizing the libido and creating a safe distance from the Other.

In paranoia, meaning is produced through a delusion, which provides an account of the world and what is wrong with it. The libido is localized in the Other, to generate most commonly ideas of persecution. The subject separates rigidly self from Other. In schizophrenia, meaning cannot be pinned down, and the subject remains at its mercy. The libido is not localized outside but returns to invade the person's body. The distance from the Other is not easily maintained, and the Other may be present within their mind and body. In melancholia, meaning is usually fixed: the person is the cause of every calamity and mistake. The libido here submerges their self-image, overwhelming their ego. The Other is included within the self, but without generating the terrible battles of inclusion–exclusion that we find in schizophrenia.

From these basic structures, the psychotic subject tries to find ways of dealing with their difficulties. Rather than trying to curtail these efforts by adapting the patient to what the clinician sees as reality, it is a question of encouraging them and helping them to find their own solutions, using the logic not of the clinician's belief system but of their own psychosis.

5. Making a Diagnosis

The current vogue for the endless cataloguing of symptoms makes proper diagnosis more and more difficult. New diagnostic categories spring up overnight, based on surface symptoms yet obscuring the structures that lie beneath them. Two people may present with the same surface behaviour, say, a crippling timidity in social situations. They may both express concerns about their self-esteem and body image, and so the label 'social phobia' may be applied. Dialogue may show, however, that for one the symptom is linked to how they wish to be perceived by someone else – to be loveable, they must have a certain image – where for the other, it is simply a consequence of the delusional belief that other people know their thoughts. The same surface symptom thus covers two very different structures: one neurotic, perhaps, and one psychotic.

It is rare that a symptom as such can tell us much about diagnosis. Rather, it is the person's relation to a symptom, the way in which they articulate what it means to them. The timidity in the example above could mask either a delusional idea or a neurotic question. Classifying them together on the basis of the surface symptoms – shyness, low self-esteem, difficulty in starting a conversation – is both unhelpful and potentially dangerous.

What matters will be how the person gives voice to their experience, how they situate it subjectively: in other words, what they say about it. A patient once told me about their departure from a successful job in the City and difficulties in finding another post. Given how she had described her enjoyment of her work, I had expected to hear about a compulsory redundancy or some office friction that had necessitated the move. Yet it was only after long and detailed questioning that she admitted that she had left the job because one day, on her way to work, a black cat had crossed her path. She knew immediately that this was a sign directed to her, and that it was the moment to leave.

Many people have daily superstitions and many people act on the sight of black cats. They might decide to buy a lottery ticket, or be especially careful in some task, or phone a relative to inquire about their health. There is usually a sense of 'I know very well it's silly, but all the same . . .' There is a difference between using the contingent appearance of a cat to focus a thought or prompt some action, and interpreting a message as if it concerns one directly in an unequivocal way. It is not the superstition itself that suggests the diagnosis, but how they situate it in relation to themselves.

To understand the appearance of the black cat and interpret it as a message will be different from those instances where we doubt our beliefs. It is not so much what we experience as how we experience. Take Bismarck's famous dream of 1863, which he immediately conveyed to Emperor William I. He was on horseback following a narrow Alpine path, with a precipice on one side and rocks on the other. The path became narrower and narrower, and the horse wouldn't continue. Unable to turn back, he struck the rock with his whip and appealed to God: the whip extended indefinitely and the rock collapsed, opening up to a large countryside, where he could see Prussian troops being deployed. It would be tempting to read this dream in terms of some sexual symbolism: the extending whip, the hole, etc. Yet, as the psychiatrist George Dumas pointed out, what matters isn't the symbolism but the fact that Bismarck bestowed so much meaning on it that he had to tell William as quickly as possible. It was less the dream than the place he accorded to it.

Imagine a minister today phoning the prime minister in the small hours because of a dream that they were sure had some special meaning. The hallmark of psychosis here is not the content of the dream but the dreamer's relation to it, the place it is given in their life: for Bismarck, as an objective communication of a message about the deployment of troops, independent of the dreamer. The key clinical feature here lies in this certainty, which almost always separates neurosis from psychosis.

The absence of doubt is the single clearest indicator of the presence of psychosis. This certainty can take the form of an absolute conviction of some truth, be it that of a delusion – 'I know that the

CIA are following me' – or of a scientific theory or religious dogma. The moment of insight is sometimes quite sudden and precise. As one psychotic subject wrote, 'I was suddenly confronted with an overwhelming conviction that I had discovered the secrets of the universe, which were being rapidly made plain with incredible lucidity. The truths discovered seemed to be known immediately and directly, with absolute certainty. I had no sense of doubt or awareness of the possibility of doubt.'

Where a neurotic person may profess to believing in something absolutely, they tend to harbour internal doubts, which may then generate symptoms. The apparatchik who follows the party line against his own beliefs or the priest who lectures on some moral imperative while privately breaking it may be tortured by doubt and frustration. A politician once came to see me complaining of insomnia and an overwhelming sense of unease. Although he was not consciously aware of the link, his symptoms had begun after a moment when he had to stand up in the Commons and make statements he knew to be untrue. It was not the lie as such, however, that had created the symptoms but the conflict it had generated with a remark his dying father had made about the importance of truth.

Where for the neurotic there may be a belief in some knowledge – scientific, religious, philosophical – there is also the sense that this knowledge does not coincide with individual truth, as if knowledge is never enough to answer our deepest personal questions. It is always somehow lacking and inadequate. Yet, in many cases of psychosis, it is as if knowledge and truth are not in conflict with each other but are homogeneous. Delusional ideas here often concern the body or some law of nature or genealogy or the protection of children. They revolve with great frequency around the question of origins: how bodies are made, how things in the world come to be, or where one – or one's race – comes from.

We might have to follow a tiny detail in the patient's speech to access these ideas, asking questions and paying special attention to any material that indicates a personal interest: a book they've been reading, a film they went to see, a text they may be writing. When we approach the delusional idea, it may be revealed bashfully or stated as if it were already a known fact. We can detect a certainty here: the person just knows something, and they may either try to share their certainty with the world or keep it quietly to themselves.

Clinicians are familiar with both of these forms of psychosis. In the former, the person may write letters and documents to the press and government, convinced that their knowledge must be disseminated for the greater good. In the latter, it may be a chance question or some contingent encounter that makes the certainty reveal itself. In one case, a fifty-year-old woman was hospitalized after walking into a bank and requesting the 20,000 francs promised to her. She explained that at the age of twenty she had the revelation that if she could stay a virgin for another thirty years she would be given 20,000 francs. For thirty years she had bothered no one, keeping the delusion discreetly to herself, never attracting psychiatric attention until the moment she went to collect her money.

Certainties can touch any area of the person's life, and may endure for a lifetime without ever being shared. Sometimes they attract attention swiftly: the husband who becomes certain of his wife's infidelity; the student who is sure that their teacher loves them; the churchgoer who knows that the priest has a special affection for them. A woman knew that her doctor loved her when one day she felt a pain in her arm while doing housework: he must have sent her this pain so she would have to return to see him. These delusions often derive from the axiom 'the Other loves me', even if the person elected to love has never had any contact with the patient. We could contrast this certainty with the neurotic's doubts about love: 'does the Other really love me? Do I really love the Other?' These are the everyday torments of the neurotic, to be distinguished from the clarity of the psychotic's knowledge: 'I am loved.'

Neurotic people, prone to doubt, are often impressed when they meet someone who seems sure of him or herself, convinced of their beliefs. This is why sects, cults and religious movements so often form around charismatic individuals who seem certain of their purpose in life. They have a sense of a mission, which may well captivate the neurotic who doesn't know quite what to do, never certain of their career or vocation. We could think of the followers of Jim

Jones, but the doctrines preached need not be so extreme: they could be the everyday policies of some political party. Once again, it is less the content of the beliefs than the attitude towards them. The neurotics, uncertain as to their goals or the meaning of their lives, will naturally be drawn towards someone who knows exactly what they want, who insists on some knowledge or truth with blind determination. Doubt gravitates towards certainty.

It's also why, as Geneviève Morel points out, psychosis is usually not diagnosed when people who want a sex-change operation go for their preoperative consultation with a psychiatrist. If the psychiatrist is neurotic, and hence not sure of their own sexuality, feeling not male or female enough, they may be impressed by someone who seems sure that they are male or female: they just happen to be in the wrong body. It may be this very clash between doubt and certainty that leads the psychiatrist to diagnostic error.

This certainty can emerge in very discreet ways. It could be during that conversation in the small hours when someone tells you their philosophy of life. This could be an all-encompassing theory of the world or simply a minimal set of rules that the person lives by, disclosed in intimacy. One of my patients only told me after a year of working together that she had a written list of instructions for her life that she carried in her jacket pocket at all times. These were certainties for her, never questioned, which enabled her to get through the many difficult situations she found herself in. Such rules could also take the form of advice from some self-help book or expert that the person takes seriously. Once again, it is not the content of the advice that matters but the place it occupies in the person's life.

Such advice, after all, may be rather sound. It is important to remember here that a delusional idea is not necessarily incorrect. As Jaspers observed many years ago, a delusion is not a false belief. It can be correct in content yet still count as a delusion, as we often see with delusions of jealousy, where the partner is actually unfaithful, or in cases where someone has been unjustly treated by some authority. Delusion, for Jaspers, arises from a primary experience of meaning not accessible to others, a moment of conviction that can be later recognized in the way the person tries to substantiate it, rather than its actual content. Although it may be comprehensible, logical, consistent and meaningful, the key is in this point of origin.

Modern cognitive therapies for psychosis tend to presuppose that psychotic delusions are not so different from everyday beliefs, and clinical intervention may derive from this view. Yet they leave out this dimension of a revelation or disclosure of meaning, the 'direct experience of meaning', emphasized by Jaspers. As John Custance described his own epiphany, it was as if 'all the secrets of the Universe were being revealed, as though I had some clue, some Open-sesame to creation'. It is less the content of the delusion that matters here than the mode of its construction. Even if the nature of what the person is certain of may be ambiguous – was the voice he heard benevolent or malign? – the belief that it means something is unshakable.

We see this when we work with people from cultures with belief systems different from our own, who are often misdiagnosed. Clinicians go on courses that teach them about different cultures to prepare them to work with people with disparate backgrounds, yet often they then assume that a delusional idea is simply a transcultural variation in belief. A culture may foster belief in spirits, for example, but that won't stop someone from that culture forming a delusion about spirits. We see the same thing with patients who have had a history of severe trauma and deprivation. The therapist may be so amazed at the violence and hardship the patient has suffered that they miss what is delusional in their interpretation of events. As Jaspers insisted, it is not the content of the ideas that matters but the person's relation to them, the way that meaning enters into and is built up around their experiences.

Lacan argued that the certainty in psychosis is always in proportion to an initial sense of perplexity. When a gap opens up in the person's world, separating signifier and signified, it is the absence at the level of signification that will be transformed into the certainty of a signification later on. This is the certainty that there is something in the world that concerns them directly – not necessarily anything more or less. A psychotic subject might know that a hallucination is a hallucination, and even describe it with the vocabulary of psychiatry or psychoanalysis. There doesn't have to be any belief in the reality of a hallucination for it to count as a hallucination: the decisive variable is whether they think that it concerns them or not.

When modern treatments boast of reducing a psychotic subject's belief in their hallucinations from 100 per cent to 70 per cent, this can hardly be taken seriously. As long as the dimension of meaning is present, percentages are a red herring. It is not reality but certainty that matters with hallucinations. The person may admit that perhaps no one else heard the voice, but they are nonetheless certain that it has some link to themself. Clinicians are often confused by a patient's procrastinations here, assuming that these mean that psychosis should be ruled out. But surface doubts and uncertainties are common in psychosis, and can take the form of typical obsessive symptoms: have I closed the door properly? Have I turned off the taps? Did I leave food for the cat? and so on. These surface doubts should not be confused with the deeper, ontological doubt of the neurotic, and they are in fact very good prognostic signs in some kinds of psychosis, such as manic depression.

There are also some cases of madness that give a central place to doubt, as if the delusional certainty had never come or was in suspension. This was finely described by Tanzi and the Italian psychiatrists, with the concept of 'doubting madness', and by Capgras with his 'questioning delusion' or 'delusion of supposition'. Sometimes, the difference with neurotic doubt lies in the real and not symbolic nature of the person's questioning: a neurotic person can doubt unconsciously to which sex he belongs, but a psychotic doubter may actually have a real doubt, as if the biological sex was itself unclear. More generally, the key is to see what place the doubt has in the person's life: this will give the diagnostic indication. In these cases of psychotic doubt, there will still be a certainty that there is something there that concerns them, a personal signification.

—

What other clues can tell us about the presence or absence of doubt? First, we could focus on how the person assumes their own history, how they speak about their childhood and family. Sometimes, childhood is described as a continuum: it was happy or sad, but that's it. No more information, no detail or inflection is forthcoming. Parents may be qualified in the most minimal way, using only a handful of invariant terms. Moments of change or drama are absent: one thing happens and then another, as if there are no real breaks or moments of discontinuity. In one case, a man described how when he received the phone call at work telling him that his pregnant wife had gone into labour, he jumped on his bike, headed for the hospital and then took another turning in the road and just kept going, never seeing his wife again and never meeting the baby. All this was described as if it were just another daily event, and not some life-changing moment. The sense of history – as a symbolic inscription in our lives of discontinuities – was missing.

To have a history, certain moments must be felt as different, special, as points of change and transition. The key here is that in the absence of an organizing signification, such as that provided by the narrative of the Oedipus complex, chronological and historical structure will be compromised. The fact that certain memories and not others will be privileged is the result of a grid of basic significations that select what we can remember and what we can't. Difficulties in the constructions of this grid – or its reduction to a minimal number of unique meanings – will then generate the continuum often apparent in the way that a psychotic subject recounts their history.

In other cases, however, the signature of psychosis is exactly the opposite. It is less the absence of defining moments than their presence that matters here. A man described how he decided one day to marry the next woman who walked through the entrance to the work canteen. In another, a woman described the moment her life changed: when her mother gave her a bath for the first time. She knew, she said, that this signalled the mother's sadistic intention towards her and the privileging of her sister, who was not required to bathe. Note how, once again, it is not what happened that indicates psychosis, but how this was interpreted, how one detail is given a kind of defining power, as if everything rested on that.

In a neurosis, the picture tends to be a bit different. The neurotic might complain of a sadistic mother who privileged the sibling, but this won't be explained as the result of one scene. Rather, because repression operates, there will be a series of screen memories, all alluding to the motifs in question. Many different moments may be remembered with a sense of the maternal favouritism, but it is unlikely that one memory will be given the elective power that we find in psychosis. Repression means that certain other memories will be forgotten, and the sense of maternal sadism or favouritism may well be deduced from the material rather than directly designated, as it is in the example above.

In a case discussed by Geneviève Morel, a young woman who hoped to have surgery to transform her into a boy described the moment when her decision was suddenly made. Her father had been sent to a concentration camp in Cambodia when she was three, the mother leaving her with relatives but keeping her younger brother. When she was six, the father escaped and the family was reunited. Her memories date from this time, and she described a scene in which she watched as her brother urinated standing up. She knew from that moment on that she was a boy. The father's return had triggered a psychosis, with the delusional idea crystallizing in this moment of certainty. The scene produced a single, unshakable signification for her: being a boy. In this example, there was no prehistory of symptoms suggesting an inquiry into gender, no questioning or dialectical thinking about sex, just one simple and decisive moment.

The moment of understanding, as Jaspers stressed, is crucial here. Psychotic subjects will often be able to explain exactly when they grasped some truth, when an idea or image suddenly became clear to them. Psychiatry has tended to focus on how things are unclear in psychosis, and many studies over the years have made claims about how psychotic subjects fail to understand conversation, questions, stories, mathematical problems, and so on. This emphasis on deficit obscures the question of insight, of how an answer or an idea may be transparent to the person. It is as if an answer imposes itself, often before any question has been consciously raised. As Wilhelm Griesinger put it, before the psychotic subject asks the question, 'he has already received the response'.

In another example, a woman described how her life had changed the moment she suddenly understood that the Bishop of Amiens was her father. She had been at church with her mother when he had turned towards them and she described how the bishop had become 'petrified' on seeing her mother. Later, after the bishop was victim of a homicide, she deduced that her parents must have been the culprits. Gestures and words would confirm her interpretation and some thirty years later she would shoot her real father for his part in cheating her out of her legacy from the bishop. Asked why she had shot him, she said that her intention had not been to kill, but simply to ensure that a proper inquiry took place.

The French neurologists Henri Hécaen and Julian de Ajuriaguerra collected many examples of such moments of revelation, especially concerning ideas about changes to the body. In one case, a young man insisted that everything had changed from one minute to the next after his first masturbation. His whole world was described in terms of a before and after, when he had lost all his moral and physical qualities. 'I changed completely, both in body and mind.' His hair, teeth and eye colour were all different now. 'My body was becoming deformed,' he said. 'My head changed completely, and even though people didn't notice this I knew that something had been modified. My arms got shorter and my skin came loose from my bones.' He would try desperately to refind his old image, gazing in the mirror every evening, and was horrified to see that he was looking more and more like his father.

In another case they discuss, a woman saw herself in a mirror one day and knew that everything had changed. Her eye colour was different, her forehead was destroyed, her nose squashed, her face was bigger and her neck wrinkled. These changes were soon ascribed to external influence: 'they' had extended her body or shrunk it, enlarged her stomach, twisted her legs, stretched her feet, and made her appear as another woman. She was physically dead, her body frozen, and another person was living her life. She felt there was an observer above her, scrutinizing her whole life and reading her mail.

Such defining moments can characterize not only thoughts about the body but also about abstract theories and creeds. Andrew Carnegie was reading the eugenicist Herbert Spencer when suddenly he knew this was the truth he had been searching for. He had at last 'found the truth of evolution'. Kurt Schneider reports a patient who was struck when he saw a dog lift its front paw. He asked another man a little way in front of him if the dog had saluted him too, and on receiving a negative reply, knew instantly that 'it was a revelation addressed to me'. These moments of sudden insight may concern themes such as the cosmos, life, death or God, one's birth, or mission in life. 'I seemed to see everything so clearly and distinctly as if I had a new and remarkable understanding,' said one of Jaspers's patients. 'It was as if I had some special sense like second-sight; as if I could perceive what I and others had never before been able to perceive.'

Memory is significant here, as real memories are often distorted to include the delusional ideas, or delusional ideas themselves become transformed into memories and backdated. French psychiatry had a special interest in these moments when it seemed as if a memory dating from before the construction of a delusion was given a causal role retroactively. In one man's wartime memory, he described how he had seen two women pass by as his unit went into the trenches, one of whom began crying when she saw them. He said to his fellow soldier, 'I'd like to have a mother like that,' and at that moment he felt that she had looked at him and he had the intuition 'this woman was my mother. It was like a bolt of lightning, stronger than me. I was crushed and shattered by what I felt, but I knew that I was not wrong.' In another example, retrospective interpretation convinced a woman that the fact she had been called 'a little queen' as a child was proof of her right to the throne.

Searles reports the case of a patient who retrospectively constructed a complicated delusion that machinery had been installed in her abdomen and that a chain had been fastened to her heart to control her. Her difficult history of invasive surgical procedures was now given a meaning. When she was seven, she had an operation on her sinus; at fourteen, a benign tumour had been removed from her breast; and her appendix had been removed when she was nineteen. Later on, she realized that everything now made sense. The sinus operation had created a hole in her head, allowing her to be 'run' as a machine; the breast operation had allowed a chain to be put around her heart; and the removal of her appendix had allowed machinery to be placed in her abdomen. 'They' now had control over her and she demanded further surgery in a 'real hospital' to cut the 'strings' that bound her to these controlling figures.

———

The clarity with which a psychotic subject may experience a moment of change or a new meaning is echoed in the way in which symptoms are often described. Where the repression operative in the neurotic's Oedipal trajectory will mean that symptoms conceal disguised thoughts, in psychosis there is often a transparency. A woman complained of terrible anxiety and claustrophobia on the Underground which was preventing her from travelling to work. The meaning of the symptom was only revealed after several months of analytic work. She dreamed that she was facing a wall, and experienced exactly the same feeling of dread as she had on the Underground. The image of the wall reminded her of the last place she had seen her brother, who had been in prison before he died. Her anxiety thus marked the proximity to her brother and her thoughts – which she had tried to push out of her mind at the time – of being in his coffin with him: an anxiety, in fact, about being underground. The symptom here was linked to forgotten ideas and memories: in between them was repression.

In a psychosis, it is possible that the person will explain the symptom immediately in terms of the memory: 'I'm having claustrophobia because of the idea of being in a coffin with my brother.' The mechanisms of encryption in the construction of symptoms may be absent, as if the symptom were a direct stamp on the body or the mind rather than the result of a complicated process of ciphering. In a case discussed by Paula Elkisch, a mother spoke of her fear that her son would become a ne'er-do-well like her own brother. If the baby slept all the time, she thought, his chances would be better, and so she would walk up and down continually with the child clutched in her arms. 'My arms were numb,' she said, 'and I did not know where I ended and the baby began.' When the boy was taken to hospital at the age of eight, he had no sense of bodily boundary: he would ask everyone around him, 'Are these my hands, are those your hands?' as if the maternal confusion of bodies were directly imprinted on him.

This clarity, which signals an absence of repression, is a common sign of psychosis. A neurotic person comes with a symptom that needs deciphering. They can't sleep, they can't work any more, they have panics, and they want to know why. It seems opaque to them, yet they sense that there is some hidden cause or explanation. Often what we find in psychosis is rather different: that the person comes with a symptom, but they know why they have it. 'My arm is paralysed because that's where my parent struck me as a child.' Where, for the neurotic, the childhood scene may well be forgotten, only recovered later in the therapy, or remembered but cut off from its emotional significance, a psychotic subject can often articulate quite clearly what the cause of their symptom is. Psychotic phenomena also tend to emerge with greater discontinuity here than neurotic ones, appearing suddenly, as if out of the blue.

Whether their explanation of the symptom is 'correct' or not is beside the point, since what matters is the person's relation to causality itself. The way in which someone thinks about causes is indeed a diagnostic indicator. Being certain that 'I'm like this because of this' is frequently a feature of psychosis. For example, being sure that one has a certain symptom because one was beaten as a child or that one has a certain illness because of one's diet may be factually true, but the clarity of the connection is psychotic. Take the example of a woman who remembers that when she was a child, her mother called her a whore for wearing lipstick. When she hears voices many years later that label her a prostitute, she makes the link between these experiences, certain that the maternal comment explains the voices. The unshakable belief in this causality is the sign here of the psychosis.

In a case discussed by Morel, a patient with body-image problems described how she had become 'ugly' in a single moment, when, at the age of three, a boy had kicked her in the face. She wanted to have surgery so she could be given the face that was hers before this moment of change: the original face, she said, would make her pretty and loved by boys. There was never a shadow of doubt for her that it was the kick that had changed everything, despite medical confirmation that her facial features were in fact congenital.

This kick from the outside illustrates another key feature of psychosis: its xenopathic character. Old psychiatry described this in a number of ways: Henri Claude's 'syndrome of exterior action', Guiraud's 'xenopathic phenomena' and Séglas's 'syndrome of influence'. The belief here is that an active agency is operating outside the person. In paranoia, this agency is located outside the self and named: 'I'm acting like this because of the CCTV camera, or because I'm being followed, or because of the plot against me.' The initiative, as Lacan observed, always comes from the Other, from the outside. As Schreber put it at the very start of his *Memoirs*, 'the total mental life of a human being rests on excitability [of the nerves] by external impressions', as if it were the external impressions rather than the nerves that had the priority. This contrasts with the neurotic's feeling that his problems come from within himself: even if he doesn't know how or why, there is a sense that the cause never lies entirely outside.

This is often apparent from the way that the person speaks about their distress. If the Other is always blamed for their problems, it is different from the instances where, beyond this, there is a sense of one's own implication in the symptom. If blame is attributed exclusively outside the self, the indication is psychosis. We can observe how this is compatible with a situation where the Other really is to blame, where the subject has been the victim of a series of atrocities or abuses. Nonetheless, in neurotic cases, there is always a margin of doubt or guilt: 'They've done all this to me, but what is my own involvement?' The clinician must be cautious where it is clear that external tragedies have marked the patient: what matters once again is how these have been processed, subjectivized, made part of the person's life.

This sense of an outside force acting on the self is often called 'mental automatism', and was described by Séglas and then elaborated by De Clérambault. As one hospitalized woman explained, 'People don't do things *for* me; they do things *at* me.' 'I'm in the position,' she said, 'of being thought *at*.' Inner and outer activities are no longer under one's control, and the psychotic subject may feel at the mercy of a foreign power. 'My arms and legs work on their own . . . thinking comes to me, I don't know where from, but it's not me who's thinking,' said one patient. 'Everything I do is like a machine, it works on its own, without me.' The person feels acted upon, spoken about, thought about, yet not master of their own acts. They are made to think, to feel, to remember, to understand. They may not recognize their thoughts as their own but as somehow inserted into their mind, and so they feel that they are in the power of some external agency.

The crucial feature here is the idea of an external force or pressure. One's thoughts may be felt to be repeated aloud or commented on and one's intentions broadcast. 'When I say something, it seems as if I hear it being repeated in the distance,' said one of Bleuler's patients, and, 'When I stop speaking, then the voices repeat what I have just said.' Séglas defined 'thought echo' as the belief that one's thoughts are heard by others, and although there are many variations in how thoughts and voices are experienced here, they have in common a sense of external-ity. The person's own thinking becomes strange and somehow separated from them. The feeling of an external influence is perhaps purest and most intense in the phenomenon of possession, where there is the belief that some outside agency has taken control over one's mind and body.

What might seem here to be the most extreme manifestation of psychosis was linked by many early researchers to normality itself. Pierre Janet and Henri Ey had pointed out that mental automatism is part of everyday reality, even if we are not usually aware of it. They evoked those aspects of ourselves that don't follow the dictates of the ego and are outside conscious control. Everyone experiences automa-tism in some way, and the psychiatrist Charles-Henry Nodet observed that: 'It's not automatism that is pathological, but the signification that the subject attributes to it.' Once again, it is not the phenom-enon as such that is significant but the place we assign it.

Verbal automatism, for example, operates constantly in everyday life. George Dumas collected examples of moments when words sprung into his mind, as if entirely of their own accord. One morning, as he was shaving, he heard the question 'What will one say in Rio?', and, on another occasion, as he was putting on his shoes, 'The number of lawyers is limited.' He catalogued around sixty such phrases, all quite brief and with a verbal meaning yet no apparent relation to their context. This, for Dumas, was authentic mental automatism, and what distinguished the psychotic and non-psychotic subject was how ser-iously they took the words that imposed themselves.

Life would naturally be easier if we didn't have to take such things too seriously, as Lacan would later comment, but the psychotic subject is someone who, precisely, takes things seriously. The grumpy 'hello' from our neighbour, the coldness of our boss, the slight change of tone we hear in a friend's voice are all a part of everyday reality. If we were to take these all seriously, getting through each day would become impossible. And this is exactly what some psychotic subjects report. The interpretation of such details may well be correct, but the amplification of everyday signs can be unbearable for the person, resulting in suspicions, rows or perpetual friction with the environment.

Often, these details are understood strictly in terms of the imaginary, as if the world consisted only of oneself and the other person. The neighbour's grumpiness is interpreted as being caused by something one has done, the boss's coldness by one's own failings. There is no reference to the possibility that a third party might be the cause, that the other person is distracted by events in their own life that do not concern the patient. Interestingly, when the idea of a third party does emerge, it may well be delusional: 'The boss was cold because someone told them bad things about me.' The third party appears as a malevolent presence rather than as a mediating, pacifying one.

This psychotic sensitivity to detail will frequently uncover some truth. Although the neighbour may not be grumpy owing to any fault of the person, their grumpiness has still been spotted. In therapy, psychotic subjects are expert at picking up the clinician's moods, and this means that a psychotic person can often see through the convention and veneer of what passes for everyday reality. Old psychiatry evoked this with the expression 'the irony of the psychotic'. When the therapist says, 'I care about you,' they might be quite rightly sceptical, knowing full well that this is what therapists are expected to say. Recognizing this, some of the most remarkable experimental treatments for psychosis in America in the 1950s aimed at total candour: the therapist would insult the patient, voice sexual fantasies and even fall asleep during sessions if they happened to be tired.

Psychotic irony indicates an understanding of the language games and make-believe that the ordinary social world is based on. Rather than being immersed within it, a certain distance allows a more accurate perspective, and this is no doubt one of the reasons why groundbreaking discoveries are so often made by psychotic subjects. They can see things that others are blind to. A young psychotic man described a moment of what he called 'epiphany' in his childhood. He realized one day that the word 'God' could in fact be any other word: the choice of those three letters was entirely arbitrary. This was significant, he explained, because it crystallized his experience of the world until then: in assembly at school, for example, he knew that the spectacle of all the children sitting quietly listening to the head teacher talk was a 'sham'. The ascription of authority was 'not based on anything'.

We could also think here of Jared Lee Loughner, whose point-blank shooting of congresswoman Gabrielle Giffords shocked the world in January 2011. In the effort to determine at what moment she had become a potential persecutor, one episode stood out. Three years previously, Loughner had enrolled at a community college and attended one of Giffords's outdoor meetings with constituents. He had submitted a written question that asked: 'What is government if words have no meaning?' If the lack of response set up a persecutory tension, the question indicates the real issue for Loughner: if the symbolic order is based on nothing, how can anyone claim legitimate authority? And hence the nightmare of conspiracy theories that haunted him, each one representing an ungrounded abuse of power.

The psychotic ability to see through convention is often misinterpreted as lack of intelligence. One of the most frequent tests used in the early twentieth century to assess the mental abilities of patients involved telling a story and then asking questions about it. At the Burghölzli clinic, they used 'The Donkey Carrying a Load of Salt'. A donkey, laden down with bags of salt, had to cross a river. He noticed, after falling, how much lighter his load had become, as the salt had dissolved in the water. The next day, his load was a bag of sponges and he deliberately fell, only to discover that sponges soak up water, and so he became heavier: so heavy, indeed, that he drowned. When one patient was asked to explain what had happened, he replied that 'the donkey wanted to drown himself'. Rather than seeing this as a cognitive error or a projection of his own mental state, it could be understood as bringing out the latent truth to the tale: the poor donkey, tired of serving as a slave for others, failed to remember what sponges do, perishing in one of those 'accidental suicides' that psychiatry itself had once studied.

—

The xenopathic character of psychotic phenomena can produce a variety of reactions. The person may try to fight against the force that assails them, or simply observe, record or passively accept it. If they are fighting, the clinician will know quite quickly, as there is often an appeal for therapeutic help or medication. If the response is more passive, it may be difficult to grasp what is going on. An important clue will lie in how the person assumes their passivity. There is a difference between a case where someone always does what they are told, perhaps harbouring resentment about this and perhaps obeying out of fear of losing the love of their masters, and a case in which the obedience does not generate any conflict. There is no feeling of guilt or protest about following orders, no embarrassment or indecision, but simply an obedience without subjective effects, as if there were an almost reflex-type relation to the words that tell us what to do.

This permeability to language is found especially in schizophrenia. Words often have an immediate effect on the person, as if there is no barrier to separate them from what they are being told to do or be. Naturally, this might fit well with a certain social conformity: if we do whatever we are told, life might go smoothly. This can help us to understand one aspect of the famous double-bind theory, elaborated by Gregory Bateson and his team. If the person is brought up continually receiving contradictory messages from their environment, the foundations of madness may be set into place. They might be told not to do something yet simultaneously receive the message that they should do it. Perhaps a focus here on the permeability to language would nuance this view: it is less the fact of receiving contradictory messages that is the problem than of having to obey what one hears. It is this obedience – which entails one will have to follow both messages – that creates the impasse.

Permeability can be striking in some cases and discreet in others.

A patient's promiscuous behaviour, for example, might be interpreted as a symptom of hysteria. Serial encounters with men, unchecked sexual behaviour, followed by complaints about the impossibility of finding the right man might be understood as a way of asking a question about femininity: what is a woman for a man? How could a woman be loved or desired? Yet closer exploration of the detail might suggest the absence of any subjective phenomena at the moments of encounter: when the man propositions her, she might just go with him, as if his words had to be obeyed. The person could lament not having a relationship, but there may be no real protest, no resistance or doubt at that first moment. It would be this obedience that suggests a psychotic structure.

Another significant diagnostic indicator is how the person has divided up their reality, and this is linked to the question of doubt and certainty that we have seen to be so central. The main characteristic of the symbolic order is the establishment of a system of divisions and contrasts that carve up our world. Such systems always start from binary oppositions, such as male–female, animate–inanimate, human–animal. As they become more complex, each term of the opposition attracts further terms and these new additions modify the initial system, to create doubt and a certain fluidity. So many children's stories involve exactly this sliding: something bad is contained in something good – the poison in a delicious apple – or something good is found in something bad – the ogre who becomes friendly, the benevolent wizard behind the monster.

In psychosis, where the symbolic is not inscribed as it is in neurosis, it may remain reduced to the minimal initial binary, with no elasticity or movement. In a case discussed by Piera Aulagnier, the world was divided into 'black' and 'white' for this man born from two races. Whatever was white would be identified with persecutors and whatever was black with the victims to be avenged. Such rigid divisions of the world into binaries display the opposite of what we find in neurosis, where there is a sliding between terms and a doubt intrinsic to the way the world is thought about. If a psychotic subject can divide the world into 'men' and 'women' or 'good people' and 'bad people', the neurotic is never quite sure: a man can be too feminine, a woman too masculine, and people good and bad at the same time. Although there are plenty of cases of psychosis where this emphasis on binaries is not apparent, we encounter them with some frequency.

In a case described by Morel, the patient had divided the world into the opposition good–bad. This young woman had started to experience problems after passing her secondary-school exams. Until then her elder sister was deemed 'bad', like her father, while she was 'good' and feminine, like her mother. The 'badness' of the father was like a hereditary trait that passed from his own father to him, and then to the sister. This elementary division established a delusional filiation, and helped her to organize her world until the exams. Now, she felt that she emitted a 'bad smell' and that people were alluding to this around her. The first diagnostic sign of the psychosis was in the fixity of the good–bad opposition, which brooked no dialectic or change.

Rigid binaries can be deduced from the person's speech and at times they are apparent very quickly. The terms of the binary, such as good–bad, occur so frequently that their importance is clear, as if without them their experience of the world would dissolve. These binaries may be a basic interpretation of the desire of the Other, and as such have a crucial protective function for the person. Schreber's division of God into an Upper and a Lower God was a significant moment in the construction of his delusion, and helped him to partition the malevolent from the more benign forces that he felt had invaded his experience.

Just as the terms of a binary can have a special weight in the subject's discourse, so single words or expressions may take on a particular value, like joints or staples in speech that are necessary to pin down meaning. As we saw in the last chapter, verbal idiosyncrasies are a common feature of psychosis, and a verbal allusion, a pun, or even the resonance of a particular word can index the presence of a delusion. The new use of an old term, the minting of new terms, or the assumption that the listener understands the meaning of a new word are all classic signs of psychosis. What counts is the fixity of a word or a phrase or a formula. Even a grammatical structure can have this function: its repeated use at all the points in someone's speech at which a problematic meaning is evoked can have the same function as a neologism. As an unsymbolizable point is approached, words or grammatical sequences become congealed, a protection against the proximity of the hole.

We should also consider emotion and affect here, as they are often used to make the diagnosis of psychosis. If the person seems inordinately shut off, unable to experience emotion or even in a stuporous state, schizophrenia has, in the past, been suspected. Today, most clinicians are more cautious, but there is still a tendency to use affect as a diagnostic tool. The reasons why this is unreliable are quite patent. Someone can seem catatonic yet later reveal the intensity of the emotions they chose not to disclose, just as someone can show excessive emotion, which is there simply to please the other, who expects it. The advice Edith Jacobson gave in the 1950s is still absolutely precise: she warned that affect is never enough to make a diagnosis, although the quality and the intensity of the affect can give a clue as to the underlying thought processes. It will be these that ultimately settle the diagnostic question.

If affect and emotion must be carefully contextualized here, diagnostic clues can be found in the related area of the localization of the libido. For the neurotic, libido is more or less localized to the erogenous zones, especially the sexual organs, and is generally marked by the sign of negativity: we can't get what we want, satisfaction is too brief, and so on. We strive after moments of pleasure, yet they are fleeting and usually fail to live up to our expectations. The sources of satisfaction, likewise, are situated outside the body, in the people we desire and yearn for. The libido, for the neurotic, is thus limited and more on the side of a minus than a plus. Yet in psychosis things are different.

Here, the libido is less linked to negativity than positivity: rather than being too absent, it is too present, and the psychotic must often defend himself against it. It will be situated either in the body, as in schizophrenia, or in some Other, as in paranoia. Self-mutilation may be one way of trying to remove libido from the body in schizophrenia, while striking the Other may be an attempt to negate the libido in a paranoia. In all forms of psychosis, due to the fact that the symbolic has not been internalized in the way it has for neurotics, there will be atypical localizations of libido. Each case can teach us something about this.

Sometimes the phenomena are striking: states of rapture or bliss, which the psychiatrist Oswald Bumke catalogued in the early twentieth century. Characteristic of these states is that the excitation hits the person from the outside. It is often not prepared for but simply emerges with overwhelming force, as if their own bodily arousal were an external phenomenon. Rather than being sought-after or pursued, as with the neurotic, it just presents itself unannounced. Such moments or states of arousal or excitation may be connected to discoveries, revelations or inspirations. In more discreet forms, the person may have odd bodily sensations that they prefer to remain silent about, experienced as either pleasure, pain or physical unease. Sometimes these may produce hypochondriacal concerns and a feeling of perplexity.

A direct expression of emotions, rather than their concealment, is also sometimes a sign of psychosis. The person may laugh or cry, or experience heightened reactions that they are unable to control. Instead of repression making one's feelings unavailable or confused, they just appear in all their clarity, as if there is a continuity between some event or experience the person is speaking about and the reaction. Emotions linked to some childhood scene are as present decades later as they had been at the time. The feelings here return in the person's body, regardless of their conscious intentions, bypassing the network of thoughts that would otherwise encrypt them.

An attention to the questions we have discussed in this chaper can allow a differentiation of neurosis and psychosis, essential for clinical work. Without it, we remain caught in the ever-expanding field of mental health labels where every surface symptom is transformed into some new diagnostic entity. This multiplication may certainly benefit pharmaceutical companies, eager to find new targets for their products, and it may also be helpful for some patients who seek to identify themselves with labels. But it neglects the basic underlying structures which we need to recognize in order to devise real therapeutic strategies for working with psychosis.

6. Causes of Psychosis

What are the causes of psychosis? Why will some people become psychotic and others not? Psychosis is a mental structure that will be established quite early in life, probably within the first few years. This does not mean, of course, that the person will ever go mad. There is a difference, as we have seen, between being psychotic and going psychotic. For the triggering of a psychosis, other factors must come into play, which we will discuss in the next chapter. But what happens in those early years that sets a psychotic structure in place? The vast literature on this question has produced many different answers: genetic defects, chemical imbalances, poor parenting, depressed mothers, absent fathers, social deprivation, communication problems, and so on.

How seriously these ideas are taken depends on the cultural climate at the time. When parents were being blamed for everything, they would be deemed the cause of psychosis in their children. When the vogue was for genes – as perhaps it is now – these biological elements are the culprits. Most of the headline-grabbing results claiming to have found the gene for manic depression or schizophrenia have been quickly fading stars, despite the fact that the media almost never publish details of the negative results or retractions that follow. Other biological 'advances' that made the news suggested that the psychotic had impaired liver, brain, kidney and circulatory functions; was deficient in practically every vitamin; suffered from hormonal imbalance; and had enzymes that were askew. As early as the mid-1950s, this cycle of excitement and disappointment was already the rule. Writing in the journal *Science*, one psychiatrist pointed out that each new generation of biologists had to be indoctrinated and disillusioned. Yet these lessons were poorly learned, and today there is an insatiable appetite for biological explanations.

These tend to involve two basic misunderstandings. First of all, it is often observed that people in different generations of a family have the same 'mental illness'. Hence it must be genetic. Yet for better or for worse, we inherit not only our parents' genes but also our parents. A young paranoid patient said very little apart from the sentence 'It's all a matter of chemistry and physics.' When his psychiatrist met with the parents and asked them what they thought about their son's condition, the mother, after a long silence, replied, 'Well, we don't know anything about it. It's just a matter of chemistry and physics to us.' The father and the patient then repeated softly, 'Yeah, just a matter of chemistry and physics.' Growing up with a parent who has certain problems will of course impact on the child, and so they may well develop problems themselves. This dimension of familial transmission is usually totally ignored in genetic studies, as if we spend the first years of our lives in some sort of abstract cocoon, away from the daily contact with our loved ones.

The presence of a biological problem, likewise, cannot be considered in isolation. Imagine that a child is born with a specific genetic or neurological problem that affects, say, their speech, vision or hearing. Now, this will surely have some impact on the place prepared for the child by the fantasies of the parents. Prior to and during gestation, the parents will have ideas – both conscious and unconscious – about who their child is going to be, what they will be like, how they will relate to them. Will they love us as one of our own parents did or failed to do? Will they recognize us as we were perhaps not recognized by our own parents? Even at the most basic level of the body image, parents will have preconceived ideas. They might imagine what they expect the foetus to look like, and are often surprised at the ultrasound when they might be confronted with a discrepancy.

However kind and loving the parents may be, the biological difficulty can have an effect on how they respond to their child, and this can be detected swiftly by children who are, we know, so sensitive to emotional interactions. If that child develops a psychosis later on, an investigator might assume that the biological problem must be the cause of the psychosis, rather than seeing it as a possible effect of the parents' *reactions* to the problem. This tension between their own fantasy images of their child and the actual reality, marked by the biological problem, may be a source of significant impact in the early interactions, often exacerbated by the remarks of grandparents, medical staff, etc.

The other misunderstanding here concerns what a gene itself consists of. Despite the admonishment of many researchers, the popular view of a gene remains that of a 'unit character', a single element that would be responsible for specific physiological or behavioural traits. Eugenics theorists in the early twentieth century argued that specific genes would cause nomadism, crime, unemployment, indolence and dissolute lifestyle, and these were linked in turn to the 'bad blood' of Jews, blacks and the mentally unwell. The notion of unit characters was a basic feature of these theories of hereditary, and was disproven about a century ago with the discovery that there is no simple one-to-one correspondence between a visible characteristic and a gene that produces it. On the contrary, a characteristic would be the result of many different genes in a system, reacting both with each other and with the environment. By the 1920s, it was known that different genes could affect the same characteristic, just as a single gene could affect different characteristics.

Despite these facts, the unit-character theory still pervades contemporary understanding of genetic causality, and in the early 1990s biologists suggested finding another term, as 'gene' had become so prone to misinterpretation. Genes were seen as isolated causal agents rather than as parts of complex networks of biological interactions that usually depended to a large extent on what was going on in the surrounding world. Many biologists recognized that the old nature/nurture opposition could no longer be maintained in the way that it once had been. Indeed, the effort to make a gene responsible, splitting it away from everything else that might concern a human life, has a certain psychotic quality to it, as if one entity could be deemed the culprit, just as in paranoia one unique agency is designated as the cause of one's problems.

The rigid positioning of one single causal factor is a hallmark of psychotic thinking. Blame is assigned to one persecutory agency in paranoia or, in cases of melancholia, to oneself: to some action one has done or failed to do in the past, as if it were just one act, one detail, one cause that would explain everything, like a philosopher's stone. This style of reasoning is of course ubiquitous in many kinds of scientific research, and may be contrasted with the more obsessional mode we find just as frequently in the medical journals. At the conclusion to the study there will be a paragraph showing the authors' indecision: well, it could be this factor, but it could be that factor, and so on, in an endless cycle of procrastination and doubt. How much more attractive the psychotic certainty must seem with its fixing on single causes! And this no doubt explains the popularity of psychotic discourses in media-science reporting and with grant committees.

Lacan's perspective was different, and, like many of the psychiatrists of his time, he distinguished carefully between conditions of psychosis and causes of psychotic triggering. If the basic condition here was the failure of the paternal metaphor, several different contributing factors could be at play. The advent of psychosis could never be predicted in advance, and it would only be later on that one could work backwards, exploring that person's unique history to find the clues that would show how the psychosis became established. So what could these factors be? What can compromise the paternal metaphor or make it impossible? After exploring these questions, we will look in the next chapter at the specific situations that may actually trigger a psychosis.

—

We have seen how there are two crucial periods in each person's childhood. First of all, there is the time when the child poses the question of the mother's absences. Where is she going? Is she coming back? Why is she leaving me? Children often symbolize these absences through games, such as the famous 'Fort/Da' described by Freud that we discussed in Chapter 2. Dolls, rattles, dummies or other objects can be used to play out sequences of appearance and disappearance, as the child orchestrates comings and goings, presences and absences. Games such as peek-a-boo and hide-and-seek will soon allow a more elaborate treatment of these themes.

If the first period shows that the child is asking a question about the mother's comings and goings, the second involves the interpretation of these rhythms. The initial phase here is one of seduction, where the child tries to become what it thinks the mother is interested in. This could mean being very good or very naughty, being extrovert or shy, teasing her or being compliant. But soon, the realization dawns on the child that this won't wash, that there is something beyond the mother that they will never access and that satisfying her is both prohibited and impossible. This space beyond the mother is connected to the father, or to any agency that plays a comparable role: it could be a grandparent or any other relative, a family friend or even a profession, as we saw earlier.

Recognizing this has a mediating effect on the child, indicating that they cannot be everything for the mother: something else has drawn her away, something that has a power over her. Trying to think through what the mother is for the father and what the father is for the mother constitute a painful and critical time in childhood. Sometimes, as we have seen, the child enlists the help of an element from outside the family to help with this process, such as the totemic animals of a phobia. This will allow the child to move away from a world with three places (the child, the mother and the imagined object of the mother's interest) to a more complex space that opens up to the social world. The fact that there is a beyond to the mother introduces a gap, like the missing piece in those games that allow one to slide counters around to constitute a shape or image. Without this gap, the pieces are frozen and no movement is possible. How the child recognizes and registers this beyond is thus crucial, and it will depend largely on how the mother transmits it, how she speaks about her world and how she situates the father within it.

What matters here is not how strong or powerful the father actually is, but rather how he is represented in the mother's discourse, how she has positioned him. When she speaks, is he accorded the same value as everything else in her discourse or is he given a privileged place? Is he respected or forever denigrated? This point of reference could be occupied by other figures, as we have seen, as long as it indicates that the child is not everything for the mother and that some external agency has a hold or power over her. It's a process through which the child becomes aware of the fact that the mother is lacking.

And this is one privileged point at which problems can emerge. If the mother identifies herself with the law, how can the child see her as subject *to* a law?

One of my patients described the birth of her children as if they had been divine births: the father was simply never mentioned. As I asked her about the conceptions and pregnancies, she gave plenty of details but not one single reference to the man who had impregnated her. It was as if she had created the children by herself. This has often been observed in the mothers of psychotic subjects, as if it were their own bodies that were responsible for the gestation and birth of their children. In one sense, this is of course a biological truth, yet it fore-closes not only the biological part of the father, but also, no less significantly, the symbolic function of the father in the configuration that preceded the child's entry into the world.

The current vogue in psychology for the theory of 'Other Minds' misconstrues this basic question. Child development is seen to pivot around the moment the child realizes that the mother can have a mind of her own, different from theirs; that she can think different things. In one famous experiment, children are shown a sweet packet and its contents. Some of the children leave the room and a plastic alligator is put in the sweet packet in front of the remaining children. The experimenters then asked: will they expect the other children, on returning, to be surprised by the contents of the package? Would they have ascribed their own beliefs to the other children, or, on the contrary, understood that they have 'other minds'?

Needless to say, the experimenters paid no attention to the role of symbolism in what they were doing – what might an alligator repre-sent for them? – but the real moment of change comes not when the child realizes that the mother has a mind of her own, but when they realize that there is something else beyond her mind, that she can be the object of someone else's thought or think about someone other than them. This triangulation is often patently missing in some forms of psychosis. The person might ascribe everything to themself: their friends don't phone because of something they themself have done, rather than something the other party might have to do. It is as if at every point in their life, whoever they are with, it's just them and the other. There is no third term to mediate human relations, no beyond to the other person. And that's why many of these subjects prefer to avoid other people altogether. They know that close will always be too close.

Sometimes a delusion can try to address this problem. Schreber's system was not just about himself and God, but about the complicated network of rays and nerves that formed a part of the Order of the World. His preoccupation was not focused exclusively on how the rays and nerves were linked to his body but on how these two sets of filaments *related to each other*. He was thus establishing forms of triangulation that might temper the unbearable position of inhabiting a world that contained just him and the immense Other Mind that he called God.

It is worth clarifying the problems of triangulation here, as they fall into more or less three groups. In the first, there is only the mother and the child, as if no one and nothing else exists. The child risks being reduced to a pure object for the mother here. In the second, there is the mother, the child and the object of the mother's interest, so a minimal triangle is created. The child may try to fill this space that he believes will satisfy her. In the third group, there is the mother, the child, the object of the mother's interest and then the real third term, often though not always linked to representations of the father. Each of these structures generates its own sets of problems, although the first two are characteristic of psychosis.

The absence of a third term is often clear when paranoia generates acts of violence. Living in a world where he is constantly persecuted, the paranoiac may feel, in relation to the persecutor, 'It's either him or me.' The mirror phase here has no symbolic mediation: it's just the person and the image in front of them, which both confers identity and robs them of it at the same time. It's why, as the psychoanalyst Sophie de Mijolla-Mellor points out, the person can claim that they acted in legitimate self-defence when they murder their unsuspecting and unarmed persecutor, someone who may even have been unaware of their killer's existence.

This failure to situate a third term can mean that the child remains caught in the position of an object for the mother. This could take the form of a purely biological entity, whose basic needs are met but little else, or a prized and valued companion, not only emotionally invested but over-invested, as if they were everything for her. If the mother is saturated with her child, there is no lack, and hence the difficulties, if not impossibility, of moving beyond the relation with her. The child's body can become the very place of maternal satisfaction, and we can see this not only in some of the psychoses of childhood but also in adult cases where the subject tries desperately to regulate or remove the presence of libido from their own body, perhaps through self-harm or piercing or even removal of body parts.

They are trying to create a separation from the mother's libido, which is stuck to them, to distance those aspects of their body that harbour this alien and invasive presence. As one patient told me, she had to habitually cut off the hair that her mother had loved stroking when she was a child. Only this, she explained, let her feel safe. When schizophrenic subjects describe their actions, thoughts and feelings as the products of others, explained via suggestion, possession, hypnotic influence or some influencing machine, isn't it this presence of the Other within them that they are evoking?

—

The father can also play a role in setting the stage for psychosis. We saw with the examples of Little Hans and of Marcel Pagnol how the real father could be measured against a symbolic benchmark and deemed lacking. In both cases, a solution was found by introducing an external element: a horse for Hans, the rock partridges for Marcel. These acted as a conduit for the symbolic function of paternity to operate, giving the son an orientation and a direction. But what would happen if rather than accepting his necessary weakness the father actually tried to compete with the symbolic agency, to usurp it, to become the law himself? One of my patients remembered waiting in a theatre queue with his father as a young boy, feeling uncomfortable. Next to them was a barrier, so why didn't his father just step over it to get to the ticket office faster? If the memory posed a question for him as to his father's masculinity, how would one compare it to a case where the father acted as if barriers did not exist?

Many cases of psychosis show us a father who took himself for the law rather than situating it as an agency beyond himself. The father's social situation may or may not be relevant here; there are cases of psychosis in the children of judges and policemen, but the professional role is never in itself enough to tell us anything. What matters is how the father relates to his role, how he assumes it, to what extent he identifies with it, and whether or not he recognizes and transmits to the child that he is himself subject to a symbolic law that is beyond him.

In some cases, the father literally takes himself for the law, while in others, the law is reduced to an ideal, such as justice, charity or fairness. The decisive factor is less the content of the ideal than how the father relates to it. If he identifies with it passionately, it is possible that the symbolic law beyond him remains unavailable, or that contradictions and discrepancies take on a traumatic and excessive weight. Schreber describes his father as having 'an apostle-like mission to bring health, happiness and bliss to the masses'. It is difficult not to link the imposition of the father's rigid and highly idealistic system to Schreber's own psychosis. Where Moritz Schreber was the point of origin of child-rearing, pedagogic, orthopaedic and callisthenic imperatives, in his son's delusion God is not author of the law but, on the contrary, himself subject to the Order of the World. This 'lawful relation' meant that God did not interfere too much in human affairs: he would remain at the right distance. Schreber's delusion thus aimed to rectify his father's usurpation of the law.

Lacan also evokes here the father who presents himself as excessively virtuous, as a pillar of faith, a paragon of integrity or devotion, as serving a charitable cause, the nation, or some ideal of safety. The more that an abstract ideal is appealed to by a parent, the more that the child may suffer when the parent falls short of it, whether through weakness or fraud. The key here is that the ideal is situated by the parent in the symbolic dimension, as an organizing principle of the world. When it is questioned, it is therefore not a local disturbance that takes place but a shattering of the person's whole existence. Growing up, we need far more than food and shelter: we require a link to the symbolic order, based on trust. We need to know that when the adults speak to us, they are not deceiving us, so that we don't need to perpetually ask ourselves 'They are saying this, but what do they really mean?' The early work by Bateson and his colleagues argued that this question is repressed for neurotics but present in many forms of psychosis. Unable to establish a basic trust in speech, what else is there that can ground our presence in the world?

If ideals are implanted in the symbolic order and are then found to be lies, the person's very foundations are removed. It isn't just that they will be disappointed in the father but that the actual links to their world will be shaken. In one case, a father imposed his own system of education on his children from the very moment of birth. They had to eat, sleep and excrete exactly the way he wanted them to, and he devised his own philosophy to make sense of these cruel impositions. He endeavoured to have all four children potty-trained by the age of one. Negative emotions were not allowed, and they even had to smile while he beat them, to show that they acknowledged the justice of their punishment. Rather than the law being beyond him and then transmitted however awkwardly through him, he made himself identical with the law emitting it himself through his philosophy. A respected judge, he occupied a position of great power, and none of the maids or nannies in the household dared challenge him. The mother accepted the system for raising their children without protest.

Despite the cruelty of the father's system, the patient loved him with a passion. 'I was whatever my father wanted me to be. His idea of me – that's what I was.' Whenever they would visit a restaurant, she would close her eyes and allow him to insert any new foodstuff into her mouth, a sign, she said, of her total trust in him. Nothing could dent this love, until, many years later, she discovered the details of his debauched extramarital life. Now she had to question all his lessons about morality, the dangers of masturbation, the importance of fidelity. It was at this point that she started observing cats in the world around her, interpreting their movements and sounds as messages that would tell her what to do in her life. Where the certainty of her father's word was put in question, now she established a new compass, what she called 'the law of cats'.

However traumatic someone's upbringing may have been, there is a certain responsibility in the way in which they choose to make sense of the world. The family environment can try to force ideas and interpretations on the child, but there is always a margin of choice that, minimal as it may be, is nonetheless their own. This brings us to the question of the child's own part in psychosis. There must be an element of choice in the decision to accept or reject the idea of the father, not simply the real, empirical father but the symbolic third term necessary for the paternal metaphor to operate. If paternity implies an act of symbolic recognition between generations, a basic trust, this act can be rejected, for a variety of reasons, personal and specific to each individual history.

There are cases where a child can simply refuse to accept that there is anything beyond the mother, any third term that would mediate and pacify. Melanie Klein grasped this with her theory of the paranoid-schizoid and depressive positions. She argued that a fundamental phase of infancy involved a registration that the gratifying and frustrating breasts – the 'good' and 'bad' breasts, in her terminology – were one and the same. The child would understand that the mother was the site of contradictory qualities and this would create a sadness. What we see so clearly with some psychotic children is that such feelings are often not possible. In their place is pure sadistic attack. A frustration in love, for example, may not generate any depressive feelings, but rather a series of vicious onslaughts.

This lack of sadness can be a result of refusing to recognize that there is a third term beyond the mother. Accepting this, after all, would have a depressive effect, indicating that one could not satisfy her oneself and that one could never be enough for her. Here again we have a clue to the logic that runs through so many psychotic creations, where the subject tries to make themself the missing piece, whether it takes the form of the redeemer of mankind or the love object of some public figure or religious group.

It might seem that this rejection of the third term would be based on the sheer pain of having to break a fusional state with the mother: hence the child consigns the paternal function or its equivalent into oblivion. But when we explore the childhood histories of psychotic subjects here in cases where there appears to be less emphasis on the mother devaluing the father or the father usurping the place of the law, we tend to find that the early relation with the mother was marked not by fusion but by discontinuity and turbulence. Perhaps it is these situations that make the child's efforts to satisfy her even more desperate, and hence the foreclosure.

In other cases, the rejection involves a lack of faith in the symbolic order itself, as we saw with the case of the man whose epiphany concerned the word 'God' and with Loughner's disbelief in the grounding of words. Rejecting the symbolic agency of paternity or third term might be a decision bolstered by the mother's own words, or it might not be. But, in case after case, when we listen carefully we will find that this lack of establishment of the paternal function has taken place. It could be encouraged by the mother's embargo on the father in her speech, by the father's annexation of the place of the law, by the child's own decision not to believe in the father or the symbolic, or any combination of these factors.

We should note that all of these are compatible with having loving parents and a good relation with the real father. Lacan was careful not to make of the real father the cause of psychosis, but rather the non-integration of the symbolic function of paternity, resulting in a breakdown in the process of symbolizing the mother's desire. This rejection or non-integration of the symbolic function can involve both an under-investment or an over-investment of the real father. In the case we discussed above, the real father was elevated to the status of a God, or, more precisely, the child accepted and elaborated his own self-elevation. In other cases, the father simply doesn't count. Questions as to the patient's childhood receive monosyllabic answers, as if the father had just been written out of the family history. It is important to recognize here the difference between flesh-and-blood family and the symbolic relations between them that are built up out of speech. A rejection of the paternal agency can occur even if the real father and the child seem to get on well and to have a loving rapport.

This point should not be forgotten, as it tends to lead so easily to the old 'blame the parents' argument. The decisive factor here is what the child has made of the relation – or lack of relation – between the parents. There is thus a certain responsibility with the child in choosing its psychological structure, a fact compatible with a wide variety of family backgrounds. Recognizing this should discourage those futile attempts to find the exact family type that will generate a psychosis. The rigid emphasis on a single set of surface features is unhelpful, although there are certainly things we can find out and explore about the family constellations in psychosis.

Generalizations about the mothers of psychotic subjects are too often unqualified, and there is just no such thing as 'the mother of a schizophrenic' or 'the mother of a paranoiac'. We might find certain features in many cases but that does not mean all cases. We can encounter many mothers of schizophrenics who didn't invest the baby in their womb narcissistically, or who saw it as their own unique creation, or who had postnatal depression, but there is no single causal route from these facts to the psychosis in their child. Many factors are involved, and we must explore the detail of the patient's early life and family constellation in each case.

That being said, certain dynamics in the mother–child relation do crop up again and again, and we can consider them without the obligation to find the philosopher's stone of causality. Gisela Pankow argued that the mother of the schizophrenic can't see her child as an independent entity. In one example, a woman was found to have neglected her daughter, depriving her of food and basic care. Years later, she explained that 'I couldn't believe that I could give birth to anything separate from myself.' Her baby, she said, 'wasn't real', and so she had treated it like an object. If the child cannot exist for her independently, how can they then grow up believing in their own existence? Likewise, if the mother doesn't have confidence in her own capacity to care for her child, or believes that her child does not have this confidence in her, this may create significant difficulties in the mother–child relation, a lack of faith in the Other, which some analysts have linked to paranoia.

Piera Aulagnier had the idea that such early difficulties may make it impossible for the child to think about its own origin, and so anything that may evoke this is avoided. These ideas are foreclosed and life just continues. The risk will be at moments when the question of origins is stirred up, most obviously during parenthood. Now a psychosis might trigger. The other solution for Aulagnier is the early development of a delusional thought about origins, as if to take the place of what was never articulated in the discourse of the parents. Where the parents unconsciously impose a taboo on thinking, the child constructs a delusion. This is also entirely compatible with normal life, only becoming problematic when external events put the delusional thought in question.

Aulagnier also made many interesting contrasts between the family constellations in schizophrenia and paranoia. She observed that the mothers of paranoiacs often spoke of the sacrifices they had endured and the courage they had shown in bringing up their children, with the father's desire designated as dangerous or harmful. Feeling the weight of the mother's martyrdom, the child's critical and hostile thoughts towards her become impossible to assume: rejected from the psyche, they then return from the outside in delusions of persecution. We could add that the child's attachment to the father is also often treated by the mother as a crime: they have no right to love someone so malign. With schizophrenia, Aulagnier noted how the mothers would often show either an attitude of rejection or of complete appropriation of their child's autonomy.

'I never knew I was pregnant,' said Joey's mother, and at the birth she 'thought of him as a thing rather than a person'. In contrast, another mother could say directly to her son, 'I don't need to ask you what you want. You are me.' Under such conditions, what space would be left for the child to think? With no autonomy ascribed to them, how could they have a self or know what was *their* experience and what was *someone else's*? If they were obliged to think what others think, nothing else might seem possible. We see this clinically in the often astonishing identity of mother and child's speech: even if interviewed separately, the same version of a life story is given, as if no alternative were possible.

These ideas seemed to offer an explanation for the specifically schizophrenic feature of believing that one's own thoughts and body are being controlled by someone else, a detail that we do not find in paranoia. Similarly, problems in the early mother–child relation also seemed to account for other characteristics of schizophrenia. Take the example of the so-called Capgras syndrome, in which the psychotic subject believes that people around him have been replaced by doubles. Although seen as a rather exotic rarity, it is in fact very common, and several of my patients believe I have been 'replaced' by a copy at times. We find this phenomenon in the Schreber case when he says of his wife, who had been with him continuously until she had to leave for a four-day trip to visit her father: 'I could no longer see in her a live person but only a miracled-up human figure in the manner of "fleetingly made men".'

The obvious explanation is that the change in the behaviour of the loved one is intolerable, and its inconsistency means that the subject chooses to believe in two different people rather than one person who can both gratify and frustrate, perhaps through their successive presences and absences. This echoes the childhood question of how early rhythms of presence and absence are to be made sense of – or not. If much of the early research focused on patterns of mothering, it is this latter problem of how the child engages with rhythms of presence and absence that can help us to divide up the clinical field: instead of trying to match types of mother to types of patient, we can explore the different ways in which a child can symbolize, or fail to symbolize, the mother's desire.

In the Capgras examples, rather than seeing these as the consequence of inconsistent mothering, we can posit a basic difficulty in the establishment of signification, and hence of symbolic functioning. There is a reversal here of the Von Domarus principle: it's not that two subjects are identified on the basis of a single shared predicate, but that the presence of an identical set of predicates implies that there are two subjects. She looks the same, she talks the same, but she is a different person. Rather than assuming that the mother is the same but comes and goes, she is split into two. As one of my psychotic patients put it: 'Darling, I don't do object permanence.'

The many fine descriptions of mothers of schizophrenics allow us to discern complex and often almost invisible levels of interaction between mother and child, but in the end there is no one style of mothering that will produce, say, a schizophrenia rather than a paranoia. The fact that a mother loves her child conditionally or unconditionally, invests them with a mission or neglects them, deprives them of personhood or only sees the reflection of her own fantasy in the child will all no doubt have effects, but not in the sense of guaranteeing one future. The reason why psychoses fall into distinct groups is not because of distinct styles of mothering but because of the resources available to the infant in the world of meaning.

—

We saw earlier how the child must link the mother's presences and absences with something beyond her, usually identified with the father. This process implies that the child has registered the rhythm of presence and absence, and, as Colette Soler suggests, there is a group of psychoses that is based on a problem with this archaic operation. If presence and absence have not been registered, the child may literally not react at moments of greeting or farewell, as we see with some autistic children. They act as if nothing has happened when someone enters or exits the room, as if the rhythm of presence and absence has not been symbolized at all. That's why they may also be captivated by anything that embodies this basic alternance – such as a light being switched on or off. Unable to internalize the most basic binary oppositions that lie at the heart of the symbolic order, they can only access them, as it were, from the outside.

Interestingly, we can perhaps see a return to this point in some forms of 'dementia', where the person can only ask 'When will I see you again?' repetitively as if their whole world is reduced to this one basic question. To take another example, a patient said, 'I couldn't think about my mother when I wasn't with her.' If the presences and absences of the mother aren't symbolized, then her absence can be equivalent to her disappearance, as we see in the terror that parental absence produces in some psychotic children: it's as if the mother's going away leaves a hole in their reality, rather than just being understood as a temporary departure. As a schizophrenic patient put it, terrified about my upcoming holiday, 'You would disappear in a hole which will then itself disappear, and so you wouldn't have existed any more.'

In another case, the patient's parents left her with a relative when she was one and a half years old to go on a trip. When they returned, she refused to recognize them, and would later date her 'death' from that point. They simply ceased to exist for her, and after leaving home she would cut all contact with them. Days on which I was unavailable to see her or on vacation would be impossible for her: each departure was not only a betrayal but also an irreversible disappearance. In this group of psychoses, it is less a rejection of the father than a problem in the process of symbolizing the mother that gives the central aetiology.

The registration of a place created by the mother's absences has not been symbolized, and so the subject has nothing with which to make sense of her comings and goings. All they can register is the fact that 'something' has changed for the worse, and this could generate, on the one hand, phenomena such as Capgras syndrome – where one person's comings and goings are taken to be the actions of different people – or hypochondria, which is a way, after all, of trying to signify that things are different, that some change has taken place. The initial problem here in marking the place of the mother is why, as we have seen, it is so vital for the schizophrenic subject to manufacture a lack somewhere in their world. They can use this to distance the Other, who is always too close to them, and to find a point of safety.

The distinction between what psychoanalysis terms 'alienation' and 'separation' is helpful here in formulating the difference between these forms of psychosis. We are alienated in the signifiers that come from our parents, the ideas and fantasies that we are born into and that shape our early lives. We take on certain traits, aspirations and ways of being from them. Language itself alienates us, as we must exist within its parameters and structures. But we must also separate from these signifiers, make ourselves distinct from them, create a distance, since otherwise we would belong body and soul to the Other. Children learn to speak, as Karl Popper once pointed out, not when they can utter words but when they can lie: that is, know things and do things that the Other doesn't know about. This is one example of the process of separation.

It is only thanks to this separation that we can genuinely include ourselves in language, in the chain of ideas, since we would otherwise be pure puppets of speech, unable to extricate ourselves from the words of others. We would simply be copies of the ideas and images imposed on us, and with the Other enjoying a direct line to our body and mind. We could see a metaphor of this process in the child's single hitting of the drum after his parents tell him to stop drumming: the one stroke is the act that shows that even if he is going to play by the rules, it's his own choice to do so.

The group of psychoses linked to the archaic symbolization of the mother's absences involves a problem with alienation: the person does not enter into the initial alienation in the chain of ideas from the parent. Words seem to have no effect, suggesting that there is a basic rejection of what comes from the Other. Presence and absence have not been symbolized. In such cases, we often find hoarding or collecting, as if the person cannot separate from some scraps of paper, tins or everyday detritus, which they may even carry around in their pockets.

In the other group of psychoses, there is certainly alienation, but no separation, so words have too much rather than too little effect. It is as if the subject is represented by all the signifiers rather than just by some of them. As John Custance put it, 'I can look at nothing without receiving some idea from it leading to an impulse to action.' Words would push him at all times; looking at an inkpot would generate the image of the letters 'inkpot' in front of him, which would then compel him to go to the lavatory, the pot. It once happened that I said the word 'tweet' to a patient, and was surprised to find that he understood this as a command to go on Twitter, which he immediately carried out. There was no barrier between the word and the effect. This is the automatic obedience that we find in some forms of schizophrenia. The person is glued to language, unable to create a separation.

This inability to separate at a symbolic level may force the psychotic subject to try to produce a separation in another register. They may make every effort to pin themselves down, sometimes quite literally: touching surrounding objects, stamping their feet, carrying out some act of self-harm, to assure themselves of a place, a fixity that their unchecked alienation in language cannot provide. This lack of a position in the symbolic means that they might be prone to drift, haunting streets, railway stations and public transport depots. Without a separating point, they have no compass, and have to find their own ways to pin themselves down.

Suicide is another way to create a separation from the signifying chain. As a patient described his suicide attempt: 'There was a sudden silence, like before an atomic bomb, and then the pills were down my throat.' The act of ingesting them was completely cut off from any sense of subjective agency or volition. 'A minute or so later, I felt surprised when I saw the empty pill boxes. I realized I had taken the pills, and enough to kill me. But then I felt nothing, no thought of anyone or anything, no anxiety.' The suicidal act had involved a separation from the chain of thoughts, evoked in this example not simply by the ingestion of pills but by the curious localization of 'silence': it was situated not *after* the atomic bomb, as one might have expected, but *before*, as if to index the eclipse of any sense of subjectivity, any ownership of thought. The forced separation of a suicidal act often seems the only alternative to a person who feels totally at the mercy of the Other, either stuck completely to them or quite literally dropped.

The lack of a distance from the Other means that everything can get too close, too invasive. 'Every word,' Custance continues, 'almost every letter, of a newspaper I might chance to look at, would contain some dire message of evil.' With no means of separating from the Other, we remain glued to its signifiers. Every element of reality becomes a sign calling us. In contrast, in the psychoses where there is no alienation, nothing calls us, there is no sign that represents us.

How could these strange relations to language and the world of signs come about? What would the causes be of these different positions? We need to turn now to explore the impact of language on the infant in more detail, and the ways in which this can affect the subject's experience in psychosis.

Early Western research on mother–infant interactions tended to ascribe little subjectivity to the newborn apart from the wish to feed.

Even recognizing and differentiating the mother from others was assumed to take place quite some time after birth. Yet careful work began to show that there were complex transactions between infant and mother beginning *in utero*, mainly involving cycles of activity.

It was once believed that infants can only hear properly several months after birth, yet the new studies demonstrated that a foetus could discern sounds as early as four months from gestation. After the mother spoke or sang, for example, there would be certain movements in the foetus, which would then cease when the mother herself continued. This research showed that mother and infant were engaged in interacting cycles of activity: each party was giving the other a place, in a kind of elementary turn-taking.

Although it is doubtful what meaning can be given to these cycles, the essential factor is the timing of exchanges. After making their contribution, each participant retires to allow the other to respond. This basic turn-taking could be seen as the minimal structure of human dialogue, which would prepare the way for speech. There was a significant divergence here between Western and Eastern research. Where the Western psychologists tended to see the capacity for speech as an innate potential for expressing one's thoughts, to be activated by one's surroundings, the Russian tradition saw thinking itself as an import: we would internalize the dialogue around us, and this would establish the structure of thinking. Thoughts, on this model, come first from the outside and have the form of a dialogue: in fact, exactly what some psychotic subjects tell us about their experience.

The implication of such research was that thinking and speech are always at some level connected to dialogue, or, at least, to the idea of someone else's speech. Even when a child speaks on its own, with no one else there, some of the formal features of dialogue will still be present. This would be shown decisively through the study of crib speech, the babbling of babies and infants as they are falling asleep. Crib speech has no doubt existed as long as babies have, and it is amazing that it was only in the 1960s that it began to receive any attention from linguists. The groundbreaking study was conducted by Ruth Weir in 1962, with her two-and-a-half-year-old son Anthony as subject, and it was published with an introduction by the linguist Roman Jakobson. Weir placed a tape recorder next to little Anthony's bed and then performed a linguistic analysis of the data recovered over a period of several months. Her results were remarkable.

Listening to the crib speech of her son, she noted first of all something that later studies would confirm: the frequency of imperatives in the child's speech. Lying alone in his bed, he would recite orders to himself, and this presence of 'another' speech within his own was found throughout the recordings. Sometimes such imperatives could be taken for declaratives, as in phrases like 'Jump on yellow blanket' or 'Make too much noise', and Weir's hesitation as to how best to classify these examples is instructive. It shows, perhaps, how what ends up as a declarative has its origin in an imperative: that is, in speech coming from the Other and addressed to the subject.

The linguist Paul Guillaume had argued that proper names are not just strict designations of objects, but calls, containing the emotional meaning the person has for the child, so that early linguistic forms cannot be categorized in terms of adult grammatical categories. 'Mama' and 'Papa', for example, are less nouns than imperatives, linguistic participants in concrete action. All speech may have this imperative root, and it is interesting to remember that linguists once wondered whether the imperative was the first mood of human speech.

As Weir studied her son's evening soliloquies, she came to another important conclusion: that these apparent monologues were not monologues at all but dialogues. Anthony produced what she called 'a dialogue spoken by a single person'. It was as if Anthony was always in the process of *addressing himself*, and bedtime speech was a privileged moment for this. While his little stuffed toy 'Bobo' was more or less ignored during the day and not particularly missed when left somewhere, at bedtime Bobo would become an interlocutor in crib speech, the addressee of numerous commands and calls. The fact that these dialogues would take place on the frontiers of sleep implies that this is a privileged point for the internalization of speech. Similar findings have been made by later researchers, but before trying to make sense of Weir's results, we could bring in another theme from child-language studies.

If little Anthony was especially interested in having interlocutors, mothers spend a large percentage of their time dialoguing with their babies who are in no position to answer back directly. Cross-cultural studies have shown how around 70 per cent of mothers' speech to babies consists of interrogative forms: 'Are you hungry?', 'Do you want a drink?', 'Are you too hot?' The puzzle here is less the frequency of these syntactic forms than the fact that they are not mirrored in the eventual speech of the babies themselves. There is no demonstrated correlation between the frequency of interrogative forms in maternal speech and in that of their children. In fact, the inverted word order characteristic of interrogative forms in some languages is hardly ever present in the early linguistic productions of native speakers.

This is surprising given what we know about imitative patterns, and it is interesting how researchers found that not only do children tend to imitate maternal speech, but they also imitate more when the mother is *imitating them*. The relative frequency with which children imitate their mothers' speech was correlated with the relative frequency with which mothers imitated their children's speech. The children, it turned out, were more likely to imitate maternal imitations than other speech acts. It showed how infants don't only learn *by* imitating their mothers but learn, in a sense, the process of imitation itself.

Now, if we consider the frequency of such interrogative forms in maternal 'baby talk', it suggests that the baby, even though unable to speak, is being given a potential space within the mother's linguistic world. Even if they cannot reply with words, infants are being given the *possibility of responding*, which may take the form of gesture, cry and, later, words, as the child grows older and learns the language codes of the mother. But in its first months, the function of maternal questions must be to prepare a place within speech for the speaking subject to be born. The interrogative forms of maternal speech not only create a context in which babbles become meaningful but offer a space to the subject. This is by no means a given: think of those situations where the caregiver will not ask any question to a child, but, on the contrary, will *tell* the child that they are hot, cold, hungry or thirsty. The parent knows everything here, and may try to make the child believe that they have no separate subjectivity. This leaves no place for the self to emerge. The infant is simply an object for the Other.

Question forms in maternal speech can also be linked to the strange linguistic phenomena found at the edges of sleep. The words we hear in hypnogogic and hypnopompic states were once a topic of interest to psychiatry, and Kraepelin was especially intrigued by them. In the states of falling asleep and waking up, the linguistic fragments usually seem to require completion or elaboration. Most people have probably experienced this on waking up: they're either left with a verbal fragment that they can't make any sense of but that seems important, or know that they've solved some mystery or puzzle during sleep but can't remember how they did it. It's like Bertrand Russell's famous proof of the existence of God: he knew he'd done it and threw his tobacco tin in the air to celebrate, yet tragically all he could recall later on was the image of throwing the tin.

Unable to reconstruct the proof, its only legacy was this image and the feeling of certainty that he had solved something. Likewise, when we have the sense that we have solved some crucial problem or puzzle in our sleep, all that remains is usually the accompanying affect and perhaps some fragment of a sentence, not the actual solution. Why this odd insistence, then, not only of incomplete bits of language but also the feeling that they need to be completed or that they are important and concern us?

The answer requires us to extend the classical model of language. Despite its many vicissitudes over the twentieth century, linguistics remained largely faithful to the dominant nineteenth-century model of language as involving three main functions: the referential, the emotive and the conative. The referential treats the denoting and connoting aspects of language, how it relates to its objects; the emotive treats the speaker's relation to their words, expressive of their attitude; and the conative treats the relation to the addressee, such as questioning or ordering. Now, this brings us to the crucial point: all of these perspectives on language explore the relation to the addressee but what they don't do is study *the experience of being addressed*.

And don't the experiences of the infant being spoken to and of the adult on the edge of sleep indicate exactly the contours of this function of language?

Being addressed is both something essential and something problematic for an infant for two very simple reasons: first, the meaning of the adult's interpellation will initially be enigmatic and, second, the infant has no immediate defence against it. Nearly all other interactions with the adult can be the subject of some form of contestation, some demonstration of one's subjectivity. The child can challenge what the adult offers or demands. They can refuse to eat, to drink, to go on the potty, and so on. But what they cannot refuse so easily is to be addressed by the Other. Rather than seeing this as a trivial detail, we should not underestimate its importance as a central function of language and of the infant's experience. The very fact that it cannot be defended against gives it a persecutory potential.

A parallel emerges here with the look, which is perhaps the only other form of the adult's presence that cannot be readily defended against. Infants can refuse to follow the direction of the adult's look, they can shut their eyes when they are supposed to be open, but they cannot block the fact of being looked at. And hence perhaps the reason children often have the fantasy that by closing their eyes they can become invisible to others. The look of the Other and the fact of being addressed share this feature of being experiences imposed from the 'outside' that concern the child directly, yet which cannot be defended against. In these states, we are in the position of an object rather than a subject for the Other. And for these very reasons, the look and the voice can become invasive and threatening.

A further parallel might be drawn here. How does the child defend itself against the look of the Other? One solution, described by Lacan, involves the production of screens, which function to distract the Other. Attention is drawn to some image or screen that the subject manipulates to keep the look away from themselves. This is the principle of the amulet, an object kept close to the body to divert the evil eye and thus ensure one's protection. There's a split, then, between the look of the Other and the screen offered up by the subject. Can't we also find a similar split at play in the field of sound? If the subject has to defend against the experience of being addressed, doesn't the production of sound have the same function as the screen in the field of vision, which could take the form, for example, of a painting?

The most basic instance of this may be the infant's scream: not the scream that expresses pain or some demand, but the one that submerges the Other's interpellations, which makes it so difficult, at times, for the Other to continue saying anything. Schreber describes this experience with great clarity. At times he would 'bellow', especially at night 'when other defensive measures like talking aloud, playing the piano, etc., are hardly practicable. In such circumstances, bellowing has the advantage of drowning with its noise everything the voices speak into my head.' It is the same action that so many commuters take on their way to work. Listening to their iPods, the music drowns out not only the sounds of the tube or bus but also the invasive thoughts that trouble them, whether these take the form of voices or not. Nearly all of my patients who hear voices use iPods or headphones for this purpose.

Feeling that his mother's voice intruded into him – and, by extension, the whole of the English language – Louis Wolfson would plug every orifice in his body to defend himself against it. He would listen to foreign broadcasts throughout the day on a pocket transistor radio, and keep French and German books with him at all times. Even eating was affected, as he couldn't bear to see the English words on the packets and tins in his mother's kitchen: he would reach for them with his eyes half closed. Every sentence and every word was experienced as a dreadful interpellation, as if his mother were trying to 'inject' them into him.

If the infant is initially unable to defend itself against the experience of being addressed through a refusal, what other possibilities are open to it apart from plugging the ears? Perhaps there are more subtle, less evident forms of refusal at play here. One option might be for the child to act as if it were in fact being addressed not by the particular adult but by something else, turning their attention elsewhere. Or, quite simply, to act as if one wasn't being addressed, a strategy well known to children. At such moments, the visual register is often invoked, the child either glancing in a mirror or a reflecting surface or, in some cases, literally gluing themselves to their reflection.

A mother described how her teenage son would stare at his reflection, and if she spoke to him or called him while he was staring at himself he would not listen. Inverting this logic, however, clarifies their situation: it was less that because he was looking he couldn't listen than that looking was an escape from the persecutory, invasive dimension of his mother's voice. We should remember that these options don't save the child from the fact of being addressed, but constitute forms of response. If someone refuses to hear, it means that they have heard very clearly what is expected of them. But there is also one more option, which we will come back to later.

It is interesting to continue the parallel with the look a bit further. How is the invasive dimension of the look of the Other dealt with? Why not invoke here the many games of peek-a-boo played by mothers and children, games that involve a rhythm of presence and absence. One might argue that the function of these games is to link the look of the Other to a structure, a ritual of presence and absence where the cardinal feature is that the look *isn't always there*. A game is being used to 'socialize' and tame a menacing presence. The invasive aspect of the look of the Other is repressed, removed from the space we inhabit to constitute our reality. And isn't there something similar that operates on the experience of being addressed? Doesn't the crib speech reported by Weir and others have exactly this function? Rather than following her interpretation of crib speech as an early language-learning exercise, we could see it as a kind of incorporation procedure that goes towards alleviating anxiety. By generating a dialogue themselves, don't children manage to modulate the experience of being addressed? They have now become the organizer, addressing an other *instead of being the unique addressee themselves*.

Just as games like peek-a-boo link the intrusive experience of being looked at to a rhythm and structure, so crib speech does the same with the experience of being addressed. It modulates the addressee function, and don't so many other children's games continue this same task? Several of these games, after all, involve one player taking on a role that is different from the other players – being 'it' for example – while the other players resist being assigned this role. Indeed, the strategies for not being designated 'it', such as evermore complex verbal constructions to block the possibilities of a predetermined outcome, become intrinsic parts of the game, or even games in themselves. One could also evoke the games of 'dare you' familiar from childhood where no one really wins and it is rather a question of just doing what someone else says or, significantly, trying to avoid doing this. Finally, one could think of the many door-knocking games in which a child will be elected or volunteer to go to knock on a door and then run off. The thread that runs through all of these examples is the different relations the subject has to the experience of being addressed. And in these games, this experience is played with, modulated, taken up into a structure. Being addressed becomes a variable in all such games of interpellation, so one is not simply an object of someone else's speech. They are ways of avoiding and playing with this place.

Once we isolate both the linguistic function of interpellation and the experience of being addressed as its corollary, a whole range of phenomena becomes clearer. The linguistic peculiarities found at the borders of sleep involve, we can now see, a separation of this function. We have the experience of words or phrases that interpellate us even if the meaning is opaque, and the occasional sense of 'respect' that Otto Isakower noticed in his study of hypnagogic phenomena is a sign of subjective involvement. As we prepare to sleep, this function can be modulated as in crib speech, while during sleep itself it doesn't disturb us too much until it emerges again around the time of waking, and perhaps even plays a part in waking. This supports Freud's quite radical view of sleep as not a passive occurrence but an active process. We don't fall asleep: we *make* ourselves sleep.

We are now in a better position to understand why the look and the voice are so present and persecutory in psychosis. Rather than being bound into a structure and repressed, they emerge as invasive, threatening and unmediated. The subject feels looked at, spied upon, spoken to, addressed. The whole world, in some cases, looks at them and speaks to them. If the invasive dimension of the voice and the look have not been extracted, the psychotic subject may have to resort to violence to remove them from his immediate world: and, indeed, so many psychotic acts aim to disarm a look or a voice that intrudes unbearably into them.

We could think here of the notorious crime of the Papin sisters, the two maids who, at the moment when the persecutory threat from their employers seemed at its height, tore out their tormentors' eyes with their bare hands before murdering them. Although such extreme cases may be rare, it is a common occurrence that when paintings or sculptures are vandalized in galleries and museums, the first target is most frequently the eyes of the person represented. Similarly, among the apparently unmotivated attacks on public figures we so often find that the person was a broadcaster. In all of these instances, the subject tries desperately to weaken or disarm what bores into them: a look or a voice that they feel is directed at them.

This linguistic function of interpellation is functioning here in its pure form: it is the experience of being addressed, isolated from any particular sensory modality and semantic field, felt as an imperative demanding obedience or conviction. As one of my patients put it, 'even descriptions for me are always accusations'. Or, as Schreber writes, 'I felt a blow on my head simultaneously with every word spoken to me, with every approaching footstep, with every railway whistle.' The subject has the sense that someone or something is calling them, addressing them, intruding into them.

—

This function of being addressed is introduced through the experience of being spoken to, yet it can then emerge in any sensory register, including vision, touch or smell. As we noted earlier, under certain conditions – extreme fatigue, drugs, sensory deprivation – anyone can have a hallucination, but for it to really count as a psychotic phenomenon it must have an effect of meaning for the person: they must understand it as making a sign *to them*, even if they have no idea what it is a sign of. Visual hallucination can be a vehicle of the linguistic structure we are discussing: through the gaze of others the person feels aimed at. It is this addressee function of language, experienced by the subject, which defines true hallucination.

Hallucination is indeed the place where the addressee function emerges in its pure form, and in general it emerges at the start of the psychosis, either flagrantly or discreetly. We should distinguish here between those hallucinations that are *about* the subject and those that are directed *to* the subject: in the former, a voice may describe their actions continuously ('now he's getting dressed, now he's going to work . . .'), while in the latter there are generally obscenities or sexual accusations, usually involving pejorative terms associated with women ('Bitch!', 'Whore!', etc.). There are also those hallucinations that instruct the person, telling them to carry out certain tasks, ranging from a homicidal act to banal everyday actions such as standing up or brushing one's teeth. A patient's slow and awkward actions can be misinterpreted as a sign of brain deterioration when they are in fact a consequence of having to listen to the instructions necessary for each step of everyday life. These three forms of hallucination correspond to three modes of address, as if the voices have become vehicles of the interpellative functions of language.

A verbal hallucination, as Lacan pointed out, is not limited to any particular sensorium: it doesn't have to take on an acoustic form but can privilege any sensory modality. What matters is the question of attribution: is it felt to aim at the subject? The broad scope of this definition accounts for the wide variety of clinical manifestations. A patient explains how he receives words from the third bed on the left, which imprint themselves in his stomach. Another speaks of hearing 'mute words'. Another reports that 'I hear a voice in my head but not in my ears', 'a distant voice'. Another says of his voices that 'I don't hear them, I feel them speaking.' Bleuler quotes his patients evoking 'soundless voices'. As one of them put it, 'I don't hear it in my ears. I have the feeling in my breast. Yet it seems as if I heard a sound.' For another, 'God always speaks to me', 'it makes no sound, it's like a thought'. What remains constant, however, is the experience of being addressed, regardless of the channels through which this operates.

Separating hallucination from particular sensory modalities was a consequence of Lacan's model of language. Language is a structure that operates and has its effects at all levels of sensory perception. Hence it follows that if one of the properties of the signifying chain is the addressee function, this can return in any modality. It could emerge through silence, for example, or through vision, or through touch or smell. There are plenty of situations where a silence gives us the sense of being interpellated, and so it is a question not of equating voices with sound but rather of finding the effects of voices in the field of sound, as many psychotic subjects teach us. The way that a person punctuates their speech, their rhythm and verbal style will give clues as to their modes of incorporating the addressee function.

The way that speech is punctuated always involves an implicit placing and supposition of the listener's presence, and, more generally, of the supposition of being addressed. Hence one person's speech may be organized to blot out any possibility of being addressed, or, on the contrary, may invite it. We could note how the use of connectives always indexes the presence of this aspect of the Other: when children start to use terms like 'and' and 'but', it points to the supposed presence or, indeed, intrusion of another speaker. Wasn't Charles Sanders Peirce right when he suggested that thinking always takes the form of a dialogue, whether we know it or not?

If we turn to vision, we can find further examples of this function. A film like *Ring* tells the story of a videotape that strangely interpellates its viewers, sending them a lethal message. The visual field here calls the subject, and they desperately and futilely try to avoid being addressed by it. Similarly, in the phenomenon of voodoo death, the little bit of symbolic matter, be it a doll or a bit of hair, has catastrophic effects on the person who finds it. The object here, although presented visually, consists of a concentration of the addressee function: it is pure interpellation, a vector designating the finder. Beyond the visual, it calls the subject. And hence its terrifying effects. The linguistic function is operating here through vision.

Language itself always contains this potentiality, and it can return in the form of murmurs, voices, whispering, buzzing, verbal commentaries and the many phenomena that psychotics describe. We must obviously answer the question now of why this interpellative function of language isn't there for everyone. It is our most basic experience of speech, after all, in our infancy. Yet it can be mediated and repressed by being woven into the minimal symbolic structures of presence and absence, as we have seen, and at another level, it is dealt with in the process of the paternal metaphor. What does this do if not fundamentally reassign an addressee function? The mother's interests are no longer directed just to the child but registered as aiming at someone or something else, beyond both her and the child. This moves the interpellative vector away. Without this operation, we remain open to the vector.

The paternal metaphor establishes a key signification, pinning down the field of signifiers. If it does not take place, signifier and signified may, at certain moments, start to become unchained. If the inscription of the third term gives a signification to the desire of the mother in the unconscious, foreclosure will mean that this desire cannot be symbolized and hence the speech of the Other is not situated in the unconscious: it may speak to the person all the time, not necessarily ascribed to another subject but simply to the 'field of perception' itself.

At certain moments, which we will explore in the next chapter, the world not only starts to speak but it speaks *to* the person. Bleuler described a patient who heard his name coming from a glass of milk and who was then addressed by the furniture. In some cases, there is just one small, discreet interpellation, but in others it can become an unbearable cacophony. As a young man explained to me about an earlier suicide attempt: 'The noise was unbearable. Everything was a message to me, all the adverts, every bit of music in shops or the street. It was too much. I had to find a way out.'

Let's return to the question we posed earlier about the possibilities of response to the experience of being addressed. We described two of them: to act as if one were being addressed by someone or something else, or to pretend that one simply wasn't being addressed. But why not hypothesize a third option, one that would consist in the rejection of this linguistic function in its entirety: language minus the interpellative function, minus the experience of being addressed. Isn't this a clinical picture we find in some autistic states?

If towards the end of his treatment Joey could say 'I' and name some of the children and his therapist, he would never use names or personal pronouns in direct address, but only in the indirect third person. Kleist had distinguished what he termed 'psychoses of reference' and those of 'alienation' or 'depersonalization': that is, those in which one is referred to and those in which everything seems remote and cut off, alien to oneself and unconnected. In these latter states, one's own body seems dead and one's thoughts, movements and speech seem to have no personal relevance. Although we would not agree with his explanations, the idea of a group of psychoses that is based on a lack of self-reference resonates with our argument. But rather than seeing this as a given, we would understand it as involving a rejection of the interpellative function of language, to preserve one's safety.

And wouldn't certain clinical consequences follow? On an immediate level, it would provide an explanation for what most people who work with autistic subjects know – that is, don't try to address them directly. And secondly, that *any* words can potentially be experienced as invasive. Simple questions may be heard as attacks and intrusions. This means that it isn't semantics that is to blame and that it isn't through semantics that one will be able to make any progress. The problem here is about the experience of being aimed at, and so is prior to any question about meaning. If interpellation is to play a part, it is through its modulation rather than through its direct exercise.

We find an example of this in Schreber's *Memoirs*. As he differentiates a Lower God from an Upper God, he notes that the former was generally more friendly while the latter was more hostile. Both assailed him with voices, often abusive and insulting, yet some of the Lower God's communications 'were in part addressed to me personally, in part – spoken through my head, as it were – to his colleague, the Upper God'. The addressee function was thus being modulated: although speaking through him, the voices were in fact addressing someone else as well, and we could conjecture that this very feature contributed to the benign nature of the Lower God. Schreber himself was no longer the unique object of the voices.

The strange dynamic of Schreber's nerves and rays illustrates the same process. His situation in relation to the divine rays was at first quite defenceless: like the look and voice of the Other, nothing could prevent them from reaching him. But as his delusion developed, he began to ponder the question of what the rays might think of the nerves. The rays were thus not singling him out as their unique object, since part of their concentration was directed to the nerves. Through this triangulation, the addressee function was once again modulated.

This transformation of the addressee function may shed light on the urgency felt by some psychotic subjects to deliver a message: they have a mission to educate, to disseminate knowledge, to teach, to reveal. Beyond the question of trying to resolve the fault in the world, isn't there also an effort to relay the experience of being addressed? The subject is no longer the sole recipient, but must make others listen too.

One of my patients had been terrified by auditory hallucinations that would order him to kill or insult himself. Listening to his iPod almost all day every day was not enough to block out the voices, yet he was able to devise a certain solution to his sense of persecution. We agreed that whenever he heard one of his voices, he would text me the words uttered. This meant that I would regularly receive insults, obscenities and commands, and yet through this process the voices became less invasive for him. In effect, by texting, he had made a circuit from the initial experience of being addressed. The vector had now been extended, to relay on to me, so sheltering him from being in the sole place of addressee. In a way, this practice was like an extension of some of the children's games we discussed earlier, and its effects were significant for my patient.

Yet how and why did the voices begin in the first place? If we have looked in this chapter at the conditions that establish the ground for psychosis, we must now turn to the question of triggers. Although many – perhaps most – people will go through life with a psychotic structure without experiencing a triggering, what are the factors that can actually catapult quiet, everyday madness into its visible, dramatic correlate?

7. Triggering

As his feet touched the ground after his first parachute jump, a twenty-three-year-old man's psychosis detonated: 'I'm God,' he said. Twenty years earlier, he had met his father for the first time, after the latter's release from prison. 'Who's that?' he had asked his mother. 'It's your father,' she replied. 'A father doesn't just fall out of the sky.'

Most people who are psychotic will never experience a triggering of their psychosis. Life will just go on, and there will be no moment of collapse or disintegration. Yet in some cases the psychosis will erupt, often in a terrifying and initially catastrophic way. Helping the person get through this difficult period can draw attention away from reconstructing the exact sequence of events leading up to the triggering. Yet a careful study of the detail of this chronology is in itself therapeutic, and will provide valuable information not only as to why they went mad but also what had prevented them from going mad until then. And this can be crucial in charting therapeutic strategies for the treatment.

Paying attention to these initial sequences is always fruitful, even if it can take months and sometimes years for the relevant details to emerge. The more we explore the moments of crystallization and eruption of psychosis, the more we can understand what psychosis is. Beyond the noisy and visible phenomena of hallucinations or overtly delusional thought there lies a logical development that has to be excavated in each case. In his classic study of schizophrenia, Bleuler observed that even if there is no such thing as a typical course of psychosis, mapping out a paradigmatic sequence could still allow new perspectives to open up. Even if each case fails to live up to the paradigm, it will encourage us to ask questions about the points of convergence and divergence with the sequence we might expect.

The triggering of a psychosis tends to go through a number of stages. First of all, there is a sense that things have changed. This can be described as a vague feeling that something is awry or simply different. The person cannot put their finger on what exactly it is. They may feel anxious, bewildered or puzzled. Occasionally, there may be a sense of joy or unexplained contentment. There is a sense of meaningfulness in the world around them, as if they were somehow aware that things are significant, but not in any defined way. Classical psychiatry provided fine descriptions of these states, yet they are often only accessible to the person after a great deal of detailed dialogue. The invasive experiences that occur later on may make it difficult for the person to remember what had happened in the early phases, which may be qualified simply as involving a feeling of puzzlement or enigma.

There may now be a certain withdrawal from social relations, perhaps some problems in sleeping or some hypochondriacal ideas. The person becomes preoccupied, in some cases unable to concentrate on their usual interests. The sense of meaningfulness they had discerned may undergo a subtle or quite direct inflection. The meanings they can feel are directed towards them, although it is unclear how or in what way. There is a sense of a 'personal signification' in these meanings, different from the continuity of their previous experience. The car that goes by, the change in the weather or the article in the newspaper seems to somehow single them out. Everyday signs start to refer to them, and these ideas of reference may gather momentum. As one psychotic subject put it, 'Everything means "something".' The world has changed, it is different: it has a meaning, a necessity, yet the actual sense of this is not clear. The dominant feeling is one of perplexity, yet with the sense that the changes in the world *concern oneself*. Certain words or phrases may start to preoccupy the person, as if they had an inordinate weight even if their meaning is opaque.

The hypochondriacal unease that often appears here may be difficult to describe. The person says that something isn't right, that there has been some alteration in their body, and may seek medical advice to explain it. In contrast to concerns about the body that may feature in later phases of psychosis, there is not a single fixed complaint, but rather a shifting range of worries. The person may spend hours searching the Internet for clues as to the sensations they are experiencing. Where for the paranoiac subject the change is often felt as occurring in the world around them, for the schizophrenic it may be the body that first registers the idea of a change taking place.

It is in this period that the world starts to speak. Jaspers describes a case in which 'the patient saw some bed-linen on the kitchen table, a candle on the wardrobe and a piece of soap. He was extremely upset. He was very much afraid and convinced that all this referred to him. He could not say how he came to this conclusion. It was absolutely clear to him in a flash; it must concern him. "I know for certain that it refers to me."' Everyday objects or actions start to take on new meanings, however enigmatic this may be. Norma MacDonald, diagnosed with schizophrenia, describes her own experiences: 'The walk of a stranger on the street could be a "sign" to me which I must interpret. Every face on the window of a passing streetcar would be engraved on my mind, all of them concentrating on me and trying to pass me some sort of message.' People, events, places and ideas all meant something, all concerned her, and she had the sense that there was 'an overwhelming significance' in what was happening to her.

As we saw in the last chapter, the very fact of being aimed at and interpellated will confer a menacing character on one's experience. This will often be felt as directly persecutory. John Custance describes how, as his psychosis triggered, everything began to single him out, from a crumpled pillow, the creases on the side of the bed to a face-cloth or a towel on the floor. 'They can suggest shapes of the utmost horror to the mind obsessed by fear. Gradually, my eyes began to distinguish such shapes, until, eventually, whichever way I turned, I could see nothing but devils waiting to torment me, devils which seemed infinitely more real than the material objects in which I saw them.' As reality starts to speak, it becomes ominous and terrifying for the subject.

Sometimes there is the idea here that the world has ended. The person may describe how things are different, as if reality now seems empty, monotonous, and that people are fleeting things, wax puppets, husks. As Renée put it, 'Around me, the other children, heads bent over their work, were robots or puppets, moved by an invisible mechanism.' One of my patients described how she felt that 'there's nothing left. Just facades. There's no one.' Humanity has been destroyed and replaced by some sort of improvised cast. The whole planet may have been obliterated and there is often the sense that they are the only person left. They may withdraw even more from society or, on the contrary, seek out other people to talk and communicate with about their experience.

The sense of meaningfulness is often, in a next phase, interpreted. The car going by, the change in the weather or the newspaper article now come to take on a particular meaning. The thoughts of the psychotic person are crucial to explore here, as they concern the basic operation of creating meaning, of finding some way to make sense of the changes they are experiencing. These positive, constructive efforts to ascribe meaning can be local or global: they can apply to the minutiae of the surrounding world or they can develop into a more general interpretation of one's overall situation. There can be many different meanings given to individual experiences, without any unifying idea, or, in contrast, the transformation of the world into a speaking language may settle into a delusion with one fixed signification.

This means that there is a mobilization of signifiers to treat the experience of enigma. Meaning can be established little by little or, more frequently, in leaps and bounds, moments when a truth is suddenly discovered. Custance calls these 'the strange flashes of insight' and Lacan the 'fertile moments' that allow a delusion to be built. The person realizes, for example, that they have a mission or that others are plotting against them. They may then start to quietly prepare for what they have to do or, just as frequently, lash out at others they believe are threatening, others who know too much about them. People in their environment are often felt to have an unbearable knowledge about their personal life, as we saw with the case of Ernst Wagner, who believed that the local inhabitants knew about his sexual relations with animals. This third phase of the psychosis may happen all at once or over time, and sometimes it never happens at all, the person remaining at the mercy of a world that constantly points to them and never stops speaking. No orientation can be established, no meaning that would give the person a place or position.

In such situations, the person may act rather than construct: instead of a delusion there may be a self-mutilation or any action that aims to introduce a negativity, a distance from the invasive and persecutory forces they are experiencing. They may try to subtract something from the world, either via their body or some aspect of their environment. They might, for example, have the idea that some surgical intervention is necessary, which would involve losing a part of the body. Through their actions, they aim to empty out some excess in the body or in the Other. As Colette Soler points out, after the initial phase of triggering, the efforts of psychotic subjects move in these two directions: adding something to the world, via delusion or creation, or removing something from the world, via self-mutilation or change. Both of these constitute attempts at self-cure.

If the first uses meaning in the effort to restructure, the second aims directly at subtracting libido. In the initial phase of triggering, the construction of reality becomes undone: signifier and signified come apart, so that the world just seems to 'mean'. This release of the sense of meaningfulness has an effect of interpellation: it concerns that person uniquely. A hole has opened up in the world of meaning, and so the person must try desperately to reorganize, to rebuild, to reconstruct. And so, in the later phase, a new meaning or set of meanings is constructed, which reintroduces an order to the world. This is called a delusion, and it aims to staple together signifier and signified once again. But what would set this whole sequence going in the first place?

Lacan's first answer to this in 1932 was that it involved a change in one's 'vital situation': loss of one's social place, retirement, a change of milieu, marriage, divorce, or the loss of one's parents. These moments are well known as potential triggers, whether in the form of a spectacular outbreak of hallucinations after a marriage ceremony or the quieter onset of mysticism and superstition after a retirement. But the key question, which Lacan would address in his later work on psychosis, was to determine what such situations had in common.

They would clearly not always trigger psychosis, yet, when they did, what was it in the individual's experience that made the world collapse for them?

All of these examples involved a change in one's symbolic situation: a new place had to be taken up, the kind of position that anthropologists associated with rites of passage. These were moments when the person had to 'face the world'. The fact that different cultures mark moments of transition with elaborate ceremonies and rituals suggested that a symbolic framework was necessary to process them. Externally represented in ritual, it involved an internal set of resources that Lacan linked to the symbolic order itself. But what would happen if the symbolic somehow failed here? If the symbolic order was not internalized, it would not be available to provide a network of meanings to process the moments of change. Rather than meaning, there would be an acute experience of a hole.

This, for Lacan, was the hole that opened up at the triggering of a psychosis. Since the symbolic was made up of signifiers that were all interconnected, if one privileged term was felt to be missing, its effects would spread throughout the network. This is exactly what we see in psychosis. First one element in reality starts to speak, then it all starts to speak: a neighbour's greeting is understood as, say, a moral condemnation, and then everyone in the street is gossiping. In a delusional process, first the spouse may be seen as plotting against one, then the in-laws, the siblings, the relatives, doctors, the media, magistrates, and so on. There's a domino effect.

In one case, after a sexual encounter with an associated fear of pregnancy, a woman began to think that people were watching her in the street. They were gesturing at her and soon saying things behind her back. She sensed that even her friends were more distant from her. A magazine featured a caricature of her, and newspapers and books also began to carry references to her, as if to single her out. Through the press the whole country had learned about her relations with the man, and society judged and ostracized her. She now knew that all these elements were part of a general plan to persecute her. The conspiracy gradually spread across Europe and then to America.

A general sign language was developed, known everywhere, to inform people about her. The persecutors became localized to a women's society, which had inquisitorial powers.

This expansion of the initial idea or experience, whether gradual or sudden, is why the early psychiatrists interested in phenomenology evoked a 'manifold of lived experience'. They were trying to understand how everything could be put in question from one single point. The obvious answer was because of a connectivity of our experience, a certain cohesiveness of reality. This, indeed, is how Gestalt theorists in the 1940s and early 1950s were explaining this collapse of reality. Each element of the psychotic subject's reality was interconnected, and careful study could reveal the principles of its order. Lacan's idea develops this in a different way: it was a cohesion at the level of the network of language, of our symbolic universe. This, it seemed, was exactly what was described by so many psychotic subjects: the whole world was changed, nothing was the same any more.

Renée describes how the initially 'unknown author' of her suffering was to become 'the System', a 'vast world-like entity encompassing all men. At the top were those who gave orders, who imposed punishment, who pronounced others guilty. But they were themselves guilty. Since every man was responsible for all other men, each of his acts had repercussions on other beings. A formidable interdependence bound all men under the scourge of culpability. Everyone was part of the System.' If it is tempting here to assume that perhaps one man in her past was guilty of something, it is also difficult not to see in the interconnected system the very features of the symbolic that we have discussed: each element is connected to the others, so a change in one will affect the whole set.

At the moment of triggering, the symbolic network had been broken, and the person senses that something is missing. But what could this something be? Lacan argued at first that it was the father, in the symbolic sense, the internalized representative of the law. This mediating, pacifying signifier would help the neurotic subject through the straits of the Oedipus complex but was absent in psychosis. Without this crucial building block, the whole edifice of one's life could collapse, but only if the *appeal* to it came at a particular time. Lacan was struck by the suddenness of the confrontation with the hole left by this missing piece. It wasn't simply its absence that triggered psychosis, but, very precisely, its convocation at a point where the person was embedded in an imaginary, dual relation, often with another person, but also sometimes with a group, a piece of work or an ideal.

This would be fractured by some event or intrusion where the person's equilibrium was challenged by the appearance of a third party. An imaginary relation would be catapulted into a new configuration, one that brutally introduced a third term, a figure who represented a symbolic authority or a situation in which the person had to take on a symbolic place. This would break the continuity of everyday existence and the heterogeneity of the symbolic register would suddenly be brought to light. A father here can be a real father, but also anything that suddenly goes into the place of a third term: a boss, an in-law, a tutor, a therapist. Since there is nothing in the symbolic to mediate this intrusion, no answer to the call to the symbolic agency of paternity, it is now that the world starts to come apart.

Many examples can illustrate this. Two lovers live in each other's arms, until the day they visit one set of parents. A student starts college, hanging out with his friends, until the first meeting with a senior tutor. A mother daydreams about her baby until a doctor hands her the child after the delivery. A researcher finally publishes the study they have been labouring on for decades. All of these situations can be triggers for psychosis and all involve the sudden appearance of a third term in the person's life. A discontinuity occurs, breaching the cocoon they may have established until then with their lover, their friends, their baby or their work. They are suddenly forced to appeal to a symbolic element that isn't there. Without it, the feeling of perplexity may start, and initiate the sequence we have sketched out above.

In a case discussed by Geneviève Morel, the patient Hélène had a sister seven years older than her, who became her model. When the latter left home to marry, Hélène followed her, unable to separate. The husband went to do his military service, and now the sister was courted by another man. Hélène colluded with this relationship, and her sister made her accompany them, worried about potential gossip. Hélène believed the man loved her rather than the sister due to the latter's marriage, and when her sister asked her to write love letters for her, she would describe her own feelings towards him. One evening, at the cinema, she saw their hands interlock tenderly. It was at this moment that her hallucinations began and she was hospitalized. The man had embodied the place of the third party in the imaginary couple she formed with her sister.

We see this also in those cases of psychosis that seem to be triggered by accidents. The massive shock of a car or rail accident that precedes the first manifest symptoms of psychosis is so clear that a connection often seems inevitable. Yet close listening and exploration may reveal that the triggering occurs not at the moment of the accident but when, later on, the person has to explain what happened to a policeman, lawyer or judge, or tries to obtain a compensation. It is the encounter with this figure, evoking the third term, coupled with having to assume a place from which to speak, that has the triggering effect. Normal life so often consists of just saying 'Yes' to those around us, and moments of having to take up a true position in relation to speech are the exception rather than the rule. Think of the difference between greeting an acquaintance and making a speech, or explaining oneself to a boss, policeman or judge.

This emphasis on a sudden triangulation links together situations that may seem externally to be both tragic and joyful, a fact which had puzzled earlier clinicians. Psychoses that trigger on a success or achievement have always been documented, and were sometimes explained in terms of a move towards an independence or maturity that the person was not ready for. The change of status involved in a graduation or a promotion creates a crisis of self-confidence, and the accumulating stress might produce confusional states or a psychotic 'reaction'. Lacan's theory is more rigorous, linking the triggering clearly to the encounter with an idea that has no symbolic place in the person's world. When the chain is broken, the element that has never been symbolized may then impose itself from the outside. In Lacan's formula, what's foreclosed from the symbolic returns in the real.

In one case, a woman was found in a ditch, crying that the 'earth wants all of me'. She felt that she was being swallowed up by the ground. The psychiatric team who worked with her couldn't help noticing that her first name was the word for earth in her mother tongue, although she made no connection between this and the content of her fears. Little by little, the sequence of the triggering became clear. She had become unwell after a sphincteroplasty, which effectively stemmed the copious faecal incontinence that she had suffered from for many years. Although she made no link between the operation and the triggering, the temporal association was undeniable, and this shed a light on what had happened for her.

Sodomized from an early age by her father, he would show displeasure and revulsion at only one moment in the sexual encounters: when the excrement on his penis was visible as he withdrew from her. The excrement thus marked the sign of both the end of the sexual act and of his loss of interest in her. At puberty, her incontinence started and it was now that the rapes ceased. From this moment on, she would almost continuously leak faeces, and would have to visit the toilet repeatedly throughout the day. Yet it was precisely when she accepted to have the operation on the anal sphincter, on the advice of well-meaning doctors, that her psychosis erupted. The symptom that had made her life so difficult turned out to have been exactly what allowed her to survive: the signifier 'shit' marked a limit to the invasive presence of the father. Once she was no longer incontinent, the father returned for her in the real of her hallucination. The earth that called her and engulfed her was her own proper name, and she pointed out that it had been this one name, out of her various others, that the father had chosen. It was this exact element, the one that indexed the father's possession of her, which became real in the triggering.

Another well-known example is the second moment of triggering for Schreber. He had finally succeeded in being appointed to the Court of Appeal in Dresden. But rather than working with counterparts, he was suddenly in a position of responsibility, presiding over a panel of five judges, almost all of whom were up to twenty years his senior. It was as if he had been catapulted out of a world in which he was among his imaginary equals to one in which he was in a new space, the bearer of a symbolic weight, and there was no signification available to him to make sense of this dramatic elevation. He began to experience sleep problems and to hear strange noises. At this point, everything began to collapse for him, and he would be preoccupied almost exclusively with thoughts of death.

Freud thought that Schreber's dilemma here was about repressed homosexuality, but Lacan emphasized the encounter with a situation he could not symbolize, the sudden emergence of the category of father. No mediating signifier was available to him, nothing to provide a sense to his situation. Lacking the signifier 'to-be a father', Schreber would now imagine himself as a woman, and in his delusion this would be transformed into the mission of being the begetter of a new race, which would restore the 'Order of the World' that had been so dreadfully fractured.

The situations into which the third term intrudes concern the ego and the other, like lovers living in a cocoon, or best friends who are inseparable, or those in which the distance between ideal and reality is suddenly collapsed. The person who dreams of a lottery win for decades and who finally hits the jackpot, the person who imagines he was adopted and one day discovers that this is true, the athlete who strives to break a record and then succeeds, the man who dreams about a date with his beloved and finally gets it. All these situations disrupt an equilibrium in which one has actually avoided occupying a new place in the socio-symbolic structure. If one is suddenly transported into that place, one has to face new symbolic coordinates and it is precisely this that can trigger the psychosis.

Not all such situations will invariably cause a psychosis in a person with a psychotic structure. It all depends on what the sensitive points are for them and how they have defended against them. In one case, a man triggered a psychosis on the birth of his second son, yet why didn't this happen with the first? In fact, he was an only child and had modelled every detail of his family life on that of his own parents. Becoming a father was resolved by simply becoming a double of his own father. He acted the same, behaved the same, and tried to recreate his own family situation in this strange mirror. When his wife became pregnant again unexpectedly, this broke the imaginary safety belt he had constructed: suddenly things were no longer the same and the enigma of paternity was there in front of him.

The unintegrated idea of paternity now returns not at a symbolic level but in the real, as it did for the parachutist we evoked at the start of this chapter. Ideas of being used sexually, of being loved by some authority figure or of being gay can be effects of this lack of integration: with no symbolic mapping of the father–child relation, different versions of paternity and of being an object for the father emerge. This is often misconstrued as indicating an underlying homosexuality, yet, as Bateson once pointed out in a difficult but marvellous sentence, 'The symbols [here, the ideas in the delusion] do not denote homosexuality, but do denote ideas for which homosexuality is an appropriate symbol.' The motifs of homosexuality thus give a form to the dangerous position of being an object.

In one case, a teenage boy developed the delusion that his father, grandfather and himself were a communicating system of glass tubes, which competed at draining the life fluid from each other during the night. In another, when a man's secretary announced that she was pregnant, he immediately went to examine his sperm under a microscope to ascertain whether he was the father or not. Paternity is reduced here to its biological parameters: after the encounter with what cannot be assimilated, it is reconstituted in delusional form. Hence the many images of paternity, whether biological or heraldic, that haunt the creations of psychosis.

—

The theory of triangulation and of the symbolic third term not only allow us to understand the sequence of a psychosis triggering but are also of great importance for the safety of the patient, as the following case illustrates. A psychotic man in his late twenties experienced endless feelings of persecution, and would invariably report episodes of rudeness or insensitivity that had occurred on the way to see his therapist. She cites as an example of his preoccupations a question about chewing gum. He had discarded his gum into an abandoned fridge and asked the therapist if he should have done this. Would the gum be found? Would he get into trouble? Should he have put it into a dustbin?

He would begin each session by reading from a list of what he called 'broods', compulsive ruminations about his experiences of persecution. The therapist believed that he was trying to drive her 'crazy', and felt 'penetrated' by his 'cold eyes'. The intensity of each session, she wrote, 'made me feel overpowered by his need to externalize his persecuting thoughts and feelings'. She felt exhausted, and interpreted this, like many therapists trained in the tradition of British psychoanalysis would have, as a re-enactment of his early relation with his mother. If she were feeling a certain way, according to this perspective, the patient's mother would have felt that too, a hypothesis that other schools of analysis would not accept.

The patient was on medication yet felt maltreated by the medical system. He hated hospitals, the stigma of 'mental illness', and the rudeness of medical staff. Instead, he sought understanding and acceptance, and believed that psychotherapy would offer the space for this. He repeatedly asked his therapist what she thought of 'mental illness': what did she think of his medication? Could she imagine him ever living without it? Not wishing to be drawn into what she considered an enactment of an internal conflict – presumably between good and bad, with the medical system embodying his apparently hated parents – she chose not to respond to his entreaties: 'I refused to answer, maintaining a position of neither being for nor against drugs.'

Now, when he had begun his psychotherapy, it had already been suggested by the hospital two years previously that a talking cure might be helpful, yet he had never received the promised assessment session. He was tired of waiting and started the work privately. Four months into the therapy, he received the appointment letter that he had waited for earlier. It was from this point, the therapist notes, that he began to deteriorate. He told her defiantly that he intended going to the appointment, but was then faced with the dilemma of whether he should continue with the private work. The therapist writes, 'I too was faced with what could be seen as an ethical dilemma: should I insist he tell the psychotherapist that he was already engaged with me? He had not said which hospital unit he was to attend for his assessment, so I had at this point no independent knowledge.' She decided to leave it to him to make his choice. After the assessment interview, he was turned down by the therapy unit, who told him he was unsuitable and that therapy would cause him to break down.

This was felt as a massive rejection both of himself and of the work of the therapy. How could his therapist work with him while someone else would not? His suspicion and paranoid thoughts escalated. 'I was left,' writes the therapist, 'feeling as hopeless and angry as my patient.' This sort of comment is characteristic of the British tradition in psychotherapy, where the therapist's feelings are assumed to be produced by the patient in an unconscious effort to communicate, to make them feel what they, the patient, are feeling. Other traditions, like the Lacanian one, would see this sort of comment as wildly inappropriate, based on the therapist's own failure to analyse the situation properly. How, after all, can anyone be sure that they are experiencing what another person experiences or even dare to claim to?

The patient felt more and more claustrophobic and was so agitated that he had to leave the consulting room to pace outside. A further rejection within the health service a few days later compounded his despair. Why, he asked, did his therapist keep talking with him, when he was being told that therapy would not be helpful? Indeed, the psychiatric advice he had received was that his partner should not even continue listening to his broods, as they were reinforcing his 'obsessions'. A few very difficult sessions took place, until he missed an appointment. He had killed himself by jumping in front of a train.

Now, it would be unfair to argue that if the therapist had worked within a different framework the death could have been avoided. Suicides happen, both within therapy and without. But the case can help us to see the importance of factors that might be neglected or misunderstood. The letter from the Health Authority clearly intruded into the couple formed by the patient and the therapist. We know how concerned he was with the medical 'system', which was in the place of the Other for him: a powerful agency that could pick him up or drop him. The receipt of the letter itself, even before attending the interview, had triggering effects, dramatically intensifying his paranoid thoughts. It was the intrusion of a third term into a couple.

The rejection at the assessment interview and at the second NHS meeting some days later would only have exacerbated this. We can guess from the preoccupation with the discarded chewing gum that the key question for him was his place for the Other: would the Other throw him away or care for him? The piece of chewing gum was himself. And it was perhaps the tenacity of this question that contributed to the therapist's response. Yet she could have told him emphatically that their work was going somewhere, that she had hope for him, and that he should not attend the NHS appointment. Perhaps her own anxieties about the NHS 'authority' stopped her from doing this, yet it would have arguably been the right clinical decision, affirming her care for the patient rather than abdicating from this in the name of the patient's free choice. In effect, her course of action may only have reinforced the terrible question for him: what am I for the Other? Can the Other drop me? And perhaps this is what he enacted by throwing himself in front of the train, like the thrown-away piece of gum.

As for the psychiatric advice, he does not seem to have been well served. The fact that he wrote down his 'broods' and named them demonstrates their importance, and it would seem clear that the practice of writing – even in the form of list-making – should have been encouraged. What sense was there in depriving the patient of something that came from the resources of their own psychosis and that formed part of a structuring process? Perhaps the psychiatrist imagined that the broods meant dwelling on his problems rather than moving on, but this in effect would constitute a denial of the patient's efforts at self-cure, and, crucially, a failure to recognize the importance of naming that we have discussed. When his partner stopped listening to the broods, a line of communication was closed down. In some cases, this can be the difference between life and death.

—

If moments of triggering involve an appeal to a missing signifier, there will be a corresponding hole at the level of meaning, of the signified. This can generate a range of triggering situations where it is less an encounter with some symbolic third party than with a problem of signification. The most common form this takes is an encounter in the field of love or sex. Here, it is the proximity of the desire of the Other that has the triggering effect: a sexual experience, a feeling of love or a sense of being the object of someone else's interest. At these moments, the symbolic fails to provide a mediation or a response, and the person will feel at the mercy of enigmatic forces. There is no signification there to offer support and no signifier to supply one.

Freud gives the example of a young doctor whose psychosis triggered at the moment that he succeeded for the first time in satisfying a woman. When she embraced him 'in gratitude and devotion', he suddenly experienced a mysterious pain that went round the top of his head like a sharp cut. Later on, he interpreted it as though an incision were being made at an autopsy for exposing his brain. The pain soon became linked to an explanatory delusional idea: his close friend, who had become an anatomist, must have sent the woman to him, as part of a series of persecutions the latter was organizing. The trigger here was the sexual encounter: with no way of mediating the desire of the Other, the psychosis erupted.

Novel sexual situations are often dangerous for the psychotic subject. Marcel Czermak reports the case of a young man who, at the moment of his first erection with a woman, looked down bewildered at his penis and suddenly heard the word 'Gay'. At the point of the missing phallic signification, the hallucinatory signifier emerged. If the phallic meaning established by the paternal metaphor, is absent, then each time the person is confronted with bodily phenomena that require a signification, there may be a perplexity or sense of strangeness. We should remember here that states of arousal or excitation are always at first anxiety-provoking, as we see when children have their first erections. If a signification is not transmitted and received properly, they remain problematic, and sometimes the person remains a virgin or avoids any kind of sexual encounter for this reason.

This is no doubt why psychosis so often emerges in adolescence and the teenage years. It is schizophrenia that is usually associated with onset during this period, and we can remember that one of the key features of schizophrenia is precisely the problem in conferring meaning on the body. Since the body changes during adolescence, there is a demand for meaning which opens up the hole of foreclosure. The pressures to date and engage in sexual activities only make this situation worse. When we add to this the fact that the teens are also the time when we have to take up symbolic positions in groups and in relation to the world, it becomes clearer why psychosis triggers so often at this point. The first masturbations, sexual encounters or feelings of being desired by someone else can all be catastrophic.

In a case discussed by Denise Sainte Fare Garnot, a young man went with a friend to a public library to read and listen to music. The friend, who went there just to pick up women, asked him, 'Are you on the prowl?' At that moment, he had the idea that he was immortal and that people were watching him and whispering about him. In a later session, he reported his friend's remark as: 'You have to be a man.' The sudden question of his symbolic place as a sexualized male was posed. Unable to reply, the paranoid thoughts responded for him. The whispers of people around him now asked: 'Is he a man or a woman?' and 'Where do you come from?'

The idea of immortality was part of a chain of delusional ideas, and he also believed that he was an extraterrestrial. In both of these formulations, the question of his symbolic place as a man is being transformed into another kind of identity, one that seems to sidestep the problem of being wholly in the place of a man or of a woman. Extraterrestrials, he would say, 'don't belong to this world', with the implication that this world is one made up of the logic of the male/female division. The friend's question had constituted a call to a signifier that could not be received. In its place came hallucinatory responses – 'Is he a man or a woman?' – and the voices and looks targeted him with this terrible question.

The ideas of immortality and of extraterrestrial identity were, in this sense, efforts to find a solution. If he was from another planet, he did not have to take up a position as man or woman. As for immortality, he linked it to femininity, yet had once heard a philosopher remark that the last man on earth is a man, but even so, 'I can't succeed in defining myself. Am I really the last of men? I don't know.' The idea of being immortal was not pleasant for him, and he was anxious to find some further elaboration. As we saw in Chapter 3, it is important to recognize that the idea of being unique – the last man, for example – is not necessarily a delusion of grandeur. It can simply be a way of trying to find a position of safety in which one occupies an exceptional place, falling into neither one camp nor another.

Being the last human alive is an idea we find with some frequency in psychosis, yet it can be a way of establishing quite different narratives. Sometimes it is linked to end of the world scenarios, and Freud explained this in terms of a withdrawal of love: after some emotional catastrophe, we draw our libido back into the ego, and in so doing become aware of a depletion in the external world. For Lacan, this would be an effect of our relation to language: as we approach the hole in the symbolic, we sense a collapse that extends right across the networks of representations that make up our reality. It is interesting to note, however, that end-of-the-world ideas often do not leave the world entirely empty: as well as the subject, there is some malevolence, some evil force that remains.

This is the subject of countless science-fiction films, in which the earth's population has been wiped out by war, plague or natural catastrophe. The hero or heroine wanders around looking for food and shelter, yet soon discovers that they are not really alone: some remnant of the catastrophe, in human, animal or monster form, is there to menace and attack them. It's as if the libido can never be entirely subtracted without leaving a residue, a remainder that is invariably persecutory. Countering this, there may be a fantasy of rebirth: for Schreber, a new race, or, for one of my patients, the idea that new beings would sprout from the ovaries that her decomposing body would leave behind.

—

The absence of the symbolic function of paternity is why delusions of rebirth, creation and filiation are so common in psychosis. Unable to situate the phenomenon of birth symbolically, and, more generally, to situate themselves at the point of origin of some process – whether biological or cultural – the person constructs a theory to go into the place of the hole that has opened up for them. They may believe that they have been born from only one parent, or, like Schreber, that they will give birth to a new race of beings, or that they are descended from royalty. The patient discussed in Chapter 1 who believed that common first names indicate both shared essence and ancestry had built the delusional thought at the exact point where the link between generations had to be explained. As we find so often in psychosis, the unintegrated idea of an origin is rebuilt and re-elaborated in the delusion.

Ends can be just as impossible to symbolize as beginnings, and delusions will often be constructed here around death and bereavement. In popular culture, we see this reflected in the beliefs about false burial: Hitler, Elvis or Michael Jackson are in fact still alive, perhaps living in a remote country, their remains being those of some other unfortunate. At the point where mortality cannot be symbolized, the delusion creates a new narrative. In one case, a woman who had tragically lost several of her children explained how, at her daughter's funeral, she must have been 'at the burial of a child who was not mine'. Her real daughter had been abducted earlier on and then replaced by a double, who was in turn replaced herself. She counted more than two thousand substitutions of the child over five years: 'Young girls came to me every day and every day they were taken away from me.' The loss of her child, unthinkable for her, became the point at which the delusional efflorescence of daughters was established.

We could remember here how all human groups develop stories and myths that attempt to give an account of the beginnings and endings of life, as well as the birth of natural and artificial objects: fire, water, air, forests, birds and beasts, towns, books, and any other part of social and cultural creation. Origins have to be treated with the symbolic, they must be made sense of and explained. In psychosis, the internalized symbolic structure that would allow this is unavailable, and hence the difficulty at moments when the person finds themself at the origin of something, whether it is through pregnancy and parenthood or scientific discovery or invention.

Scholars and scientists may become unwell precisely at the moment of discovery, when it is a question of assuming the 'paternity' or authorship of their work. As Nathalie Charraud points out, the psychosis of the mathematician Georg Cantor was triggered not when he first had the insight about infinite sets that would radically change his field, but when colleagues and students honoured him. It was at the moment that they formally recognized him as the creator or discoverer of transfinite numbers that a terrible psychotic depression immobilized him. The signification of paternity could not be integrated and so returned for him in delusional form: in his effort to re-find equilibrium, Cantor published two works in which he tried to prove that the plays of Shakespeare were in fact penned by Francis Bacon. A claim about authorship thus responded to the point at which his own authorship could not be articulated by him in the symbolic.

In another case, a woman's psychosis erupted at the moment she missed her period for the first time. She began to worry that she might be pregnant, and visited her doctor more and more frequently with the idea that 'there was something inside my stomach', a 'something' that soon became identified with 'a bug'. Her doctor had her hospitalized, and the context of her delusional idea would later be clarified. The patient's mother had miscarried a baby when she learned that her own father, a doctor, was terminally ill, and this tragedy had never been mentioned to him. As the patient put it, 'words never touched that pregnancy'. Not long after this, the mother had become pregnant again with the patient, and this time she did tell her dying father. The patient often imagined that the mother must have been thinking of her father during her sexual relations with her husband and during the pregnancy, and that he, as a consequence, must be her 'true father'. 'If I'd died,' she said, 'he might have stayed alive.'

As a child she had felt that her mother 'was mothering the wrong person. She should have been mothering the child before me.' And she was sure that a remnant of the dead foetus had stayed inside her mother and had then been transferred to her. The idea of being a child was, indeed, impossible for her: when she heard someone remark that analytic patients were like the analyst's children, this was unbearable. The absence of any symbolic framework to make sense of reproduction left her at the mercy of the traumatic elements of her history, and they would invade her mind and body when she triggered.

Indeed, her mother had completely blanked her daughter's biological being, never once mentioning periods or providing her with sanitary towels. Her own identity was equivalent to that of the miscarried baby: 'I feel like an aborted foetus,' she said. In the triggering of her psychosis many years later, she was desperate for a doctor to acknowledge that 'there was something inside', as if the mother's first pregnancy that had never been symbolized was now returning in the real for her. Where a doctor – her grandfather – had not known about the something inside her mother, now she tried to make a doctor recognize that there was 'something there'.

The triggering in this case came after the missed period, yet in many other examples it occurs after a maternity is realized. In a case discussed by Isabelle Robert, a woman experienced hallucinations of the word 'Mother' after giving birth. She interpreted the hallucination to mean that she had a 'maternal mission' to care for children, which she elaborated in a number of ways. This allowed a certain stability, until the next triggering of her psychosis came after the birth of her second child. Yet it was less the birth itself that had triggering effects than the fact that, later, she found that she could not watch over two children with the same degree of care as she had with only the one child. In other words, her 'maternal mission' was compromised. It was this short-circuiting of the solution she had elaborated in response to the earlier episode that rekindled the psychosis.

Solutions like the idea of the 'maternal mission' may be set into place quite swiftly after a triggering and have a protective value so that what appears to be a brief 'psychotic episode' passes without apparent sequelae. In a case reported by Brigitte Lemonnier, a man could avoid a triggering of his psychosis after the birth of his son via the idea of paternal love. He imagined himself as a link in a long chain, which began with a bad father, followed by himself, who was better than his father, then his son, who would be a better father than he was, and so on, until there would ultimately be a perfect father. This delusional idea allowed him to find a position as father and gave an order to his world. It was at the moment that his wife left him, taking the children with her, that this system was suddenly put in question: he was thrown back to the idea of being a 'bad father'. A few days later he attempted suicide.

What we learn from these cases is that triggering may occur not when the person encounters some figure of symbolic authority or third term, but when the solution they have created hits an obstacle. The mechanism of stabilization or compensation that they may have spent years or even decades constructing is suddenly challenged. We will look at these mechanisms in detail in the next chapter, but let's give a couple of further examples here. A man sought help when he began to have imposed images of being a woman used sexually by a man. These disturbing thoughts had started during a visit to his wife's parents, who he had not met before, just after the birth of his second child. Although it seemed tempting to interpret the triggering in terms of the introduction of a third term, it was in fact rather different.

He described his history in terms of being a victim: poorly treated by his parents, bullied at school, picked on by his boss at work. These experiences crystallized for him around the idea of being a 'loner', an identity that held him together both during his relationships and when he was single. On his own, he would lead a solitary life, and, at the times of relationships, would periodically disappear to watch films with idealized solitary protagonists. The position of being an object for the Other, evoked by the many stories of his victimhood, were treated, as it were, by the assumption of the image of a loner. This was the identification that allowed him to sustain himself through these experiences.

The triggering had occurred at precisely the moment this identification was put in question. It was less the alterity of the in-laws, less their symbolic distance that disturbed him, than his position in the family network. He already had a child from his first marriage, and he described in great detail how his wife then had always slightly rebuffed him after the birth. Her family, likewise, had never embraced him as one of their own, yet, now, with his second marriage and the new baby, he had suddenly become 'one of them'. Their warmth and inclusiveness bewildered him. He had expected to be excluded, as he had been with his first set of in-laws, yet, to his surprise, he was greeted as an equal, a part of the family. This meant that he could no longer see himself as the loner. It was at this point that the intrusive thoughts overwhelmed him.

In another case, a man's psychosis triggered after a quiet afternoon in his garden. He had been attending to the plants and fruit trees, and realized suddenly that the spray he had been using on an apple tree was marked 'Poison'. The next morning he awoke to the sound of knocking coming from inside his chest: a tiny man was trapped inside, banging on his ribcage to get out. He was guilty of suffocating this strange homunculus, and, in desperation, rushed to the nearest Accident and Emergency demanding that they operate to release his captive. Detailed questioning could find no trace of psychotic phenomena over the previous years. So why this punctual burgeoning of hallucination?

It was not an encounter with some symbolic third term that triggered the psychosis here but the failure of a formula which he had lived by. His father had died in a tragic accident when the patient was a small child, and there had been visual and some auditory hallucinations in the time following this. Later on, he would look after injured animals, and his subsequent training as a surgeon allowed him to perpetuate the project of what he called 'giving life'. These years seemed devoid of any crises or hallucinatory terror. After his retirement, he turned his attention to gardening, which he described in the same terms as his medical work: his job was to keep the plants and trees alive and healthy, and especially the apple tree.

This was in fact a tree that his father had also cultivated, and it was the one element in his garden that he associated with him. On the day that he used the wrong spray on the tree, his mission collapsed: if he had always kept things alive – animals, people, plants – he was now not in the place of the saviour but of the murderer. The formula that had protected him – to be 'the one who gives life' – was no longer tenable, and in its place a delusional guilt emerged. The knocking in his chest was the return of the dead man, and he was responsible.

—

The encounter with something that is impossible to symbolize, due to the failing of the symbolic, tends to push the psychotic subject in the direction of creation. Delusions, most obviously, involve a work of elaborating the foreclosed element into some kind of system or some new form. Hence the panorama of versions of paternity and reproduction we find there: Gods, emperors, Christs, royal and alien births, to name only a few. In contrast, the acts carried out at times by psychotic subjects, studied by Colette Soler, aim at swifter, more radical solutions: they strike what is perceived as bad libido in the body or in the Other. These can be dangerous both for the person and for those around them.

Perhaps not surprisingly, such acts can become appropriated as cures for psychosis, and history is full of examples. In the early twentieth century, there was a serious theory that the extraction of teeth could cure psychosis. Henry Cotton, superintendent at a New Jersey asylum, who had studied under Kraepelin, argued that psychosis was caused by bacterial infection, and that harmful bacteria could gather in infected molars and cuspids. From there, the bacteria would spread around the body. Removing the teeth of newly admitted patients produced recovery in 25 per cent of his cases, he claimed. As for the remaining 75 per cent, the bacteria must have migrated elsewhere, and so he removed their tonsils, colon, gall bladder, appendix, fallopian tubes and uterus. In the end, he claimed that nearly all his patients were cured by his knife.

Questions about the ethics of removing healthy body tissue and a review of medical records showed that these results were false and that there had been massive patient mortality, yet Cotton was allowed to continue extracting teeth. In these cases, where the symbolic function of negating the body's libido has failed to take place, it is sought in the real, through actual bodily subtraction. Although Cotton's ideas would of course be ridiculed today, more sophisticated versions of them still flourish, as if the idea of salvation were linked to the idea of extraction. And this is an idea that we often find in psychotic thought: by removing something, persecution is pacified. But rather than seeking this at a metaphorical level, it is played out quite literally.

The theory that we have sketched out supposes that we inhabit a world of meaning and that events and changes in our lives are mediated by symbolic processes. We must be able to symbolize the things that happen to us, the new roles we find ourselves occupying, the new positions we may be called to take on, the proximities to the Other that life will at times involve. If the appeal to the symbolic framework fails – for the reasons we have been exploring – then a psychosis can trigger. A hole opens up at the level of one's imaginary world. There is a profound sense of change. And then, in most cases, there is an effort to find some sort of solution, a compensation, through the construction of delusion or via any activity which promises to provide a foundation at the point that the symbolic fails. This could involve a research project, a new profession, an artistic activity or a search for origins or historical truth.

If triggering often involves an appeal to the symbolic function of paternity, we have also seen how it may occur in a variety of other situations. If the person's compensatory mechanism is challenged, or if an identification that has sustained them is weakened, the psychosis can erupt. Changes in Lacan's later work reflect this diversity. Although he began by referring to the paternal function – or Name-of-the-Father – he would later use the plural, evoking the Names of the Father, and questioning their link to paternity as such. What mattered was not exclusively the place of the father in the family, but rather any operation or set of operations that would tie together the real, the symbolic and the imaginary, and provide a compass in relation to the enigmatic desire of the Other. The father was just one of the many different forms this buttoning-down process could take, and would become less and less privileged. Once we recognize the wide range of constructions that human beings use to survive, we are in a better position to grasp the factors that matter in each psychotic triggering.

8. Stabilization and Creation

A woman whose psychosis triggered when she summoned up the spirit of her dead father in a seance was persecuted by an ever-present figure of the Devil, always at her side, ravenous for her mind, her thoughts and her body. This unbearable situation was tempered, over time, by a new configuration. Her attitude of despair was gradually replaced by one of acceptance, almost satisfaction. She now spoke about the Devil as if he were a naughty child, telling him off and chastizing him, and he would even ask for forgiveness. If the Devil first came into the hole opened up by foreclosure – described so perfectly by her as 'The one who has no name' – he was now transformed into a child, with her no doubt in the place of the mother. This transformation allowed a certain stabilization, and it was entirely her own invention, not something suggested to her by her attending psychiatrists. She had found a way of making tolerable the initial triggering of her psychosis.

Psychotic subjects often find ways not only to stabilize after a triggering and make their suffering more bearable, but also, perhaps with even greater frequency, to avoid the triggering of psychosis altogether. In both sets of cases, we have to ask the same question: what has stopped the person from going mad? We've seen that the most obvious way of defending against the primary phenomena of psychosis is the creation of a delusion: this can have the effect, if it is successful, of re-establishing meaning, pinning the signifier and the signified together again and limiting and framing the libido. But there are a variety of other responses, sometimes developed in conjunction with a delusion, sometimes independently. In this chapter, we will explore these forms of restitution, the ways in which psychotic subjects can find equilibrium and stability.

Let's start with a clinical example. A man in his late thirties sought help for anxiety and intrusive thoughts. He had recently left another therapy, which had not proven successful. Owing perhaps to the many triangles in his life, the previous therapist had the idea that he was repressing his homosexual interest in the ex-boyfriends of his partner. These interpretations only aggravated his symptoms, which included language disturbances – the idea that his thoughts did not belong to him – and imposed images of being made to perform fellatio on another man.

The triangles noted by the previous therapist did indeed exist. He would try to become friends with his various girlfriends' exes, copying them and adhering as closely as possible to their images. This allowed him to have relations with women, and the earlier moments of triggering had occurred at very precise moments. Firstly, when the current best friend had 'dropped out', breaking all links with him and thus leaving him alone with his girlfriend. And, secondly, when he had been introduced to the family of one of his girlfriends. In both instances, auditory hallucinations assailed him, as if, pushed into the symbolic place of a man and with no symbolic support to help him, the voices named him where the symbolic had failed to.

He was able to stabilize through an identification, though not one that depended on the triangular situations that had captured him until now. Although he had never met his maternal grandparents, he had been told that the grandfather had taken part in an important mountaineering expedition. At university, he had joined the mountaineering club, and had continued this pursuit over the years. Even when he was with a team of other mountaineers, he still felt that he was 'alone, battling with the elements'. This hobby gave him, in fact, the only form of 'manhood' that did not involve the perils of encountering the opposite sex, prescribed as a kind of command by his father and which risked opening up the hole of foreclosure for him. I encouraged his elaboration of the romantic ideal of the mountaineer, and he began to develop activities around it: he would read the literature, watch films about it, and so on.

Being in the situation of a man for a woman was impossible for him, and at such moments the hallucinations would start. The identification with the ideal image of the solitary mountaineer, on the contrary, could sustain him, and was less dependent on his counterparts than his copying of the girlfriends' exes. The form of restitution here, first studied by Ludwig Binswanger, involves the construction of an ideal: a particular image gives the person a compass point, an orientation around which to build their life. This construction of an ideal may borrow from descriptions of a relative or family tradition with positive associations, but most often it is taken from the world of the mother. It might involve an activity she had been interested in, a person she idealized or a career she had to give up, and it can help to give the person an ideal point around which to organize themself. Sometimes, after a baby is born, psychotic men 'become' like mothers, as a way of avoiding being in the place of the father, which would risk triggering the psychosis. It is perhaps no accident that in 1903, after his discharge from hospital, Schreber and his wife adopted a ten-year-old girl who later told the psychoanalyst William Niederland that Schreber was 'more of a mother to me than my mother'.

Louis Wolfson's fascination with languages is another example of this process. He became what he called 'a schizophrenic student of languages', learning French, German and Russian in order to escape from the English language that so terrified him. We will discuss Wolfson's work with languages a bit later in this chapter but it is his position as 'student' that interests us here. It allowed him to situate himself in relation to the world around him: sitting in his room at home, in his trips to the library and on his nocturnal walks, where he would 'study' the hookers, pimps, drug addicts and cops of Broadway, forming his identity around this idea of learning. Meeting others, he would describe himself as a student, and this mediated the potentially dangerous field of human contact. Looking at a man sitting opposite him on the subway one day, he imagines an aggressive encounter, before deciding that reading a foreign-language book would be a better option than staring. Always studying, Wolfson could convert the passive and menacing situation of being the prey to those around him into an active, stabilizing position.

This construction of an ideal can help to give the person a place as a subject rather than merely an object: persecuted, insulted, followed, maligned. It is interesting to contrast this with another common form of stabilization, the adherence to the image of another person. With no ideal to support them, the person just copies some-one else, as the patient described above had done with his girlfriends' exes. Although this may allow them to get through life, it maintains them in the place of an object rather than a subject, as they are liter-ally dependent on other people. The image of the other must be there for them to stick to. With my patient, this form of superficial identification was less robust than the idealized identification with the grandfather.

Helene Deutsch described this type of identification in her studies of 'as-if' characters, who only enter social relations through a kind of external imitation. They glue themselves to someone else's image, carefully using it to organize their behaviour and generally avoiding those situations that would constitute an appeal to the symbolic dimension. They can show friendship, love and sympathy, but there is something wrong, as their expressions of feeling are 'in form only', like 'the performance of a technically trained actor who lacks truth to life'. As one woman who had become a prostitute in her teens explained, by copying the other girls she could survive without any real contact with the outside world. She knew at some level that such contact would be impossible for her.

There is nothing here to suggest any disorder, Deutsch comments. Behaviour is not unusual, intellectual abilities are unimpaired, emo-tional expressions are well ordered and appropriate. But something does not quite ring true. Those who become close to the as-if charac-ter will invariably end up asking 'What is wrong?' precisely because everything seems so right. Kurt Eissler pointed out that since as-if characters rely on imitative techniques, their span of adjustment might be much broader than that of their counterparts, who will shy away from certain activities, tasks or roles in accordance with their unconscious preferences. Since the as-if person's preferences are located strictly at surface level, they may do what the surface expects of them, thus fitting in well with society and attracting little atten-tion. In the words of one woman, 'Sometimes I feel like I was a mixture of many shadows, sort of *not one person*, but a lot of people's thoughts of me, like self-reflections of these things . . . And each one sees me in a different light and actually I appeared this way.'

Where some as-if subjects can function well in a wide range of situations, others prefer a narrow environment, made up of simple, monotonous situations that brook little change. They can have plenty of friends, yet somehow authentic proximity is never possible. There is a strange absence of passion, as if life is simply some sort of procedure that must be run through, even if this means smiling, laughing and crying at the appropriate moments. Speech will likewise display a shallow quality, as if they are not really involved in what they are saying. As-if identifications provide a kind of borrowed strength, and often allow the person to excel in the work or social environment. Their fragility lies in the fact that if the person who is being copied moves away or distances himself, the removal of this key reference point may leave the subject with no armature.

In another case, a young man had finished his first written assignment at university and was on the point of knocking on the tutor's door to discuss his work when he froze, invaded by what he called 'an indescribable feeling' of anxiety. He was found by college staff some time later, sitting next to the door talking to himself, yet with no recollection later on of what he could have been saying. His subsequent hospitalization was not pleasant, and he complained of insensitive treatment by nurses and doctors and a heavy load of medication that left him overweight, slow and ill smelling.

When I met him many years later, he was still medicated, yet living at home with his parents, not able to do very much, but increasingly interested in the psychology books that his sister would supply him with. Growing up, no one had noticed the slightest anomaly or any sign of the troubles to come. He had done well at school, mixed with other children and then got into university. So what was it that had allowed him to function so smoothly until that afternoon? As he described his childhood and teens, so banal and uneventful, it became clear that what had sustained him was a continuing set of identifications with his peers. He had just done what they did, fixing usually on one or two classmates and copying their clothes, their mannerisms, their approach to work, and adopting their aspirations.

This mimicry had allowed him to keep up his studies, to go on a handful of dates, and to play sports at school with none of the turbulence one might have expected at these significant moments of 'being a man'. He was just a boy – and then a teenager – like any other, and it was through this process of imaginary reflection that he was able to navigate the dangerous moments of transition that punctuate the lives of young people. In his holidays, when the other boys would be less available, he would imagine what they were doing and try to do the same.

This series of images supported him, until the moment when the encounter with the tutor confronted him with a third term. With no resources to respond, the psychosis triggered. He must have already been made more fragile by the move away from home and school to university, where he knew no one and had no immediate identificatory supports. In another case, a man described how he had followed his close friend in everything, copying his every gesture, until the latter closed the door to his room one day to prepare for an exam. He then became certain that it was himself who had been taken away, that he was being watched and followed, and that people wanted to kill him. Deprived of the guiding image, his place as an object was accentuated and he had no defence against the attacks directed against him.

The vacuum of emotional engagement in such cases should be distinguished from the common neurotic doubts about one's identity. Neurotic people often feel as if they are fakes, playing the social game while inwardly despising it, and have a sense of illegitimacy, as if they lacked a place in the world. This sense of having a double life creates conflict, yet in as-if cases there is never a struggle between the 'real me' and the social self, as one might expect. It is an identification without conflict. Sometimes, their stiffness and superficiality in social relations may be noticed by other people, and it can give the picture of the commitment phobe. In fact, the person just knows at some level to stay away from situations that would involve an appeal to the symbolic, those, precisely, where a commitment is involved.

Such cases show us how the imaginary – the register of our capture in visual images – can provide support mechanisms in psychosis. In a case of childhood psychosis, a boy who was unable to construct a boundary to his body treated himself through his addiction to TV and films. He would mirror all the actors, taking on an identity and contour through a process of external imitation. In the case of Stanley, described by Margaret Mahler and Paula Elkisch, this boy who seemed unable to express emotions began to do so in a totally polarized way: he would switch himself from panic to ecstasy as if by flicking a switch. 'The emotions which Stanley seemed to turn "on" and "off", like one of the switches, were created by him in a most peculiar and rather "unemotional" way.' Knowing that certain emotional expressions were expected of him by his environment and that he had to comply, he would just turn them on or off.

This process, in which a psychotic subject 'learns' emotions, has often been described as if their feelings could be turned on or off according to the needs of the situation. Eissler described a case in which the patient's 'feeling of deadness set up a *tabula rasa*, so to speak, upon which the ego artificially could put the socially required emotion, like a painter puts the correct pigment on the canvas'. The creation of these surface emotions chimes with the social imperatives of our culture today, which see emotion less as the authentic sign of our inner life than as a set of behaviours to be learned. If we are trained properly, we will learn emotional skills and so be able to show the 'appropriate' emotion. What was seen by the analysts and psychiatrists of the 1950s as a sign of psychosis has now become a norm of healthy subjectivity.

The next form of stabilization that we find in psychosis is linked to the creation of ideals and involves the establishment of formulae to live by. Geneviève Morel has developed this idea, whereby the person builds a template based on how two parties relate to each other. They may occupy one or the other of the two places yet if the formula breaks down, the psychosis risks erupting and the person may experience the most brutal and terrifying feeling of being dropped and rejected. The most common kinds of formula involve a relation between mother and child, father and son, and lover and beloved. Whatever form they take, they always involve some kind of commitment.

A crucial period in the work with a psychotic patient took place when she was able to use a formula 'A mother cares for her son' to organize and regulate her experience. In her own childhood, her brother had been idealized and adored by the mother, and his image became both a point of fascination and of persecution for her. All the family's attention was on him, while she, on the contrary, was 'dropped' and uncared for. The patient was unable to accept being in the place of a loved person in her later life, as this reintroduced the pain of her exclusion from the mother–son relationship. 'To be loved' was profoundly false to her, just as the mother's massive idealization of her brother had been. The few boyfriends she had were chosen because they would pay little attention to her, and when this turned to manifestations of love on their part she would leave them.

Her hallucinations and other psychotic phenomena would fade at a very precise moment. I had been unwell and, unusually, had to stop work for a few days. She was very concerned and had images of nursing me back to health. From then on, her role in the therapy was a maternal one: she saw me, she said, as her 'little baby', to whom she would provide care and nourishment. The tone of the sessions would now change considerably, moving from fierce attack to tender solicitation. Her formula was both a way of situating herself in relation to her mother's love and a modification of it: a tenderness not directed to a perfection, which would have been unbearable, but to a weakness.

Later, she could move to the other pole of the formula. Rather than seeing herself as the mother, she could call herself 'my baby', and it was now I who was situated in the maternal role. Again, this time the maternal place was not persecutory but benign. If we write the formula like a mathematical function Fxy, as suggested by Morel, F would designate the nature of the relation – in this case, 'to care for' – x the place of the mother, and y the place of the baby. As long as she could situate herself in one of the two positions in relation to someone else, the psychosis was stable.

Another case discussed by Esthela Solano-Suarez illustrates the logic of the functional formula. A fifty-year-old man sought help for what he called 'depression'. For a few months he'd lost all interest in life, as well as his appetite and capacity for sleep. His body seemed strange to him. He couldn't make sense of what he was going through, and in fact he had recently had a promotion in his professional life.

Having worked for some time at a prestigious jeweller's, he was now promoted to the post of manager. Yet this sought-after position had become a nightmare for him: he felt unable to deal with it, over-whelmed with the feeling of a void that separated him from his body. Suicide seemed the only way out.

In the analytic sessions he spoke of his mother's death when he was five. He had no conscious pain at this loss and no memory of her or of himself in those early years. His memories only began at the moment that he was informed of her death by his father. The latter then sent him to an orphanage, of which he had few memories, all of which were equally void of affect: he spoke of those years as if he were some-one else. He could not understand how his father could have abandoned him and why no one else in the family stepped in to care for him.

Four years later his elder sister took him out of the orphanage to live with her. Twenty years older, she had just lost her only child, and now devoted all her attention and care to her younger brother. She would indulge his every wish, spending lavishly on him the money she earned as a prostitute. He had happy memories of this time and refound a taste for life. Later, he would become a prostitute himself, selling his body for a very high price to wealthy private cli-ents. Soon, one of them offered him a job at an exclusive jeweller's, and the patient became the most successful of the sales staff.

Money was very important for him, and was his sole satisfaction in his work as a prostitute. In his own sexual life, he would only have sex if he paid for it as well. Money was exchanged for enjoyment. Solano argues that he identified with his sister as a prostitute – The Woman for All the men – with the exchange of money playing a cru-cial role. She notes that he mentioned that he chose her as his analyst since she was Argentinian, a word containing 'argent', 'money' in the patient's mother tongue. Now the problems he experienced would take on a new sense. On one level, the new post put him in a paternal position, with no corresponding signifier available to support him. On another, the new post prevented him from the daily work of exchange with clients in the shop: the financial transactions were no longer part of his occupation. His compensatory mechanism was thus compromised.

Solano encouraged him to adapt his new post: he could be the manager but at the same time make sure that he kept up contact with clients on the shop floor. As he did so his sense of being alive returned to him, and, indeed, his shop recorded its highest-ever sales figures that year. The formula thus involved his relation with others, with F indexing the mechanism of exchange of goods for money, and x and y the vendor and the client. It is interesting to compare this two-place relation with the use of the signifier 'shit' in the case we discussed in the previous chapter. There, the patient had to be incontinent to protect herself from the invasive threat of her father. 'Shit' was the predicate that had to be attached to the subject, yet did not connect her to any kind of circuit with other people. When the predicate was removed, the psychosis triggered. If functional formulae have the form Fxy, cases like that of the woman who needed to leak faeces have the form Fx, where F stands for the action and x the subject. Notice also that the examples of functional formulae involve a certain commitment to some form of social relation, whereas those of the form Fx do not.

—

Another common mechanism, frequently documented by analysts and psychiatrists, is the creation of a prosthetic symbolic order, as if to plug oneself in to the symbolic system that one had never incorporated. Unable to access the system internally, it is sought directly on the outside. The literature is filled with cases of those who develop attachments to machines or mechanical devices, who believe they are being influenced by machines, or who seem unable to distinguish between animate and inanimate objects. In many cases, the machine remains at the level of a simple binary structure, taking the form, for example, of a switch going on or off. Stanley would spend hours drawing switches which he would pretend to turn on or off. He would later become obsessed with turning lights on and off, doing little else for weeks.

The fascinating feature of these cases is that the authors almost always interpret these relations as being based on a human model: the machines that captivate and terrify the child are understood as concretizations of inner impulses, traced to relations with the parents and caregivers. The machine is seen as a symbol of someone that had been important for the child. Margaret Mahler, for example, thought that the machines which figured in the cases of schizophrenic children allowed them to convert a human relationship into a mechanical one and hence to master the threatening factor of unpredictability and difference.

In a groundbreaking but now sadly forgotten book, Harold Searles questioned the basic logic of this approach. Rather than linking the machines and mechanical objects to real people, Searles suggested, why not see them as significant precisely as non-human objects: children, he argued, need a measure of stability in their non-human environment, and it is only through this that they can begin to construct the idea of parents as living entities. Although we would not agree with the last part of Searles's argument, he saw something absolutely essential: that children seek out in their environment something that matters for the very reason that it isn't human, objects or figures that incarnate the dimension of the symbolic as such, a symbolic order that transcends human relations.

For the neurotic, these elements may be used to reinforce the function of the father, as we saw with Little Hans and Pagnol. But in psychosis, there may be an even more archaic appeal to the minimal structure of the symbolic itself, in the form of binary oppositions. The machines that Searles studied embodied an elementary plus and minus, and it was to this that many of these children would glue themselves. With no internal registration of the basic binary structure, the child would attempt to access it externally or embody it themselves, as in those cases in which a single action is turned on and off repetitively.

We see this today in the common motif of incorporating non-human elements into the body. The Six Million Dollar Man or Robocop or the hero of the science-fantasy *Innerspace* all become men through the introduction of alien, symbolic circuitry into the actual fabric of their bodies. Children's literature, likewise, is filled with stories in which some magical object confers special skills or powers on its discoverer. In all of these fictions, the additional non-human element allows the person to become who they are, as if their very identity resulted from it. Accessing this symbolic dimension introduces a stability and equilibrium into human relationships. These narratives stage the basic idea that we need to incorporate the symbolic order into our bodies, a circuitry of representations and laws: and so the non-human environment, as Searles saw, has psychological significance in its own right.

These systems could take the form of machines and mechanical devices, or of mathematical or genealogical systems, or computer work, for example. They could also involve archive research or any kind of interpretation of documents, often to study or prove some form of filiation. That's why there are so many psychotic people in libraries. Louis Sass describes a patient who formulated a strategy for his imitative behaviour. Although his copying might have evoked the as-if characters we discussed earlier, he actually aimed to understand how people interacted socially by studying their conduct like an anthropologist. He hoped to encode the steps involved in making friends and so devise new 'schemata' for relationships on his hospital ward. He explained how this would allow him to be a more efficient 'communications machine'.

The most famous of such cases is no doubt Joey. When he first arrived at Bettelheim's school, he seemed to function by remote control, a 'mechanical man' who was run by machines and currents around him. He would try to insert his fingers into plug sockets, and then, when this was made impossible, would lay down imaginary wires to connect himself to electrical outlets. This would be especially important at mealtimes, as he felt that his digestive apparatus could only function due to the current. Where Bettelheim interpreted these wires as both embodying and linking him to a source of emotions, we could see them as attempts to access the non-human environment: the minimal form of the symbolic that he needed to survive.

There are many possible ways of accessing a prosthetic symbolic, and we could situate a spectrum, at one end of which lie those activities that are embedded in a culture and which aim at social reform, the creation of a new world, and at the other those that aim simply at plugging the body into the most minimal form of binary structure.

Many people diagnosed with Asperger's syndrome are in fact psychotics who have managed to find a solution along these lines, limiting their interests to a single, usually symbolic, activity, as if to condense the real – their experience of bodily excitation – and the symbolic into one point.

Schreber's idea of a new Order of the World is one example of the creation of a pseudo-symbolic network that had the result of establishing a law-like system and of limiting libido: the elaboration of his system occurs simultaneously with a reduction in his bodily suffering. This Order was initially self-sustaining, and God simply left it alone, not interfering in the fate of individual beings. The system thus had a stability which was not affected by the arbitrary will of any agency, human or divine. Divine caprice was kept in check, as if a system 'more powerful than God' regulated distance between the subject and the latter's potentially malevolent and powerful will.

Such systems are often built up around some ideal point – for Schreber, to be the begetter of the new race – which can be traced back to the mother. Attempts to create order around this point may involve ideas of saving the world or improving it. The aim, as Colette Soler points out, is to tie the libido to a principle of order. This is often situated in the future, and so allows the person to exist in the present. We could remember that even for Schreber, the race he was destined to beget would only happen later on, echoing the wish he and his wife had for 'children in the future'. It is very dangerous for a psychotic subject when they lose the idea of a future, often prompted by a well-meaning therapist trying to make them be more 'realistic' or happier in the here and now.

In an elegant series of studies, Soler has shown how Jean-Jacques Rousseau created his own compensatory symbolic. Rousseau tried to modify what he saw as the disorder of the world, denouncing the corrupt morals of his time – in true paranoiac style – and then proposing social solutions to purify it. For Rousseau's father, his son was the cause of the mother's death. The question of this imputed responsibility may have contributed to Rousseau's position of protestation: the foreclosed guilt came back from the outside, in the real, to create the delusion that everyone was plotting against him. In his writings, he situates this 'bad' libido in the Other and then tries to offer an ideal order as a remedy. Where the order determined by the symbolic has been foreclosed, the paranoiac creates a new one.

Although this may at times appear delusional, it is perfectly compatible with genuine social change. Rousseau's impact on Western civilization is undeniable, and we could also evoke here James Tilly Matthews, whose 'Air Loom' we discussed earlier. Matthews was able to convince the French government in the early 1790s that he could broker peace with England, and his diplomatic efforts were initially taken absolutely seriously. In Bedlam, he was an able negotiator and advocate, settling disputes between staff and patients, and persuading a House of Commons inquiry that they should investigate hospital conditions. He recognized that there was a fault in the world and proposed solutions to it, first at the level of international diplomacy, and then in the local context of the management of the hospital where he was confined.

If in some cases a new order is created, in others an existing one is appealed to. This can take the form of the law itself, but understood in a literal sense. Hence the litigious, querulous psychoses well known to nineteenth- and early-twentieth-century psychiatry. The person takes out court cases, makes threats of litigation, complains to public authorities. Their position is always that of innocent victim of some tort or injustice, and the law is appealed to in order to restore justice and correct a fault in the world. Legal failure often results only in further litigation and appeals, so convinced is the subject not only of an injustice but also of the law's ability to correct it. The psychotic subject has made themselves the instrument here of an idea of justice or some other abstract cause.

The law here is not an internalized agency but an external structure that the person appeals to. Whereas in neurosis the law is in many senses metaphorical, operating as a principle of limitation and never reducible to any simple statement, in psychosis it can be identified with specific words or injunctions. The psychoanalyst Guy Trobas gives a number of examples: 'Incest,' said one of his analysands, 'is forbidden by the law, I didn't know this when I was young.' 'Incest,' said another, 'is forbidden by the police . . . one can go to prison for it.' The incest prohibition is here equated with a legal prohibition rather than a more structural, abstract force. We see the same literalization of the law in another of Trobas's examples: 'I don't have the right to seduce you because you're married.' The law here dictates its own logic, in contrast to the moral confusion of the neurotic, who might well have an affair and then suffer from the unconscious effects of the prohibition.

Gérard Pommier observes that there are at least two paths here in psychosis: to create a name via an activity or work, or to efface one through an ideal that requires one's sacrifice, often for the greater good of mankind. The motif of sacrifice can be a way of introducing a lack, a negation of libido, but it can also function in other ways. Psychiatrists and analysts have often observed that in some cases one has the impression that the patient's suffering allows someone else to exist, like the two poles of an equation. This may be reflected in the belief that if they are to live, someone else will die, or it can take more subtle forms. We could remember the case we discussed in the previous chapter, in which the patient thought that she should have died to allow her grandfather to live. In other cases of schizophrenia, it is as if their own madness and torment externalizes what is not acknowledged by the parent: they have to be mad to allow the parent to survive. The patient here is in the place of an object for the Other, completing them, perhaps through condensing the parent's own libido. Louis Wolfson noted an equivalence between his psychosis and his mother's absence of an eye, as if his madness was what permitted her not to be aware of her own affliction. This equation was echoed in what he called his 'cardiac neurosis': since he was his mother's only child, and if, according to her, he was her 'raison d'être', if he were to disappear, then so would she.

This balancing act sheds light on another detail of Wolfson's account, which we find in many cases of psychosis: a sense of oral greed. Wolfson felt acutely ashamed when he would eat ravenously, and this would lead to suicidal thoughts. The idea of one's own greed is often unbearable to psychotic subjects, as if it is literally an act of murder. But why would satisfying an oral appetite be so problematic? Why is it this that generates guilt rather than moments, for example, when another person is attacked or insulted? The answer, perhaps, is that these are one and the same thing. As a young schizophrenic woman put it, describing her relation with her therapist, 'I watched carefully while you nursed me to see if you got thinner. I had to be sure that I wasn't taking too much.' With no symbolic third term, the world is reduced to the self and the other: what one has is what the other lacks, and vice versa.

Wolfson's account of his psychosis illustrates not only this motif of sacrifice, but also the importance of writing and the name. Writing is often a way of accessing a prosthetic symbolic and it is extraordinary to see just how many people want to write books. Literary agents and publishers are swamped with manuscripts, and newspapers and magazines regularly carry advertisements for writing courses. The fact that these ads appear on front pages indicates the extent of the market, and one would suspect that almost every adult in the country has some aspiration here. Writing is incredibly important for the psychotic subject as it has a pacifying function. If the symbolic chain is damaged in psychosis, writing offers a way of repair, of knotting, of binding words and the libido together.

Sometimes writing aims at the creation of a purely formal system. Louis Wolfson searched for a knowledge about languages, describing himself, as we've seen, as 'the schizophrenic student of languages'. He lived alone in a room, desperately trying to avoid the voice of his mother, a near-impossible task as he had identified the whole English language with her. It was unbearable for him to either listen to English or to speak it. He felt that he had to remove the English that was inside him, as it invaded his body through every aperture: his ears, his eyes, his mouth and his anus were all conduits for the horrifying attacks. Closing these bodily openings with earplugs or fingers was not enough to block it out, as it had already penetrated inside him. Even listening to foreign-language broadcasts with headphones was not an adequate defence. Written words in English would have the same persecutory effect, and he was invaded regardless of whether his mother was physically present or absent.

To protect himself, he developed a new language, what he called a 'linguistic weapon', a system to transform English words 'almost instantaneously' into a hybrid of German, Hebrew, French and Russian. Translating into a single language would not have been effective, he explained, as this would allow the individual English words to survive. His task, on the contrary, was to 'annihilate' them, rendering them incapable of assaulting him in the future. He could thus decontaminate his mother's voice by breaking it down into words or syllables, translating these with his own system of linguistic rules using the different languages and thereby generating new words and sentences. A linguistic system was being used to generate a negativity exactly where the symbolic had failed to do this for him. At the same time, this system performed an operation on the interpellative aspect of language we discussed earlier: he was able to keep this in check via artificial means. Wolfson published his accounts of his experience in French, never in English, and, after living in New York, moved to Canada after his mother's death and then to Puerto Rico where he apparently won the national lottery in 2003 and became a millionaire.

The psychotic subject finds stabilization here through a transformation of language, and we often find the creation of such systems in schizophrenia. Lacan was especially interested in Joyce in this context, and argued that the writer found a solution to foreclosure through his work, making a name for himself where his father had failed to transmit one. Sadly, most Lacanian commentaries on Joyce just repeat banalities and evoke the same tired examples. Geneviève Morel's study is one of the exceptions, and she examines carefully Joyce's experience of language. She shows how Joyce suffered from imposed speech, with little barrier against the intrusive dimension of words. He would repeat conversations between his father and uncle without knowing what the words meant, and in 1931 he would hear his father's voice after the latter's death. His 'epiphanies' also revolve around fragments of speech, as if extracts from conversations he heard had an enigmatic quality that he had to write down. Rather than fleeing this dimension of language, however, Joyce's strategy was to accentuate it: he made himself a receiver for all the speech he could hear around him, writing not in isolation but often in the kitchen surrounded by women chattering. He opened himself up to the intrusion of speech, creating his books from what would impose itself on him.

Although these works gave him a name, as Lacan pointed out, they perhaps also had another function. Joyce famously remarked that his books would keep his students busy for a few hundred years. We could see this as a form of promotion of his name, Joyce the Writer, but also it surely allowed an inflection of the addressee function that we have discussed. Rather than being targeted by speech himself, he could relay this, through his work, to the community of readers who would study him. In a sense, he had passed on the enigma to them, yet not in its original form. He had performed a work not just on language but on the addressee function within it.

If a work like *Finnegans Wake* can baffle and fascinate readers, so we often find that schizophrenic creations of language produce a similar effect. The effort here is to build a metalanguage, a language within a language, which may take the form of a language about another language. There is a powerful logic in such projects, since if what the person suffers from is the omnipresence of language, its intrusive, unmediated presence, what better strategy than to build a defence from the very material that is attacking them. At times, such inventions change the world, as we see with computer languages and other mathematical and formal systems, as well as with certain inventions in the field of literature and poetry. Like Wolfson, for whom language was experienced as invasive and persecutory, an operation is performed *on* language, a way of talking about language and changing one's place in relation to it. In many of these cases, as Sass puts it, language is not inhabited but 'contemplated as a thing apart'. Clinically, it is important to recognize this fact and not to assume that a patient must use language for communication: on the contrary, it may be absolutely critical for them to turn language into some sort of object, system or tool, however odd and idiosyncratic this may seem.

These linguistic operations are often equivalent to the construction of sets. The person groups together elements of a natural language or some other manifold and introduces an order into it. A schizophrenic boy I worked with would spend months dividing up flowers into his own taxonomies, with special rules for the creation of each classification, ranging from colour to the sharing of the first letter of the flower's name. It was probably no accident that his mother's name was also that of a well-known plant, and we could see such efforts as attempts to generate sets where the paternal metaphor has not been available to carry out this task. This process, after all, creates a set out of the signifiers of the mother's desire, collecting them together via the introduction of the father and the phallic signification: rather than posing an enigma to the child, they are accorded a meaning. In the absence of this construction, many psychotic subjects treat the desire of the Other by inventing their own varieties of set formation. Grouping elements together not only supplies an order but also establishes limits and barriers that are crucial for the person's safety.

These transformations can transmit meaning – as a literary work does – but can also empty out meaning, reducing language to an algebraic system of signs, inaccessible to others. A schizophrenic patient proposed that instead of describing the psychotic phenomena that tormented her, she would number them and use a number system to report on her experiences. I accepted this, and, with some humour, she proceeded to create her new code: 15 was the experience of having colleagues invade her mind, 22 was the sensation of her body dissolving, 17 was paranoid ideas about being followed. This numbering had an effect of emptying out meaning, reducing the intensity of the phenomena through the formation of a new code, one that was built by her rather than imposed by anyone else. Over the years, we laughed a lot, and I wonder whether this in itself was not an example of what we could call, to borrow Jung's expression, a 'metamorphosis of the libido'.

The idea of an artificial creation of a symbolic system can also help us to explain the effects of some forms of therapy. Marguerite Sechehaye's work with Renée was once taken as an example of how a serious case of schizophrenia could stabilize through a long and attentive psychotherapeutic work. When Sechehaye first met her patient, she had already been seen by fifteen psychiatrists, who all predicted a bleak outcome of psychic disintegration. She suffered from what appeared to be a chronic hallucinatory psychosis, with auditory hallucinations, dissociation of ideas, catatonic states and autistic withdrawals. After some ten years of therapy, Renée could start to live and work independently, taking up the study of biology, receiving her diploma and an academic prize, publishing acclaimed papers and deriving some satisfaction from being alive. Sechehaye used a technique that she called 'symbolic realization', where she literally became Renée's source of nourishment, allowing her patient to eat apples from her breast, and using gesture and movement to dramatize the interactions she felt Renée was seeking.

Sechehaye's idea was that Renée had to live through a period where her oral demands would be met, unlike in her infancy, where, due to a series of catastrophes, she had been severely deprived. Too much water had been added to her milk, yet her tears and refusal of the bottle led only to a diagnosis of stomach 'weakness' with a proposed remedy of yet more dilution. It was the prescience of her grandmother that saved her from starvation: realizing what was happening, she corrected Renée's regime and provided the loving and nutritive care that the skeletal child was clearly lacking.

The grandmother's sudden departure when Renée was eleven months was a terrible shock to her, and she would scream and cry, hitting her head and searching desperately for her lost carer. Her father's sadism, the birth of new siblings and the collapse of the parental marriage compounded this wretched childhood, and by her teens she was already delusional, believing that a 'System' had been created to destroy the world and refusing food as a penance for a dreadful crime she had committed yet which she could not specify.

Over the course of her years of therapy with Sechehaye, the primary psychotic phenomena abated, and the changes were visible not only to the patient but also to relatives and carers around her. There is no doubt that dramatic transformation took place, but what could explain it? Commentators on the case tend to ascribe the therapeutic success to Sechehaye's loving care of her patient: it was her sheer devotion, they argue, that allowed Renée to recover and find a renewed interest in life. But, as Sechehaye observed, this attitude of 'loving mother' was not present throughout their work: it was the additional presence, she claimed, of the symbolic satisfactions that gave the work its real power. Since Renée's traumas had occurred at a stage prior to her grasp of verbal language, she needed a non-verbal, concrete response. Unable to literally relive her infancy, she was asking for satisfaction in symbolic form.

Yet when we reread the case in the light of a different understanding of the term 'symbolic', we can see that what characterized nearly all of the interactions with her therapist was the presence of make-believe. As she offered Renée a piece of apple, she would say, 'It is time to drink the good milk from Mummy's apples, Mummy is going to give it to you,' upon which Renée would lean against her and press the apple to her breast before eating it. Sechehaye realized that this feeding had to be orchestrated, set to particular times of day and stylized quite precisely with her patient. What they invented together was less oral satisfaction than a kind of graft of make-believe. And it was now that Renée would experience 'the sensation of reality' for the first time.

The raw apples would become apples cooked in water, then baked in milk, then porridge with milk, soups, sandwiches, etc., but each innovation had to be prefaced by the ritual with the piece of raw apple from the breast, as if to confirm the symbolic status of the interaction, its artificiality. She never asked for more or less of the apple, as if to confirm its minimal symbolic value. In the code they created, the apples stood in for maternal breast milk, and Sechehaye expanded this repertoire of make-believe interactions. She would give Renée a letter 'from' a dead rabbit she'd been fond of, would pretend that dolls and inanimate figures were real beings, feeding them and caring for them, and so on. The whole treatment was conducted as a form of play – a deadly serious one – yet one which reintroduced Renée to the function of the symbolic.

It is, after all, only with a system of signs that we become able to pretend, making believe that one thing stands for another and recognizing the conventional nature of linguistic elements. What the treatment did was introduce Renée less to breast milk or the possibilities of oral satisfaction or maternal love than to those of symbolic functioning. Perhaps it was no accident that Sechehaye had attended Ferdinand de Saussure's groundbreaking lectures on linguistics, and her notes, together with those of her husband Albert, would form a part of the edition of de Saussure's work that so influenced linguistics and the human sciences in the twentieth century.

—

All of the examples of modes of stabilization we have discussed are compatible with the next form, which revolves around the logic of the exception. The person creates a space, usually for him or herself but occasionally for some other entity, of an exceptional being, one not included in a set. As one of Manfred Bleuler's patients put it: 'I am what the outside world has lost.' For Schreber, this was the special place of being God's chosen human. For one of my schizophrenic patients, it was the place of being a unique traffic warden, one whom people would not detest. For another, it was the place of being not a patient or a friend but a singular helper, incomparable with anyone else. Rather than seeing these examples as megalomania, the key is to recognize the necessity for the subject to make a place for themselves that can give them an existence. Christs and Napoleons were once common in mental asylums, and we still often find Christs today, yet they usually have no problem with menial tasks. As we saw earlier, a pope or emperor can be happy to do the laundry since they are usually much more preoccupied with establishing the miraculous nature of their mission than with realizing its effects.

What is the logic at play here? If there is a rejection of the special signifier of the father, so the psychotic may be drawn to create another one, following the principle that what is excluded from the symbolic returns in the real. To do this, the subject has to create a set or find one, in relation to which they will have a special, exceptional place. One of my patients described the way she could never be 'in' a set, at work or in her social life, but could only be 'of' a set, occupying an exterior position. 'It's not a feeling of exclusion,' she said, when a situation occurred where it looked as if someone had taken her place, 'since exclusion can only exist if inclusion is a possibility. Inclusion with humans is a categorical impossibility. I'm not in the realm of inclusion or exclusion.' A tempestuous and difficult transference relation would gradually become attenuated when she began to picture herself inhabiting 'a shed at the end of your garden'. This exceptional position, neither one of inclusion or exclusion, gave her a place that was safe both in a topographical and a logical sense, one that she could name: 'the mad woman in the garden'. That this was a logical rather than an empirical necessity was clear from the fact that she knew very well that I do not have a garden.

Augustin Ménard gives an example of this logic in his book on invention in psychosis. His patient was a thirty-five-year-old woman hospitalized for a severe weight loss that threatened her life. Her anorexia had begun only a few months before, after a suicide attempt, which had led to surgery and hospitalization. She was unable to talk about her history, her family or the events of her life, but little by little she introduced a hierarchy into the world of food: forbidden food, tolerated food and authorized food. She began to get better and speak more to her psychiatrist, revealing her fear that certain foods were poisoned. Yet she had not apparently interpreted why this would be the case. A few weeks later, her eating had become normal again and she told him that in order to eat without risk, there had to be just one food that was forbidden. This 'sacred' forbidden food was the orange.

Like the Name-of-the-Father, this was a symbolic organizing principle, a point of exception that could then organize her world, even though she couldn't say anything about it. The fact that she was able to start speaking and eating at the same time suggests that, until then, words and food were too real for her. With the introduction of the point of exception, they could then become possible. The orange was a signifier of exception, which contained within itself a negativity, perhaps the very negativity she had tried to embody with her suicidal act some months before.

We could compare this case with another in which a man persecuted by an omnipresent look began to forge a solution to his dreadful situation. Leaving his home was terrifying and barely possible due to the malevolent, persecutory gaze of everyone outside. During his therapy, a strange thing happened. He began to explore large department stores, noting the position and movement of the security cameras. He calculated the precise points where he would remain unseen by them and began to shoplift minor items from those places. Although this was a crime, it was nonetheless a positive moment for him: he was able to begin to subtract himself from the gaze of the Other, to create a space for separation, rather than being glued to the invasive signifiers of the Other, which were always watching him.

He had created a point of exception, less an organizing principle, as in the previous case, than a space carved out of the world of signifiers in which he could have a minimal space to be. Louis Wolfson describes a similar project. Feeling the invasive gaze of the security guards at the New York Public Library, not to mention the terrible pressure of the English language, he began to work out ways in which a book could be stolen. With great ingenuity, he devised a system that would allow him to exchange library cards to purloin any volume he chose. He thus created an empty space in the oppressive world around him, which permitted him, perhaps, to survive there.

It is interesting to note the proximity here between the logic of exception in madness and the logic of femininity: don't they both involve occupying a unique, exceptional place? Could this be one of the reasons why the psychotic subject – whether male or female – so often gravitates towards a feminine position?

We could contrast the view of the logic of exception with the idea that in early childhood there is a sense of discordance, of not fitting in, of somehow not having a place. This no doubt occurs at some moments for all children, and has any number of causes: they were not wanted, were felt as a burden or an intrusion, etc. It could be argued that the psychotic child makes the decision to interpret this sense of discordance rationally: they don't fit in because they are exceptional, because they have a mission, because they have royal parentage. The feeling of not having a place can be transformed in this way into a powerful sense of having a place, having a mission, and we could think here of some of the well-known cases of high-school killers. On the other hand, there are equally many cases where the psychotic subject starts life with having too much of a place, that of a replacement for a dead child or as a saviour or a persecutor of the parent. Perhaps it is the very weight of this meaning that is unbearable for these children.

—

The last two forms of stabilization we will discuss are often found together: they concern activities of limiting and naming, and the creation of a new, unique way of knotting the symbolic, the imaginary and the real together, what Lacan called the 'sinthome'. Psychotics often heal themselves, as we have seen, through libido-limiting work, and this can involve the invention of some new object that allows them to localize the libido outside the body, using the very point of what is most particular to them to find a solution. This is generally linked to an addressee, some person, group or community that the person is connected to through the invention.

The psychoanalytic idea here is a sophisticated version of the story of Dumbo the elephant. In the Disney film, this poor pachyderm is snubbed and maligned by humans and animals alike because of his huge ears. Yet the very marks of dejection become the instrument of success: when Dumbo realizes, with the help of his friend Timothy the mouse, that the ears can serve as wings to propel him through the air, he becomes the star of the circus. His lack becomes his virtue, enabling him to live with a new dignity. Although it is a fairy story, the logic of Disney's film illustrates Lacan's concept: the transformation of what afflicts one into a way of living, not by suppressing it but by exploiting it, by learning to use it.

We could see the same process in the case of Joyce, through the exploitation of exactly what assailed him: the voices that imposed themselves would become the very stuff of his literary identity. The superheroes who populate the world of children and teenagers gain their powers in a similar way. Reading through the profiles of the hundreds of heroes and villains in the *Marvel Encyclopedia*, we see how each one takes on their name through some devastating experience of loss, pain or horror: the death of a parent, a nuclear accident, being savaged by wild beasts, abandoned as a child, and so on. Rather than repressing this moment, it becomes directly inscribed in their name, as if they identify with the seal or stamp that is imposed on them instead of resisting or denying it. It is this stamp that then gives them a direction in life, even if it brings with it a certain isolation.

One of my patients had been told quite unequivocally by her parents that she had been an unwanted baby, and this mark of being undesired had been played out by her in many of her later relationships. Her parents had not minced their words: her birth, they said, 'had been a mistake'. Throughout her life she attached herself to situations where she was 'not wanted but just tolerated', and her psychosis triggered at the moment that her partner told her that he did not want the baby she was carrying. In the solution she constructed so many years later, she reinvented herself, changing her name so that it was spelled in the way that a certain foreign mispronunciation of her name would sound. She thus took what was quite literally a mistake – the erroneous pronunciation of her name – and turned this into her resource. Rather than suffer from being a mistake, she transformed this into the principle of her identity, one that she now used for a creative form of work.

In another case, we see a movement from as-if style, conformist identifications to the forging of a name. The girl we mentioned earlier who became a prostitute to avoid social interactions described how, later, her mimicry of others allowed her to 'invent someone new', and she gave herself a new name: 'Emily'. 'I only came into being with Emily. It was the name that allowed me to survive.' 'Because I didn't exist before. I was dead all those years before. But now with Emily I could make up a past and a present, it was entirely fabricated.' This helped to sustain her for several years, but proved more fragile when people became curious about her, prying into the details of her private life.

Sometimes the name is not the actual proper name of the person but a word that has the same function, buttoning down language and the body's libido. In one case, a long period of therapy resulted in the invention of a new word – 'Vemaebel' – which the patient was proud of and felt protected by. It could designate herself, the therapist or some situation she found herself in. In itself it had no conventional meaning, yet it was incredibly important to her. When things were difficult, she would either text me the word or write it down on a piece of paper. Several months after the minting of this word, she invented another one – 'Michmuch' – and the two neologisms allowed her not only to put a name where none previously existed, but to make a minimal binary. Strange as it may seem, the moments of creating these two words were decisive in the therapy, and signalled the tempering of her hallucinations.

We could remember here the significance of naming processes in the Oedipus complex that we discussed in Chapter 2. If the neurotic person says 'Yes' to the paternal function, the mother's desire can be designated. But if, in psychosis, the subject says 'No', they will have to invent their own name or names to pin down the enigmatic and menacing aspects of the Other. Different cases of psychosis show this creative effort time and time again, as new words are produced that designate, specify and limit rather than simply describe. In the case we discussed in the previous chapter, the subject not only made lists of his problems, but added a name to those lists – his 'broods'. Naming here is equivalent to the construction of sets, as a set has to be labelled, and constitutes already a significant progress, akin to the building of a metalanguage. Devaluing this work of nomination is both cruel and dangerous.

This importance of names explains another aspect of psychosis. Some psychotic subjects find it very helpful to receive a diagnosis, a label that other subjects reject as pseudo-scientific nonsense, an invasive attempt to bracket them off and categorize them. Healthcare researchers are forever trying to figure out what is better: to give labels or to refrain from giving labels. Yet it is clear that the significance and worth of a label will depend on each individual subject. If, for some, it can carry a naming function, like a staple to pin things down, it may be useful. If, for others, it is experienced as intrusive and alienating, it won't be welcome. The key is to have an idea of what place the name has in each subjective economy.

Making a name can form a part of the kind of stabilization that Lacan called the 'sinthome', a way of linking together real, symbolic and imaginary, which always involves some kind of creation. It could just as well be an object outside the body, situated as an exceptional point. In a case described by Éric Laurent, a young man explained in his first consultation how he was the unrecognized son of a business-man who had just died abroad. He knew this man was his father from the mother and from one letter received from him. Learning of the death from a local paper, he went immediately to the embassy of the country in question and demanded to be recognized as a citizen and as the dead man's son. As proof of the filiation, he held up the article in the paper and the letter. After this, life was only bearable for him through smoking a lot of dope. Work was difficult, as he would think that people were talking about him, and relationships were also marked by psychotic phenomena: he would see a skull on the face of the girl he was interested in, and his own skeleton through his skin during sex. In his analysis, he was able to construct something from the minimal material of his one-and-only childhood memory: he is on public transport with a bottle of water in his hand or next to him. That was the unique memory, nothing more, nothing less.

He lived in a small room at the top of a building, above his mother, and would often experience his neighbours as overbearing and perse-cutory. This room was next to the toilets, which leaked, and he began to develop his thoughts around this point – the cistern, the water, the flush – and would detail and describe with great care and concern the ways it could malfunction. He would do this with the different neighbours who until then had been intrusive, educating them as to the different possibilities and details, showing them what was wrong, and making himself the caretaker of the cistern. This was accom-panied by the creation of a system of distances: for the neighbour he felt closest to, he would phone from his own room; for another, he would call from a phone box in the street, which he considered to be far from his home. He had become the educator of his building, and Laurent notes that the patient's father had worked in education. As Laurent observes, he had created an object outside the body, and constructed a knowledge around it that allowed him to address those who, until then, had been impossible to talk to.

In another case, described by Ellen Corin, a young man who lived in a dark basement with the curtains closed all day explained how he had always been marginalized. He complained of his interfering, miserly parents and of being teased as gay by his classmates. 'People

are nasty,' he told Corin. 'People look at you, they stare at you . . .'
The key organizing feature of his life was listening to shortwave
radio broadcasts and trying to identify the transmitters. He collected
information on transmitters and recorded it carefully in a register,
picking up signals from South America, the US and Canada. The
radio was a device, Corin notes, that allowed him to insert himself
into a virtual network of people, participate in a communications
circuit and elaborate a certain kind of social world while staying in
his room. He was using what culture offered him to transform a position of distance from the social world into a form of participation.
Like Laurent's patient, he had not only created something, but linked
this creation to an addressee.

The emphasis here is less on reintegrating the person to established
social roles or norms than of helping them to foster a style of living:
as Corin puts it, to explore the ways of relating and gaining perspective on the world, 'from content to style'. She describes very finely
the way that psychotic subjects out of hospital may try to create
modes of living, often sitting and walking in public places where
they can mix with people without necessarily interacting with them:
to be there, but at a safe distance. They may go to the same restaurant
or park bench at the same hour of the day, creating a private system
of coordinates, their own geography. Apparently empty exchanges
with a bartender or coffee-shop staff may provide a crucial part of
this anchoring system. They relate to others without having to commit to interpersonal relations. Some prefer more anonymous spaces,
like shopping malls or busy streets. Rhythm and routine, as she points
out, are crucial here and should be respected.

One of my patients visited a gym for years not in order to exercise
but simply to say 'Good morning' to the boy who worked at reception. She had no romantic interest in him, yet he was a guarantee for
her that the world was stable. One day, when he wasn't there, her
hallucinations started. All she had wanted, she said, was to see him, to
know that he was there, a single point of consistency that she could
rely on. The minimal exchange of words had a vital function for her,
as if without them all else would collapse. There was no desire to get
to know him better, no wish to have any sort of relationship, and this

fact is often misunderstood by neurotic clinicians, who assume that everyone must thirst for human contact.

Yet a distinction between mixing and interacting is crucial. Pushing a psychotic subject to have what the therapist takes to be 'genuine' human relations can be disastrous, and it neglects totally the importance of the distances that the person may have inscribed in their world. The same goes for the way the person may have divided up external space. Psychotic partitions of space are often confused with phobias – indeed, by the person themself. An agoraphobia, for example, may function as a basic division of the world into inside and outside, good and bad. This elementary structuring of space may be a response to the hole of psychosis, and thus crucial to maintain, as old psychiatry recognized with its advice not to try to remove mono-symptomatic phobias. If someone has had a phobia that has organized their life for decades, the clinician should think long and hard before making any sort of intervention. Eduardo Weiss reported that Freud had an agoraphobic patient whom he cured of his phobia, only to see a psychosis then trigger. It was stabilized when the phobia was re-established by hypnosis.

It is interesting to compare the inventions we have discussed with those that often appear earlier in the psychotic process. When someone feels that their thoughts, emotions and actions are made or manufactured by an external agency, that they are a puppet of an outside force that can set them in motion or drop them at any moment, they often form the belief that this is taking place via some kind of machine or device. Tausk called this the 'influencing machine', an apparatus that could control the person's thoughts and bodily sensations from a distance, via air currents, electricity, radio waves or magnetism.

In a sense, this is in itself an attempt at self-cure, as it provides an explanation for the symptoms that the person is suffering from. How else could the bizarre theft or intrusion of mind and body be explained? Available scientific or folk knowledge is used in the reasoning process here. In some cases, however, the psychotic subject invents a device that *they*, rather than the external agency, control. Like the Russian dolls we evoked earlier, there is an inversion here, as if the person is finding a means to move away from being an object at the mercy of some external force to controlling it him or herself.

In Joey's case, he was initially an object at the mercy of electricity and the currents that flowed through him. His drawings show his whole body constructed out of an electrical current originating elsewhere and passing through him. After his work with Bettelheim's team, he left the school and would return there three years later, proudly bearing a machine that he had built himself. It was a special device to transform an alternating into a continuous current. He had thus moved from being a victim of electricity to its master, or, at least, its engineer. Like the man with the cistern, Joey had found a way, through his psychosis, to bring new objects into the world that transformed persecution into creation.

Most of the forms of stabilization we have discussed can coexist with each other, and it seems likely that there is always in fact more than one operating in the psychotic subject's life. Solutions are like stitches, and to make reality hold together, a single mechanism is rarely enough. If Schreber's delusional system allowed him to restructure his experience, his sustained and solid love for his wife was also crucial for him, as was the writing of his *Memoirs*. As we shall see in the next chapters, which explore some well-known cases in detail, networks of different solutions or compensations are built up over time. These protect the psychotic subject and can allow life to continue. Whether the emphasis is more on the symbolic – through the construction of a metalanguage – or on the imaginary – through some aspect of the body image – there is always an attempt to treat the real, the experience of intrusive thoughts or bodily sensations that threaten to overwhelm them.

These mechanisms and inventions can all allow a quiet and uneventful life, and, indeed, we could argue that normal life itself is simply a diversity of solutions to make the real bearable for us. There is no ultimate norm here, just a multiplicity of forms of creation.

9. Aimée

On 18 April 1931, a young woman approached the well-known actress Huguette Duflos outside the Théâtre St-Georges in Paris where she was appearing in a play called *Everything is Going Well*. 'Are you Mme Duflos?' she asked, and, when the actress answered affirmatively, she drew a large hunting knife from her handbag and struck her. The blow cut the tendons of Duflos's hand, and the attacker was swiftly overpowered by stagehands and passers-by. Interned first in a police cell at St-Lazare for two months and then in hospital at Ste-Anne, she calmed down remarkably. What had made her do such a thing? she asked. How could she have thought of attacking Duflos? Her homicidal passion seemed spent, and was replaced by a strange tranquillity. How could visible, terrifying madness undergo such a dramatic reversal into peace and equanimity?

The case of Marguerite Anzieu – known as 'Aimée' after the protagonist in one of her novels – allows us to study in detail not only the triggering of a psychosis, but also its apparent transformation into 'sanity'. This question will run through both of the following chapters, where the cases we explore show a certain external stability, even a social conformity, despite the presence of an underlying psychosis. What could allow this kind of metamorphosis? Should we think of it as a kind of sustained hibernation or, on the contrary, the result of one of the operations of stabilization and creation that we have discussed?

It was Anzieu who attracted the attention of a young psychiatrist, Jacques Lacan, at Ste-Anne. Lacan was thirty-one at the time and was working on his thesis in medicine on the theme of 'self-punishment paranoia'. French psychiatry was preoccupied in those years with constructing a differential clinic, defining the varieties of psychosis and their different symptoms, clinical presentations and prognoses. Lacan was already fascinated by Freudian theory, and was using it as a new way to approach the current debate on psychiatric classification. Just as psychoanalysis had described those neurotics who commit a crime out of a pre-existing sense of guilt in order to draw punishment on themselves, so Lacan thought that the search for punishment might define a certain form of psychosis.

When he met Anzieu in June 1931, it seemed as if he had found the clinical case he was looking for. Here was a psychotic subject who had clearly been delusional, who had even apparently attempted a homicide, yet who, not long after the act, had transformed into a picture of remorse and humility. It seemed as if the punishment she received had a powerful effect on her madness, as if, at some level, what she had sought through her actions had been precisely the acknowledgement of her guilt. Although she was just one of the forty cases that his thesis was based on, Lacan would see her almost daily for a year and a half, devoting the bulk of the thesis to a detailed study of Anzieu's life. The clinical detail that he focused on was the moment of change, the point when Anzieu's delusion apparently evaporated.

This question is also crucial for our own discussion of madness, as it highlights the processes that can turn the noisy, visible image of psychosis into something more encapsulated and contained. Marguerite spent several years in hospital after her arrest, with no further acts of violence or behaviour that would have been deemed socially unacceptable. Recently discovered documents describe her during her incarceration as 'calm', a 'good worker', who often requested her release. She was transferred from Ste-Anne to Ville-Évrard in 1938, and released from there in 1943, taking a variety of jobs as a housekeeper and cleaner and never again coming to the attention of either psychiatry or the law. She died in 1981.

Marguerite Pantaine was born in July 1892 to peasant parents in the Cantal region of France. She was their fourth child, and was followed by three brothers. The eldest child had died at the age of five in December 1890 and a stillborn child had been born in August of 1891. Most of Marguerite's early years were spent being looked after by her elder sister Élise, who was five years her senior, until Élise's departure to work for their uncle. Describing her childhood,

Marguerite saw herself as a 'garçonnière', a kind of tomboy, playing mostly with her brothers, or indulging in 'solitary reverie'. She had a special link to her mother – what she called 'an exclusive attachment' – and would say many years later: 'I should have stayed with her.' Whatever she did, the mother would still love her. 'We were like two friends,' she said, as she explained to Lacan how she regretted ever having left her mother's side.

Marguerite would often play up to her 'tyrannical' father, the only one of the children to contest his authority. She insisted on having her own way in details such as her haircut or the knot of her belt, and was accorded a special status out of the children, with privileges from her mother such as her own special linen, to the envy of her sisters, a fact that they would still recall bitterly some thirty years later when Lacan interviewed them. She was the one on whom the maternal hopes rested, the one most likely to succeed. We see here already the idea of a weight imposed on her, the coordinates of which will become clearer later on.

According to the family myth, Marguerite was never ready on time, always slow or late for what she had to do. She performed well academically and was the first to go to a nearby lay school at thirteen, where it was assumed that she would make a career as a teacher. She was accepted for a teacher training college, yet at sixteen she failed her exams, surprising everyone and blocking her progress. This failure was linked to the 'drama' of the death of a close friend, which was later to be the subject of a book manuscript she drafted called 'Le Détracteur'.

It is at this moment in her history that Lacan locates the first signs of her difficulties. She spoke of her need from now on for what Lacan termed 'moral guidance', a guidance that her teachers had failed to provide. Her family were worried about her and it seems that at least from this point onwards she was preoccupied with the idea of a higher calling. She found a job in the postal service and went to live with her sister Élise and Uncle Guillaume, who had now married, in a small provincial town. It was during this brief stay that Marguerite experienced her first love. She met a roguish poet – what she called a 'poétereau' – and began a relationship with him. He was a sort of local Don Juan, and she would later discover the cruel fact that this first sexual relationship had merely been the object of a wager with his friends.

As she was doing well in her new job and had successfully passed an administrative exam, Marguerite was assigned to another town where she would stay for three years, corresponding with the poet, who had become 'the unique object of her thoughts'. Isolating herself more and more, she didn't tell anyone about this powerful love, which continued, it seems, without her having seen him during that time. She then moved to Melun, where two crucial things happened: her love of the poet turned to hate – 'He can drop dead for all I care,' she said. 'I went swiftly from love to hate' – and she met a woman, C de la N, who she became powerfully drawn to.

C de la N came from aristocratic stock fallen on hard times. She was domineering and haughty, often speaking about her noble family, and exerting a coercive influence on the office staff. For Marguerite she was different, special, unlike 'all those clone-like girls [toutes ces filles faites en série]'. C behaved as if she were socially and morally superior to all those around her, and next to her Marguerite felt 'masculine', scorning her own sex. Despite her closeness to her new friend, and being in her shadow, Marguerite was not totally dominated by her. She 'reserved a part of herself' with C: whatever their proximity, she explained, 'I always kept a secret garden.' There are thus two distinct threads in Marguerite's life: that of the tomboy-'garçonnière', with the idea of a masculine identity, and that of the secret garden, the solitary reverie, the part of herself that she reserves. During this period, Marguerite would speak of her 'curiosity about the masculine soul'.

At twenty-five, Marguerite would marry her colleague René Anzieu, a man 'totally opposed to anything vain, decorative or creative', and who displayed what Lacan described as 'moral equilibrium and practical security'. C's influence on the marriage was certain, but was cut short when she was herself posted to another town. Why the choice of René as a husband? Lacan asked. 'If I didn't take him, another would,' Marguerite replied. This period was marked with problems for her: she became increasingly silent, sometimes for weeks on end, and was plagued by jealousy. She would have bizarre outbursts of laughter, experienced frigidity and washed her hands compulsively. She also read a lot during this time. This grim situation was made all the more difficult when her newly widowed sister Élise moved in with them some eight months later, an arrival that Lacan would describe as 'probably the most decisive event in her life'.

Élise gave advice on everything and soon became the dominant member of the household. She was especially bitter about her own thwarted motherhood. She had already had a hysterectomy and had a 'deep need for maternity', according to her sister. Élise was 'always against' Marguerite, who was humiliated and deprived of her place, yet nonetheless praised the qualities and virtues of her older sibling. She was, quite literally, supplanted, as their entourage would later confirm. This intrusion of the sister into her household was particularly interesting for Lacan: why, he asked, was her attitude so accepting?

Even if circumstance might have made it seem necessary, Lacan was struck by the difficulty, even impossibility, for Marguerite to openly articulate her obvious reproach to Élise for invading her space. She just appeared to accept it, denying her complaints, and living in what he called a 'mute struggle' with her sister. Élise's most powerful weapon, Lacan observed, was less her own authority than her sister's conscience, and it was the combination of her struggle with Élises's authority, her recognition of her sister's qualities and her own humiliation that gave the particular character to her psychosis.

At twenty-eight, Marguerite became pregnant, and it is now that we find the first real triggering of the psychosis, even if we might suspect that things had started to get difficult for her after the marriage. People were maligning her, she now believed, whispering about her; her work colleagues were conspiring against her, passers-by in the street were gossiping about her and newspapers contained allusions to her. These phenomena were interpreted by Marguerite: 'they want the death of my child'. 'If the child doesn't live,' she said, 'they will be responsible.' She had nightmares about coffins, and in one episode she slashed a colleague's bicycle tyres, threw a pitcher of water and an iron at her husband and reproached him for having been with someone else. Evoking her behaviour in this period, she referred to her 'melancholies'.

Tragically, Marguerite's child, a girl, was born dead, strangled by the umbilical cord. It is at this point that a new delusional idea crystallizes: C de la N is responsible for the child's death, and her former friend becomes a persecutor. It turned out that C had phoned not long after the delivery to find out how Marguerite was, and she had interpreted this as a sign. It had seemed odd at the time, she thought, yet now she understood. She immediately broke off her correspondence with C, ascribing blame uniquely to this woman she had once been so fascinated by. She now also gave up her religious practices. It is at precisely this moment that Marguerite's own mother becomes delusional, convinced that the death of a farm animal is due to the malevolent wishes of a neighbour.

At thirty, Marguerite became pregnant again, and is now depressed, anxious and interpretative, reading malign intentions into the world around her. When the baby boy, Didier, is born, she is devoted to him, but still hostile and querulous. She felt that everything was threatening her child, and on one occasion made a scene with the driver of a car that had passed too close to the pram. After five months, Élise takes over the household, revelling in her new maternal role. She would later tell Lacan that she had found consolation for her barren state in becoming the mother to Marguerite's son. Soon René discovers that his wife has been applying for a passport to emigrate to the US.

Marguerite had resigned from her job and started planning for a trip to the States to seek her fortune as a novelist. She does this, she says, for her child. Things become progressively worse, and now, at thirty-two, she is hospitalized for the first time. During this first hospitalization, which lasted six months, she had the idea of being a great novelist and of her son becoming an ambassador. The hospital recorded that she left 'uncured', and her delusional ideas continued: people were mocking her, insulting her, accusing her of 'bad morals', of being 'depraved'. She was convinced that 'they' wanted to take her child away, yet the motive and detail were unclear. She was perplexed about who her enemies were and believed that she was meant for a 'higher destiny', although this, too, remained imprecise.

It was during this difficult period that she appealed to a certain novelist to denounce the 'injustice' of the hospitalization, which was designed, she believed, to separate her from her child. The idea of a destiny or calling continued to preoccupy her, and she decided that she must find out more about the special place she had been given. To do so, Marguerite moves to Paris where, after working hard in her job, she studies, spends long hours in libraries, takes the baccalaureate exams, drinks a lot of coffee, and travels back home regularly to see her son, who remains with her husband and sister. It is now that her delusion really begins to take shape.

Marguerite knows that she will be a great writer, 'denouncing the sins of artists, poets, journalists' who were responsible for war, murder and the corruption of morals. Writers and artists like Sarah Bernhard and Colette are corrupting society, pursuing their selfish aims of glory and pleasure. She denounces 'the insouciance of frivolous mothers' and realizes that her mission is to create a 'brotherhood between peoples and races', a 'reign of women and children' and the 'end of wickedness', in which 'the love of humankind' will flourish. Everyone will wear white and there will be no more war. She will achieve this through her writing, becoming a 'femme de lettres et de sciences' who spreads purity and devotion. A 'reign of goodwill' will follow.

Marguerite's delusional system thus contained both the theme of persecution – her child is threatened – and of grandeur – she is the agent of social reform. We should observe here how Lacan met with Marguerite every day, interviewing her carefully, yet it was only after a year that she could tell him the content of her delusion, making sure that the chairs in the room were moved around to avoid eye contact. This reticence should certainly encourage caution in quick psychiatric diagnoses, often done via questionnaires rather than lengthy, detailed dialogue. Most delusional people just won't say what their belief system is, and it can take months or even years of careful exploration to find out.

Especially high on Marguerite's list of targets was Huguette Duflos, whom she believed was working for Pierre Benoît, a well-known author who had exposed details of her private life in his books. Benoît had turned from being a potentially benevolent helper to a more menacing figure, not only alluding to her in his writing but sending spies to plagiarize her own work, copying her unpublished novels and notebooks. She believed that there was even a whole journal, *L'Œuvre*, directed specifically against her. How the link of Duflos to Benoît became established is unsure, although the actress had played one of his characters in the film adaptation of a book, which Marguerite had seen.

The threat that Marguerite experienced here was less directly to her than to her son. If anything happened to him, it would be her fault: she would be a 'criminal mother', as she had not stopped the persecutors in time. Lacan pointed out the curious logic of her belief: if all her thoughts of persecution were focused around the threat of harm to her son, in reality whenever he was unwell or at risk she did not appear especially concerned. On two occasions, it seemed as if he had appendicitis yet she appeared unmoved. This might suggest, in fact, that the key for Marguerite was the *idea* of harm to a child, not the empirical fact of harm to her actual son Didier, and we often find this curious feature in delusions. To cite another case, a woman who believed herself to be a mother with duties to save children would hear a voice which said, 'Think of the children first and you will be all right.' Yet, as she noted, 'I actually thought very little about my own children.' The delusion was structured at the level of representations, of ideas, rather than of the real, empirical characters in her life.

But why Duflos? Lacan asked her this question more than a hundred times. He knew that during Marguerite's friendship with C de la N, the latter had mentioned the actress as being a neighbour of her aunt, thus situating her in the sphere of socially elevated beings that C in some sense embodied. Yet why a threat from her? At last an answer seemed to emerge. One day, when Marguerite was wondering at work where the threats to her son were coming from, she heard someone mention Duflos's name. She now understood. She remembered how, in her previous job, her office colleagues had once been praising Duflos, and Marguerite had remarked that she was a 'whore'. It must be a revenge, she now realized. And at the moment that Marguerite arrived in Paris, Duflos was in all the papers, involved in a court case regarding a theatrical contract. Seeing this, she had felt anger at this importance given to the life of 'artists'.

Duflos, she now believed, was mocking her, ridiculing her in her stage performances, yet she could not believe that the actress was operating on her own: she must be 'supported' by someone more powerful, and this person was none other than Pierre Benoît, the man she had appealed to in order to save her and recognize her literary worth. Although she did not think that the two were lovers, she imagined a powerful link between them. We could note how her appeal goes in two directions: first of all, to Benoît, and then to the Prince of Wales, to whom she sent a sonnet each week. She had a platonic love for him and he occupied the place of a benevolent authority. Interestingly, the motif of the helper in delusion has received much less attention than that of the persecutor, perhaps due to the fact that a psychotic subject is often less likely to speak about their defenders, for fear of endangering their benign and supportive effects.

Marguerite's room was actually filled with images of the prince, and he had received a steady stream of letters and poems. She appealed to him to act as her champion, warning the world of the dangers of corruption. This kind of platonic reverence had been finely described by the psychiatrist Maurice Dide, involving a prolonged fidelity and devotion yet with no demand for a meeting or sexual liaison. It echoed her three-year adoration of the roguish poet, who had become 'the unique object of her thoughts', despite the fact that she made no effort to see him again. Marguerite did not sign her letters to the prince until just before her attack on Duflos, and Lacan was careful to study the chronology here of her delusional construction.

Although the delusion of the threat to Didier had been elaborated over a five-year period, it was only in the couple of years before the attack that she had felt the need to 'do something'. In order to fulfil her destiny, it wasn't enough to write her novels: they had to be published, which would make her enemies retreat. She wrote two novels, 'Le Détracteur', with a heroine called Aimée, and 'Sauf votre respect', but the publishing world was not kind to Marguerite. A number of incidents during this period indicate how crucial this literary project was to her. She was reported to the police for harassing a journalist some six months before the Duflos episode to get an article about

Colette published, and she had attacked an employee of the Gallimard publishing house after they had rejected one of her manuscripts.
She had also made a series of formal complaints to the police about
Pierre Benoît. Throughout this time, her concerns about her child's
safety were growing, and she would have dreams in which her son
was drowned or killed or snatched from her. Finally, she posted her
novels to the Prince of Wales, her ultimate saviour.

Her terror at what she felt to be an imminent attempt on her son's
life grew stronger and stronger. If anything were to happen to him,
she repeated, it would be her fault: 'I would be a criminal mother.'
The storm clouds, she said, were gathering. Posters around Paris carried warnings to Benoît that if he continued to threaten her, he
would be punished. In March, she bought a large hunting knife, and
determined to confront her enemy face to face: 'What would she
think of me,' she asked, 'if I wasn't there to defend my child?'

It was in April 1931 that she struck Duflos at a moment when she
was supposed to be visiting her son. The persecutory vortex seemed
to be at its most acute, and yet, not long after her internment, the
delusion deflated. 'How could I have believed that?' she asked in
wonder. The motifs of erotomania and megalomania seemed absurd
to her now. How could she ever have thought, she asks, that Duflos
wanted to harm her? Once again, it is at the precise moment of the
daughter's hospitalization that the mother's psychosis triggers: she is
convinced of the malevolence of her neighbours and that they were
responsible for the whole of Marguerite's drama.

———

So how did Lacan understand the case in 1932? As well as the idea of
a new diagnostic category, his interest was in the crystallization of
the delusion. At what exact moment had each element been added or
systematized? What brought her thoughts together or challenged
them? How did she rewrite her past to make it consistent with the
delusional thoughts? What phenomena of memory were at play?
Why, for example, were the memories so scanty of the moments
when the key persecutors had entered her delusional beliefs? Lacan
tracked these details with meticulous care.

For him the aetiological key lay in Marguerite's relation with her mother and her sister. The sister had taken on the place of a mother for her, but in an intrusive, unbearable way. It was she who looked after the young Marguerite and who moved in with her later on, taking control of the household and of her child. This terrible proximity could not be admitted to consciousness for Marguerite, and so the centrifugal tendency of her delusion: it was always other people outside the family that posed the threat. Unable to voice her reproach to Élise, it returned in the persecutory motif of the delusion. The mechanism that governed her madness was projection: the ideas that could not be tolerated were now believed to come from the outside. Her attack on Élise became her persecutors' attacks on herself.

This powerful sister presented the image of the woman she could not be and who took her place quite literally. After Élise had moved in with her and René, Marguerite had said that she herself should leave, allowing René to 'make his life with someone else': no doubt, with Élise. She hated her, yet, as Lacan argued, aspired to be her, and this fury showed itself in the icy way in which she would compliment Élise. She was unable to subjectively assume her rage at this sister who had supplanted her. Élise was her 'most intimate enemy', Lacan says.

Writing a year or so after the publication of the case, Lacan could add: 'Her affective ambivalence towards her sister organized all the self-punitive behaviour of the Aimée case. If during her delusion Aimée transferred on to several successive figures the accusations of her amorous hatred, it was in an effort to free herself from this first fixation, but this effort was to fail: each of her persecutors was really nothing less than a new image, always entirely a captive of her narcissism, of this sister whom our patient had made into her ideal.'

Her delusion was thus a form of flight from her own aggressive and murderous tendencies, an attempt to liberate herself from the chains of her 'amorous hatred'. It was the very distance between her and her persecutors that mattered, according to Lacan. She chose them well: they inhabited a world separated from and inaccessible to her, and this distance allowed a certain 'non-realization' of her drives. Thus, her first real persecutor, C de la N, was chosen precisely because of her difference from 'all the other girls': she was special, distinguished, unique. Unable to articulate a reproach to her sister, Marguerite chose C de la N instead. Rather than blame her sister for the loss of her child, she blamed C. Élise was at some level aware of this, as she told Lacan that she was worried about her own safety. Although Marguerite had never threatened her or identified her with her persecutor, Élise sensed intuitively that her sister's attack was aimed at her.

These persecutors, however, were ultimately nothing less than projections of Marguerite's own image. Beyond her rage at Élise – and beyond her, the mother – lay a homosexual love for them. She was guilty of the very corruption she accused them of. The image of the idealized woman she struck was thus her own. Duflos represented the ideal of social prestige and power that she, Marguerite, aspired to. She imputed corruption to these women, yet wanted the same fame for herself, dreaming of a 'grande vie' and to influence the world. Indeed, the poets she deemed responsible for the world's evils were termed 'les amateurs de la gloire', the term 'amateurs' being almost an anagram of her own name 'Marguerite'. In striking Duflos, Lacan argued, she was striking herself, her own ideal image externalized in another woman.

So why the sudden fall of the delusion twenty days after the attack? Was it the act of striking Duflos, or, as Lacan claimed, the subsequent incarceration? Immediately following the act itself, she was still consumed with hatred and reproach. But then everything just 'dropped': the erotomania, the jealousy, the persecution theme, and her altruistic idealism. These were no longer necessary, as she had made her punishment real: she was now among criminals and delinquents, and separated from her family. She realized, finally, that she had struck herself, making herself guilty before the law. Many years later, in 1975, Lacan would revise his opinion, remarking that the idea that her real desire was to be punished was 'to push the logic [of the case] a bit too far'.

Even if we question the concept of a self-punishment paranoia, there is still a crucial problem with Lacan's interpretation in 1932. If Marguerite was so concerned about the sister's intrusion and the purloining of her son, why wasn't the delusion centred on exactly this – the thought that her persecutors wished to steal Didier away from her? Why wasn't there an emphasis on their efforts to remove him and to get rid of her? Although she has the thought at one time that Stalin's secret police were going to take her son away, it was less the idea of theft than of harm that her delusional thoughts gravitated around.

A tentative answer to this question appears in a footnote to the case, where Lacan evokes a possible murderous drive in Marguerite towards her son. This, he suggests, might explain the 'centrifugal' tendency of her delusion and her flight away from her child. It would also account for the feature of the case that had so intrigued him: her sudden 'cure'. The imprisonment, after all, would have helped her bring about 'the definitive loss of her child'. She was thus punishing herself for the crime of which she accused her persecutor. On the other hand, when Lacan began his interviews with her after the incarceration, he noted her fears about the effect of a possible divorce, which would mean a separation from Didier. The relegation of these thoughts to a footnote and the fact that he does not develop them at all in the main text testify perhaps to their problematic status. Yet how else could one explain what seems to be a major 'contradiction' in the material: the threat of harm to her child?

In his remarkable reading of the case and gathering of historical data, Jean Allouch has proposed another interpretation, which brings together many of the themes that Lacan dwelled on. His point of departure is the coincidence of the mother and the daughter's triggerings. Each time the daughter is hospitalized with the visible signs of psychosis, the mother's madness is precipitated: firstly, after the loss of Marguerite's first child, and secondly, after the attack on Duflos. Lacan makes little of this, and his positioning of the mother is odd: he assumes that Marguerite's fixation on Élise must be a displacement from the mother to the sister, yet this is hardly elaborated. One has the sense that it was more a requirement of Freudian theory than a clinical deduction. Yet, at the very least, the intertwining of the themes of their delusional thought suggests that the place of the mother deserves further exploration.

In Lacan's account, there are several details that suggest the mother's importance to the case. Speaking about the main motif of her delusion – the harm to her son – Marguerite would never become tearful, yet it was only when speaking of her mother that her eyes would well up. She cried at the idea of a separation from her mother – not from her son – and she would say repeatedly, 'I should have stayed close to her.' Lacan observed how nothing was more critical for her than the idea of her mother's 'grief', and in the writings that he included in the thesis, one novel ends with a description of a mother's feelings on the death of her child. This was written in the months preceding the attack on Duflos and was one of the texts that she sent to the Prince of Wales. Another text, written even closer to the act, involves a parent grieving the death of their child. She would also say that her best writing had been inspired by the death of her friend in her teens when she was doing her exams for teacher training college.

We can remember here that Marguerite's older sister had died at the age of five, just over a year and a half before her own birth. She had come too close to the grate of the hearth and had burned alive, either in front of her mother (Lacan's version) or in her absence (Didier Anzieu's version). Her name had been Marguerite, a detail bizarrely absent from Lacan's account of the case. As we reread the text with Allouch, we see how the presence of the dead child and the guilty mother is everywhere. In the first triggering, Marguerite's paranoid thoughts revolved around the idea of other people being responsible if her child were to die. At the time, she threw both water and a hot iron at her husband. When she was fined for her later attack on the employee in the publishing house, she told her family it was because she had started 'an accidental fire'. In one of her stories, she describes how 'I warned [the animals] when the fire broke out in the wood.'

Throughout the delusional construction, a child is at risk and a mother is guilty, and the delusion aims, in effect, to save a child. That is its logic, even in the supreme goal of a world in which mothers and children live happily and peacefully together. Allouch found that in the original court record, Marguerite told the judge that she had a daughter and not a son, and used her mother's name Jeanne rather than her own. When Lacan had asked her why her son was threatened, she had only ever replied once, saying impulsively, 'To punish me.' But why? Lacan asked. Because she was a 'criminal mother'. She had to stand up to Duflos or else she would have been a 'cowardly mother'. 'What would she think of me,' Marguerite asked, 'if I wasn't there to defend my child?'

The fact that the real health of her son was less important to her than the idea of harm to a child echoes this. It was as if the tragedy of the mother returned in the delusion of the daughter. At the first triggering, indeed, her mother blamed a neighbour for their farm animal's death. So the motif of death and responsibility converge, as if Marguerite's madness involved a message to her mother demanding that responsibility be taken for the death of her namesake. For Allouch, the child is linked to the presence of sexuality: it is the sign itself of a sexual relation, and so Marguerite strikes sexuality in other women. Her delusional thoughts, after all, are about 'depraved' and 'dissolute' women. And her first triggering is not when Élise arrives but during her pregnancy, when she thinks that people are calling her 'depraved'. In striking Duflos, then, she was striking not simply her sister but her mother. One day, after Lacan asked her for the hundredth time why she had struck Duflos, she replied, 'To make her confess' – as if to accentuate the very dimension of a confession that seems to have been absent with her mother: 'Je l'ai frappé pour la faire avouer.'

The corruption and dissolution that Marguerite saw in her female persecutors can thus be understood in a number of ways. To have sex after the death of a child is perhaps a crime that requires punishment. But the mother's absence at the moment that the first Marguerite's dress caught fire was also perhaps interpreted as an unforgivable fault, a point of maternal absence around which all the signifiers of 'frivolity', 'dissolution' and 'badness' revolve. There would then have been an attempt, through the delusion, to name the unsymbolizable part of the mother that could let a child die by her 'insouciance'. The mother's frivolity let the child die, so Marguerite gave herself the mission to eradicate frivolity in mothers.

The key motif, then, concerns a mother's responsibility for the death of a child. We can remember here that when she was growing up, Marguerite could do no wrong: however naughty she was, the mother would still love her. Lacan's choice of the name 'Aimée' ('Loved') for Marguerite perhaps reflects the significance of this burden. How, after all, can a child be alive if, whatever they do, it's as if they have done nothing wrong: it dehumanizes, as if they were someone or something else. For Marguerite, it suggests a capture in the weight of the image of the dead child, an assignment emphasized by the choice of the identical name. To occupy this place was intolerable for her, as Allouch points out, and hence both the feeling of a persecution – what is more persecutory than having someone else loved through you? – and that of a mission in life: to replace the dead sister.

The idea of being a replacement child for a daughter who had been burned alive was perhaps the parameter of the space in which Marguerite grew up, and having a child of her own only forced a detonation of the delusional motifs. When Élise came to live with them, Lacan was surprised at how easily Marguerite conceded both child and household to her, yet this choice makes more sense when we realize that in this process she was both giving her sister the child she didn't have and abdicating from the impossible place of a mother. Just as she replaced a missing child for Élise by handing over her charge, so the latter could tell Marguerite that Didier was her consolation: in other words, the replacement child for her. Wouldn't it have been this, then, that contributed to the triggering of the psychosis in the first pregnancy, her unconscious acknowledgement that she was making a baby for someone else?

Marguerite's madness, for Allouch, represents the impossibility of being assigned to the place of the dead sibling, which would have entailed the denial of the mother's responsibility for the death. Note indeed how, in this family, each child was born almost immediately after the other, not allowing any time for a mourning of the dead children. The first Marguerite died in December 1890, and then a stillborn child in August 1891, before Marguerite's birth in July 1892. Lacan mistakenly dated the first child's death as occurring during her mother's pregnancy with Marguerite, and the error is telling in itself, suggesting the significance to her of her namesake's tragedy. The madness aimed, in part, at a disclosure, a confession from the mother, or, perhaps, an accusation at the mother's failure to mourn. Mourning, indeed, seems present in the case only as an asymptotic point for both mother and daughter.

This movement towards disclosure is present throughout the case. Marguerite has to denounce the plot against her child and the corruption of women like Duflos. The public and the authorities need to know what is happening, and so she appeals to politicians, publishers, the police and civil authorities. At the horizon of these appeals, for Allouch, is the protestation: how can a criminal mother dare to have a child? The psychosis thus discloses what the mother refused to recognize, and it seems that, at some level, the mother did receive her daughter's message: hence the timing of her own delusional outbursts. Could one even consider the 'cure' after her incarceration, as Allouch indicates, less as the result of an imprisonment than as an effect of the mother's triggering, as if she were showing her daughter that she had been heard?

In hospital, we learn that Marguerite intended to write a life of Joan (Jean) of Arc and a series of letters from Ophelia to Hamlet. 'Jeanne' was, of course, the name of her mother, and *Hamlet* is a play in which a mother is guilty and her child is faced with the burden of avenging the death that she ignores. There is sadly no more detail about these literary projects, but we do know that Lacan encouraged her writing. He thought that her understanding of childhood feelings, her enthusiasm for nature, her romantic platonism and her social idealism were a motor for her creative activities and were produced by the psychosis. She had a 'jouissance quasi sensible que lui donnent les mots de sa langue', and Marguerite indeed would call herself 'une amoureuse des mots'. All she needed to succeed with her written work was 'social help', yet he also noted that as her condition seemed to improve at Ste-Anne, her writing got worse.

Lacan's study is an astonishingly rich clinical document, and it invites us to read it with both the tools of traditional psychoanalytic biography and the structural theory of psychosis. Take, for example, the question of Marguerite's pregnancies. We can apply a structural view, and assume that they would have posed the question of paternity for her. Unable to symbolize this, the psychosis would have triggered. Or, we could assume that each pregnancy posed the question for her of her mother's pregnancies and what these meant, reviving for her the accusation against her mother for harm done to a child. In fact, we do not have to choose between these perspectives – or indeed others – as they have a certain compatibility. The basic problem of symbolization for Marguerite, rendered immediate by the pregnancies, would have opened up the hole into which her delusional construction was placed.

We can note a curious detail here which brings together both of these perspectives. One of the few anecdotes about Marguerite as a child concerned her pursuit by a bull ('taureau'). Family members would often evoke her misadventure when, taking a short cut across a field to catch up with them, she was chased by this frightening beast. Allouch draws attention to the repetition of 'taureau' in her baptism of the roguish poet as 'poétereau', and linked this to the figure of the father. Her dreams, she would later tell Lacan, would often feature not only a bull but a viper ('vipère'), a word which contains 'père' ('father'). If we link these motifs, there is a chain that connects the phoneme 'eau' with the father.

Now, what do we find in her writings but an almost systematic juxtaposition of the image of a dead or threatened child with water. Each time she mentions the motif of the child, some depiction of water ('eau') will follow, either in the same sentence or the subsequent one. The signifier 'eau', and its derivatives such as 'torrent', can thus be understood as both an appeal to the father and as an evocation of what would extinguish a fire. At each level, it treats the unchecked desire of the mother. We might even conjecture that her project of an escape to America involved an elaboration of the same logic: it would mean, after all, putting water between herself and her family. After her son Didier trained as a psychoanalyst many years later, he would become well known for his introduction of the concept of an unconscious bodily boundary he called the 'skin ego'. Although this has been linked to the idea of his mother's overprotective care, couldn't we also find in 'moi peau' the 'eau' that perhaps mattered so much to her?

The effort to regulate the desire of the mother is significant in the very 'fixation' to the trauma of her namesake's death. Although at one level we could understand this in strictly biographical terms – the weight placed on her, the choice of the same name, etc. – there is the possibility that the importance of the first Marguerite's death was in itself a way of interpreting the mother's desire. In the absence of phallic signification, perhaps the image of the dead child took its place, so that, confronted with the question of making sense of the mother's moods and behaviour, Marguerite appealed to the unspeakable event in the past as an explanation. This would have established the traumatic scene as a central, defining signification, to be revived at moments when her own pregnancies would have demanded the injection of some sort of meaning.

The case also shows us the importance in psychosis of the place of an addressee. So much of Marguerite's effort involved creating lines of communication: to Pierre Benoît, to the publishing houses, to the Prince of Wales and then, no doubt, to Lacan. The fact that the young psychiatrist visited her almost every day for a year and a half after her incarceration must have been meaningful to her, just as his admission to her that he could not find her writings to return to her later on must have had an effect. Maintaining an addressee was vital for Marguerite, and, if we look at her acts of violence, they all occur at the moments when something disrupted the line of communication, when the Other failed to receive her productions.

Later, perhaps, God would become her most stable addressee. In 1975, towards the end of her life, she could remark that 'prayer saves me from everything' ('la prière me sauve de tout'). She would say masses for the souls of the dead, and one day she confided her secret to Didier: she had become 'God's chosen one' ('l'élue de Dieu'). As well as evoking her mother's maiden name – Donnadieu – doesn't this also suggest a new perspective on erotomania, the diagnostic category that once generated so much debate in Continental psychiatry and which has been used to categorize Marguerite? Although the dominant motif in erotomania is one of love – the belief that one is the love object of another – isn't the theme of communication just as important? The subject in erotomania, after all, believes not just in love but in the fact that this love is being communicated, signified to them. In that sense, a line of communication is established at the centre of the experience of love. And this idea of being spoken to allows us to integrate erotomania into the classic psychoses, without having to give it some special status.

Perhaps the periods of relative stability for Marguerite were the result of keeping this line of communication open: from the letters to the roguish poet to the articles sent to magazines to the sonnets sent to the Prince of Wales. The activity of writing must in itself have been crucial, and we might suspect that in some way that was linked for her to the idea of occupying the place of an exception. She believed, in the years prior to the attack on Duflos, that she would be the woman of letters to change everything. We could guess, indeed, that after Ste-Anne, she continued to write letters to some interlocutor, whether located in her family or somewhere beyond them.

As a child, likewise, Marguerite had been the one with privileges, the special one, yet if her triggerings show that being assigned to the place of the dead child was unbearable for her, the position at the end of her life as the 'chosen one' still testifies to an exceptional place. She was unique now, not for her mother but for God, and we might wonder whether this singular space was what she had referred to in her dialogue with Lacan as her 'secret garden', a part of herself that she chose not to share yet which remained, nonetheless, essential to her.

If, with Aimée, her psychosis would erupt visibly and dramatically at certain moments in her life, leaving little ambiguity as to the diagnosis, the case of the Wolf Man is more complex. It shows how madness can trigger and then disappear, stabilized in discreet and invisible ways. Sergei Pankejeff was seen by some of the greatest and wisest of the twentieth century's psychiatrists and psychoanalysts: Theodor Ziehen, Emil Kraepelin, Sigmund Freud, Ruth Mack Brunswick, Muriel Gardiner and Kurt Eissler. Yet the diagnoses he received were wildly different: neurasthenia, obsessional neurosis, obsessive-compulsive personality and a borderline condition, to name only a few. Although Freud had seen him as an adult, his published discussion was limited to Pankejeff's childhood. Just before his fourth birthday, there had been a dramatic change in the boy's character, and Freud was intrigued by what he took to be an infantile neurosis. What had happened to turn a bright, confident child into an anxious, obsessive young neurotic? As for Lacan in his study of Aimée, it was the moment of change that constituted the key clinical question.

Pankejeff had seen Freud from early in 1910 to the summer of 1914, and then again from the end of 1919 to February 1920. Later in the 1920s he was referred to Ruth Mack Brunswick, a brilliant student of Freud who took him into analysis. He was convinced he had a large hole in his nose, and would look at his image in a pocket mirror hundreds of times a day. This acute paranoid state got worse, improved and would then reappear some thirty years later in a strange episode when he was apprehended by Russian troops after the war. Again, it was short-lived, but Brunswick had no doubt as to her diagnosis. Where Freud had seen the after effects of an obsessional neurosis, for Brunswick it was a clear case of psychosis, which she diagnosed as hypochondriacal paranoia.

Reading Brunswick's paper on the case, it is difficult to disagree, yet none of the later analysts and psychiatrists who saw Pankejeff would share her view. After Brunswick, Pankejeff would see Muriel Gardiner, herself an analysand of Brunswick, and their relationship would last for decades. Gardiner, who knew him for forty-three years, saw absolutely no sign of psychosis, and nor did the dozens of other seasoned clinicians who would see him over the years until his death in 1979, including Kurt Eissler, who met with him for a month every year for fifteen years. Pankejeff was labelled obsessive, narcissistic, neurotic, even borderline, but not psychotic by those who worked with him, apart from Brunswick. Yet, as we will see, once we recognize the distinction between being mad and going mad, it becomes possible to reconcile the diagnostic contradiction. What allowed him to lead an ordinary life, working for an insurance company in Vienna, and, after the Russian episode, never again, as far as we know, experiencing such a severe outbreak of paranoia?

—

Freud first met Pankejeff when the young Russian aristocrat arrived in Vienna after already having seen many of the big psychiatric names of his day and spending several months in different German sanatoria. He was totally dependent on other people, unable to dress himself – a detail Pankejeff contested later on – or even go to the toilet, relying on a male aide's enemas. As well as suffering from intestinal disorders, he felt separated from the world by a veil, which would be periodically punctured only by the enemas he would receive to relieve his constipation. After the first session, he was candid enough to tell Freud that he considered his analyst a Jewish swindler, that he would like to use him from behind and defecate on his head.

Freud was interested in the question of Pankejeff's childhood, and traced a sequence of events and their effects in his patient's life in the case history he was to publish some four years later in 1918. The significance of Freud's work here lies particularly in how he complicated the theory of trauma. Developing his own ideas from the 1890s, he argues that a traumatic scene can have delayed effects, becoming traumatic only when it is interpreted anew sometimes several years after the event. Witnessing a sexual act, for example, can have no great effect at the time, yet, when the person learns about sex later on, suddenly become traumatic retroactively and start to generate symptoms.

This was essentially Freud's argument in the case, and he elaborated it through a detailed exploration of his patient's childhood. Pankejeff was born to an aristocratic and wealthy Russian family in 1886, two years after his sister, Anna. The caul, or 'lucky hood', he was born with gave him a special place as a 'lucky child', and he would survive both pneumonia and malaria in his first year. His father was a district judge, who suffered from severe bouts of depression and perhaps manias, his mother a cool, undemonstrative and hypochondriacal woman with a dark sense of humour who was often ill with abdominal disorders. He would remember his mother lamenting to her doctor, 'I can't go on living like this,' words he would later on apply to himself. With his father often absent and his mother unwell, the nannies and nurses played an especially important role for Pankejeff and Anna. Gruscha was the first beloved nanny, followed by Nanya, both of whom played a significant part in Pankejeff's story.

He seems to have been a good-natured and quiet boy, yet a transformation took place one summer when his parents returned from their holiday, having left him in the care of an English governess. The three-and-a-half-year-old was now bad-tempered, irritable and violent, with a wish to be punished by his father. Pankejeff dated this change from the Christmas of that year, when he was not given a double quantity of presents, his due as his birthday fell in fact on Christmas Day itself. He became terrified of the image of a wolf in a children's book, screaming that it would come to eat him up. This was accompanied by various terrors of animals and insects, and Pankejeff also developed an obsessive piety. Before going to sleep, he had to kiss each of the religious images in his room after praying and making the sign of the cross innumerable times. Blasphemies would simultaneously enter his mind, and this combination of positive and negative thinking naturally made Freud posit an obsessional structure.

These obsessive rituals were nourished by the Bible stories that his mother started reading him. Pankejeff brooded about the relation of God to Christ, and the question of whether Christ had a 'behind' and would excrete. Who was Christ's father? he wondered: it seemed to be Joseph, yet he had been told that Joseph was only 'like' a father. These ruminations were constructed around his own identification with Christ, with whom he shared a birthday, and they contained a reproach to God for his harshness and cruelty to his son.

The obsessive period would become tempered when, at ten, an Austrian scholar Herr Reidel arrived on the estate, and Pankejeff would spend a great deal of time with this new and influential figure. His piety faded after Reidel shared with him his doubts about religion. These echoed his own doubts so precisely that Pankejeff experienced a profound relief and felt able to abandon his religious preoccupations. With Reidel, he developed an interest in military matters, uniforms, weapons and horses, and now spun his daydreams around these new motifs. Freud thought that the subsequent teenage years were more or less unproblematic for Pankejeff, and that the new interests allowed a sublimation of the themes that had previously tormented him. He also immersed himself in literature, reading the Russian novelists and poets, and painting, which he felt filled the 'vacuum' created by the loss of piety.

At seventeen, however, Pankejeff suffered a breakdown, brought on apparently by contracting gonorrhoea. This blow to his narcissism was too much for him and 'he went to pieces'. He lost his belief that he was favoured by destiny, the 'lucky child' who had been born with a caul. Two years later his sister commited suicide by drinking mercury. Anna had been an important figure for Pankejeff. Boyish as a child, she had shone academically in both sciences and creative writing. She seems to have been idealized by her father, and Pankejeff would compete with her, oppressed, as Freud comments, 'by her merciless display of superiority'. In his teens, they became closer, yet she rejected a sexual approach he made to her. It was at this moment that he turned to a peasant girl who worked in their home and who had the same name as his sister. The special place that Anna occupied for her father would perhaps exact a toll on her: in the period before her death, doubts as to her body image made her withdraw from society.

After the suicide the father began to show a new affection for Pankejeff: 'He took the most intense interest in everything I was doing or planning to do and wanted to be my advisor and protector in every way.' It was clear, he writes, that his father 'had transferred his feel-ings for Anna to me'. And this, of course, only made matters worse. He went through the 'deepest depression', with thoughts of suicide. Pankejeff now switched from law to natural science, mimicking Anna – as both he and Freud thought – who had a passion for that subject. Also significant here was the influence of an old tutor, who showed disappointment that Pankejeff had previously chosen law and not maths or natural science. Later, he would transfer back to law after a period of obsessive indecision.

As his depressions continued and studying proved difficult, Panke-jeff would be taken to see a variety of doctors and stay in several sanatoria. It was at Kraepelin's establishment in Munich that he first caught sight of Therese, a nurse who was dressed up in Turkish cos-tume at a fancy-dress party there. Her beauty and serious air struck him, and he soon learned more about her: she had a daughter from a failed marriage and her mother had been Spanish, a detail that espe-cially intrigued him. Declaring his love, he courted her despite her insistence that she lived only for her daughter and her work as a nurse. Her withdrawals from and returns to the relationship created a rhythm of sadness and elation, which confirmed comically one of the psychiatrist's diagnosis of manic depression.

Less than a year later, in the summer of 1908, Pankejeff received the news that his father had died, most probably by suicide, at the age of forty-nine. There is little information about this event, and all we really learn is that Pankejeff harboured an animosity towards his mother regarding her lack of clarity over the will, and that he started painting again. Soon he returned to Munich, ostensibly to see Kraepelin but, as he admits, in fact to see Therese. Pankejeff was tortured by her, and the next year and a half are characterized by his movements both towards and away from what his mother called 'a woman with whom no man could get along'. He would renounce her and then be driven back to her in a painful and seemingly endless oscillation. Tormented by the ques-tion of whether he should marry her or leave her, 'I now considered my condition absolutely hopeless. There was no way out.'

It was now, thanks to a young Russian doctor interested in psy-choanalysis, that Pankejeff would meet Freud. Contrary to all the other authorities, Freud was not opposed to Therese, and in fact encouraged his patient to return to her, even though he asked Pankejeff to wait until analysis had continued for a few months. When he eventually saw her again, he was shocked: since leaving her work as a nurse and opening a *pensione*, she looked terribly run-down, like a 'skeleton'. The thought hit him there and then that her misery must have been caused by him: 'In this moment I determined never again to leave this woman, whom I had caused to suffer so terribly.'

Freud's careful construction focuses on the infantile neurosis. He gave no real account of Pankejeff's analysis with him, but used the material to explore the question of his patient's character change in childhood. The key conceptual issue here was trauma and how it could be revived and reinterpreted at a later date. He also showed how disparate and even contradictory trains of thought could exist side by side in the unconscious. The account of the Wolf Man's childhood is not always easy to follow, but we need to sketch the main ideas before moving on to the diagnostic question.

Freud posited a 'primal scene' of parental coitus, witnessed when Pankejeff was one and a half, although the dating changes slightly during the narrative of the case. Pankejeff wakes up in the afternoon to see his parents engaged in three instances of *coitus a tergo* ('from behind'). About a year later, he sees the servant Gruscha kneeling on the floor cleaning, and this revives the memory of his mother's position in the primal scene. It now establishes the prototype of his 'compulsive' loves: a girl not only kneeling – following the primal scene – but of servant status. In excitement, he pees and is admonished by her with a threat.

Pankejeff's position here is an active one, yet a seduction by his sister, Anna, when he is three and a quarter or three and a half will change this. She plays with his penis, 'at the same time telling him incomprehensible stories' about his Nanya. The English governess, who was to arrive not long after this, became the target of the reproach to his sister for the seduction, in which his position was not active but passive. Although he adopted this position, he now became sadistic and bad-tempered. A couple of months later, he turns his advances to his beloved Nanya, playing with his penis in her presence, yet she unfortunately rejects him too. She tells him that his habit is not good, and that children who masturbated got a 'wound' in that place.

The wish to have his penis touched by her is thus countered by her threat of castration, and it is now that what Freud calls Pankejeff's 'genital organization' breaks down. He cannot process this terrifying idea of a wound, and 'rejects' it. The female genitals are turned into a 'front bottom', yet this psychical operation does not resolve his problems. He remains preoccupied with ideas about castration, despite the apparent absence of dread. With his fears focused around anatomical sexual difference, he is thrown back to his sadistic-anal drives, becoming irritable and aggressive.

How does Freud explain the change from naughtiness and defiance to obsessive piety? The key turning point comes just before his fourth birthday. Now Pankejeff has the wolf dream that will give him his analytic name. 'I dreamed that it was night and that I was lying in bed. Suddenly the window opened of its own accord, and I was terrified to see that some white wolves were sitting on the big walnut tree in front of the window. There were six or seven of them. The wolves were quite white, and looked more like foxes or sheepdogs, for they had big tails like foxes, and they had their ears pricked like dogs when they pay attention to something. In great terror, evidently of being eaten up by the wolves, I screamed and woke up.'

The two aspects of the dream that most haunted him were the absolute stillness and immobility of the wolves and the strained attention with which they looked at him. Freud's complex and detailed analysis of the dream, helped by its many variants which now emerged during the analysis, produced an interpretation: that the dream indexed an early sexual scene, in which the patient's eyes had opened – the window suddenly opening – followed by his own strained attention at something he could see. This was the scene of *coitus a tergo* between the parents. As he was then in a phase of his sexual development when the father was his object, the memory behind the dream would have become especially traumatic, as it gave an image of what the father's sexual satisfaction would consist of. It brought home to him the existence of castration that he had rejected:

to be the father's sexual object, he would have to be a woman. This shock produced the subsequent change in his behaviour.

The longing for satisfaction from his father would mean castration, yet this was unacceptable due to his attachment to his penis. Now a fear of the father became prominent. But the 'primacy' of his genitals did not really take place for Pankejeff: it was not possible for the boy to enter a fully phallic orientation. He didn't want to lose his penis, yet the thought of sexual difference was still too much for him. So, like many boys, he decided in favour of the anus rather than the vagina, which would coexist side by side with the dread of castration. 'This really involved no judgement upon the question of its existence, but it was the same as if it did not exist.' So the result of the dream was less a triumph of any masculine current than a reaction to a feminine and passive one. Freud argued that the Wolf Man was not able to reach a fully masculine position, and any masculinity that he did have consisted only in an anxiety at the threat of being in the passive, feminine place.

Pankejeff was thus faced with a dilemma, while lacking the tools to resolve it: he wanted to be the object for his father, yet could not accept the price this entailed. And it was here that the wolf phobia took on its significance. By creating a terror at the image of the wild beast, he could defend himself against being his father's sexual object. Fear acted here as a barrier, establishing a distance from the dreaded yet longed-for proximity with the father. When the mother now began introducing him to the Bible stories, the phobia could become an obsessional system: piety could absorb the fear present in the phobia and allow new pathways for processing it. He was Christ to his father's God, allowing both an expression of love, masochistic passivity and a questioning of the motifs of sexuality and violence that had so tormented him.

The question of castration was explored by Freud with particular reference to a scene that took place during this period. Some time after hearing a story of a female relation born with six toes, who had one chopped off with an axe, he was playing in the garden near his nurse, carving with his pocketknife in the bark of a walnut tree. 'Suddenly, to my unspeakable terror, I noticed that I had cut through the little finger of my (right or left?) hand, so that it was hanging on by its skin. I felt no pain, but great fear. I did not venture to say anything to my nurse, who was only a few paces distant, but I sank down on the nearest seat and sat there incapable of casting another glance at my finger. At last I calmed down, took a look at the finger, and saw that it was entirely uninjured.' Although this episode might suggest a recognition of the idea of castration, the story of the relation indicating that women have no penis since it has been chopped off, the deeper current, for Freud, foreclosed castration entirely. At one level, Pankejeff abominated the thought of castration while simultaneously accepting it, but, at another level, 'the oldest and deepest', he did not even 'raise the question of the reality of castration'. Not integrated into his mental universe, it literally returned from the outside in the hallucination.

These hypotheses allowed Freud to explain the function of his patient's early difficulties. The whole of the infantile neurosis was his attempt to 'give a decisive answer' to the question of the primal scene. It was about finding and settling on an interpretation. The sexual scene was given an anal interpretation – the hole that the penis entered was the anal aperture – and then, when he was forced to confront the question of the vagina, he decided to stick to the anal theory. He chose the intestine over the vagina, and rejected, Freud argued, the idea of castration.

The question of the reality of the primal scene has divided commentators since the study's publication. Perhaps surprisingly, it took more than fifty years for anyone to notice that *coitus a tergo* would hardly have allowed a child in a cot a crystal-clear view of a woman's anatomy, and that even if we ascribe a manic energy to the father, three bouts of coitus in such a short space of time remain implausible. On the other hand, it is interesting to note that the very first thing Pankejeff tells us in his autobiography is a memory of 'looking through a crack in a fence' at a Russian fair and watching the gypsies 'gesticulating wildly and everyone was loudly shouting at the same time'. 'The scene,' he adds, 'created an impression of indescribable confusion.' Given the place of this image at the start of his memoir, it would be difficult not to see it as a screen memory.

When the analysis with Freud ended in 1914, Pankejeff and Therese married and moved to Russia, until the Revolution forced them to leave the country some four years later. Settling in Vienna, yet now penniless, Pankejeff received financial help from Freud, who organized an annual collection for him for six years, and he would find work in an insurance company, where he remained until his retirement in 1950. An unresolved constipation brought him back to Freud's consulting room from November 1919 to February 1920, and Helene Deutsch remembers in her autobiography how she was forced to give up her analytic hour to let the Wolf Man see Freud. Curiously, the annual collection began at the time that the second analysis finished, setting up a rather Freudian symmetry: the constipation – theorized as the withholding of a gift – was followed by the receipt of money – equated elsewhere by Freud with excrement – as if the patient's symptom was being inverted after he had left the analysis.

Pankejeff was next unwell in 1923, obsessed with a spot on his nose, not long after his mother arrived in Vienna sporting a wart on her own nose. This wart, she told him, had a 'curious habit of coming and going', and she had already consulted several doctors about it. He developed a hypochondriacal fixation on his nose, terrified of a defect in the skin, in the form of a scar, a groove or a hole. In October 1926, he was sent by Freud to Brunswick. She was only twenty-six at the time and in both analysis and supervision with Freud. Brunswick observed that 'nothing whatsoever was visible on the small, snub, typically Russian nose of the patient'. Yet he would continually powder it, then inspect it and remove the powder, trying to 'catch the hole, as it were, in its moment of growth and development'. Would the hole heal? he asked himself endlessly. 'I can't go on living like this,' he would repeat. His life was centred around the little mirror he carried at all times in his pocket, as if his fate depended upon it.

He would soon add his teeth to the hypochondriacal worries, and went from one dentist to another, just as he was now going from one dermatologist to another, and, when he was with Freud, had gone from one tailor to another, never satisfied with the results. He linked his symptom to his sister, who had suffered from pimples, and explained that memories of her had been revived by a recent film, *The*

White Sister, starring Lilian Gish. Although the film contains no reference to spots or warts, it does involve a sister being cheated out of an inheritance and, oddly, opens with an unexplained image of a bare tree, strikingly similar to that drawn by Pankejeff to illustrate his famous dream. As for the dermatological question, Anna had complained that her own nose was red, and they had also shared a game as children revolving around the word 'esanesor', the reversal of 'rose nase', red nose. And just as Pankejeff worried now about his teeth, so Anna's teeth had been eroded by the mercury she had taken in her suicide.

Brunswick described her patient's current illness as 'an unresolved remnant of the transference' to Freud, and notes that there was 'no new material'. The analysis was in fact supervised by Freud, to create a peculiar triangle: she would report her work to her patient's previous analyst, who also happened to be her own analyst. When it came to her clinical strategy, Brunswick was unequivocal: she systematically challenged Pankejeff's belief that he occupied a special place for Freud. The result, as Brunswick acknowledges, was not a cure but an exacerbation of his paranoia.

After the treatment with Brunswick, Pankejeff would see Muriel Gardiner, herself a patient of Brunswick, for a series of conversations that extended over many years. This was not an analysis as such, but Gardiner made herself available as a privileged addressee, and would often help him with practical issues. Life now continued on its 'normal course' with 'no extraordinary events' until disaster struck in 1938. After Hitler's troops had entered Vienna, with her own life savings dramatically devalued and fearful that she might have to provide her family tree to the new powers, Therese committed suicide. Pankejeff had lost 'the only stable structure' in his life. Meetings in Paris and London with Brunswick helped him not to give up, and soon his mother, who had been living in Prague, would move into the Vienna apartment with him. She would remain there until her own death some sixteen years later.

Coping with his wife's suicide was especially difficult, but there was no concerted outbreak of paranoia until August 1951. Pankejeff had strayed into the Russian zone of the city to paint a landscape. Detained by Russian troops for a couple of days, he was eventually released and instructed to return with his other paintings. The next few weeks were a nightmare for him, and he felt as if his reality were collapsing: should he risk going back or not? When he did return, the Russians were not in the least interested and he was dispatched back to his daily life.

Throughout these later years, Pankejeff would complain of impossible situations with women, discussing his problems 'with every person whom he could call in any sense a friend, and with several psychiatrists and psychologists'. He continued a torturous relationship with a woman, Luise, for decades, filled with guilt, ambivalence and doubt. He proposed to her, retracted his offer two days later, yet maintained a thirty-year-long 'love–hate' battle with her, complaining incessantly: 'I can't go on living like this.' Luise herself would endlessly bemoan her illnesses to Pankejeff, with the reproach that, by not marrying her, he was depriving her of the state medical care and share of his pension that were her due. To Gardiner, it was clear that this nightmare was necessary for him. The only woman spared his doubt and ambivalence was an elderly neighbour, Tini, who became a kind of housekeeper and showed a devoted and maternal love to Pankejeff.

Continuing a relatively normal and inconspicuous life, he would be visited by analysts eager to test their theories or to make sure that he was okay. Kurt Eissler would spend time with him every summer, and he would regularly see a Viennese psychiatrist, Wilhelm Solms, who had taken an interest in his case. In the early 1970s, after the publication of his memoirs, he was tracked down by the journalist Karin Obholzer, who later composed a book of their taped conversations. She was quite sceptical of the benefits of psychoanalysis for him, and observed how he would at times answer the phone 'Wolf Man speaking', as well as signing his paintings 'Wolf Man'.

Hospitalized after a heart attack in the summer of 1977, Pankejeff would move to the Vienna Psychiatric Hospital, not for 'psychiatric' reasons, but because Solms, who knew him well, thought he would be more comfortable there. He died in May 1979 at the age of ninety-two. There are 180 hours of taped conversations with Pankejeff in the Library of Congress and thirty boxes, which include correspondence between Pankejeff and Freud, and a second article by Brunswick that will be released in a few years.

—

To take up the diagnostic question, we can turn first of all to the obsessional phenomena in Pankejeff's childhood and later life. Freud links this to his religious phase. He is praying a lot, touching holy pictures and clearly using religion to organize his world. Just as he would be tormented with doubt at this time, brooding and questioning in a perpetual and exhausting internal dialogue, so many years later he would think about Therese in the same way: should he or should he not see her? Should he or should he not give her up? Other choices would generate similar procrastination: should he study law or natural science? Should he return to the same tailor, dentist or dermatologist? These are classic obsessional features, as was the pre-occupation with what Freud called 'undoing': worrying about how he should end a letter, he then posts it, regrets having done so and wishes to undo his action.

Although we might find all these traits in an obsessional neurosis, the broader and more detailed clinical picture suggests that they are part of something else. We should remember here that traits such as these are never definitive criteria to establish diagnosis, since what matters is the underlying structure. We can study this not by classifying traits but by exploring what place these have in the person's world. Although Freud does not seem to question the diagnosis of obsession, he does express one isolated doubt: why, he asks, did Pankejeff show no apparent reaction to his sister's suicide? When he heard the news, Freud writes, 'he felt hardly a trace of grief. He had to force himself to show signs of sorrow, and was able to quite coolly rejoice at having now become sole heir to the property'. Perhaps as a riposte to Freud, Pankejeff's memoirs contain a long section entitled precisely 'Unconscious Mourning'.

Whatever we make of his apparent lack of emotion when describing Anna's death to Freud, it seems to me that Brunswick's descriptions of Pankejeff's state in the 1920s leave little doubt as to the diagnosis: she was clearly dealing with a psychosis, as we can see from the sustained and acute hypochondria, the almost continual recourse to his pocket mirror and the delusional thinking. Other details point in the same direction: the sudden moments of change that he reports have the character of the reversals and shifts we find in psychosis. To take one example, Pankejeff is about to visit Kraepelin in Munich, on his father's advice, and the latter boards the train with him before its departure. As his father speaks in earnest to the doctor accompanying his son, a strange transformation takes place: 'Only now did I become aware of a peculiar change that had come over me in the short time since I had boarded the train. It was as though a good fairy with her magic wand had dispelled my depression and everything connected with it. I was reconciled to life again and I felt in complete agreement and perfect harmony with the world and with myself.' At the precise moment of being with his father who was showing concern about his son, his mood suddenly changes.

Other examples would include his sudden resolution to never leave Therese, and the phenomena of mortification that he would experience in his depressive phase: 'Everything seemed "unreal", to the extent that people seemed to me like wax figures or wound-up marionettes with whom I could not establish contact.' Once we recognize these features of psychosis, we then have to explain what function the obsessive symptoms of his childhood had, and also, why it was that so many later analysts and psychiatrists failed to make the correct diagnosis.

Lacan's views on the case seem to have changed over the years, and, most unusually, he makes a variety of diagnoses. In his first approach, he interprets the childhood neurosis as an attempt to access the symbolic father. After the traumatic scene with Anna, he behaves badly in order to bring punishment on himself, a way of trying to introduce the symbolic dimension. Lacan paid particular attention to the episode of the severed finger. The threat of castration is denied access to Pankejeff's symbolic world, so it returns in the real. The key feature for Lacan was less the image of the cut than the fact that he didn't tell his nurse. Like the young Andy Warhol, who broke his arm at the age of four but for two days told no one, it indicated a short-circuiting of the symbolic relation. The finger episode illustrates how Pankejeff's appeal to the symbolic father failed: unable to metaphorize castration, he was left with the terrifying image of a bodily wound.

We can find this unresolved question of the body in many aspects of the case. Pankejeff would go from one tailor to another, never satisfied with the garments they produced for him. Later, he would go from one dentist or dermatologist to another, always followed by reproach and dissatisfaction. It was as if he were continually appealing to an Other to provide his body with something it lacked, and in each instance the resulting failure left him with a damaged body image. We can guess that beyond these appeals was a basic fault in the construction of his body. Every attempt to find a cure for it would only generate paranoid thoughts.

Pankejeff's body image was often quite literally an open wound for him – like the severed finger he had hallucinated in his childhood – and, in his search for medical or sartorial remedy, he was aiming at both an image that would fit and an image with meaning. As we find in many cases of schizophrenia, the body lacks a fundamental signification. Muriel Gardiner noticed this dimension of an appeal to meaning, observing that 'one feels that he is always trying to understand'. He was perpetually seeking advice from others, talking about his problems incessantly, and we could remember here that in his description of the seduction by Anna, he mentions her telling him 'incomprehensible stories'. The moment of bodily excitation and distress is thus linked to an opacity of meaning: there was something he could not understand.

He would also tell Obholzer that when as a child his penis had become irritated and swollen, he had gone to tell his father. Later, in his teens, a spot had become swollen and red, and, once again, it was to his father that he appealed for meaning. Meeting Obholzer, he told her that 'I must seek advice, I must inquire', and everything in his life had to be checked and discussed with Gardiner, Eissler and Solms, who would meet with him weekly. Even on his deathbed, Pankejeff would still cry out, 'Give me some advice! Help me!' As Obholzer noted, he kept on repeating these same phrases, the same desperate appeals. We could infer that a basic establishment of meaning had never taken place for him. In Lacanian terms, the paternal metaphor had not functioned.

What was left for Pankejeff was the body as a potential hole, and it is here that the images of both his mother and his sister would reappear. Just as his mother had the wart and the sister pimples, so he would obsess about the spot on his own nose. He would complain of exactly their ailments, and his use of a pocket mirror certainly has a feminine quality. Commentators interpret the concern with his teeth as an identification with Freud, who had mouth problems, but it is also and perhaps more fundamentally the symptom of his sister after she swallowed mercury, which, he reported, 'made her teeth fall out'. These bodily torments encircle the idea of the presence and absence of a hole, as if castration for him were not a metaphorical dimension in the symbolic but a real possibility, felt in the body. Where phallic signification was absent, his nose became an unbearable hole for him.

—

So why did generation after generation of the Wolf Man's psycho-analytic friends and helpers get it wrong? In a sense, it was hardly their fault: they met a charming, civilized man, who liked to speak about art, literature and psychoanalysis. He had few visible symptoms, showed no sign of a delusional system and had a high degree of insight into his condition. Muriel Gardiner, who met with Pankejeff for decades, could say that she never saw anything 'abnormal' in his behaviour or conversation between 1927 when she first met him and 1938, when his wife died. 'He made a most orderly and reliable impression, was always appropriately and carefully dressed, was very polite and considerate of others.' Indeed, she says that in all the forty-three years she knew him, 'I myself have seen no evidence of any psychosis.' But why not see the very fact that he seemed to be stable and self-contained as the key to the diagnostic error: what the analysts missed was that it was perhaps *their very attention* that sustained Pankejeff's recovery. In their enthusiasm to understand the case, they left out of the equation the very question of what psychoanalysis meant for him.

The analysts often observed that it was his accessibility to analytic treatment that ruled out psychosis, without realizing that the key to this accessibility was the role that analysis played for him. Gardiner says that, despite Brunswick's account of the case, it was not a real paranoia due to the fact of Pankejeff's recovery: 'I would say that both the insight and the accessibility to analysis contraindicate psychosis.' Nor did she think of his view of himself as Freud's favourite as a delusion of grandeur. She admits, though, that her views are based on Freud's case history and from her later meetings with him, after the 1926 episode. This view was shared by the Wolf Man himself, as he would later say to Obholzer when they discussed diagnosis: 'There is no such thing as a paranoia that comes and goes. It doesn't exist. If someone really suffers from paranoia, it doesn't go away.'

Yet once we distinguish between being psychotic and going psychotic, and recognize the signs of untriggered psychosis, we can understand precisely these vicissitudes. They were directly linked to his own relation to psychoanalysis. Pankejeff, after all, saw himself as part of psychoanalytic history, and Freud called him 'a piece of psychoanalysis'. Helene Deutsch gave him her analytic hour due to his significance for research, calling him 'the source of important discoveries for psychoanalysis', and Anna Freud would refer to him in the introduction to Gardiner's compilation of documents as 'our Wolf Man'. He really belonged to psychoanalysis, and this strange link was no mere figment of his imagination.

Gardiner would send him money, sell his paintings and even forward lecture fees to him. The name he was given by psychoanalysis would likewise become his own: he would not only answer the phone with 'Wolf Man speaking', but would also sign his paintings and even his article, 'Recollections of Sigmund Freud', with 'The Wolf Man'. Was it not this very baptism that solved at some level the problem for Pankejeff of situating himself in relation to the father, a problem that was at the core of his childhood 'neurosis'? Where in his childhood he had been tortured by the task of defining the relation between Christ and God, now a new solution appeared: in his work with Freud, 'I felt myself less as a patient than as a co-worker, the younger comrade of an experienced explorer setting out to study a new, recently discovered land.' It was this place of a 'co-worker' to Freud's 'experienced explorer' that provided him with his stabilizing identification.

We should remember here that the real problem of the primal scene for Pankejeff had been how to position himself. If he wished to be an object for his father, this was hardly bearable after the revival of the sexual scene, since it would entail being a woman, and hence losing his penis. So what was he for his father? Pankejeff must have entertained different configurations of this relation, and Brunswick mentions that his 'favourite fantasy' was Peter the Great and his son Alexis, who was killed by his father despite renouncing his right to succession and fleeing to Vienna. We could see his religious phase as an attempt to reformulate this in another way, ciphering the father–son relation in new terms. Sharing a birthday with Christ, it had seemed that an identification with the Son would allow him to situate his relation with his father. Being Christ to God would be less dangerous than being a woman for his father.

But this was not a successful solution. He was plagued by the violence and sexuality that seemed to characterize the relation between Christ and God. Why, he wondered, had God killed his Son? Did Christ have a 'behind'? He effectively imagined Christ as being like a woman to a man, an equation that must have resonated with exactly those traumatic aspects of the primal scene that the appeal to religion was designed to avoid. But now, rather than the direct and unsymbolizable confrontation of father and son, the place of co-worker established both a distance and a minimum of erotic tension. Rather than father and son, it was explorer and co-worker, working together.

And this explains the triggering of Pankejeff's psychosis in the 1920s. This took place at two specific points: in 1923 and 1926. In the first instance, the analytic community had just become aware of Freud's cancer and it was widely believed that his death was imminent. Pankejeff was shocked to see the crippled image of his former analyst after the operation on his palate in April that year. Paranoia erupted for him at exactly this moment, as Freud's death would mean that Pankejeff would lose the place he had for Freud and psychoanalysis. Now there would be nothing to protect him, and the spectre of a menacing, invasive father became realized. The fact that he masturbated to obscene pictures at this time is significant, as we shall see.

The importance of his place for Freud is clear from his memoirs and the conversations with Obholzer. Pankejeff explains how disturbing it was to be labelled 'paranoid' by Brunswick, prefacing his remark with Freud's opinion of his patient's 'impeccable intelligence'. Freud had praised him as a 'thinker of the first rank', praise that was no doubt irreconcilable with the diagnosis of paranoia. Pankejeff explains that because of this, he literally willed himself out of the nose problem: 'I gathered all my strength. Stopped looking in the mirror, and somehow overcame these ideas.' The effort to preserve the image he believed he had *for Freud* thus effected a cure. Even if Pankejeff's account is inaccurate, the logic is revealing. As he observed to Obholzer, 'Mack made an incorrect diagnosis, and through this incorrect diagnosis she cured me.' The restitution mechanism here was precise: to become the ideal co-worker, rather than the paranoiac.

In 1926 the problem was similar. As Freud engaged in a controversy with his student Otto Rank, the latter published a monograph in which he questioned Freud's interpretation of the famous wolf dream. The arrangement of the wolves on the tree, he noticed, bore an uncanny resemblance to the arrangement of Freud's followers in photos that hung on the wall of his office. Visible from the couch, they would have stirred up Pankejeff's jealousy of Freud's analytic 'children', whom he wanted to both belong to and surpass. Rank argued that Pankejeff was translating his infantile jealousy of his sister, present before him on the 'family tree', on to Freud's followers. Wasn't the wolf dream, then, a retrospective projection into his childhood of his contemporary relation to Freud and psychoanalysis? This part of Rank's interpretation is quite sharp: even if the dream was not based on the photographs, he still sensed the importance of the psychoanalytic gaze to the patient.

Freud was troubled by this criticism and now wrote a letter to the Wolf Man asking him to confirm the dating and content of the dream. It was this simple act that triggered the psychosis, as it put in question the imaginary place that Pankejeff had constructed for himself as the beloved co-worker of Freud. Suddenly, he had become an object of suspicion. As he would write many years later, noticing the coincidence of the worst period of the nose symptom and Freud's letter, 'Could the outbreak of my "paranoia" have had any connection with Professor Freud's questions?' We could hypothesize that this brutal challenge to his imaginary identification opened up the abyss of foreclosure into which the image of the mother and the sister were placed. He was now intensely worried about whether there was a hole in his nose and whether his teeth were eroded, exactly the image of his mother and dying sister.

Brunswick's analytic strategy only made this worse, and she recognized later that it exacerbated his psychosis. As she did her best to lay waste to his self-image as a beloved son of Freud, his paranoia intensified, becoming acutely persecutory: doctors and dentists were trying to disfigure him. Her clinical strategy had been 'a concentrated attempt to undermine the patient's idea of himself as a favourite son'. She questioned his idea that Freud favoured him, even asking him why, if that were the case, he was never seen socially at the Freuds', and reminding him that his was not the only one of Freud's cases to be published.

One might see in her clinical strategy an aspect of her own transference to Freud, as if to show her patient that he was not the beloved child of the master but that she was. It was too hasty to interpret his relation to Freud as a grandiose idea that required deflation rather than as a stabilizing identification that should not have been interpreted but reinforced. Brunswick's technique was thus a big mistake. She aimed to cripple an identification rather than to support one, and it was only with hindsight that she could recognize how 'necessary and protective' his idea of being the beloved co-worker had been.

Despite the error of Brunswick's initial strategy, the analysis was no doubt effective. She situates a key moment of change which was signalled by two dreams. In the first, which followed the escalation of the ideas of persecution, the patient's mother takes holy pictures down from the walls of a room and smashes them. He wonders at this act on the part of his pious mother. This marked 'a turning point', says Brunswick. In the second, he is looking out of a window at a meadow, beyond which is a wood. The landscape is similar to that of the old wolf dream, but it is day and not night. He looks at the branches of a certain tree, admiring the way they are intertwined, and cannot understand why he has not yet painted this landscape.

So there is the tree from the original, terrifying dream, but with no staring wolves. And in the other dream, the gaze of the religious icons is negated through the act of destroying them. The dreams show that the persecutory gaze has been tempered. After the original wolf dream, Brunswick notes, Pankejeff couldn't bear to be looked at fixedly, a detail absent from Freud's account. He would fly into a rage and cry, 'Why do you stare at me like that?' Now, instead of the menacing gaze of the wolves, there is just the screen of the tree and landscape. He is no longer paralysed by the threatening stare of the wolves but, on the contrary, is in the position of someone who looks rather than someone who is looked at. And the question of painting suggests that he will *do something* with what he sees. He is no longer just an object.

Brunswick points out, with a real eye for clinical detail, that Pankejeff's recovery is shown now by his ability to read novels, which, as he explained, meant being able 'to identify himself' again with characters. Why? Since, he said, a character is in the power of another – the author – reminding us of the very structure of his childhood question: what is the relation between father and son? And at the same time, this new possibility of being able to identify with characters testifies to a new capacity for imaginary identification, which was blocked as his body image became reduced to that of the sick and dying woman. He could now inhabit other images, and so read fiction. As Brunswick says, 'From this moment on, he was well.'

When Brunswick saw Pankejeff two years after this period of analysis, there was 'no trace of psychosis', and the next triggering would only take place some twenty years later, when, in 1951, he inadvertently strayed into the Russian zone. Captivated by a landscape with a deserted building that recalled his childhood, he began painting, unaware that it was the anniversary of his sister's suicide. The house, he added later, 'really consisted only of a wall, in which one saw black holes instead of windows'. Russian soldiers apprehended him and were suspicious, as the building was in fact a military post. He was detained and questioned for two and a half days, offering to bring his other works to prove that painting was his 'avocation'. The officer told Pankejeff to come back in twenty-one days, bringing his landscapes and his papers.

Now, the sense of persecution became acute: he thought that people were watching him and talking about him, and he experienced the same intense panic he had in 1926 with the nose paranoia. These three weeks were, he says, 'the most terrible nightmare'. He couldn't believe that he, a Russian, would stray into the dangerous Russian zone to paint. Should he or should he not return as instructed? Finally, he went back to the Russian post, yet no one was particularly interested: the officer who had asked him to report back was not even there. He chatted with another officer about painting, and was then casually discharged. It was only after many months that he could believe that there was no longer any danger.

During the period between his capture and his return to see the Russians, Pankejeff was overwhelmed by despair and suicidal thoughts. But what was it that he did immediately afterwards and which seems to have restored his equilibrium? He wrote an article with the title 'My Recollections of Sigmund Freud' in which he basically describes who he was *for* Freud. The pure anxiety of not knowing what he was for the Russian officer – a spy or an innocent painter – was resolved by the articulation of what he was for Freud. Doing so, he restituted his imaginary place as a 'piece of psychoanalysis', the favoured co-worker. Gardiner was no doubt right in sensing that this text helped to 'lift him out of depression'. And hence the subsequent stabilization.

The lack of any theory of restitution mechanisms is why generation after generation of the Wolf Man's interlocutors missed his psychosis. They looked for the noisy, attention-grabbing symptoms rather than the quiet signs of a psychosis that was, for most of the time, stable. In a sense, they are hardly to blame for this, since it was their very act of showing interest in him that helped him to maintain his equilibrium.

Their focus sustained his conception of his role in psychoanalytic history, which gave him his stabilization. Even a perceptive clinician like Gardiner failed to recognize the diagnosis. Familiar as she was with Brunswick's paper, she assumed that the idea of being 'the favourite son' of Freud would had to have been a delusion of grandeur to make Pankejeff psychotic. Since it wasn't, and since he was accessible to analysis, she ruled out the diagnosis. An acknowledgement that psychosis does not necessitate either delusions of grandeur or inaccessibility to treatment might have encouraged her to modify her view. A stabilizing imaginary identification, after all, is not the same thing as a delusional identification.

This stabilization had a certain enduring quality for Pankejeff. Until the end of his life he saw himself as a piece of psychoanalysis. Even in the 1970s he was meeting with Eissler and other analysts and psychiatrists, going over his troubles and evoking what he meant for psychoanalysis. But, as we have seen in previous chapters, there tends to be more than one element at play in a stabilization. We could conjecture that if the identification with a co-worker was what gave him his most robust sense of identity, there were nonetheless two other aspects of his life that allowed him to survive: a complaint about a woman and the practice of painting.

With Gardiner and Obholzer, Pankejeff would talk continuously about the opposite sex. How should he handle Therese? What sort of mess had he got himself into? How could she have killed herself? Decades later, in the conversations with Obholzer, the litany of complaints continues: how could Luise exploit him so? What would allow him to escape her? How much money should he give her? Throughout his discourse, he says again and again that women have ruined his life. With Obholzer, he blames a fixation on Anna: 'The sister complex ruined my life,' he says, and can speak about little else than the impossible Luise. In the end, it is difficult to avoid the conclusion that there was something necessary for Pankejeff in the act of complaint, as if a Woman had become his symptom.

We can see a split between the woman as symptom, hated and loved, yet ultimately persecuting him, and the kinder, benevolent woman, embodied by Gardiner, the housekeeper Tini and, at the end of his life, by Sister Anni. Anni was a private nurse, paid for by funds from Gardiner and the Freud Archives, who spent several days a week with him. According to Gardiner, there was 'no ambivalence' here, just as there had not been with Tini, whose place Anni apparently filled. These women were devoted to him, and he accepted their help with gratitude and recognition, as if they allowed him to escape the 'love–hate' of his relation with Luise. Curiously, the text written by Gardiner after his death reflects exactly this split. It is essentially a subtle demonization of Karin Obholzer, as if to separate bad Obholzer and kind Gardiner.

But why, we could ask, was it so important for Pankejeff to maintain an 'impossible' woman around him? The complaint itself perhaps involves a trait that he took from his mother. As a child, he had overheard her say, 'I can't go on living like this,' and these words echo throughout his discourse about women. She had also once remarked that Therese was 'a woman with whom no man could get along', and this sense of impossibility seems to have left its mark on all his later relations with women, with the exception of Tini and Sister Anni. It is clear that Luise was in the place of a persecutor for Pankejeff. 'I cannot describe to you how awful this woman is,' he tells Obholzer repeatedly. After he had agreed to marry her and then reconsidered, she would make incessant financial demands on him, reproaching him continuously for his neglect. He gave her a large part of his pension as well as other significant sums of money, against everyone's advice. Although desperate to pay her off, remaining entangled with her seems to have been more important to him than any real separation. Gardiner offered to help him move to Switzerland or France to escape her, yet he did not take up the offer: the unbearable situation was, in fact, somehow well suited to him.

After his retirement in 1950, it is clear that Pankejeff faced severe depressive feelings and a growing sense of despair, and we can guess that it was the torturous embroilment with women that allowed him to fill this void, as if the mother's sentence 'I can't go on living like this' was exactly what, in fact, allowed him to live. With Obholzer, his complaint that 'the sister complex ruined my entire life' can be understood as less a new interpretation of his past than simply another form of this effort to make Woman his symptom, the cause of his suffering. Obholzer was right to describe Luise as a 'fixed point' for him, and perhaps the function of this point was to allow a certain stability.

Identifying a woman as the bane of his existence may well have been vital for Pankejeff for a simple reason. If he could localize the invasive libido outside himself, he would be able to reduce the suffering and perplexity he felt at the level of his body and his body image. But it is also interesting to note here that Pankejeff would tell Obholzer that his father had restricted his inheritance until the age of twenty-eight since he feared that his son would fall into the hands of an unscrupulous woman, 'a robber'. He believed that a mistress of his father's had played precisely this role, even having a box at the theatre paid for by him. Was it an accident, then, that all he could complain about to his later interlocutors was how Luise was stripping him bare, taking all his money?

This suggests a different perspective on Pankejeff's complaint. Couldn't we see it as in fact a way of maintaining the incest barrier? He had elevated the father's concern about a 'robber' woman to a kind of ever-present worry: it involved a prohibition on women, yet at the same time offered the only template of the relation 'man–woman' that was available to him. It was a relation that also carried the maternal stamp of impossibility, and allowed him to move away from the place of being an object for his father which Freud believed had been so central for him in his childhood. We see this echoed in a particularly odd moment of transition in the interviews with Obholzer. At one point, he is describing how a Russian physician's son was taken off to act as an interpreter by the Russian troops, and then suddenly says, 'You see, one has gone through all sorts of things and then one is faced with an enigma with such a stupid woman and doesn't know what to do.' The discourse about Luise immediately takes up the question of a relation between father and son.

If the complaints about a woman seem to become more and more present as his analysis with Freud receded into the past, there was one other element that had a steady, pacifying effect for Pankejeff: the practice of painting. We can remember the detail from the dream he had with Brunswick, where he wonders why he has not yet painted the scene he sees before him. The painted image thus comes into a place where there had been horror. The gaze of the wolves is gone, and now he is a subject who paints rather than an object that is stared at. Painting was a constant theme in his correspondence with Gardiner, and she comments that in his periods of ill health, almost every single letter contained a lament that he wasn't able to paint. Whether he was painting became a kind of barometer of his psychical life. Indeed, just after describing his wife's death, he writes that 'it took a full year and a half before I could begin to paint again', as if this were the true measure of his recovery.

Painting seems to have had two functions for Pankejeff: to temper the invasive gaze directed towards him and to absorb and channel the libido. He would describe to Gardiner how 'I was so often enchanted by a landscape that I sometimes felt an irresistible urge to paint this landscape as soon as possible.' The note of urgency suggests the drive, and we know that when he heard news of Freud's cancer, he began masturbating to obscene images. The image is appealed to here at the point of greatest unrest and anxiety, like a screen. When he reports that Luise once reproached him for showing her paintings after sex, we can wonder whether this did not share the same compulsive quality, as if he had to introduce an image to mediate between them.

Prior to the key turning point in the analysis with Brunswick, another of his wolf dreams shows the place of this image. In one part of this dream, a pack of grey wolves is behind a wall, crowding against a door and rushing up and down. Their eyes gleam, and it is evident that they want to attack Pankejeff, his wife and another woman. He is terrified, fearing that they will succeed in breaking through the wall. This is followed by the dream in which his mother smashes the holy images, and we could perhaps see the wall as representing the image itself. It is this that protects him from the menacing presence of the wolves, which, as both Freud and Brunswick suggested, index the invasive aspect of the father.

If painting, a complaint about a woman and an identification with the co-worker to Freud's seasoned explorer allowed Pankejeff to lead a relatively normal life, we should not see his case as a success of psychoanalysis. It was less the interpretations of his analysts that helped him than how he was able to use the place that they put him in. If psychoanalysis alienated him, turning him into a kind of mascot, he put this alienation to use, through the identification that he forged around it. It was an alienation that enabled him to build his life, even if we might wonder what other paths might have been open to him had his analysts adopted different strategies and been more sensitive to the diagnostic questions that we have discussed.

When his memoirs were edited and published by Muriel Gardiner in 1971, their title certainly reflected this alienation: *The Wolf-Man by the Wolf-Man*. The curious repetition was no tautology, as it was the imprint of psychoanalysis that allowed Pankejeff to find an identity. These were the recollections not of Sergei Pankejeff but of the Wolf Man. After his death, when Gardiner prepared the French edition, she chose a different title: *L'Homme aux loups par ses psychanalystes et par lui-même* ('The Wolf-Man by his psychoanalysts and by himself'). This new formula, perhaps, made the process of refraction even clearer: the book was first of all by 'his psychoanalysts', and only secondly by 'himself', as if he were essentially a by-product of psychoanalysis.

Critics often comment that despite a lifetime of treatment, Pankejeff suffered a great deal and was ill served by those who endeavoured to help him. They assume that he should have become more autonomous, suffering less and distancing himself from the world of psychoanalysis. Yet, as we have argued, perhaps the form that his suffering took had a part to play in the equilibrium that he managed to maintain, as did his relation to analysis. As for the question of autonomy, Pankejeff was dependent on symptoms in the same way that we all are. Although some symptoms prevent us from living, others allow us to live. These may involve solitary activities just as they may involve a link to other people. For Pankejeff, there was always a call to those around him, from his earliest childhood to his last days in hospital. Just as he had sought a response first from his family and then from his analytic interlocutors, his dying words to Sister Anni condensed this perpetual and desperate appeal to the Other: 'Don't leave me.'

Madness and normality are no better equated than in the case of Britain's most prolific murderer. Harold Shipman went about his business for decades before arousing suspicion, and yet his good citizenship and modest life were combined with unbridled homicide. Although there is some disagreement about the number of his victims, he killed at least 250 people, and very probably many more. Despite this unparalleled and extraordinary murderous passion, in Shipman's case there was no violent outburst, no socially inappropriate behaviour, no noisy delusional system that he felt compelled to broadcast. In fact, when Shipman was interviewed by psychiatrists, they found no indications of 'mental illness'.

Rather than taking this verdict seriously, why not recognize once again that madness must not be identified with its visible manifestations. The signs of madness may be – and usually are – highly discreet. Madness and normal life are compatible rather than opposed in most – though not all – instances. Shipman's story is fascinating not only as a case study in quiet madness, but also in what it shows us about how society responds to questions of madness and murder. When I organized a conference a few years ago on Shipman, I received letters from elderly people who insisted that, if Shipman were alive and practising, they would have no hesitation in seeking him out as their GP. This was well after the trial and Dame Janet Smith's Shipman Inquiry, which had found him guilty of more than 200 murders.

Media responses, for their part, mostly focused on the inner evil of this strange doctor. In the absence of a serious theory to explain his actions, there was an appeal to an almost religious notion of pure evil. How could a human being do such things? What motive could he possibly have had? The lack of any ready explanation meant that the aetiology became invisible and intangible: a kind of wicked force within him. Curiously, this is exactly the kind of thinking that we sometimes find in the explanations that murderers give of their actions: the homicidal act, they say, aimed at the evil at the heart of their victim. The 'mad' and the 'sane' share here a delusional idea: that there is a mysterious and malign inner agency that must be destroyed. For the killer, in the victim; for society, in the killer.

Professional opinion was not much of an improvement. The psychiatrist Richard Badcock, who interviewed Shipman prior to his trial, spoke of 'a huge intellectual buzz from murders' and 'a power-based replacement for ejaculation'. The only psychiatrist to interview him since his arrest suggested that Shipman suffered 'a spiritual disorder that transcends the conventional diagnoses of medicine, psychology and religion', concluding, 'It's about evil.' And the Detective Chief Superintendent who dealt with the case summed up Shipman with the words 'evil just oozed out of him'.

Reading through the expert opinions on the case in the Shipman Inquiry is also a troubling experience. Not only do they show a failure to go deeper into the material, but they testify to a sad stagnation of psychiatric knowledge. Despite more than 270,000 pages of evidence and a budget of over £20 million, the conclusions reveal little more than what one would garner from an Internet questionnaire: Shipman is deemed to suffer from 'an addictive personality', 'poor self-esteem', 'a corruptible conscience', 'a rigid and obsessive personality' and 'a deep-seated need to control people and events'; in fact, qualities that probably characterize many of us. They tell us absolutely nothing about him or why he committed his crimes, and it is all the more remarkable to find that the reports could detect no sign of psychosis. The Shipman Inquiry psychiatrists specify that 'he could be psychotic', although they stress that there is 'no evidence that he is', despite the vast amount of material at their disposal. Several other psychiatrists who have commented on the case also state categorically that Shipman was not psychotic, although he may have had a 'personality disorder'. In a summary of the expert opinions, Brian Whittle writes that Shipman 'was certainly not psychotically ill' and that psychosis without medication 'is an erratic and ungovernable state'. A psychotic subject, he assumes, 'would be showing signs of their illness in other areas of their lives'. But this is exactly the view that we have contested and which is essential to recognize in order to make sense of the Shipman case.

Hopefully a more balanced interpretation can encourage us to complicate such views and try to understand how this trail of homicides could have taken place. Shipman never said why he did it, or even that he did it, and many of the relatives of his victims felt that his suicide in January 2004 robbed them of answers. For a time, Shipman came to embody this very idea of a deprivation of meaning, and hence perhaps the appeal to far-fetched notions of pure evil. There was the expectation that one day he would reveal everything, some motive or cause that would bring 'closure' to the case. Newspaper cartoons portraying him as the grim reaper suggested, on the contrary, that like death itself, no explanation would ever remove the enigma and opacity that surrounds the departure from life.

The biographical information on Shipman is not as voluminous as the many biographies might suggest. There are testimonials from acquaintances, colleagues and cellmates, a few police interviews, and the details of the murders themselves from police reports and Janet Smith's Shipman Inquiry. The parts of his correspondence that have been made public can tell us something, but what we don't have is the direct speech of Shipman himself or his close family: nothing to explain, justify or describe what took place.

This would of course make the investigator's task easier, but as well as trying to shed light on the question of why Shipman did it, it is important to use the case to make us think about what more we would need to know to come to a deeper understanding. What questions should we ask in order to learn more? Were the murders a sign of his madness or, in fact, a desperate attempt to cope with situations that had blocked his everyday, normal madness from functioning?

—

Shipman was born in January 1946, the second child of lorry driver Harold Shipman and his wife, Vera, the illegitimate daughter of a lace clipper. Not much is known about his childhood, spent on a Nottingham housing estate, although school photos show him smartly dressed with a bow tie, in contrast to his classmates. He was not especially social, it seems, yet was by no means isolated from his peers. Several accounts describe a special closeness with his mother, a 'mental telepathy' between them, with Harold pampered and doted on, sneaking into the parental bed with her if his father was out at work or in the pub. Vera, it is claimed, had high hopes for her boy, and at eleven he won a scholarship to High Pavement Grammar School, where he worked diligently although without achieving any notable academic success.

Soon after Shipman's seventeenth birthday, Vera was diagnosed with lung cancer, and would die less than six months later at the age of forty-three. During these months, their doctor regularly visited the house to administer injections of morphine, and Vera and her son would apparently spend long hours talking. Shattered by the death, he would have to stay an extra year at High Pavement to retake his A levels, before starting medicine at Leeds University.

Shipman would meet his future wife, Primrose, on the bus on his way to lectures, and it was not long before she was pregnant. This was, it seems, a scandal for both sets of parents, creating a rift that would never heal. They married in November 1966, with none of the blessings that a young couple might expect from their families, and their first child, a daughter, was born some three months later. They would have three more children, all boys, born in 1971, 1979 and 1982.

After his graduation, Shipman started work at Pontefract General Infirmary, where he remained for four years until 1974. He took a diploma in child health and in obstetrics and gynaecology, and it was probably at Pontefract that he began his first serious drug use. Shipman would use pethidine, a drug often used to relieve labour pains or as a painkiller before going on to morphine, and he would inject himself regularly with the drug.

In April 1974 he took a new job at the Abraham Ormerod Medical Centre in nearby Todmorden, and he would later claim that his pethidine use started that May due to a depression triggered by opposition from senior staff to his suggestions as to how to improve the practice. Nonetheless, he was swiftly promoted, moving from assistant to principal GP, and his hard work and dedication earned him the admiration of both patients and colleagues. 'He was a saint, a really good person,' one of his Todmorden patients recalled. He became a respected member of the local Canal Society, helping to clean and preserve the waterway that ran through the Todmorden valley. And yet, at the same time, he had started killing. Although there may have been prior homicides at Pontefract, it seems certain that it was at Todmorden in the mid-1970s that his pattern of murder was established.

It was in the summer of 1975 that Shipman's colleagues first began to notice that something was wrong. He had blacked out at the surgery, and then at home, which they interpreted first as the effect of 'stress'. Shipman's massive pethidine injections had, in fact, been increasing, and his arms and legs were covered in the signs of intravenous drug use. He told his colleagues that it was epilepsy, but a local chemist had noticed the huge quantities of pethidine that he was prescribing, often forging the relevant documents. Shipman had already got through the hoop of an interview with a Home Office drugs inspector in July, yet the chemist was convinced that the prescriptions were not legitimate. The surgery partners confronted Shipman, who admitted his drug use, and he was removed from the practice.

A police investigation followed, and Shipman again admitted his addiction to pethidine and agreed to seek help. He stayed at the Retreat in York, coming off pethidine, it seems, while remaining refractory to the psychiatric interviews. One report claims that he admitted to having suffered nightmares since his mother's death, yet no detail is given. In early 1976, he pleaded guilty to having stolen drugs and forged prescriptions, yet his psychiatrists advised that he be allowed to continue his medical practice. 'It would be catastrophic,' wrote one psychiatrist to the court, 'if he were not to be allowed to continue.'

The Shipman family would now move to County Durham, where he continued low-key medical research and liaison work, before September 1977, when he got a job with Donneybrook House practice in Hyde, near Manchester. Enthusiastic, committed and hard-working, Shipman once again earned the respect of patients and colleagues. As well as putting in long hours, he joined the St John Ambulance brigade, teaching first aid to volunteers and training childminders. An assiduous attendee of all medical Continuing Professional Development (CPD) events, he barely missed a single meeting at Manchester and Liverpool universities and at Tameside General Hospital. He began killing in his new practice not long after arriving in Hyde.

His victims were elderly men and women, often suffering from chronic illnesses or recently bereaved. The Hyde killings began slowly, sometimes with only one per month, yet they would escalate during the 1980s, with Shipman carrying out four or five murders per month, clustering in the period from December to February. There would be petty thefts from the scenes of the homicides, involving objects of little value or apparent use.

Just as at Todmorden, Shipman had ideas on how to improve the practice, and would resent any obstacle to their implementation. This interest in reforming healthcare allowed him to give a number of interviews to print and TV journalists: he said some very sensible things about 'mental illness' on *World in Action* and was quoted in the medical press on the issue of addiction and alcoholism in the profession. He assumed enthusiastically a position of medical knowledge and was eager to broadcast it.

In January 1985 Shipman's father died of a heart attack. Pauline, Shipman's sister, had been living with her father and after his death she sold the house and moved in with their younger brother, Clive. The will stated that the house would be left to her, and it seems as if Harold had been excluded entirely from the legacy. At work, Shipman appeared to be more withdrawn, and partners and staff at the practice sensed something was awry: almost always a perfect doctor with his patients, he could be arrogant, touchy and controlling with staff.

No doubt this was one of the reasons why, after nearly fourteen years at Donnybrook, he was to set up his own surgery, taking some staff with him to found the Market Practice. Here he could follow his own philosophy of healthcare relatively unchecked: to prescribe the drugs he chose himself, to avoid unnecessary hospital admissions and to devote individual, unique care to his patients. The local Health Authority was impressed, and the practice flourished. He responded promptly to house calls and scheduled appointments in record time. When the Health Authority asked him why he didn't have a nurse on call on the premises, Shipman replied that he would do all the work himself. He really was in the place of the one and only Doctor.

Even the sign on the wall of the building declared 'Dr Shipman's Surgery Entrance', as if it were not simply medicine that was being dispensed but Dr Shipman's medicine. The killing spree starts to escalate now in 1992/3. He had a list of around 3,100 patients, and the homicides would continue until his arrest in 1998, reaching a peak in 1995. The later investigation produced an image of Shipman's murder scenes as a kind of *tableau vivant*. He would visit an elderly patient who usually lived alone. This would be reported in his notes as a routine visit or due to an unsolicited call. He would inject his victim with the powerful opiate diamorphine, which would cause death usually within a few minutes. He'd claim that they were either dead when he arrived or that they died after his visit. The body would be found fully dressed, usually in an armchair. Explaining how he gained entrance to the property, he would often say that they had left the door on the latch. At times, he would then go with a neighbour who had a key to the property to 'discover' the body. He would also often change his notes, indicating that the death was expected, either before or after the killing. The most common fabrication in his notes was to invent a history of heart problems. This method is interesting due to its consistency. We can observe that it not only involves a murder, but also, with some frequency, staging the moment of discovery of a body and being there at the scene.

As the death toll rose, a local undertaker became suspicious at the remarkable fact that it was always Shipman who was handling the deaths of local patients. She spoke to a Hyde GP, who in turn reported this to the coroner, who then informed the police. Yet lack of evidence, combined with an administrative error that resulted in false death-rate figures, prevented deeper investigation, and after a few interviews with another undertaker, they dropped the case in March 1998. It is likely now that Shipman knew that he was under suspicion, and this may have had an effect on the subsequent events.

The discovery of Shipman's murders would come about through a series of bizarre blunders, which has suggested to many commentators that he sought his own apprehension. Shipman had given a blood test to Kathleen Grundy, a former mayoress of Hyde, in June 1998, and asked her to sign some papers relating to it at his surgery. He then asked another patient to sign a folded document, which appeared to be some sort of medical form: in fact, it was Kathleen Grundy's will, which now had the witness signature it required. Shipman had typed out the will himself, leaving all her worldly goods to her doctor, 'to reward him for all the care he has given me and the people of Hyde'. It was, by any standards, a feeble attempt at forgery: it was poorly typed, with missing letters and even a fingerprint.

That same day, Shipman posted the forged will to a local firm of solicitors, together with a letter signed 'K. Grundy', which stated: 'I wish Dr Shipman to benefit by having my estate but if he dies or cannot accept it, then the estate goes to my daughter.' The firm, however, had never acted for Grundy, and could make little sense of the receipt. The next day, Shipman visited Grundy and administered the lethal injection of diamorphine that had become his trademark. Waiting one more day, he falsified her medical records, backdating notes and suggesting that she had been a drug addict: later he could say that he suspected a heroin or pethidine addiction. The notes say, 'Denies taking any drugs other than for irritable bowel syndrome,' and, later, 'Denies everything.'

Barely a week after this, Shipman sent another letter to the solicitors to inform them of Grundy's death, this time signed by 'S' or 'F. Smith', 'a friend' who had typed out the will yet who gave no contact address. The solicitors contacted Grundy's daughter, who was a solicitor herself and already possessed a copy of her mother's genuine will, which left the estate to her alone. She knew instantly that the second will was forged, and called the police. Grundy's body was exhumed and, anticipating the results, Shipman added more references to her alleged drug addiction to his records. When the presence of morphine was found in the body, there had to be a good explanation for it.

The scope and scale of Shipman's killing would quickly come to light. As the investigation continued, the people of Hyde sent cards and letters of support to the beloved doctor's surgery. Few could believe the allegations, yet as relatives of the deceased checked Shipman's accounts of their loved ones' deaths, discrepancies emerged.

Although he had claimed, in some cases, that he had visited the deceased's home after being called out, telephone records contradicted this. Crucially, the hard disc of Shipman's computer also conserved details of the dating of additions to patients' notes after their deaths, a fact that apparently he had not anticipated.

He had been arrogant with the police, identifying once again with the unique authority on medicine and telling them that they just didn't understand medical matters. Yet the hard disc records showed that he had fabricated medical histories going back years, sometimes all on the same day, sometimes just hours before killing his victims. Further exhumations proved Shipman's guilt beyond any doubt. He was convicted of murder and sentenced to spend the remainder of his days in prison.

Incarcerated, he was still the doctor, offering medical advice to both inmates and staff: surgery took place on Saturdays in his cell. He was to be addressed as 'Doctor', and Shipman wrote several times from prison to his local MP with concerns about the quality of care received by his patients during his absence. In particular, he was worried that the locum replacing him would be using a restricted list of drugs, rather than his own more expensive and carefully chosen selection. This concern with the right medication was often echoed in his advice to inmates, whom he would tell which drugs to ask the prison doctors for. Otherwise, Shipman spent his time translating *Harry Potter* into Braille.

It was catastrophic for Shipman when he was moved from his usual cell to a new location next to the hospital wing, as it deprived him of his prison surgery. He made a first suicide attempt, trying to hang himself with a piece of towelling, before finally ending his days by hanging on 13 January 2004. A copy of Shakespeare's *Henry IV* lay on the bedside table beneath his body.

So what can the biographical information tell us about Shipman's homicides? What clues can point us in the right direction? And why the strange *tableau vivant* that he had to create time after time with his victims? The only real psychological theory that has been proposed about Shipman is that he was fixated to the trauma of his mother's death. In the months preceding this, the young Harold would watch as she received her daily injections of morphine to ease her suffering. She died in a morphine-induced coma with her two sons, Harold and Clive, at her bedside, after the family doctor had administered a final, fatal dose of the drug. Almost immediately afterwards Shipman left the house, and ran for ten miles in the pouring rain through the streets of Nottingham and surrounding countryside.

Watching the doctor administer morphine to her, he had decided to become a doctor, and the agony of her death condemned him to repeat this scene again and again with his victims. Now, this explanation seems attractive, fusing as it does the image of a saviour and a killer. This, after all, was exactly the role that Shipman would play in his career as doctor and murderer. There is certainly a contradiction in this figure of a doctor who administers a lethal dose of morphine: the one who is supposed to save life is here also the one who takes life away. Was Shipman fixed to this unbearable moment at the juncture of life and death?

The problem with this account is that the facts are largely fictional, gathered from hearsay and from people who were probably not close to the family at all. We don't really know if Harold attended his dying mother – one account specifically says he didn't – or whether he witnessed the injections, just as we don't know any of the medical details of her illness and death. All we actually know is that one of Shipman's patients reported that he would often speak about his mother, and that he had told her husband that he had witnessed her suffering from cancer when he was seventeen. There are simply no other details, and so the construction of the story of his presence at the moment of death, the injections and so forth is purely mythical.

On the other hand, the first concerted burst of killing occurs on 21 January 1975, when, a week after his birthday, he murders three patients all in the space of a single day: Lily Crossley, Elizabeth Pearce and Robert Lingard. They were all dead within half an hour of the doctor's visits. It is difficult not to associate this with a date that must have meant something to Shipman: the diagnosis of his mother's cancer, after all, had been just a few days after his seventeenth birthday and, crucially, she had died on 21 June. The convergence of dates, we might guess, had an effect on Shipman. We could also remember here that he would take his own life on the eve of his fifty-eighth birthday. A link between this date, the number 21 and Vera's death would thus seem possible, if not likely.

But we need to think about what kind of link this is. If the mother was so important, why didn't Shipman kill younger women? It would be hasty to assume that the elderly people he killed must have evoked parental figures, especially given that his mother had been only forty-three when she died. Why did he kill men as well? And why the complicated modus operandi, why the elaborate staging of these deaths? There must be some indication of what he was really aiming at, what he was seeking to achieve or attain through these repetitive scenarios. The fact that he was so often present at the death of his patients had aroused the early suspicions of a colleague and undertakers, as it was unusual for a doctor to be there at that moment. If the *tableaux* would make him present at a death, we could in fact guess that he had *not* been present at the moment of his mother's death. And if he had a special interest in killing the recently bereaved, widows in particular, we could ask what experiences he might have had of the bereaved in his own childhood. The elderly were certainly significant for him, and we could hope to learn more about his grandparents, their deaths and the effects of these deaths in the family.

The question of Vera's death is of course significant, but we would need to think about how it functioned for him. A simplistic view would see the bereavement as a major cause of 'stress', but a more complex perspective would consider the registers of the real, the imaginary and the symbolic. An element from one register can return at moments of discontinuity in another register: an image, a desperate urge or a bodily agitation, for example, might emerge when the symbolic register is suddenly accentuated or put into question. This is exactly what we saw with the Wolf Man: when the imaginary identification that stabilized him was challenged, the image of his sick mother and dying sister were polarized, returning to invade his body. It is less a question, then, of fixation to a trauma than of asking why the elements of the trauma would reappear in his life when they did. Was it fixation to his mother's death or the failure to have a symbolic mechanism that could mediate not only this, but also other, disparate parts of his experience?

The timing of the homicides becomes especially important here. Why was his staging of an injection and a death to happen when it did? He could, after all, have become a drug addict in his youth, allowing a convergence of the image of an injection and a pull towards his dead mother. There is never any exacerbation of the murders in June, the month in which Vera had died, and the anniversaries do not seem to have been marked for him with symptomatic behaviour, although, as we have seen, the number 21 must have carried a certain weight for him. If the injections embodied for him the image of his mother's relief from pain, would he have aimed to recreate them at the moments of his own distress? There is a difference between the traumatic repetition of some event and the convocation of this event to other, perhaps different, points of symbolic fracture.

In order to explore these questions, we would need to explain the real mystery of the Shipman case: the blank period, from December 1989 to January 1992, when it seems as if his killing more or less ceased. If we can understand why he didn't kill in that period, presumably we will then be better able to understand why he did kill before and after that time. The Shipman Inquiry says that these periods of interruption were 'dictated by his fear of detection and his desire for self-preservation'. But this is not so sure. Although the murders just before this period involve near detection, this had occurred at other times and did not always result in a respite from the homicides. Perhaps another feature that did matter here was the fact that in some of these cases the victim didn't die soon enough. It may have been less a question of almost being caught than of the victim almost not dying, and thus remaining in the limbo between life and death. Similarly, we could note that the lull coincides with Shipman reaching the age at which his mother had died, and the start of his plans to open his own practice: was it an accident that the building he chose, after much careful searching, was number 21 Market Street?

We can remember here that for the many years when he was

injecting himself with pethidine, he was not killing other people. And then, when the killing started, his method of choice was lethal injection. There is thus a certain symmetry present in the two practices: a person is injected, and we could hypothesize that this revolves around a mirror identification, an imaginary stasis. He is in the place of the one injecting or the one injected, or both. If we were to look for a continuity here, it would lie in this identification: to be injected. And so, perhaps, in injecting his patients, he was injecting an image of himself. His own image had become confused with that of his usually elderly patients. He was them.

And chronologically, when Shipman stopped injecting himself, he started injecting others. Interestingly, when he was held in a police cell after his arrest, and so unable to inject anyone, he refused food, as if it might contain poison, only taking tea and coffee from a machine he knew everyone used: no longer injecting his victims, he feared the toxic substance would be surreptitiously introduced into his own body. What he had done to them, he feared would be done to him. This imaginary confusion is apparent in other details of the case. We know, for example, that Shipman lied. He would fabricate details of medical histories, and some of these, it seems, cannot be explained simply in terms of covering his tracks. Perhaps the lies he concocted can give us clues to his motives: a lie, after all, always contains some truth unacknowledged by the subject. The remarks about Grundy's suspected heroin and pethidine addiction, for example, clearly do not refer to her: when he wrote that she 'Denies everything', who could this have referred to if not himself?

—

So what had sustained Shipman during these years? What allowed him to lead an apparently normal life? The answer to this question may lie in an ideal identification, as it so often does in psychosis. The person identifies with a particular social role or function, which gives them an identity, an anchoring point. In February 1976, after Shipman pleaded guilty to forging prescriptions and stealing drugs, psychiatrists recommended that he be permitted to pursue his work as a GP. Hugo Milne wrote to the court: 'It would be to his advantage if he were allowed to continue to practise. Conversely, it would be catastrophic if he were not allowed to continue.' Rather than seeing this advice as a tragic misunderstanding, it testifies to a recognition of what was crucial to keep Shipman going. He had to be a doctor with patients.

The ideal identification for Shipman was medical: to be 'the Doctor', and even his wife, Primrose, would have to address him at times in those terms. Shipman was like someone impersonating a doctor, with the difference that he really was one. 'I am a good doctor,' he would often say, 'I have all the qualifications from Leeds Medical School.' The identifications in psychosis – whether stabilizing or not – often involve the place of an exception: the person is the Only One to know, to care, to save. Shipman's behaviour is indicative of this: at his CPD meetings, he would take the place of the only real expert on medical procedure and knowledge, and, in a certain sense, he became the doctor that Hyde lacked: the One that could be trusted, relied on, appealed to.

He always insisted that he ran a 'flagship practice', and as the Shipman Inquiry put it, 'he plainly thought he was by far the best doctor in Hyde'. He prided himself on the fact that the practice 'had the highest level of screening' for various health problems. 'We are a flagship,' he stated. 'The Health Authority can always compare the quality of this practice to any other and ask why the other practice is underperforming.' It was thus the best, the site of a collection of superlatives that singled it out as the exception. As Shipman would later point out during his trial, where other doctors would be happy with a certain blood pressure result, he would not, as he aimed for 'perfection'. This focus on superlatives – typical of paranoia – was echoed in his account of the trial itself: it would be, he wrote to friends, 'probably the most expensive case this century'.

The idea that this identification stabilized Shipman is borne out by what we know of his time in prison after his conviction: he made himself into the prison doctor, dispensing medical advice to inmates and guards alike, and corresponding with his MP regarding the best care for his ex-patients in Hyde. He refused to attend the prison Cognitive Self-Change Group or the Enhanced Thinking Skills Workshop although he did sign up for Bereavement Counselling classes. The place of medical carer was obviously vital to him.

Shipman's prison correspondence shows that he was in despair, lonely and in great pain, and that taking on the role of good doctor was the only thing that held him together. It was when this place was denied him that, within weeks, he tried to hang himself: his first suicide attempt. Perhaps this stabilizing identification was itself predicated on an identification with an aspect of his mother. Although we do not have any material about this, it would be significant to learn more about how she administered to illness in the family: her children's, her husband's, her parents', her own. Could Shipman have identified with a trait of caring for the sick from his mother? And, if so, would his caring have turned to murder only when this image of the good doctor was questioned?

It is interesting that the sole document we have from Shipman's schooldays, a story published in a school magazine, includes exactly this trait: a dog breaks a budgie's wing, they visit a vet, a splint is applied, and they become inseparable afterwards. The bond between them is fixed after the medical intervention, and this story was written long before the mother's illness. The maternal side to care is perhaps reflected in the fact that Shipman was very well regarded in paediatrics, and during his time there, and in obstetrics and gynaecology, there was little, if any, killing, as if being in the place of a mother meant that he did not have to. He apparently loved delivering babies.

Commentators on the case have suggested that he did not kill during this time because it would have been difficult on a practical level in a children's ward, but it may well have been that the identification which sustained him was not hampered there. The move from paediatrics, however, to obstetrics and gynaecology probably coincides with the start of his pethidine use. No longer in the place of a carer of children, he could still remain in the place of a mother by taking the drug: pethidine is given to help the pain of women in labour and period pains and is often used by those who work in those wards.

So did the identification with the caring doctor – perhaps based on an identification with the mother – precipitate or hinder his murders? Was taking life part of his image of a doctor or, on the contrary, what emerged when the identification broke down? Shipman was particularly zealous in his choice and prescription of what he considered to be the best drugs for his patients. His drugs bill was double that of his colleagues, and he was proud that he was not letting money compromise the care he gave. He would often clash with the local Health Authority, which did not sanction his selection of expensive medicines. And in prison, he would instruct unwell inmates to request specific medications from the official prison doctor, usually costlier than those that would habitually be prescribed.

It is not impossible that this concern led to a calculus of murder: to provide the best treatment, his budgets had to be balanced, which meant periodically removing a certain number of patients. 'I've got too many patients to look after,' he would complain. On learning of the deaths that he had himself been responsible for, he would sometimes remark 'that's one off my drugs bill'. The patients he killed, indeed, often had a high consumption of pharmaceuticals. In this sense, the murders would have been a necessary part of his medical ideal, a kind of bureaucratic management of budgets that ensured quality care by means of homicide.

When Shipman claimed during his earlier trial for drug offences that his use of pethidine had increased after joining the Todmorden practice, we might well choose to believe him. He said that he grew more dependent on the drug after meeting resistance to his plans to improve the practice. Rather than seeing this as an implausible excuse, Shipman's commitment to an ideal of best-practice medicine means that the effect of opposition to his projects might really have been devastating for him. The stakes of his medical identity, after all, were high: it was his very existence that was in question here, the position that sustained him.

On the other hand, it may have been that it was a disturbance to his identification that led to the homicides. When a stabilizing identification is put in question, there is usually some disruption of that person's symbolic coordinates. Something happens that affects the symbolic structure of their world: becoming a parent, getting a new job, a retirement, or any other break in the continuity of everyday life that requires a symbolization. In other cases, the ideal identification itself

constitutes a symbolic question and not just a real, empirical one, the minor thefts that followed the murders stage nothing less than a death and the transmission of an object to Shipman.

This emphasis on the question of legacy may also shed further light on the Grundy murder. Shipman ran a patient fund for his surgery and actively encouraged donations. There was even a notice up in his office telling patients to leave money in their wills. He knew that Grundy had promised a sum from the Mayoress's Fund and that her committee then decided against it, considering it an 'inappropriate cause' and bequeathing it instead to the Tameside Hospice. Apparently she had informed Shipman of this just before she died. She was thus in the place of someone who owed him something which had been withheld. The Shipman Inquiry notes how he would sometimes ask for an item of property belonging to the deceased. In one instance, he asked a family for a budgie – we could remember his childhood story – in another for a sewing machine, in another for an antique bench. These petty thefts would include valueless pieces of jewellery – brooches, earrings – and perhaps petty cash.

Janet Smith notes that he pilfered items from the homes of the deceased, but pays little attention to this, as, she says, it was clearly not the motive for murder. This same question of a sum of money or property to be passed on after a death is relevant to his own suicide. Commentators on the case have often pointed out that Shipman took his life before his sixtieth birthday, knowing that if he died later, Primrose would not have received her full widow's pension. If he died before sixty, she would receive £100,000 and a pension of £10,000, yet if he died later, a pension of only £5,000 and no lump sum. Although one could see here a simple act of altruism, the motif of the legacy may well have been important to him here in his choice.

I would also guess that we would need to learn a lot more about Shipman's grandparents, and whether there had been a problem in the issue of a will or legacy at some point in their generation. The key here once again lies in the registers: the legacy for Shipman was not in the symbolic but in the real. It is perhaps no accident that the end to his murders and his eventual conviction revolved around exactly this question of a will and a legacy. Might this not suggest to us that it is also where it had begun?

—

The Shipman case shows us the kind of details we need to look for to understand both normal life and homicidal action. Rather than simplistic theories of fixation to a trauma, we need a more complex model that includes how the real, symbolic and imaginary interact, and recognizes the importance of ideal identifications. The case is often used to bring up problems in medical accountability and with the system of death certification, but it also illuminates a real impasse in contemporary psychiatry. This is a psychiatry that has lost its history, and it is crucial to return to the early research on stabilized psychosis, the kind that is compatible with professional success and social functionality. Without this, there is little left but an appeal to childish notions of pure evil.

The fact that such notions come from 'experts' should make us remember from the case itself that listening to an expert is sometimes unwise. Shipman benefited from an unquestioning belief in medical authority and knowledge, both in his dealings with his victims and in the first half-hearted investigation into his practice. Perhaps a scepticism would have saved lives here, and there is an irony in the fact that the attempts to make sense of his motives and to deliver some sort of 'closure', a comprehensive explanation of what happened, merely repeat the very gesture that Shipman himself relied on: respect for the expert's knowledge.

The diagnosis here is not 'pure evil' but paranoia: he occupied the place of an exception, and was committed to imposing his own knowledge on the world around him, which he deemed to contain a fault. As The Doctor of Hyde, he would make the world a better place. Even in prison, his efforts continued, and he needed to occupy a special position. As he wrote to his friends, 'There is no publicity at the moment and it feels like nothing is being done. The episode has caused me to break down in a very big way.' There is no doubt a hint of grandiosity in his comment, as if the publicity was necessary for him. In another letter, during the trial, Shipman writes, 'The case is already a first for computer evidence, a first for the publicity, a first for the number of charges, a first for Lancaster Legal School who are using my case for their "Long case" for finals. There are several other firsts as well.' The concatenation of superlatives echoes the exceptional status that he sought: not only the Best Doctor but now, with the trial, the First.

It is also important to separate this case from the long line of serial killers that Shipman is often included in. It seems clear that he was not trying to extinguish or annul some dangerous element in his victims. As one of my patients put it, speaking about Jack the Ripper, 'He was trying to kill something more than a person or a living body.' With Shipman one doesn't really have the sense that he was engaged in a comparable task. Replaying again and again the scene of a death is not necessarily the same thing as wanting to kill, and he would often save rather than destroy.

In another letter from prison, we see both his life-saving capacity and his curious faith in medicine: 'Life in here is entertaining, my cellmate tried to hang himself on Monday night. I heard the noise from his last breaths, lifted him up and then untied the knot and laid him on the floor before crying for help. After that I went back to sleep at about 2 o'clock in the morning. My cellmate seems a lot better now, his medication is working.' The style is detached, and the traumatic events do not seem to have interfered with his sleep.

That his efforts were compatible, at one level, with the world around him shows the coherence of psychosis and normal life. As he wrote to friends from prison: 'The police complain I'm boring. No mistresses, home abroad, money in Swiss banks, I'm normal. If that is boring I am.' And yet it was this very normality that he bemoaned his judge and jury were unable to see. Writing of his perceived failure in the witness box, he could say, 'I feel I failed to get over my normality.' From our perspective, it would be the recognition of this normality that might start to make us worry.

12. Working with Psychosis

A psychoanalytic theory of psychosis does not imply a psychoanalysis of psychotic subjects. All it really shows is how concepts from psychoanalytic research can help us to think about clinical cases of psychosis and develop strategies for clinical work. The various attempts over the years to introduce rules for such work – just like those designed for neurotics – were never successful, and only compounded confusions about questions of technique. There is simply no formula for such work, even if there might be certain contraindications. As the psychoanalyst Colette Sepel pointed out, there is no such thing as the psychoanalysis of psychotics: there is just a psychoanalyst and a psychotic. What happens in the relation between them has to be rethought and reinvented in each individual case. This was well known in the 1950s, yet today there are increasing pressures to pretend that there is one right way to do things.

The previous chapters should have taught us, however, that any kind of clinical work, whether psychoanalytic or not, must be sensitive to a number of different elements. If psychosis can be triggered by the encounter with a father figure or third party, it is obviously prudent for the clinician to avoid this position: no authority figures or masters, no experts. It was recognized very early on in the history of psychoanalysis that some people went mad after starting analysis or therapy, especially if the clinician adopted a guru-like position. Sustained silence from the analyst or enigmatic interpretations that the subject could make no sense of, or the unqualified invitation to free-associate could all trigger a latent psychosis, and the literature is filled with such examples. The more the analyst identifies with a place of knowledge, the more dangerous things are for the patient.

A diametrically opposed position explains some of the successes of the therapeutic communities of the 1960s and 1970s. Clinicians would deliberately avoid taking on the mantle of authority, and traditional mental health hierarchies were collapsed. The psychiatrist or therapist here would be on the same level as the patient, sharing the same living areas, the same table at mealtimes, the same newspapers and cigarettes, thus favouring imaginary relations rather than forcing the subject to confront symbolic ones. There was an effort to move away from structures and situations in which there was a strict asymmetry between 'doctors' and 'patients', between 'us' and 'them'. Although all such communities had rules, clinicians would try not to adopt *ex cathedra* attitudes. Rather than parents, they would be peers.

Today, nearly every practising therapist or analyst will work with psychotic subjects, although usually both clinician and patient will be unaware of this, due, as we have argued, to the prevalence of stabilized forms of psychosis. Many clinicians today are not taught how to make a diagnosis in the traditional sense that we have tried to sketch in Chapter 5, and sometimes become lost in the ever-expanding maze of labels: personality disorders and character types, addictions, social phobias, seasonal-affective disorder, etc. The fact that the therapeutic situation is nowadays quite relaxed and supportive, avoiding hierarchy, explains why so many of these cases never do end up triggering, and so the clinician often appeals to these labels to try to name what they are working with.

Avoiding positions of mastery in the therapeutic setting is at times easier said than done. A well-meaning clinician can consciously adopt a friendly and supportive attitude in the therapy, yet make interpretations that impose a particular worldview on the patient. This worldview might come from their own theoretical dogma or from their own personal prejudices. As Piera Aulagnier warned, there is a violence here in trying to force the other to share a truth that is not their own. Sometimes we find this out only when it's too late, and the patient's reactions show us that we have imposed something on them that is unfaithful to their experience: we might feel that our own anxiety will be reduced, after all, if they start to think like us. This is one of the reasons why there is always an appetite for manualized programmes for the therapy of psychosis which impose a model of 'how to think' on the patient. Some of these read like instruction manuals, as if therapy were simply about applying a technique of correct thinking to a passive recipient.

It is of course much easier to believe that one can apply a mechanical method than to recognize that each treatment needs to be invented with each individual patient, and the history of therapeutic approaches to psychosis shows a neat divergence of currents: those that aim to create a distance from the patient, with an emphasis on technical procedure and rules, and those that put the therapist's being at stake in the encounter with psychosis. As Marguerite Sechehaye put it, therapy here involves an 'existential wager'. These traditions both have their extremes, which are easily ridiculed, and in a sense we could say that where the one is constructed around ensuring the therapist's safety, the other is more focused on the patient. Therapists in this latter tradition have warned frequently of the dangers of subtly or directly trying to adapt the patient to one's own worldview.

There is always a great danger in trying to 'normalize' a patient, and adapt them to what we take to be a common reality. As Frieda Fromm-Reichmann put it: 'Perhaps the greatest threat to a favourable outcome of psychotherapy with schizophrenics, which is directly attributable to the therapist, is the conventional attitude of many therapists towards the question of so-called social adjustment of their schizophrenic patients. The recovery of many schizophrenic patients depends upon the psychotherapist's freedom from conventional attitudes and prejudices. These patients cannot, and should not, be asked to accept guidance towards a conventional adjustment to the customary requirements of our culture, much less to what the individual therapist personally considers these requirements. The therapist should feel that his role in treating schizophrenia is accomplished if these people are able to find for themselves, without injury to their neighbours, their own sources of satisfaction and security, irrespective of the approval of their neighbours, of their families, and of public opinion.'

These words are as true today as they were in the 1940s when they were written. Indeed, there has been a progressive move in some therapy traditions towards a model that risks reinforcing these very prejudices. For these traditions, therapy is about feedback, and as the psychotic subject articulates their thoughts and feelings to the therapist, the latter must function as a containing space, showing that their apparently inchoate communications can be heard and sending them back in processed form to the patient. Of course, the human contact of the relationship can be beneficial, but the risk is that a meaning will be imposed on them, one that may well have more to do with the history of the 'container' than with that of the patient. I hope I'm not caricaturing such therapies, and there are certainly cases where they are helpful and skilfully conducted, but they can also produce 'robots', who ventriloquize the language and worldview of the therapist.

The emphasis on social adjustment carries other dangers, as it risks neglecting the unique and idiosyncratic formulae for living that many psychotic subjects have developed. Rather than telling someone how to live, what matters is to find what it is in their own history that has helped them, what points of identification or idealization, what activities or projects: what is there in their delusion, perhaps, or in their family history that is reliable and stable, what 'good objects' are there that could be encouraged and supported? Social adjustment, indeed, can lead to catastrophe if the therapist pushes the subject to engage in some activity or relationship that is socially valorized, yet, because it introduces a symbolic position, has nothing to support it.

Suggesting that someone take a job, or go on a date, for example, may be unproblematic in some cases, but in others may trigger or exacerbate a psychosis. In these instances, the subject is being pushed into a symbolic position or an encounter with the desire of the Other – to be a boss for employees, to be a man for a woman – and may not be able to cope with the symbolization that this entails. Likewise, the social imperatives to 'achieve' and to 'act' may lead the therapist to encourage the subject to undertake some activity when in fact it is essential to them that it remain forever unrealized, always situated in the future. We could think of Schreber's future creation of a new race, or of the way in which Aimée, despite her activity of writing, would situate her major literary works as future projects. This is what Freud referred to as the asymptotic aspect of psychotic phenomena, recognized equally by American psychiatrists in the 1950s with the idea that non-triggered psychoses may remain stable due to an interest in ideals that remain unrealized. Aspects of the future must always be accorded a place. A platonic love, for example, can keep someone stable for decades, and its non-realization must be respected.

An openness to real dialogue is crucial here, and the therapist must avoid any attempt to show the subject that they are thinking 'incorrectly' or failing to conform to a right way of perceiving the world. Paradoxically, this situates the treatment of psychosis outside the traditional parameters of 'mental health', which relies on the idea that the clinician knows in advance what is best for the subject. As Kurt Eissler pointed out many years ago, 'As long as therapeutic considerations preoccupy the psychiatrist in his intercourse with the schizophrenic, he is bound to fail in his approach, since therapy necessarily implies that something is "good" or "bad".'

Likewise, anyone undertaking such work would be well advised to question their own fantasies of helping or curing others. As Lewis Hill pointed out, 'The phrase "to help human beings" can both conceal and indicate motives to set oneself up as superior to and condescending towards patients, motives to dominate and control and force patients into preconceived patterns of behaviour, and even motives to achieve distinction by way of morbid self-sacrifice and self-punishment.' A psychotic subject can understand this very swiftly and, quite rightly, show scepticism. As a schizophrenic woman objected to her therapist at the end of their first consultation, 'How can you claim to care about me if we've only just met?' And if the therapist just cared about all distressed human beings, how could she recognize the particularity of the patient in front of her? Her work would be sustained by a rescue fantasy that would effectively block her from hearing her patients.

Reassuring the patient here that things will improve may simply be a way of reassuring oneself. Such situations are common in therapeutic work with psychotics, and the general tendency today to introduce what one analyst called 'the falsification of the doctor–patient relationship' will often have regrettable results. The insincerity that the patient picks up on so quickly will only confirm his distrust of the environment. Freud's remark, in a letter to his colleague Johan van Ophuijsen, echoes this sentiment: 'I would advise you to set aside your therapeutic ambitions and try to understand what is happening. When you have done that therapeutics will take care of itself.' The wish to save the patient may give one a sense of self-importance and value, but it will ultimately compromise the therapy.

As Lewis Hill put it, the therapist must recognize that 'the urge to help is not so productive as is the willingness to be of use to the patient'.

—

If there are no formulas or recipes for work with psychotic subjects, we can still hope to devise strategies that respect the need for stabilization, compensation and the creation of unique, individual ways to knot together the symbolic, the imaginary and the real. We can help the person to create meaning, without imposing our own, and to invent new ways of dealing with the mental or physical excitations that torment them. If we think back to the three case histories we have explored, we could imagine how the detailed knowledge of their lives that might emerge through dialogue could give us some clues here. With Aimée, for example, for whom the epistolary relation was so important, work might have involved encouraging her to continue this in some way: either through a career or, perhaps, through asking her to write daily or weekly to the analyst. We remember what happened when the channel of her literary communication was broken: when there was no longer anyone to acknowledge her letters, she struck Mme Duflos.

We hypothesized that her solution also involved taking on a place of an exception, being the 'chosen one' of God. She didn't shout this out to the world, but kept it more or less to herself. This position might also be affirmed and supported by the analyst, through some way of allowing her to see her position as unique. Perhaps this could have involved encouraging her to see herself as the analyst's special teacher, which, in a way, would be absolutely accurate. Every patient teaches the analyst something, and while there would be little reason to tell this to a neurotic, there would, at times, be good reasons to tell it to a psychotic. The analyst here might try to help the subject find ways of recognizing this dimension of teaching and learning.

With Sergei Pankejeff, we have a clue to both the question of stabilization and that of transference. He was most stable when in the position of the co-worker to Freud's explorer. This provided him with a way to avoid the unsymbolizable question of what it meant to be a son to a father, and so the clinician would no doubt avoid a paternal position, emphasizing rather the joint work of research on psychical life undertaken together. The wager would be that this imaginary position would have an effect on his bodily troubles and that his physical symptoms would preoccupy him far less. The therapeutic relation between subject and analyst would thus become the space where an identificatory position could be constructed: to be a co-worker.

There is also the possibility of a shift from the physical body to some body of knowledge. Pankejeff was fascinated by psychoanalysis and literature, and had an extensive knowledge of both. If his position of co-worker could be maintained, one might hope that a displacement were possible from his interminable questioning of his physical body – which brought him much suffering – to a questioning of some other form of knowledge: not medical knowledge of the body but the body of psychoanalytic, literary or philosophical knowledge, for example. In such an exploration, it would be important to keep questions open, acknowledging that, in the absence of the symbolic operation that would establish a limitation of meaning, there would always be a question mark internal to Pankejeff's world. Elaborating this in fruitful rather than persecutory ways could constitute one of the aims of a therapy.

As for Shipman, although the material suggests that a therapy would hardly have been possible, we can still abstract many details from the case. We might guess that an identification on the side of the mother may have allowed some stabilization, and that his role as 'The Doctor' was his way of occupying the place of an exception: to be The Doctor his mother lacked, perhaps. It shows how a psychosis can be perfectly compatible with a 'normal' life: maintaining a job, a family, garnering respect in the community. As for the homicides, the real question here is to ask whether Shipman's crimes were the true form of his psychosis or, on the contrary, desperate attempts to refind this form after it had been shattered by external events. We can learn from the case how a psychosis can be kept stable by a professional role, which means that we need to think carefully when dialoguing with a patient who seems to have no external symptoms.

A professional role may be a way of maintaining a functional formula, sustaining the place of an exception, or establishing a link to some group or abstract cause. In his discussion of work with psychotic subjects at the Courtil Centre in Belgium, Alfredo Zenoni describes how educative and rehabilitative endeavours are set aside in favour of projects of 'self-elaboration', in which patients often construct roles for themselves: retired worker, artist, volunteer therapist, inventor or veteran of mental health institutions. These identifications may allow them to see themselves in terms of some already established social bond, not necessarily to live within it, but to occupy a place, perhaps, on its margins or in a kind of suspension from it. As we have seen, such roles will be compatible with the logic of that person's psychosis, and may draw them to different kinds of projects.

These should not be confused with standardized efforts at rehabilitation that have predetermined aims and outcomes. As Ellen Corin points out, each psychotic subject's project of restructuring their world must be taken seriously. It would be absurd to work towards 'rehabilitation' while ignoring the strategies and meanings that patients elaborate by themselves as part of this project. This might involve being both 'inside' and 'outside' the social field, being linked to some network while not being obliged to interact with other people or commit oneself personally in the interaction. The critical insights expressed by psychotic subjects must be respected and made part of any therapeutic process, so that, as Corin observes, they can find a place within a real world whose contradictions they perceive rather than some ideal society that exists only in the therapist's imagination.

Already in his 1932 thesis Lacan had observed that psychotic subjects often gravitate towards religious, political or charitable groups, especially ones with a defined cause, such as social reform or some promotion of a public good. Teaching and nursing were also popular, as were the religious orders and the armed forces: these professions supplied a structure, which could take the place of the missing symbolic dimension, or a sense of devotion to an abstract duty, such as care or education. Rules and regulations, as found especially in the military, were often useful here as they gave the subject an external structure, compensating for the internal system that was not established. Many therapeutic communities, indeed, would emphasize an explicit system of rules, with the idea that these could function as a form of prosthetic symbolic order, yet with the proviso that these were never seen as the whim or invention of any one particular person, but rather applied to everyone there as an empty 'How things are'.

Working out therapeutic strategies in the individual case will then depend crucially on understanding how the person has coped in the past: the key questions are what stopped them from becoming mad before, and what the circumstances were of their triggering. Once we have an idea of an answer to these questions, it will help in the formulation of therapeutic strategies in the present. The more we learn about the triggering, the more we can have an idea of what cannot be symbolized for that person, and this can help us to avoid pushing them in the wrong direction.

Learning what allowed an equilibrium before – whether it was the construction of an ideal, adherence to an image, having a functional formula that works, the creation of a prosthetic symbolic system, establishment of a logic of exception, having activities that can limit and name libido, or any other form that the person has found of knotting together the real, the symbolic and the imaginary – will be important in thinking about future possibilities. Once we have an idea of this, directions for therapy may become clearer, but what form can such therapy take? Does it have rigid boundaries? Is it programmatic or procedural?

—

Interestingly, the very work of finding out about the circumstances of a triggering and the processes that allowed a prior equilibrium constitutes a therapy in itself. Rather than leading the patient through a questionnaire to accumulate data – more likely to benefit someone else's institutional career via publications than to be of any scientific value – true dialogue here can help to establish the subject's sense of a history: a history that may, in fact, have been entirely lacking.

We have seen already how some psychotic subjects have no history: a 'happy childhood', an uneventful work and family life, and so on. No markers are introduced to indicate where things changed, those moments of discontinuity that characterize a human life. Other psychotic subjects are very clear about these moments of change, but, when they are absent, it can be very helpful to allow the subject to construct them through careful and tactful work. This process can be therapeutic by establishing a temporality, moments of 'before' and 'after' that can function as symbolic coordinates, allowing the person to situate themselves and their difficulties. Rather than being an object with no history, they can become its subject.

This work must involve a great deal of detail, with the clinician inviting the subject to name, date and isolate the episodes and events of their life. Creating distinctions in what may appear to be a mass or unbroken flow of experience is crucial here. We can remember that the defining feature of the symbolic is precisely that: the forging of divisions and contrasts in a body of undifferentiated material. It is always an important moment when a psychotic subject can create a second signifier, a new term that is different from but related to one that has indexed a destructive, intrusive or unbearable force in their lives. A melancholic patient would speak continuously of a 'nothing-ness' that weighed down on him, until a moment of progress when he was able to differentiate 'nothingness' from 'emptiness'. Regard-less of the content of these words, what mattered was the forging of a minimal binary, the basic cell of symbolic functioning.

In another case, in which the subject repeated endlessly 'I am dead', it was the opposition between 'dead' and 'inert' that allowed an opening-up of his discourse, enabling him to speak for the first time about other things. The clinician here can help the subject by carefully emphasizing a word in their speech that may take on this function of the second term of a binary, inviting the patient to differ-entiate it from the original and seemingly monolithic signifier. Other examples would include a patient's differentiation between a 'void' and a 'vortex', and the separation, in a case of melancholia, between the sentences 'I've let him go' and 'I've let go of him.' What might seem to be trivial linguistic inflections can be of vital importance in the work with a psychotic subject.

It is through the minimal inscription of these sets of differences that the person can develop a grid with which to order, frame and make sense of their experience. Gradually, a certain kind of history can be built up, and the attention to proper names and dates can help to accentuate the dimension of naming and pinning down that we have seen to be so important in psychosis. If in schizophrenia, especially, meaning is so often unfixed and potentially threatening, naming can help to block its drift and sliding. This work of designation can also involve the therapist naming certain aspects of the patient's life. Rather than imposing a worldview, it may simply be a question here of offering a few words – when necessary – and generally taken from the patient's own speech.

The practice of naming here can follow the logic of the psychotic's own use of neologisms: as Tanzi and his colleagues noticed, invented words tend to refer to the experience of persecution and to the different forms of attack used by the persecutor. In analytic terms, the unmediated desire of the Other: this is the exact point at which the subject is compelled to create a new word, to use the resources of language to establish some sort of limit. Learning from this, the therapist may introduce words at precisely those moments, encouraging the patient to name those experiences, and proposing names taken from their own discourse.

Similarly, it may be decisive to name the experience of persecution from a family member. By linking a particular word to their mother or father, for example, a pinning down can take place, which weakens the feeling of persecution. Such moments – necessarily rare in a therapy in order to conserve their impact – are more about the act of emphatically naming than about suggesting or proposing. They focus on manifestations of the desire of the Other, be it the actions or speech of a parent, a partner, a friend or a colleague: anything that makes the subject have a sense of an enigma or menace. The clinician's act of naming can weaken the invasive threat, yet it should obviously be a rare event, or the very situation of persecution that the therapy aims to reverse would be reinstated.

This process can occur inadvertently. One day I left a session to answer the door and receive the post. The patient heard me say 'Hello Postman' and explained to me, years later, that this had been the most important moment in her therapy. This, rather than any of my direct therapeutic interventions over the years, had really changed things for her. She remembered as a child going through books where a farmyard scene was represented, feeling relief that the elements in it could be named and counted. They were finite, and so she could say 'Hello Geese, Hello Ducks, Hello Sheep'. The moment when I named the postman mattered to her as it staged a bonding between word and thing, between signifier and object. The world, from then on, became more stable.

It is interesting to observe here that some approaches to psychosis benefit from this principle without fully recognizing it. The *DSM* approach and that of many cognitive therapies encourage psychotic subjects and their families to see the symptoms of psychosis as external illnesses, whether they are understood as biologically determined or the result of learning errors. Although this perspective is easy to criticize, the very gesture of naming and 'objectifying' symptoms may be helpful for some psychotic subjects. It has the function of pinning down meaning that we have discussed. And that's why the cognitive therapies are sometimes useful in such cases: they give the subject a language, a way of naming and ordering their experience.

The work of helping the psychotic subject create a history, through naming, dating, isolating and detailing, emphasized by Harry Stack Sullivan, is in some senses a secretarial duty. Lacan in fact defined the analyst's place in work with psychotics using an old psychiatric expression: 'the secretary of the alienated subject'. This is a rather splendid way of putting it. A secretary, after all, doesn't – or shouldn't – intrude too much; they write things down; they check, confirm and ask for clarifications; they remind you of something when necessary; they help to organize schedules and the difficult aspects of life; they are hopefully reliable; they tend to occupy the same stable space; they might, like the clinician, ask you to elaborate, to date, detail, name and isolate in order to take down their notes; they don't try to impose a worldview on you or tell you that you're wrong; and sometimes they may do something unusual, like expressing an opinion forcefully. And, of course, being a secretary means not being a boss.

Secretarial duties introduce another important factor into therapeutic work with psychotic subjects. A secretary will often ask their boss to slow down, to repeat a word they didn't quite catch, or remind them of something. This is a work of punctuation, and the full stops, commas and dashes that it creates will allow a history to be constructed. Without punctuation marks, none of us would have any history. Yet punctuating goes well beyond this semantic dimension. Through the rhythm of sessions, their frequency, their timetabling and their endings, a different kind of punctuating also takes place, one that affects the libido as well as the question of meaning and history.

Psychotic phenomena are often experienced as non-stop. Schreber complained of the never-ending torments of his body and the perpetual commentary of his voices. There is no let-up in the sense of acute dread, the physical sensations, the voices, the sense of menace or threat to one's being. The subject may be unable to even imagine that what is assailing him could ever stop. Clinicians know, for example, that it is unhelpful to tell a manic-depressive subject in their dejected state that soon things will brighten up. Invasive psychotic phenomena have a continuity about them that makes them all the more unbearable, and punctuation is one way of trying to work against this. It introduces a basic rhythm of presence and absence, a kind of serial negativity, perhaps like that of the mechanical devices described by Joey: 'Machines,' he said, 'are better than people. Machines can stop. People go farther than they should.' The rhythm of sessions is a way of introducing a symbolic cut into the continuity of the phenomena, even if the actual content of the sessions is not especially significant. If a subject in a manic state, for example, has repeated sessions of a variable length on the same day, they are sometimes able to calm down, even if the session lasts only a matter of minutes.

Obviously the therapist has to have the possibility of working this way, with a flexible timetable and the use of sessions with no set length. A patient in crisis could have anything between one and a dozen sessions in a day, the emphasis being on the breaking of the horrifying sense of continuity that the psychosis is imposing. It is important to think carefully about this question of the frequency and length of sessions, as it constitutes a valuable tool in work with psychosis. It must obviously be used prudently by the clinician, and the patient must be introduced to the practice of variable-length sessions. There would be little point, for example, in ending a session after five minutes with no prior explanation with someone who is complaining that they are always rejected. But, once they recognize the principle, if they say something striking about this exact issue, it might be a good idea to end the session at that moment. Ending, after all, introduces a punctuation, generating effects at many different levels.

We could contrast the idea of the effects of punctuation with the classical dogma that therapy aims at providing insight. The therapist is supposed to listen to the patient and then convey to them the meaning of what they are saying. The realization that psychotic phenomena had a hidden meaning was exciting to the first and second generation of Freud's students, yet this led to the mistaken idea that treatment consisted in a comparable process of explaining meaning. Ironically, it was this very idea that led so many authors to decide that therapy with psychotic subjects actually didn't work. Insight may at times be helpful, yet as a programme for therapeutic work it can become invasive and persecutory all too swiftly.

We have to remember here that for many psychotic subjects, the world already means too much. If everything is sending them a message, perhaps the last thing they might want is another message. And if, in their childhoods, their caregivers always knew 'too much', watching them incessantly or claiming to know their thoughts and intentions, the clinician must adopt a very different position, intervening not from a place of knowledge and meaning, but, on the contrary, from a point of not knowing: more like a student than a teacher.

Émigré American analysts and psychiatrists such as Frieda Fromm-Reichmann recognized this fact in the 1940s and 1950s, arguing that it was the dynamic of the communication rather than interpreting the 'content' of what the patient was saying that led to change. It would be less the meaning that the therapist was trying to convey than, perhaps, the actual effort to understand that had an impact. Punctuation is one aspect of this, and it works both through meaning and outside meaning: and that is precisely its advantage clinically. In a psychosis where meaning seems always to be shifting – as in some forms of schizophrenia – the therapist needs to use tools other than meaning itself.

The psychoanalyst Jean-Max Gaudillière describes how when he had to travel to Alaska he agreed to telephone one of his psychotic patients every day while he was away. He was worried about this case as there was a real danger of suicide. Upon arrival, he called and told his patient that it was nine in the morning, that it was Wednesday and that he would call back the next day at the same time. What is illuminating in this vignette is that Gaudillière specifically did not ask the patient how he was feeling. Instead, he just delivered the minimal, symbolic coordinate: where he was, what time and day it was, and that he would call back the next day. This is reminiscent of the famous postcards of the artist On Kawara, sent every day for decades, simply stating the date and that he was still alive. The calls, like Kawara's cards, were a simple, stark form of punctuating, signifying not only that he was still there, but introducing a cut into the continuity of the subject's experience, a coordinate that may, in some cases, be the very difference between life and death.

Existential psychiatrists grasped the importance of this in their emphasis on helping the psychotic subject to 'historicize'. This meant not only the elaboration of one's biography, the mapping of significant moments in one's life, but also the daily work of punctuating time. As Werner Mendel pointed out, simply to say 'I'll see you tomorrow at ten o'clock' may be the most important intervention the therapist can make. It may be this minimal act that separates past and future, and opens up the possibility of establishing a historicity. As a psychotic subject put it, 'Finding a way to exist isn't about us being in the consulting room together, but in the passing of beats between sessions. This is what lets a separation creep in' – the separation vital for her to survive.

Texting has now also become a common tool in the therapy of psychotic subjects. I described earlier the case of the man who would text me the words of his auditory hallucinations in order to move their interpellative force away from himself, allowing him to escape the place of their unique addressee. Using texts can encourage the subject to communicate, to write and to make some minimal form of inscription. It is crucial to recognize here, however, that communication is often not the primary aim of such practices. As Zenoni puts it, with psychotic phenomena the real clinical question is less

'What does this mean?' or 'What is being expressed?' than 'What function does this have?', 'What is being treated?', 'What use does this have for the person?'

One of my patients texts me a couple of times a day to ask if I am still alive, and there are no doubt a variety of ways to interpret this. A British object-relations analyst might assume it was actually a sign of their aggression towards me: they asked me if I was alive because they were afraid that they had hurt me. Or it could be interpreted as a fear of someone dying, echoing some aspect of their history. While there may be some truth in each of these interpretations, there is also a certain symbolic, punctuating activity in the daily rhythm of texts and replies, an activity that perhaps goes beyond the dimension of meaning: more to do with syntax, perhaps, than with semantics. I reply minimally, just to state that, Yes, I'm still kicking.

Another patient would text several times a day, not sentences but just isolated words and numbers. This allowed her, she said, to 'get rid of excitation' from her mind and her body. Until then, she would have to masturbate repeatedly before even leaving her home in order to try to drain away some of this morbid excitement. We find here once again an illustration of the idea of libido: less a pleasurable feeling than a troubling intrusion that must be removed or kept at a distance. Texting, and later writing, enabled her to channel these states of arousal, attenuating the acute, unwanted sensations that invaded her.

The redirection of the addressee function that texting allows can also shed light on certain clinical features of transference that we find in psychosis. Schreber's dedication of his book to the attention of 'all educated persons interested in questions relating to the hereafter' is frequently cited as an example of an appeal to an addressee, a positive sign in the stabilization process. Just as little Anthony would address commands and calls to his stuffed toy, as if he were creating an interlocutor and hence taming the interpellation function, so Schreber would endeavour to relay on the vectors that singled him out. When a patient said to me 'I have to make you into a hearer', it could be understood in the same sense: to distribute what it means to be a hearer oneself and to defend against it. And isn't *making oneself* addressed a response to the fact of being addressed?

In a case reported by Harold Searles, a very disturbed and violent patient at Chestnut Lodge was gazing about rapidly, and the therapist asked him if he was hearing voices. 'I'm not hearing voices,' he replied, 'I'm looking at my two pet flies, Lum and Abner.' The therapist saw that, indeed, two flies were buzzing around by the window. No mention was made of these characters for a year, until a moment when he was able to start talking about the terrifying voices that had been invading his mind at that time. Female voices had been telling him to hang himself, to tear his eyes out, and to smash his skull into a door. These voices had been condemnatory, he explained, but the first sign of hope had been when they had told him to tell Lum and Abner to fly to a factory in his home town and to alight on a certain machine there. This, the voices had said, was his only chance of hope. 'That may sound odd,' he said, 'but up until then I didn't have any feeling of hope, and I did feel that this *was* my chance.' He had waited till he was alone to tell the flies this; otherwise, he thought, people would have reckoned him crazy.

Although we could no doubt interpret further the meaning of the flies, of the home town and of the machine, the key detail in this vignette is perhaps the modulation of the addressee function. He is no longer the unique addressee of the voices: they are not simply telling him something, they are *telling him to tell the flies*. This simple yet staggeringly important transformation of his experience of being an object of the voices coincided with his clinical improvement. No longer the object himself, he has a job of transferring, of acting as a relay for the voices. It is surely this operation that allowed the emergence of hope in his terrifying, persecutory world. He was no longer being told, but *being told to tell*.

Modulating and redirecting the interpellative function within a therapy can be crucial for the psychotic subject. At times, the therapist may suffer from the feeling that acting as a relay is too much to bear, and there are cases where they may shy away from this place. In the case we discussed in Chapter 7, listening to the patient's 'broods' may have been difficult, but we could also guess that the intensity of the interpellative vector that they conveyed was proportional to the sense of persecution that he experienced himself. Through modifying the addressee function, circuits can be created that ultimately go beyond both patient and therapist, to a public of readers, listeners or, as with Searles's patient, flies.

—

What place does the therapist occupy here? It can hardly be a comfortable one. Tact, sensitivity and the occasional use of illocutionary force are not easily combined, and every clinician makes mistakes in the treatment of psychosis, mistakes that they hopefully learn from. Particularly difficult for many therapists is accepting to be the object of the patient's projections. Yet any therapy worth its salt will involve this, as feelings of love, hate and persecution come to be focused on the clinician. Some forms of therapy insist that these feelings be analysed as and when they occur, or explained away to the patient as the result of – precisely – projection. This strategy is of course more helpful to the therapist than to the patient, giving them a way of managing their own anxiety. But it can be catastrophic to the patient, for a number of reasons.

First of all, it denies the legitimacy of their thoughts and feelings. It tells them that what they feel is not correct, a curious manoeuvre given the fact that so many theories of psychosis tell us that the problem in the subject's childhood was exactly the fact that their feelings and thoughts were not adequately processed or taken seriously by the caregiver. But, even more significantly, it tries to shut down the mobilization of libido that projection and transference necessarily involve. In order to help someone come to reorganize their world, it might be crucial that the therapist accepts to be the hated object for a long time, perhaps for many years. Being appreciated is not always as relevant as it might seem, and no one should practice therapy if it matters to them whether they are liked or not. As Edith Weigert pointed out many years ago, if the therapist's self-esteem is dependent upon proving his therapeutic success, he should refuse the job and save the patient the experience of being deserted.

As a schizophrenic woman writing about her experiences put it, 'Hating is like shitting. If you shit, it shows you are alive, but if the doctor can't accept your shit, it means he doesn't want you to be alive.'

Accepting and enduring hatred is thus essential. As she continues, 'The doctor has to show that he can feel the hate but can understand and not be hurt by it. It's too awful if the doctor is going to be hurt by the sickness.' If part of the work of therapy is to allow the subject to create some point of focus for the invasive libido that will be liveable for them, to localize their libido in a new way, the therapist must accept that they may themselves become this very focus.

The same goes for trust. A basic trust between patient and therapist is usually considered essential, and even as the key factor in treatment, creating a trust where trust failed with the parent. But there are cases where a reorganization of the patient's world relies on the localization of the faulty, untrustworthy element in the figure of the therapist. There will be plenty of cases where the therapist does need to show that he or she is to be trusted and is not malign, but there will also be cases where the opposite is true. The key here is a sensitivity to the patient's speech and to the logic of the world that they inhabit. Being the bad, hated part of their world may allow those feelings to be shifted away from somewhere else and may be one step in a long process of change. The therapist's accepting to be hated may be precisely what allows the patient to return to life. Interestingly, some therapists – nearly always male – report that it is easier for them to bear the patient's hatred than their love.

To situate these aspects of the therapy, the clinician must try to work out what place they have come to occupy in the patient's world and then to think through the consequences of this. The wish to help the patient or a display of tenderness or benevolence may be quite ill-starred without having taken this prior question into account. The psychiatrist Yrjö Alanen describes his work with Sarah, his first long-term patient. This young woman had been hospitalized after becoming delusional while at university, believing herself to be the object of experiments and a medium for spirits and people far away who took turns to speak through her brain. Her voices eventually coalesced into one voice, that of the Guide, a being who lived inside her. The therapeutic work progressed well and Sarah was discharged, continuing in therapy for more than a year. Various factors led to an exacerbation of her psychosis and it seemed to Alanen that a further hospitalization would be necessary. Sarah was exasperated, and at one point leaned her head against the table in desperation. The psychiatrist, feeling sympathy, began to stroke her hair gently. Instantly, Sarah lifted her head and said that now she heard his voice inside her: 'Yrjö Alanen is speaking, he has become my Guide.'

Alanen later realized that he should have been more alert to what was going on in their relationship, as she had in fact started to use medical expressions linked to him in her speech before this episode. He might then have been able to avoid the new and risky place of an influencing agency. But there is still the question of how the therapist might respond once a patient's delusion has assigned them that place. Alanen found himself in a place of the Other for Sarah rather than a secretary or a peer, with its risk that a helpful and supportive work might turn into a persecutory one. Once installed in her psyche as the Guide, what should he do next?

Again, there is no set answer here, and it will depend on the particularities of each case. Alanen knew from then on that he would have to avoid the place of the Other for his patients, yet what alternative positions are tenable? The place of an imaginary counterpart may seem a better option than the potentially menacing place of the Other, yet this again will have its own problems. If the therapist is literally in the place of a mirror image for the subject, what choice will the latter have but to either disappear or destroy the therapist? The mirror phase, we remember, is not mediated symbolically for the psychotic as it has been for the neurotic subject. It's a space of 'Either you or me', which is often associated with paranoia. That's why mirror situations can be of great danger both for the psychotic subject and to those around them.

In Renée's therapy, this danger of mirroring was countered by her own insistence on avoiding the pronouns 'I' and 'you'. Sechehaye, she tells us, did 'the most amazing good' by using the third-person pronoun. She would refer to her patient as 'Renée' and to herself as 'Mama'. Their work was that of 'Mama and Renée', not of 'you and I'. 'When by chance she used the first person, abruptly, I no longer knew her and I was angry that she had, by this error, broken my contact with her. So that when she said, "You will see how together we shall fight against the System" (what were "I" and "you"?), for me there was no reality.' We can note here how the problem occurs at the precise moment that a triangulation is evoked: between the 'you and I' and 'the System', exactly the configuration of places that risks having the effect of triggering or exacerbation of the psychosis, as we saw in Chapter 7.

There are cases, however, where whatever the therapist does, the patient resolutely tries to put them back into the place of either Other or mirror image. The therapist is consistently identified with a powerful source of knowledge or with a kind of double. The patient might continually ask the therapist to instruct them and tell them what to do – perhaps like Sarah's Guide – or might mimic the therapist and experience a dreadful sense of exclusion if they are not doing what they imagine the therapist to be doing, or do not have what they believe the therapist to have. In such cases, once the therapist has recognized the nature of the transference, they may do their best not to occupy that place, or, more precisely, to occupy that place without abusing it: without, for example, delivering instructions or sharing too much with the patient. Rather than imposing their 'understanding', which in the end may turn them into a persecutor, the therapist has to encourage a process of questioning, acknowledging a point of non-understanding yet avoiding too great a sense of enigma or mystery.

The therapist's position here will always involve a communication of their own lack: lack of knowledge, of power, of insight, of expertise. Given that the psychotic subject so often suffers from the over-proximity of some Other – a parent or caregiver, a persecutor, etc. – it is vital to indicate that a different space is available in the therapy, or can be constructed there. We could think of the case we mentioned earlier in which the patient's shoplifting was a first phase in his progress: he had found a way of subtracting himself from the omnipresent gaze of the Other. The creation of a space free from the prying presence of the Other is crucial for the psychotic subject, and so therapy must adapt to this requirement, respecting the necessity of an empty space. Therapies that aim to 'know' the patient or tell them 'who they are' may be quite disastrous, as not being known, or at least preserving some margin, may be the difference between life and death. It's why so many psychotic subjects search for an anonymity in their lives.

The same goes for institutions, in which work can follow the corresponding logic: the environment should signify to the patient that it is not complete, that there is an empty space where the patient can build something. This may be very difficult for therapists and for staff, as they may feel more secure in the position of experts, but it is ultimately unhelpful for many psychotic subjects.

—

Therapists who have written about long-term work with psychosis have often remarked on the 'dyadic' or 'fusional' or 'symbiotic' nature of the transference. It's as if the therapist and the patient are locked together, with no admission of any third party. The demand for sessions can seem ravenous, the thirst for the therapist's presence never quenched. As Robert Knight pointed out, the therapist engaged in long-term work with some psychotic subjects will have to be able to weather intense emotional turbulence, insatiable demands, provocative testing manoeuvres, outbursts of hatred, not to speak of confusing communications.

Pioneers like John Rosen would have ten-hour sessions with patients, and Sechehaye would often spend a whole day with Renée. Such intense work would be gruelling: periods of progress would often be followed by terrible times of pain and withdrawal, as if the closeness that was being established would only herald a rejection. Love can only end in mutual destruction. So the patient withdraws. Too much closeness is unbearable. Just as things are going well, the patient assumes that the therapist could drop them capriciously. Tiny changes like a dry throat can be understood as signs of rejection, holidays and breaks as unthinkable abandonments or betrayals.

This 'symbiotic' relation is often explained in terms of the person's early life. The mother wants the child to respond to her, to recognize her, perhaps, as a mother. She puts pressure on the child to experience the world as she, the mother, does, and especially the world of feelings, motives and thoughts. These demands can take on an all-or-nothing quality, and the child becomes highly attuned to the mother's moods and thinking processes. He is caught, as Helm Stierlin observed, between either accepting the mother's crippling definition of reality or losing her love. Hence the remarkable intensity of the transference and the ability of many psychotics to guess the therapist's moods so accurately. As Stierlin says, they are a 'superspecialist in understanding unconscious communications'. But what should they do with this? Unable to give a sense, a scope and a perspective to this data, they are at the mercy of meaning. The acuteness of this in the transference will also be experienced as a threat, with the therapist's interventions and presence at times becoming menacing and invasive. Hence the periods of withdrawal and vengefulness.

The patient may assume that they are the unique object of the therapist's attention, and the sight of another patient can be experienced as the most appalling betrayal. This is often theorized, once again, in terms of the mother–child relation. The patient relives an early state of fusion with the mother, or tries to enact the kind of situation of parental care that they had in fact been deprived of. Some therapists advise seeing this through, and actually try to be the parent the patient never had, while others will try to analyse it rather than enact it. Choosing the parental role might mean, for some therapists, actually feeding and looking after the patient physically as well as emotionally. Even if the feelings here remain positive, the experience can be too much and, as Arieti points out, some therapists become so overwhelmed by this that they consider moving to other cities or even countries to escape from the devouring love of a patient.

It was the psychiatric nurse and later analyst Gertrud Schwing who published a groundbreaking popular book in 1940 on the importance of mothering the patient, giving them what they lacked in early life. Sechehaye did exactly this in the case of Renée, letting her feed from an apple at her breast, but her interventions were based, in contrast to those of Schwing, on a theory of symbolism. It is significant that so many of the therapies that are based on a mother–child model involve material objects and not simply speech, as if a basic process of symbolization were being attempted. Sechehaye charts the successive stages of this, as Renée became able to eat food that was not exclusively delivered by her and to use dolls as representative rather than merely material objects.

As one of my patients put it, 'I need something physical to take care of and give back. I need very, very concrete.' Her requests for food were clearly explained: 'It's not that I want nourishment. But if you give me food, it will help me to create a body to encapsulate the food.' While not going as far as Sechehaye in putting apples on her breast, many therapists describe using objects in their work with schizophrenics, and the key factor here is perhaps how they change their function over time. An object is never in isolation, yet, as my patient made clear, part of an interaction, an exchange. We could remember here how in the Freudian example of the child playing with the cotton reel, the grasping and throwing of the object was accompanied by a vocalization: it was the presence of words that allowed the symbolization of the mother's absence. And so, in some cases, a material object becomes necessary to act as a support for the symbolic process, to help it to get off the ground.

These close, intense forms of therapy teach us a great deal, yet, as Arthur Burton points out, the patient here may skirt a narrow path between destroying the therapist and finding 'rebirth' through her. Rather than seeing these options as separate outcomes in a therapy, they may actually be parts of the same process: destruction, in a certain sense, is necessary, yet what is it that must be destroyed? Is it a real, physical destruction or a symbolic annulment, once the therapist has become identified with some aspect of the patient's libido? Gérard Pommier notes how the psychotic subject may try to devour the clinician in these 'symbiotic' therapies, and that the practice of short sessions might respond to it, demonstrating that the therapist has survived, 'at least until the next session'. Indeed, the place of what could be called oral love and hatred should not be underestimated. As one of my patients put it, 'I don't want romance with you or to fuck you. Just to eat you up all in one go. It's either that or nothing.'

It often happens that a psychotic person, well aware of these dangers of a close human relationship, will try to establish their own forms of artificial distance. We could think here of the case discussed in Chapter 8, where a young man invented a kind of metric to deal with his neighbours in the apartment building in which he lived. To take another example, a schizophrenic man described how he had chosen his therapist. Out of all the possible therapists he could have consulted, he chose one who had a public profile in his own field: she published many articles and was often referred to in the literature. Yet now that he had begun his therapy, he would close his eyes at any occurrence of her name, and isolate journals in a cupboard that contained any reference to her. He had been conscious of this when choosing her, as if he had to create an artificial distance, a special kind of relationship that would have a barrier built into it. Rather than the 'phobia' being a product of the therapy, he explained how it had been part of his initial strategy: he knew that a therapy would only be possible if he could create a preliminary distance within it.

Many traditions in therapy try from the outset to avoid the danger of exclusively dyadic relationships by introducing a therapeutic team, as opposed to a single therapist, as well as the possibility of activities, workshops and groups, which aim to counter the excessive reliance on one unique figure. This multiplication of points of attachment may be very effective, although there are always some cases where, whatever the variety of therapeutic processes, one person is elected as the prime object of transference. Lacan described this aspect of transference in psychosis as a 'mortifying erotomania', an expression that has both a wide scope and a technical precision. Erotomania involves believing oneself to be the special object of another's love, and it can also refer to a unique and persistent love towards another. It's true that in the kind of long-term therapeutic work we are discussing, the relationship often has this as its structure: a special bond, understood by the patient in a variety of ways, which has mortifying effects, in the sense of introducing a certain negativity. This can be at the price of an inertia, yet it can also benefit the patient by creating a stability, a new libidinal configuration. In such cases, it is difficult to imagine how the therapy might end – and, indeed, there may be good reasons to accept that it never will.

Some therapies will go on 'for life' and most experienced therapists will have cases that they have been working with for decades.

One of my patients described how, even if she stopped coming to her sessions, I would still be there like 'bubbles on the moon': 'You are like this thing that is always there and if events happen in your life they are more like ideas or things that I know happen but I don't really have proof of – you're like bubbles on the moon.' This curious invention named for her the odd, eccentric position she had given me, which was very different from the more persecutory place I had for her when she began her therapy years previously. However spaced out the sessions might be, the 'thing' is still there for her.

When I began clinical work, my teachers were unequivocal on this: a psychotic patient, they said, is for life. Alanen describes one case that he has been working with for thirty-eight years. The clinician must be prepared for this long-drawn-out work, which will include steps both forward and backward, and must be available for the patient beyond classical working hours. They must be contactable in the event of a crisis, and the place of an addressee must be kept open. We saw with the Aimée case and other examples how catastrophic the closing of the line of communication can be. It is a positive moment in work with a psychotic subject when an addressee is constituted, someone who is designated as a listener. This does not have to be the therapist themself, and can be someone beyond them: when Pankejeff spoke to Ruth Mack Brunswick, his addressee was no doubt Freud.

Having an addressee can allow the psychotic subject to start to construct a history, a work of writing or creating, which is facilitated by being *aimed somewhere*. Schreber addressed his *Memoirs* to the science of his time and the religious enlightenment of mankind rather than to a particular person, and the identity of this addressee can vary a great deal. The therapist can, in many cases, be more like a witness, someone who is there to authenticate some form of work or activity that may be aimed elsewhere. Rather than telling the patient that a delusion, for example, is wrong, one can simply witness it, in the same way that a document might require a witness: not to evaluate its ultimate truth but simply to act as a guarantee for it. A delusion, after all, is a construction, a reparative work, which involves building something.

When the place of an addressee is constituted within a therapy, and the therapist occupies this place, it can in some cases be extended, moving on to a wider or more abstract audience – readers, viewers, listeners, fellow sufferers, etc. But during the period when the therapist him or herself occupies this place of addressee, there are obviously real dangers in imposing time limits on the treatment. However beneficial the work, to cut it off brutally with an arbitrary requirement of a maximum number of sessions, with no space for changing these bureaucratic rules, can be barbaric. Some therapists speak of 'working towards an ending', and although there are no doubt cases where this is valid, it can equally be a way for the therapist simply to try to manage their own anxiety or guilt at terminating the treatment.

—

In the end, the most common cause of failure in the therapy of psychosis is not the clinician making an ill-judged intervention or blunder but their loss of interest in the continuation of the work. This may be the result of many factors, but we hear again and again of a feeling of despair at lack of change in the patient and the difficulty in dealing with the tests of love and commitment that are forced upon them. Some psychotic subjects will demand a commitment that they perhaps once expected from their caregivers, and will develop an extensive testing repertory with which to ascertain this.

When the patient tests the therapist's engagement at these key moments, the therapist has to re-emphasize their dedication. Their patience, endurance, love and hate might be taken to the limit, and it is understandable why many clinicians have no taste for this kind of work. If they do continue, they may be drawn into what is often described as a 'symbiotic entanglement', which can be experienced as both extremely frightening and intriguingly pleasurable. How this resonates with their own unconscious life will no doubt determine how they react and respond in the clinical work, and it is no accident that many therapists will go back into therapy themselves during such times.

As Arthur Burton observes, 'The schizophrenic wants an intensity of relationship which matches his estrangement – i.e., love of the most unvarnished order.' The level of commitment required is so great that often the only therapists who are willing to take it on are those starting their careers or saints. Burton and others have noted wryly that therapy here is less like a medical intervention than a marriage, 'with all the overtones that this implies but with the sexual aspects confined to fantasy', although one could argue that in fact the sexual aspects of most real marriages are also confined to fantasy. It is actually easier, says Burton, to get out of a real marriage than out of the temporary marriage with some psychotic subjects, and we see this reflected in the notorious touchiness of therapists about their schizophrenic patients. They will rarely report with candour what happens in the work, fearful of the condemnation of their colleagues.

These comments about work with schizophrenic subjects may ring true for some cases but not for others. The perils of symbiotic entanglement and the barrage of testing manoeuvres are often absent, and the vicissitudes of therapy will vary dramatically from one case to another. Yet whatever happens, it is crucial that the therapist remembers the difference between the core phenomena of psychosis and the attempts at restitution that they are so often confused with. Efforts to establish meaning, to build bridges between ideas or to invent new lifestyles may appear delusional or idiosyncratic, but they testify to an authentic work of creation.

So many of today's mental health services fail to understand this essential feature of psychosis. The success of a treatment is measured in superficial terms of social functionality, common measures that can be applied across 'patient populations' rather than in terms of an individual life. What represents a real breakthrough for one person may mean nothing to another, and these details will always vary from case to case. As the psychoanalyst Françoise Davoine pointed out, what matters may even be a small, modest pleasure, just like in the song 'My Favourite Things' from *The Sound of Music*. This is essentially a list of trivialities – ribbons, chocolates, raindrops and roses – yet they represent investments, signs of an affective link to life. They don't remove the abyss in the background – in the film, the approach of Nazism – yet they allow nonetheless a localized form of hope and joy.

At times, the therapist's interest in such small things can be of great value for the patient. When Lacan invited an analysand to enjoy one of the delicious chocolates he had just received from Belgium, the power of the gesture lay not simply in the dimension of a gift but in the communication of his pleasure in 'a few of my favourite things'. This will no doubt be more significant to a patient than the effort to make them enjoy 'happiness' or 'success', abstractions that many psychotic subjects are quite rightly sceptical of. Seeing through the false veneer of consumerist culture, they know very well what the real stakes of human life are about.

When push comes to shove, it is the other side of consumerism that matters here: not the ingestion of a preconceived notion of health or well-being but the creation of something new. As Arthur Burton put it, psychotic subjects 'somehow need to be involved with the beginnings and ends of things'. That this involves some form of production follows from both the theories we have discussed and the clinical cases we have invoked. If it is precisely the beginnings and ends of things that cannot be readily symbolized using a pre-existing grid of meaning, the psychotic subject must reinvent. This act may include speaking, but it always also implies a material creation: writing, drawing, painting, sculpting or any human practice of forging or inscription. I have never encountered a case of psychosis in which such an activity did not play a significant role, not necessarily in terms of the time devoted to it, but to the place it occupies in that person's world. Even the sporadic postcards sent during the course of a treatment can count for everything.

Encouraging and facilitating such acts is part of the work of any real therapy of the psychoses. Sadly, even if those contemporary therapies that tell the psychotic subject that they have an illness and then instruct them what to do about it may seem helpful to some, they deprive them of this vital aspect of experience. Whether the patient decides to take up the offer or not, whether they feel helped or hindered by therapy, the clinician must recognize that so many of the phenomena of psychosis are not the sign of some deficit but, on the contrary, a path towards creation. And this is what every therapeutic engagement should be able to offer.

Afterword

Taking seriously the theory of ordinary madness has radical consequences for the society we live in. If we accept that there is a fundamental difference between being mad – which is perfectly compatible with everyday life – and going mad – which will be triggered by certain situations – we can learn to respect the different practices that individuals invent to stabilize their lives. Sometimes, these fit in well with accepted social practices, and sometimes they don't. But once we recognize that they are attempts to create solutions, we can hopefully question any project to bring them back to a normative set of beliefs and values.

Acknowledging this fact will have crucial clinical consequences. As we have seen, many of the strange and seemingly bizarre practices of psychotic subjects are efforts to find a cure for the primary experiences of terror, fragmentation and invasion. Any treatment plan that confuses these two sets of phenomena will be hazardous, and undermining the person's attempt at self-cure can have catastrophic effects. Psychotic subjects are always busy here, naming, creating, assembling, inventing and documenting, and to question or try to excise such activities risks depriving the subject of what is most vital to them. The fruits of such activities do not have to be of any social 'use' or even to make sense: they can be quiet or noisy, private or public, communicative or contained.

Campaigns to destigmatize so-called 'mental illness' often take a wrong turning here. They try to demonstrate how sufferers of some condition have made amazing contributions to the sciences or the arts. Trying to destigmatize the diagnosis of autism, for example, we read how Einstein and Newton would have received that diagnosis today, and yet made fabulous discoveries in the field of physics. Even if they are acknowledged to have been 'different', their worth is still reckoned in terms of how their work has impacted on the world of others. However well intentioned, such perspectives are hardly judicious, as they make an implicit equation between value and social utility.

Taking this step is dangerous, as the moment that human life is defined in terms of utility, the door to stigmatization and segregation is opened. If someone were found to be not so useful, what value, then, would their life have? This was in fact exactly the argument of the early-twentieth-century eugenicists who campaigned for the extermination of the mentally ill. Although no one would admit such aspirations today, we cannot ignore the resurfacing in recent years of a remarkably similar discourse, with its emphasis on social utility, hereditary and genetic vulnerability.

Biology today, perhaps more than ever before in the last century, is used to explain human nature. Only in the mid-1990s, protestors could disrupt a meeting that aimed to demonstrate the genetic basis of criminal behaviour, yet today such assertions are received glowingly by the media. The new industry of bioprediction is thriving, with its claims to be able to predict future antisocial and deviant behaviour. Academics in Britain and the US participate in such projects, with no apparent awareness of the historical roots of their discipline or the ethical problems it poses.

All this takes place in a climate of enthusiasm for future intervention: once genetic vulnerability is identified, medical and social engineering will pave the way for a healthier society. The focus here is on external behaviour rather than on the complexity of inner life, with the idea that equating psychosis with a biological illness will foster more tolerant attitudes and acceptance. Prejudice is supposed to disappear when we learn that it is like any other health problem and that hence no one can be blamed for it.

But unfortunately the human capacity to exclude and blame cannot be airbrushed aside, and biological arguments involve just as much – and, many researchers argue, more – stigmatization. A recent review of twelve studies of stigma and 'mental illness' revealed that in eleven of them biological theories of psychosis led to more prejudice and stigma than social ones. Psychotic subjects were seen as dangerous, antisocial and unpredictable. As a recent World Health Organization study notes, 'Far too much confidence has been placed in the brain disease model, which may compound rather than challenge the stereotypes of dangerousness and, particularly, incompetence.'

Almost imperceptibly, the rise of the biological approach has brought with it the spectre of the eugenics movement that had such devastating effects in the early twentieth century and in the Nazi period. In its basic form, eugenics distinguishes a healthy 'us' from an unhealthy 'them', making the distinction in terms of racial or hereditary features. You can tell from a passport or birth certificate to which group the individual belongs, and it is this that ultimately separates the segregative approach from one which respects human life: for the latter, you need to listen to what an individual tells you about their experience, rather than know in advance where to consign him.

The two alternatives that eugenics provides once the segregation has been performed are clear: either make the unhealthy person healthy, or remove them from the society of the healthy or from the planet altogether. Although we might like to think that such debates were suited to the climate of Nazi Germany, they were in fact rooted in British and American thought. Those classified as mentally ill lost the right to marry in many American states from the end of the nineteenth century, and by 1914 more than twenty states had such legislation in place. There was a progressive programme to segregate the insane, supported by the eugenics movement, with Indiana the first state to pass a compulsory sterilization law for the mentally ill.

By the late 1920s, thirty states had passed similar legislation, generally of institutionalized subjects, although there was fierce opposition from some governors and state courts. Governors in Vermont, Nebraska and Idaho vetoed the first of the bills, and in Oregon a state referendum resulted in a repeal of that state's sterilization law. Yet, amazingly, the US Supreme Court ruled in 1927 that the sterilization of the mentally ill was indeed constitutional, as it blocked the transmission of bad genes. No European country had comparable legislation, and in 1937, a poll in *Fortune* magazine reported that 66 per cent of Americans favoured the sterilization of the mentally ill. As the writer Robert Whitaker comments, 'At that moment, America stood alone as the first eugenic country.'

America's eugenics programme was to have a major influence on Germany. Although the German parliament defeated a sterilization bill in 1914, the eugenics programme became more popular after the

First World War and Hitler praised its implacable logic. The emphasis was on the inherited nature of 'mental diseases', and the Rockefeller Foundation even gave a $2.5 million grant to the Munich Psychiatric Institute in 1925 for eugenic research, as well as other grants to German medical bodies. A compulsory sterilization law was passed after Hitler came to power in 1933, and German researchers studied the American procedures and theories closely, especially those of California. The wording of the German bill was taken almost *in toto* from one of the American sterilization laws, and under the Nazis an average of 165,000 German citizens were sterilized each year against their will.

Doctors were required to report any 'unfit' patients to special Hereditary Health Courts, which would then assess them for sterilization. American medical journals praised the German model, and it was not long before the next logical question was asked: why stop at sterilization? Shouldn't the mentally ill simply be killed? Surprisingly, perhaps, this was first raised as a legislative possibility not in Germany but in the US. The eugenics activist Madison Grant's bestselling book, *The Passing of the Great Race*, which urged the 'obliteration' of the unfit, was translated widely and Hitler apparently wrote the author a letter of admiration.

Both the German and the American eugenics movements saw mental illness as an inherited biological feature. Alexis Carrel, the Nobel Prize-winning physician, could write in his 1935 book, *Man the Unknown*: 'The abnormal prevent the development of the normal.' Hence, 'Why should society not dispose of the criminals and the insane in a more economical manner than prisons and asylums?' 'Why,' he asked, 'do we preserve these useless and harmful beings?' Carrel proposed extermination in 'small euthanasic institutions supplied with proper gases'. As we know, the Nazis set about this from January 1940.

The logic of segregation that this programme introduced is perhaps delusional, since it involved a rigid separation of 'us' and 'them'. We have seen how this is sometimes a feature of psychotic thinking, in which the world is divided up according to simple binary oppositions and two-place value judgements: pure and impure, good and bad, black and white, guilty and innocent, and so on. As the writer

Mary Loudon pointed out, discussing attitudes to mental illness, 'For many people, it is important to decide where others belong because it is the only way they know where they are themselves.'

Sadly, many of the well-intentioned approaches to psychosis today are based on exactly the prejudices of the eugenics era. The psychotic is divided into a 'healthy' and an 'unhealthy' part, with the aim of treatment being to allow the healthy part to triumph. The psyche is internally segregated, and therapy's aims are explained in terms of changes in brain chemistry. The psychotic must learn to see his unhealthy thought-processes as what one psychiatrist called 'a waste of time'. The 'interaction with more mature minds' – that is, of the therapeutic team – will be able to introduce the patient to more real-istic ways of thinking, behaving and feeling. The patient must explore the mind of the therapist to find 'their own mind represented within it' and then to 'integrate this image as part of his sense of himself'.

Some advocates of this view recognize that it echoes the ideas of eugenicists, but argue that being aware of one's 'unhealthy' part will obviously not result in such extreme measures as sterilization or incar-ceration, but will allow the person to be an active agent in managing their illness. The naivety of this perspective lies in its misunderstand-ing of what we could call 'psychical colonialism', a definition of which is given by the quotation at the end of the last paragraph. The concep-tion of illness will come from the outside, as will the various models of how to manage it, and these are all vigorously marketed. Treat-ment manuals tell us, indeed, that the therapist should present to the patient a stable view of their 'internal world', which can then 'be adopted as the reflective part of the self'. This means in effect internal-izing the therapist's interpretation of the patient's problems. We could contrast this to the view that does not aim to dismiss or reject the per-son's thought-processes, but to learn from them, clarify them, and perhaps help that person to use them to their advantage.

In this segregative vision of the psyche, patients become faulty pieces of equipment that must be restored to their original functionality through external intervention, rather than through their own internal resources. Psychotic phenomena must be removed as far as possible, and the patient led back to a shared reality, which in practice means that of the therapist. Yet if many, if not most, psychotic symptoms are in fact restitution mechanisms, we pursue such programmes at a very high price. As we have seen, what had interested many of the early psychiatrists was how a psychosis could stabilize or create mechanisms of compensation or equilibrium. The most florid symptoms might fade and activities, projects and lifestyles take their place.

The key to the study of these processes was the individual case: not the grouping of cases together in an experiment, with results taken through mathematical averaging of the participants, but a study of the unique, singular narrative of each individual patient. This might be bad news for those seeking a single procedure to be applied to psychotic subjects, as it presupposes that each case is different, each solution is different, even if concepts and theories can be deduced from the cases in question. As Jacques Hochmann observes in his history of psychiatry, the field has moved away from a model of long-term attention to the individual case towards programmes of social rehabilitation, based on cognitive theories, which limit their objectives to social capacities. Charities then bear the weight of chronic, often homeless patients.

Apart from the obvious neglect of the social dimensions of illness and crime, these new discourses ignore the formative value of human speech. When a research project at the Anna Freud Centre subjects two-year-old infants to brain scanning to predict future deviance, one might wonder how this is explained to the child. Whatever is actually said, how could this not impact on them? Wouldn't it, indeed, exercise a subtle effect of suggestion, which may have consequences for them later in their lives? Not necessarily to turn them into criminals, but possibly the exact opposite: to generate feelings of guilt or moral vigilance. The question, of course, to the parent would be: 'Why have you involved me in this?'

With psychosis, social attitudes and treatments suffer from the same blindness. New and influential reviews of therapy advise therapists to not actually take the patient's account of their treatment as objective. The speech of a human being is not scientifically reliable, and so, for psychologists like Peter Fonagy, to assess the results of therapy, brain scanning should be employed to measure objective, externally validated changes in the brain. This, they argue, should dictate which treatments are deemed effective. Genetic tests, likewise, should determine waiting lists, as they offer objective indications of how seriously the patient is at risk.

A crucial line has been crossed here. The illusion of an objective, external measurement of internal life has taken the place of a sensitivity to human speech. This is an ethical reversal, as it strips human beings of what is perhaps their unique capacity: the ability to create meaning. Once we move beyond speech, meaning becomes contingent, an irritating and useless variable that can only obfuscate scientific assessment. The pressure on many mental health workers today to simply monitor medication aggravates this situation. Ensuring that the patient is taking their medication and keeping an eye on the side effects of antipsychotic drugs can persuade clinicians that treatment is actually taking place and that hence further contact hours are not essential. The most serious side effect of medication here is the temptation for the physician to let the drug be enough.

This is not to say that medication may not at times be helpful. There is little doubt that in some cases it can temper the intensity of psychotic phenomena, but it should also serve to establish a platform for dialogue. The more space that is provided for regular therapy, the more that drug use can diminish, and it is worthwhile thinking of the prescription of minor tranquillizers, rather than the immediate appeal to neuroleptics that often takes place at the start of a treatment. Without this, due to the pervasive and crippling effects of long-term drug use, the idea of psychosis as a chronic and irreversible brain disease becomes a self-fulfilling prophecy.

Rather than succumb to this bleak cycle, persistent and patient work may kindle hope where it had previously been given up. Recognizing discreet, everyday madness can teach us about the mechanisms that allow a psychosis to become stable, and these can then inform our work with those whose psychosis has triggered. The therapist should not be hampered here by conventional views as to how a doctor should treat a patient. They must give up any preset view of what 'rehabilitation' or 'reintegration' might mean, and learn this instead from the person they are working with. Instead of seeing the psychotic subject, in Alanen's words, 'as a container of abnormal biological mechanisms', an investment in dialogue and a curiosity about the logic of that person's world can open up new therapeutic directions and offer the possibility of change. Therapy can do no more and no less here than to help the psychotic subject do what they have been trying to do all their lives: create a safe space in which to live.

Notes

Introduction

p. 4 Subject or object, see Patrick Coupechoux, *Un monde de fous* (Paris: Seuil, 2006); and Georges Lantéri-Laura, *Essais sur les paradigmes de la psychiatrie moderne* (Paris: Éditions du Temps, 1998). Marguerite Sechehaye, *A New Psychotherapy in Schizophrenia* (New York: Grune & Stratton, 1956), p. 38.

p. 5–6 Horton, see Brian Koehler and Ann-Louise Silver, 'Psychodynamic Treatment of Psychosis in the USA', in Yrjö Alanen et al. (eds), *Psychotherapeutic Approaches to Schizophrenic Psychoses* (London: Routledge, 2009), pp. 217–32. On Pinel, Tuke and the York Retreat, see Gladys Swain, *Le Sujet de la folie* (Toulouse: Privat, 1977); Anne Digby, *Madness, Morality and Medicine* (Cambridge: Cambridge University Press, 1985); Andrew Scull, *The Most Solitary of Afflictions, Madness and Society in Britain, 1700–1900* (New Haven: Yale University Press, 1993); and Lois Charland, 'Benevolent theory: moral treatment at the York Retreat', *History of Psychiatry*, 18 (2007), pp. 61–80. Colonizer, see Kurt Eissler, 'Remarks on the Psychoanalysis of Schizophrenia', in Eugene Brody and Frederick Redlich (eds), *Psychotherapy with Schizophrenics* (New York: International Universities Press, 1952), pp. 130–67.

p. 7 Mental hygiene, see Luis Izcovich, 'Santé mentale et désir du psychanalyste', *Mensuel, École de Psychanalyse des Forums du Champ Lacanien*, 12 (2006), pp. 7–11; and 'L'Éthique du clinicien', in *Le Souci de l'être* (Paris: Grapp, 1992), pp. 155–9.

Chapter 1

p. 9 Media images, see Otto Wahl, *Media Madness: Public Images of Mental Illness* (New Jersey: Rutgers University Press, 1995); G. Ward, *Making Headlines: Mental Health and the National Press* (London: Health Education

Authority, 1997); Sarah Clement and Nena Foster, 'Newspaper reporting on schizophrenia: A content analysis of five national newspapers at two time points', *Schizophrenia Research*, 98 (2008), pp. 178–83; and George Rosen, *Madness in Society* (London: Routledge, 1968).

p. 11 Popular textbook, Jacques Borel, *Précis de psychiatrie* (Paris: Delmas, 1939), p. 152. Eugen Bleuler, *Dementia Praecox or the Group of Schizophrenias* (1911) (New York: International Universities Press, 1950). Broken equilibrium, Eugène Minkowski, 'La genèse de la notion de schizophrénie et ses caractères essentiels', *L'Évolution Psychiatrique*, 1 (1925), p. 228. Silvano Arieti, *Interpretation of Schizophrenia*, 2nd edn (London: Crosby, 1974; 1st edn 1955), pp. 4–5. Note that many of these terms have now taken on a specific sense in psychoanalytic theory, often quite different from their original meanings in psychiatry.

p. 11–12 Not visible, Bleuler, *Dementia Praecox*, op. cit., pp. 13, 239 and 336. See also Gustav Bychowski, 'The problem of latent psychosis', *Journal of the American Psychoanalytic Association*, 1 (1953), pp. 484–503; and 'The psychology of latent schizophrenia', *American Journal of Psychotherapy*, 6 (1952), pp. 42–62. Paul Sérieux and Joseph Capgras, *Les Folies raisonnantes* (Paris: Alcan, 1909). For early studies of stabilization, see Paule Petit, *Les Délires de persécution curables* (Paris: Thesis, 1937); Raoul Rosenfeld, *Les Compensations morbides* (Paris: Lipschutz, 1936); Adrien Borel and Gilbert Robin, *Les Rêveurs éveillés* (Paris: Gallimard, 1926); Henri Claude and Marcel Montassut, 'Compensation ideo-affective', *L'Encéphale*, 20 (1925), pp. 557–69; Marcel Montassut, 'Les compensations imaginatives', *L'Évolution Psychiatrique*, 6 (1934), pp. 19–37; and J. Laboucarie and P. Barres, 'Curabilité des psychoses délirantes systématisées', *L'Évolution Psychiatrique*, 22 (1957), pp. 317–55. Piera Aulagnier, *The Violence of Interpretation* (1975) (London: Routledge, 2001), p. 156.

p. 14 Diplomacy, see Manfred Bleuler, *The Schizophrenic Disorders* (New Haven: Yale University Press, 1978), p. 490. De Clérambault, see 'Sur un internement contesté' (1911), in *Oeuvres Psychiatriques* (Paris: Presses Universitaires de France, 1942), pp. 791–814. Double book-keeping, see Eugen Bleuler, *Dementia Praecox*, op. cit., pp. 56 and 147.

p. 14 Yaël Cohen, 'La reticence', *L'Évolution Psychiatrique*, 59 (1994), pp. 285–303.

p. 15 T. M. Luhrmann, *Of Two Minds: An Anthropologist Looks at American Psychiatry* (New York: Random House, 2000), p. 49.

p. 15 Muriel Gardiner, 'The Wolf-Man in Later Life', in Muriel Gardiner (ed.), *The Wolf-Man and Sigmund Freud* (London: Hogarth, 1972), p. 358.

p. 16 See Emil Kraepelin, *Psychiatrie: Ein Lehrbuch für Studierende und Aerzte*, 8th edn, vol. 3 (1913) (Leipzig: Barth); E. Régis, *Précis de Psychiatrie*, 6th edn (Paris, 1923); and Eric Engstrom, *Clinical Psychiatry in Imperial Germany* (Ithaca: Cornell University Press, 2003). Favourable outcomes, see Luc Ciompi et al., 'Deep concern', *Schizophrenia Bulletin*, 36 (2010), pp. 437–9. Cured, see Bleuler, *Dementia Praecox*, op. cit., pp. 6–7.

p. 16 Chaslin, *Éléments de sémiologie et clinique mentales* (Paris: Asselin et Houzeau, 1912).

p. 17–18 Schreber, *Memoirs of My Nervous Illness* (1903); *New York Review of Books* (2000); and Freud, *Psychoanalytic Notes on an Autobiographical Account of a Case of Paranoia (Dementia Paranoides)* (1911), *Standard Edition*, vol. 12, pp. 9–79. Jules Séglas, 'La paranoia', *Archives de Neurologie* (1887), pp. 221–32. De Clérambault, see the translations and commentary in Paul Hriso, *Mental Automatisms* (Hermes Whispers Press, 2002).

p. 18 Double case, see R. Dupouy and Marcel Montassut, 'Un cas de "syndrome des sosies" chez une délirante hallucinée par interprétation des troubles psycho-sensoriels', *Annales Médico-Psychologiques*, 132 (1924), pp. 341–5.

p. 19 Psychosis in population, see A. Y. Tien, 'Distribution of hallucinations in the population', *Social Psychiatry and Psychiatric Epidemiology*, 26 (1991), pp. 287–92; Maarten Bak et al., 'When does experience of psychosis result in a need for care? A prospective general population study', *Schizophrenia Bulletin*, 29 (2003), pp. 349–58; Louise Johns and Jim van Os, 'The continuity of psychotic experiences in the general population', *Clinical Psychology Review*, 21 (2001), pp. 1125–41; Iris Sommer et al., 'Healthy individuals with auditory verbal hallucinations; who are they? Psychiatric assessments of a selected sample of 103 subjects', *Schizophrenia Bulletin*, 36 (2008), pp. 633–41; and Roberto Nuevo et al., 'The continuum of psychotic symptoms in the general population: A cross-national study', *Schizophrenia Bulletin*, online publication (2010).

p. 19 Torsion, see 'Über paranoide Erkrankungen', *Zeitschrift für die gesamte Neurologie und Psychiatrie*, 9 (1912), pp. 615–38. On Kraepelin's definition of paranoia, see Rogues de Fursac, *Manuel de psychiatrie*, 2nd edn (Paris: Alcan, 1903); and Kenneth Kendel, 'Kraepelin and the diagnostic concept of paranoia', *Comprehensive Psychiatry*, 29 (1988), pp. 4–11. It is sometimes argued that Kraepelin's recognition that paranoia remitted so successfully was what led him to develop the diagnostic category of paraphrenia, although he and his students would later question its legitimacy: see Wilhelm Mayer, 'Über paraphrene Psychosen', *Zeitschrift für die gesamte Neurologie und Psychiatrie*, 71 (1921), pp. 187–206.

p. 19 Henri Claude, 'Les psychoses paranoides', *L'Encéphale*, 20 (1925), pp. 136–49; Henri Claude and Marcel Montassut, 'Délimitation de la paranoia légitime', *L'Encéphale*, 21 (1926), pp. 57–63; and Charles-Henry Nodet, *Le Groupe des psychoses hallucinatoires chroniques* (Paris: Doin, 1938).

p. 20 Wagner, see Robert Gaupp, *Zur Psychologie des Massenmords: Hauptlehrer Wagner von Degerloch* (Berlin: Springer, 1914); 'Der Fall Wagner', *Zeitschrift für die gesamte Neurologie und Psychiatrie*, 60 (1920), pp. 312–27; and 'Zur Lehre von der Paranoia', ibid., 174 (1942), pp. 762–810.

p. 22 Ernst Kretschmer, 'The Sensitive Delusion of Reference' (1918), in Steven Hirsch and Michael Shepherd, *Themes and Variations in European Psychiatry* (Bristol: John Wright, 1974), pp. 153–95.

p. 22–4 Pharmacology, see David Healey, *The Creation of Psychopharmacology* (Cambridge, Mass.: Harvard University Press, 2002). Side effects, see Sheldon Gelman, *Medicating Schizophrenia: A History* (New Jersey: Rutgers University Press, 1999); Richard Bentall, *Doctoring the Mind* (London: Allen Lane, 2009); and Joanna Moncrieff, *The Myth of the Chemical Cure* (London: Macmillan, 2009). Knock out, see Robert Whitaker, *Mad in America: Bad Science, Bad Medicine, and the Enduring Mistreatment of the Mentally Ill* (New York: Perseus, 2001), p. 100. Swiss watch, see Eugene Brody and Frederick Redlich (eds), *Psychotherapy with Schizophrenics*, op. cit., p. 28. Punishment, see J. Laboucarie and P. Barres, 'Curabilité des psychoses délirantes systématisées', op. cit., p. 329. Gérard Pommier, 'Du fantasme à l'hallucination' (19 March 2011), Espace Analytique, Paris.

p. 25 Manfred Bleuler, 'Research and changes in concepts in the study of schizophrenia', *Bulletin of the Isaac Ray Medical Library*, 3 (1955), pp. 1–132.

p. 26–7 Made it possible, see Robert Whitaker, *Mad in America*, op. cit., p. 156; and Gerald Grob, *The Mad Among Us: A History of the Care of America's Mentally Ill* (Cambridge, Mass.: Harvard University Press, 1999). Compare with Edward Shorter, *A History of Psychiatry from the Era of the Asylum to the Age of Prozac* (New York: Wiley, 1997). Increase in psychosis, see E. Jarvis, 'On the supposed increase of insanity', *American Journal of Insanity*, 8 (1851–2), pp. 333–64; J. Hawkes, 'On the increase of insanity', *Journal of Psychological Medicine and Mental Pathology*, 10 (1857), pp. 508–21; and Andrew Scull, *The Most Solitary of Afflictions*, op. cit., pp. 334–74.

p. 27 Andrew Lakoff, *Pharmaceutical Reason, Knowledge and Value in Global Psychiatry* (Cambridge: Cambridge University Press, 2005), p.174; and Nikolas Rose, 'Pharmaceuticals in Europe', in Martin Knapp et al. (eds), *Mental Health Policy and Practice across Europe* (Maidenhead: Open University Press, 2007), pp. 146–87. J. A. Liberman et al., 'Effectiveness of antipsychotic drugs in patients with chronic schizophrenia', *New England Journal of Medicine*, 353 (2005), pp. 1209–23.

p. 28 Some studies, see James Hegarty et al., 'One hundred years of schizophrenia: a meta-analysis of the outcome literature', *American Journal of Psychiatry*, 151 (1994), pp. 1409–14.

p. 29 Richard Bentall, *Doctoring the Mind*, op. cit., p. 84.

p. 30 D. L. Rosenhan, 'On being sane in insane places', *Science*, 179 (1973), pp. 250–58. The experiment was repeated by Lauren Slater some three decades later, although there is controversy over her claims: *Opening Skinner's Box: Great Psychological Experiments of the Twentieth Century* (London: Bloomsbury, 2004). Pierre Janet, *La Force et la faiblesse psychologiques* (Paris: Maloine, 1932).

p. 30 Film footage, see J. E. Cooper et al., *Psychiatric Diagnosis in New York and London* (Oxford: Oxford University Press, 1972); Michael Shepherd et al., *An Experimental Approach to Psychiatric Diagnosis* (Copenhagen: Munksgaard, 1968); Martin Katz et al., 'Studies of the diagnostic process', *American Journal of Psychiatry*, 1215 (1969), pp. 937–47; and R. E. Kendell et al., 'Diagnostic criteria of American and British psychiatrists', *Archives of General Psychiatry*, 25 (1971), pp. 123–30. See also P. Pichot, 'The diagnosis and classification of mental disorders in French-speaking countries: background, current views and comparison with other nomenclatures', *Psychological Medicine*, 12 (1982), pp. 475–92.

p. 31 DSM, see Stuart Kirk and Herb Kutchins, *The Selling of DSM: The Rhetoric of Science in Psychiatry* (New York: De Gruyter, 1992); and *Making Us Crazy: DSM, the Psychiatric Bible and the Creation of Mental Disorders* (New York: Free Press, 1997).

p. 32 Recent survey, see Jim Geekie and John Read, *Making Sense of Madness: Contesting the Meaning of Schizophrenia* (London: Routledge, 2009), p. 25.

p. 32–3 Diagnostic practice, see Wolfgang de Boor, *Psychiatrische Systematik, Ihre Entwicklung in Deutschland seit Kahlbaum* (Berlin: Springer, 1954); Jacques Roubinovitch, *Des variétés cliniques de la folie en France et en Allemagne* (Paris: Doin, 1896); Ernest Stengel, 'A comparative study of psychiatric classification', *Proceedings of the Royal Society of Medicine*, 53 (1959), pp. 123–30; and Karl Menninger et al., 'The unitary concept of mental illness', *Bulletin of the Menninger Clinic*, 22 (1958), pp. 4–12.

p. 34 Jean-Étienne Esquirol, 'Hallucination', *Dictionnaire des sciences médicales* (Paris: Panckoucke, 1817), pp. 64–71; and complicated in *Des maladies mentales considerées sous les rapports medial, hygiénique et médico-légal*, 2 vols (Paris: Baillière, 1938). An early elaboration of this view that psychiatric classification should start not with 'symptoms' but with the person's relation *to* the symptom can be found in Alfred Binet and Théodore Simon, 'Définition des principaux états mentaux de l'aliénation', *L'Année Psychologique*, 16 (1910), pp. 61–6; and 'Conclusion sur les états mentaux de l'aliénation', ibid., pp. 361–71.

Chapter 2

p. 35 Freud, *Project* (1895), *Standard Edition*, vol. 1 (London: Hogarth, 1966), pp. 353–6; and 'The Neuropsychoses of Defence' (1894), *Standard Edition*, vol. 3, pp. 45–61 and 58.

p. 38 Ernst Kretschmer, 'The Sensitive Delusion of Reference', op. cit.

p. 39 Ego, see Freud, 'The Neuropsychoses of Defence', op. cit., p. 58. On 'Verwerfung', see Lacan, *The Seminar of Jacques Lacan, Book 3: The Psychoses, 1955–6*, ed. J.-A. Miller (New York: Norton, 1993); and Jean-Claude Maleval, *La Forclusion du nom-du-père* (Paris: Seuil, 2000).

p. 40 Bad woman, see Draft H in Jeffrey Masson (ed.), *The Complete Letters of Sigmund Freud and Wilhelm Fliess* (Cambridge, Mass.: Harvard University Press, 1985), pp. 108–9.

p. 40 Henri Flournoy, 'Délire systématisé de persécution', *L'Évolution Psychiatrique*, 2 (1927), pp. 9–27.

p. 41 Charles Melman, *Les Paranoias* (1999–2001 Seminars) (Paris: Éditions de l'Association Lacanienne Internationale, 2003), pp. 271–2.

p. 43 Renée, *Autobiography of a Schizophrenic Girl* (New York: Grune & Stratton, 1951), p. 55.

p. 44 Back of mirror, see Harold Searles, *The Nonhuman Environment* (New York: International Universities Press, 1960), p. 321. See also E. Menninger-Lerchenthal, *Der Eigene Doppelgänger* (Bern: Huber, 1946); *Das Truggebilde der eigenein Gestalt Heautoskopie Doppelgänger* (Berlin, 1935); Paul Sollier, *Les Phénomènes d'autoscopie* (Paris: Alcan, 1903); and Gabriel Dromard, *La Mimique chez les aliénés* (Paris: Alcan, 1909).

p. 45 Schreber, *Memoirs*, op. cit., p. 243.

p. 46 Lacan, 'The Mirror Stage as Formative of the I Function' (1949), in *Écrits* (New York: Norton, 2006), pp. 75–81. Henri Wallon, *Les Origines du caractère chez l'enfant* (Paris, 1934); and James Baldwin, 'Imitation: a chapter in the natural history of consciousness', *Mind* (January 1894), pp. 26–55. See Émile Jalley, *Freud, Wallon, Lacan: L'Enfant au miroir* (Paris: École Lacanienne de Psychanalyse, 1998).

p. 47 René Zazzo, *World Health Organisation Discussion on Child Development*, vol. 1 (New York: International Universities Press, 1953).

p. 49 Prohibition of incest, see Charles-Henry Pradelles de Latour, 'La Psychanalyse et l'anthropologie sociale au regard de la loi', in Marcel Drach and Bernard Toboul (eds), *L'Anthropologie de Lévi-Strauss et la psychanalyse* (Paris: La Decouverte, 2008), pp. 45–55.

p. 49 Claude Lévi-Strauss, *The Savage Mind* (1962) (London: Weidenfeld, 1966).

p. 52 Renée, *Autobiography of a Schizophrenic Girl*, op. cit., p. 133.

p. 53 Paternity, see Edwin Hartland, *Primitive Paternity*, 2 vols (London: The Folk-Lore Society, 1909). Lacan on Little Hans, *La Relation d'objet* (1956–7), ed. J.-A. Miller (Paris: Seuil, 1994). See also Markos Zafiropoulos, *Lacan and Lévi-Strauss* (London: Karnac, 2010).

p. 55 Marcel Pagnol, *La Gloire de mon père* (Monte Carlo: Pastorelli, 1957).

p. 56 Bruno Bettelheim, *The Empty Fortress* (New York: Free Press, 1967), pp. 235–50.

p. 58 Lacan on Oedipus, *La Relation d'objet*, op. cit.; and *Les Formations d'Inconscient* (1957–8), ed. J.-A. Miller (Paris: Seuil, 1998).

p. 62 Later views, see Lacan, *Le Sinthome* (1975–6), ed. J.-A. Miller (Paris: Seuil, 2005).

p. 64 Kurt Eissler, 'Limitations to the psychotherapy of schizophrenia', *Psychiatry*, 6 (1943), pp. 381–91.

p. 65 Communication, see Gregory Bateson et al., 'Towards a theory of schizophrenia', *Behavioural Science*, 1 (1956), pp. 251–64; and 'A note on the double bind – 1962', *Family Process*, 2 (1963), pp. 154–61. For an example of these processes, see Schreber, *Memoirs*, op. cit., pp. 154 and 209.

Chapter 3

For Lacan's views on psychosis, see 'Presentation on Psychic Causality' (1946), in *Écrits*, op. cit., pp. 123–58; *The Seminar of Jacques Lacan, Book 3: The Psychoses, 1955–6*, op. cit.; 'On a Question Prior to Any Possible Treatment of Psychosis' (1957–8), in *Écrits*, op. cit., pp. 445–88; and *Le Sinthome*, op. cit. For context and commentary, see Lucien Bonnafé et al., *Le Problème de la psychogenèse des névroses et des psychoses* (Paris: Desclée de Brouwer, 1950); Jean-Claude Maleval, *La Forclusion du nom-du-père*, op. cit; Geneviève Morel, *Sexual Ambiguities* (London: Karnac, 2011); and Corinne Fellahian, *La Psychose selon Lacan, évolution d'un concept* (Paris: L'Harmattan, 2005). A classic early study of delusion as compensation is Maurice Mignard and Marcel Montassut, 'Un délire de compensation', *L'Encéphale*, 12 (1924), pp. 628–34. For Lacanian perspectives, see Jean-Claude Maleval, *Logique du délire* (Paris: Masson, 1996); and Anne Lysy-Stevens and Alexandre Stevens, 'La psychose infantile: déficit ou production?', *Quarto*, 46 (1991), pp. 46–50.

p. 67 Schreber, *Memoirs*, op. cit., pp. 46–7 and 248–9.

p. 69 Louis Wolfson, *Le Schizo et les langues* (Paris: Gallimard, 1970). See also his *Ma mère musicienne est morte . . .* (Paris: Navarin, 1984); the interview in *L'Âne*, 18 (September/October 1984), pp. 1–4; Serge André, 'La pulsion chez le schizophrène', *Ornicar?*, 36 (1986), pp. 103–10; Angel Enciso Bergé, 'La langue maternelle dans la psychose', ibid., pp. 94–102; and Geneviève Morel, 'Point final à une planète infernale', ibid., pp. 82–93.

p. 70 Striking and noisy, see Freud, *Psychoanalytic Notes on an Autobiographical Account of a Case of Paranoia (Dementia Paranoides)* (1911), *Standard Edition*, vol. 12, pp. 9–82.

p. 70 Formal letter, André Ceillier, 'Du rôle des hallucinations psychiques dans l'exploration de l'inconscient', *L'Évolution Psychiatrique*, 1 (1925), pp. 142–54.

p. 71 John Custance, *Wisdom, Madness and Folly* (New York: Pellegrini, 1952), p. 45.

p. 72 Word 'father', see Paul Mattusek, 'Studies in Delusional Perception' (1952), in John Cutting and Michael Shepherd, *Clinical Roots of the Schizophrenia Concept* (Cambridge: Cambridge University Press, 1987), p. 100.

p. 73 Brooks, quoted in Bert Kaplan (ed.), *The Inner World of Mental Illness* (New York: Harper and Row, 1964), p. 84.

p. 73 Lewis Hill, *Psychotherapeutic Intervention in Schizophrenia* (Chicago: University of Chicago Press, 1955), p. 67.

p. 74 See Judith Allardyce et al., 'Deconstructing psychosis conference 2006: the validity of schizophrenia and alternative approaches to classification', *Schizophrenia Bulletin*, 33 (2007), pp. 863–7; L. B. Jansson and J. Parnas, 'Competing definitions of schizophrenia: what can be learned from polydiagnostic studies?', ibid., pp. 1178–200; Manfred Bleuler, 'Research and changes in concepts in the study of schizophrenia', op. cit., pp. 1–132; Eugène Minkowski, 'La genèse de la notion de schizophrénie et ses caractères essentiels', op. cit.; and Henri Ey, 'Classifications des maladies mentales et le problème des psychoses aiguës', *Études Psychiatriques*, 3 (1954), pp. 1–45.

p. 74 Karl Jaspers, *General Psychopathology* (1913) (Baltimore: Johns Hopkins University Press, 1997), pp. 567–8.

p. 75 In fact, Paul Schilder proved in the 1920s that the 'psychotic' symptoms of patients suffering from syphilitic brain infections were grounded in their pre-infection personalities, disproving the idea that the area of the brain that had been damaged would determine the person's symptomology. See his *Studien und Symptomologie der progressiven Paralyse* (Berlin: Karger, 1930).

p. 76 Social network, see Arthur Burton et al. (eds), *Schizophrenia as a Life Style* (New York: Springer, 1974).

p. 76 Jay Watts, 'The Group of Schizophrenias' (2010), unpublished paper.

p. 76–7 Paranoia and schizophrenia, see *Clinique différentielle des psychoses* (Paris: Navarin, 1988); Colette Soler, *L'Inconscient à ciel ouvert de la psychose* (Toulouse: Presses Universitaires du Mirail, 2002); and Luis Izcovich,

Les Paranoïaques et la psychanalyse (Paris: Éditions du Champ Lacanien, 2004). On different delusional constructions, see H. Mueller-Suur, 'Das Gewissheitsbewusstein beim schizophrenen und beim paranoischen Wahnerleben', *Fortschrift Neurologie und Psychiatrie*, 18 (1950), pp. 44–51; Philippe Chaslin, *Éléments de sémiologie et de clinique mentales*, op. cit.; and Jean-Claude Maleval, *Logique du délire*, op. cit. Contrast to melancholia, see George Dumas, *Les États intellectuals dans la mélancolie* (Paris: Alcan, 1895); Jacques Adam et al., *Des mélancolies* (Paris: Éditions du Champ Lacanien, 2001); and Darian Leader, *The New Black: Mourning, Melancholia and Depression* (London: Hamish Hamilton, 2008). An early study of the relation of schizophrenia to manic depression is Moritz Urstein, *Die Dementia praecox und ihre Stellung zun manisch-depressiven Irresein* (Berlin: Urban & Schwarzenberg, 1909).

p. 77 Henri Claude, see 'Les psychoses paranoides', op. cit., and Henri Claude and Marcel Montassut, 'Délimitation de la paranoia légitime', op. cit.

p. 79 Melancholia, see Jules Séglas, *Leçons cliniques sur les maladies mentales et nerveuses* (Paris: Asselin et Houzeau, 1895). Piera Aulagnier, *The Violence of Interpretation*, op. cit., p. 199.

p. 83 Gregory Bateson et al., 'Towards a theory of schizophrenia', op. cit.

p. 84 Pierre Bruno, 'Schizophrénie et paranoïa', *Preliminaire*, 5 (1993), pp. 67–83.

p. 86 Matthews, Air Loom, see John Haslam, *Illustrations of Madness* (1810), ed. Roy Porter (London: Routledge, 1988).

p. 86 Schreber, *Memoirs*, op. cit., p. 123.

p. 87–91 The body and libido in schizophrenia, see Paul Balvet, *Le Sentiment de dépersonnalisation dans les délires de structure paranoïde* (Lyon: Riou, 1936); 'De l'importance du sentiment de dépersonnalisation dans la pathogénie des délires', *L'Évolution Psychiatrique*, 4 (1936), pp. 3–26; and Paul Schilder, *Seele und Leben* (Berlin: Springer, 1923). Balvet found four key areas here: loss of *élan vital*, loss of the sense of bodily unity, non-recognition of oneself, and the loss of the feeling of bodily substance (e.g., variations in the dimensions of the body, dissolution of the body, loss of materiality of the body). Parts not belonging, see H. Hécaen and J. de Ajuriaguerra *Méconnaissances et hallucinations corporelles* (Paris: Masson, 1952), p. 288; and on body changes, ibid., pp. 257–370. My hand, see Pierre Janet,

'L'Hallucination dans le délire de persécution', *Revue Philosophique* (1932), pp. 61–98 and 279–331; and the discussion in Stéphane Thibierge, *Pathologies de l'image du corps* (Paris: Presses Universitaires de France, 1999).

p. 91 Karl Abraham, 'A Short Study of the Development of the Libido' (1924), in *Selected Papers on Psychoanaysis* (London: Maresfield Reprints, 1979), p. 455. On Wagner, see Anne-Marie Vindras, *Louis II de Bavière selon Ernst Wagner, paranoïaque dramaturge* (Paris: EPEL, 1993), pp. 153 and 138.

p. 92 Bleuler, *Dementia Praecox*, op. cit., pp. 129 and 231.

p. 92 Existential, see Arthur Burton, 'The Alchemy of Schizophrenia', in *Schizophrenia as a Life Style*, op. cit., p. 87.

p. 92 Schreber, *Memoirs*, op. cit., p. 233. Rationalizations, see Bleuler, *Dementia Praecox*, op. cit., p. 131.

p. 93 Grandeur and mania, see Edith Jacobson, 'Psychotic Identifications' (1954), in *Depression* (New York: International Universities Press, 1971), pp. 242–63.

Chapter 4

p. 95 Victor Tausk, 'On the origin of the "influencing machine" in schizophrenia' (1919), *Psychoanalytic Quarterly*, 2 (1933), pp. 519–56.

p. 95 Father took thoughts, see Kurt Schneider, *Clinical Psychopathology* (New York: Grune & Stratton, 1959), p. 101.

p. 95 Jean Piaget, *The Language and Thought of the Child* (New York: Harcourt Brace, 1926).

p. 96 Red light, see Silvano Arieti, *Interpretation of Schizophrenia*, op. cit., p. 318.

p. 97 Serge Leclaire, 'À la recherche des principes d'une psychothérapie des psychoses', *L'Évolution Psychiatrique*, 23 (1958), pp. 377–419.

p. 97 Warhol, see Brian Dillon, *Tormented Hope, Nine Hypochondriac Lives* (London: Penguin, 2009), p. 242.

p. 97 *Folie à deux*, see C. Lasègue and J. Falret, 'La folie à deux ou folie communiquée', *Annales Médico-Psychologiques*, 18 (1877), pp. 321–55; and Helene Deutsch, 'Folie à deux', *Psychoanalytic Quarterly*, 7 (1938), pp. 307–18.

p. 98 Anna Freud, 'The role of bodily illness in the mental life of children', *Psychoanalytic Study of the Child*, 7 (1952), pp. 69–81.

p. 98 My arms, see Werner Mendel, 'A Phenomenological Theory of Schizophrenia', in Arthur Burton et al. (eds), *Schizophrenia as a Life Style*, op. cit., p. III.

p. 98 Pankow, see Jean-Max Gaudillière and Françoise Davoine, 'The Contribution of Some French Psychoanalysts to the Clinical and Theoretical Approaches to Transference in the Psychodynamic Treatment of Psychosis', in Yrjö Alanen et al. (eds), *Psychotherapeutic Approaches to Schizophrenic Psychoses*, op. cit., p. 141.

p. 98 Jeanine, see Piera Aulagnier, *L'Apprenti-historien et le maître-sorcier* (Paris: Presses Universitaires de France, 1984), pp. 263–68.

p. 100 Linnaeus, see Silvano Arieti, *Interpretation of Schizophrenia*, op. cit., p. 380.

p. 101 Gregory Bateson et al., 'Towards a theory of schizophrenia', op. cit.

p. 101 Louis Sass, *Madness and Modernism* (Cambridge, Mass.: Harvard University Press, 1998), p. 179. See also Louis Sass and Josef Parnas, 'Schizophrenia, consciousness and the self', *Schizophrenia Bulletin*, 29 (2003), pp. 427–44.

p. 102 Lacan on speech in psychosis, see *The Seminar of Jacques Lacan, Book 3: The Psychoses, 1955–6*, op. cit.; and 'On a Question', op. cit.

p. 103–4 Eyes, see Freud, 'The Unconscious' (1915), *Standard Edition*, vol. 14, pp. 197–8; and Bleuler, *Dementia Praecox*, op. cit., p. 76. Worms, see B. P. Karon and G. R. VandenBos, *Psychotherapy of Schizophrenia* (New York: Jason Aronson, 1981), pp. 159–61.

p. 104 Paul Sérieux and Joseph Capgras, *Les Folies raisonnantes*, op. cit. p. 21. See also Paul Guiraud, 'Les formes verbales de l'interprétation délirante', *Annales Médico-Psychologiques*, 129 (1921), pp. 395–412.

p. 104 Poison, see Silvano Arieti, *Interpretation of Schizophrenia*, op. cit., p. 268.

p. 104 Critique of concrete/abstract, see Maria Lorenz, 'Problems posed by schizophrenic language', *Archives of General Psychiatry*, 4 (1961), pp. 95–102; and 'Expressive behavior and language patterns', *Psychiatry*, 18 (1955), pp. 353–66.

p. 105 Bruno Bettelheim, *The Empty Fortress*, op. cit, p. 241.

p. 105 Jules Séglas, *Des troubles du langage chez les aliénés* (Paris: Rueff, 1892).

p. 106 E. Tanzi, 'I neologismi degli alienti in rapporto col delirio cronico', part 1, *Rivista Sperimentale di Freniatria e di Medicina Legale della Alenazione Mentali*, 15 (1899), pp. 352–93; and part 2, ibid., 16 (1900), pp. 1–35.

p. 106 Yrjö Alanen, *Schizophrenia, Its Origins and Need-Adapted Treatment* (London: Karnac, 1997), pp. 10–11.

p. 107 Carl Jung, *The Psychology of Dementia Praecox* (1907), in *Collected Works*, vol. 3 (New Jersey: Princeton University Press, 1972); and see *Studies in Word Association* (1906) (London: Heinemann, 1918).

p. 107 Karl Kleist, 'Aphasie und Geisteskrankheit', *Münchener Medizinische Wochenschrift*, 61 (1914), pp. 8–12.

p. 107 'Eseamarrider', see F. J. Fish, *Schizophrenia* (Bristol: John Wright, 1962), p. 50.

p. 107–8 Ludwig Staudenmaier, *Die Magie als experimentelle Naturwissenschaft* (Leipzig, 1912); and Leonard Zusne, 'Altered States of Consciousness, Magical Thinking and Psychopathology: The Case of Ludwig Stauden-maier', in Colleen Ward (ed.), *Altered States of Consciousness and Mental Health* (London: Sage, 1989), pp. 233–250. Denotation, see L. Vigotsky, 'Thought in schizophrenia', *Archives of Neurology and Psychiatry*, 31 (1934), pp. 1063–77; Harold Vetter, 'New-word coinage in the psychopathological context', *Psychiatric Quarterly*, 42 (1968), pp. 298–312. Patients' words, see Harry Stack Sullivan, 'Peculiarity of thought in schizophrenia', *American Journal of Psychiatry*, 5 (1925), pp. 21–80; and David Forrest, 'Poesis and the language of schizophrenia', *Psychiatry*, 28 (1965), pp. 1–18.

p. 109 On Saussure's distinction, see Claude Lévi-Strauss, *The Savage Mind*, op. cit., p. 156.

p. 109 Serge Leclaire, 'À la recherche des principes d'une psychothérapie des psychoses', op. cit., pp. 392–3.

p. 110 E. von Domarus, 'The Specific Laws of Logic in Schizophrenia', in J. S. Kasanin (ed.), *Language and Thought in Schizophrenia* (Berkeley: University of California Press, 1944), pp. 104–14.

p. 110 Angel, see Silvano Arieti, *Interpretation of Schizophrenia*, op. cit., p. 239.

p. 111 Adolphe, see George Dumas, *Le Surnaturel et les dieux d'après les maladies mentales* (Paris: Presses Universitaires de France, 1946), p. 245.

p. 111 Paul Courbon and Gabrield Fail, 'Syndrome d'illusion de Frégoli et schizophrénie', *Bulletin de la Société Clinique de Medicine Mentale* (1927), pp. 121–5. On misidentifications, see W. Scheid, 'Über

Personenverkennung', *Zeitschrift für die gesamte Neurologie und Psychiatrie*, 157 (1936), pp. 1–16; M. D. Enoch et al., *Some Uncommon Psychiatric Syndromes* (Bristol: John Wright, 1967); Stéphane Thibierge, *Pathologies de l'image du corps*, op. cit.; and Ramin Mojtabai, 'Misidentification phenomena in German psychiatry: a historical review and comparison with the French/English approach', *History of Psychiatry*, 7 (1996), pp. 137–58. It has been observed that misidentification phenomena occur more often with women than with men: for a delightful attempt to explain this, see Stanley Coleman, 'Misidentification and non-recognition', *Journal of Mental Science*, 79 (1933), pp. 42–51.

p. 112 Harry Stack Sullivan, 'Affective experience in early schizophrenia', *American Journal of Psychiatry*, 6 (1927), pp. 467–83.

p. 112 Subway, see M. L. Hayward and J. E. Taylor, 'A schizophrenic patient describes the action of intensive psychotherapy', *Psychiatric Quarterly*, 30 (1956), pp. 211–248 and 236.

p. 112 Kurt Eissler, 'Notes upon the emotionality of a schizophrenic patient and its relation to problems of technique', *The Psychoanalytic Study of the Child*, 8 (1953), p. 214.

p. 112 Zombie, see Werner Mendel, 'A Phenomenological Theory of Schizophrenia', op. cit., p. 106; Karl Jaspers, *General Psychopathology*, op. cit., pp. 67 and 122.

Chapter 5

p. 116 Bismarck, see George Dumas, *Le Surnaturel et les dieux d'après les maladies mentales*, op. cit., p.196.

p. 118 20,000 francs, see Bleuler, *Dementia Praecox*, op. cit., p. 137.

p. 119 Karl Jaspers, *General Psychopathology*, op. cit., pp. 103–6. On the experience of meaning, see René Targowla and Jean Dublineau, *L'Intuition délirante* (Paris: Maloine, 1931).

p. 120 Secrets of universe, Bert Kaplan (ed.), *The Inner World of Mental Illness*, op. cit., p. 94. John Custance, *Wisdom, Madness and Folly*, op. cit., p. 52.

p. 120 Lacan, 'On a Question', op. cit., pp. 450–51; and Eugène Minkowski, *Traité de psychopathologie* (Paris: Presses Universitaires de France, 1966).

p. 121 Joseph Capgras, 'Le délire d'interprétation hyposthénique: délire de supposition', *Annales Médico-Psychologiques*, 88 (1930), pp. 272–99.

p. 123 Geneviève Morel, *Sexual Ambiguities*, op. cit., pp. 188–201.

p. 123 Bishop, see Paul Sérieux and Joseph Capgras, *Les Folies raisonnantes*, op. cit., p. 156.

p. 124 Examples, see H. Hécaen and J. de Ajuriaguerra, *Méconnaissances et hallucinations corporelles*, op. cit., pp. 283–6.

p. 124 Carnegie, see Richard Hofstadter, *Social Darwinism and American Thought* (New York: Braziller, 1959), pp. 44–7.

p. 124 Kurt Schneider, *Clinical Psychopathology*, op. cit., p. 105.

p. 125 See everything, Karl Jaspers, *General Psychopathology*, op. cit., pp. 115–16. Memory, see Emil Kraepelin, 'Über Erinnerungsfalschungen', *Archiv für Psychiatrie und Nervenkrankheiten*, 18 (1887), pp. 199–239.

p. 125 Trenches, see Maurice Mignard and Marcel Montassut, 'Un délire de compensation', op. cit., pp. 628–34.

p. 125 Operations, see Harold Searles, *The Nonhuman Environment*, op. cit., pp. 192–3.

p. 126 Paula Elkisch, 'On infantile precursors of the "influencing machine" (Tausk)', *Psychoanalytic Study of the Child*, 14 (1959), pp. 219–35.

p. 127 Geneviève Morel, *Sexual Ambiguities*, op. cit., pp. 45–8.

p. 128 Schreber, *Memoirs*, op. cit., p. 19. External influence, see André Ceillier, 'Les influencés', *L'Encéphale* (1924), pp. 152–62, 225–34, 294–301 and 370–81. Thought at, see Harold Searles, *The Nonhuman Environment*, op. cit., p. 209. Henri Claude, 'Mécanisme des hallucinations: syndrome d'action extérieure', *L'Encéphale*, 25 (1930), pp. 345–59.

p. 129 Charles-Henry Nodet, *Le Groupe des psychoses hallucinatoires chroniques*, op. cit., p. 97.

p. 129 George Dumas, *Le Surnaturel et les dieux d'après les maladies mentales*, op. cit., pp. 27–57.

p. 130 Irony of the psychotic, see Louis Sass, *Madness and Modernism*, op. cit., pp. 111–15.

p. 131 Donkey, see Bleuler, *Dementia Praecox*, op. cit., p. 99.

p. 133 Binary, see Geneviève Morel, 'L'insuffisance des identifications à établir la sexuation d'un sujet', *Carnets de Lille*, 2 (1997), pp. 36–40.

p. 135 Edith Jacobson, 'On Depressive States: Nosological and Theoretical Problems', in *Depression*, op. cit., pp. 167–84. A. Bottéro, 'Une histoire de la dissociation schizophrénique', *L'Évolution Psychiatrique*, 66 (2001), pp. 43–60.

p. 136 Oscar Bumke, *Lehrbuch der Geisteskrankheiten* (Munich: Bergmann, 1929).

Chapter 6

p. 137 On the question of psychical and biological causality, see Don Jackson, *Myths of Madness: New Facts for Old Fallacies* (New York: Macmillan, 1964); Don Jackson (ed.), *The Etiology of Schizophrenia* (New York: Basic Books, 1960); and Alphonse De Waehlens and Wilfried Ver Eecke, *Phenomenology and Lacan on Schizophrenia, after the Decade of the Brain* (Leuven: Leuven University Press, 2001). M. K. Horwitt, 'Fact and artifact in the biology of schizophrenia', *Science*, 124 (1956), pp. 429–30. On causes and conditions, see Poul Faergeman, *Psychogenic Psychoses* (London: Butterworth, 1963).

p. 138 Chemistry and physics, Don Jackson, 'The transactional viewpoint', *International Journal of Psychiatry*, 4 (1967), pp. 543–4.

p. 139 Gene, see Evelyn Fox Keller, *The Century of the Gene* (Cambridge, Mass.: Harvard University Press, 2000); and Catherine Waldby, 'Code unknown: histories of the gene', *Social Studies of Science*, 31 (2001), pp. 779–91.

p. 140 Lacan, 'On a Question', op. cit. Alfredo Zenoni, 'Le nom-du-père et sa forclusion', *Préliminaire*, 5 (1993), pp. 85–92.

p. 143 Sophie de Mijolla-Mellor, *Penser la psychose* (Paris: Dunod, 1998).

p. 145 Schreber and his father, see Zvi Lothane, *In Defense of Schreber* (London: The Analytic Press, 1992); Luiz Eduardo Prado de Oliveira, *Le Cas Schreber* (Paris: Presses Universitaires de France, 1979); and *Schreber et la paranoïa* (Paris: L'Harmattan, 1996).

p. 147 Responsibility, see Jacques-Alain Miller, ''Sur la lecon des psychoses', *Actes de l'Ecole de la Cause Freudienne*, 13, 1987, pp. 142–4.

p. 149–52 Gisela Pankow, 'Dynamic Structurization in Schizophrenia', in Arthur Burton (ed.), *Psychotherapy of the Psychoses* (New York: Basic Books, 1961), pp. 152–71. Mother's divine birth, see Piera Aulagnier, 'Remarques sur la structure psychotique' (1964), in *Un interprète en quête du sens* (Paris: Payot, 2006), pp. 361–86. Mothers, see Piera Aulagnier, ibid.; and Suzanne Reichard and Carl Tillman, 'Patterns of parent–child relationship in schizophrenia', *Psychiatry*, 13 (1950), pp. 247–57; Trude

Tietze, 'A study of mothers of schizophrenic patients', *Psychiatry*, 12 (1949), pp. 55–65; and Sophie de Mijolla-Mellor, *La Paranoïa* (Paris: Presses Universitaires de France, 2007). I never knew, see Bruno Bettelheim, *The Empty Fortress*, op. cit., pp. 238–9. Fathers, see W. R. and T. Lidz, 'The family environment of schizophrenic patients', *American Journal of Psychiatry*, 106 (1949), pp. 332–45.

p. 154 I can look, see John Custance, *Wisdom, Madness and Folly*, op. cit., p. 36.

p. 155–6 Early Western research, see Colwyn Trevarthen, 'Conversations with a two-month-old', *New Scientist*, 62 (1974), pp. 230–33. Eastern, see A. N. Sokolov, *Inner Speech and Thought* (New York: Plenum, 1972); Blyuma Zeigarnik, *The Pathology of Thinking* (New York: Consultants Bureau, 1965); and Michael Cole and Irving Maltzman, *A Handbook of Contemporary Soviet Psychology* (New York: Basic Books, 1969). Colwyn Trevarthen, 'Descriptive Analyses of Infant Communicative Behaviour', in H. R. Schaffer (ed.), *Studies in Mother–Infant Interaction* (London: Academic Press, 1977); and Irene Deliege and John Sloboda, *Musical Beginnings* (Oxford: Oxford University Press, 1996).

p. 156–7 Ruth Weir, *Language in the Crib* (The Hague: Mouton, 1962). Paul Guillaume, 'Les débuts de la phrase dans le langage de l'enfant', *Journal de Psychologie*, 24 (1927), pp. 1–25.

p. 157 Similar findings, see S. Pickert, 'Imaginative dialogues in children's early speech', *First Language*, 2 (1981), pp. 5–20. Alison Elliot, *Child Language* (Cambridge: Cambridge University Press, 1981). Imitation, see Stan Kuczaj, *Crib Speech and Language Play* (New York: Springer Verlag, 1982). Native speakers, see Alison Elliot, *Child Language*, op cit.

p. 159 Kraepelin's texts are collected and translated in Frank Heynick, *Language and Its Disturbances in Dreams* (New York: John Wiley, 1993).

p. 160 The look, see Darian Leader, *Stealing the Mona Lisa: What Art Stops Us from Seeing* (London: Faber & Faber, 2002).

p. 161–2 Louis Wolfson, *Le Schizo et les langues*, op. cit., pp. 46–52. Mirror, see Paula Elkisch, 'The psychological significance of the mirror', *Journal of the American Psychoanalytic Association*, 5 (1957), pp. 235–44.

p. 162 Children's games, see Iona and Peter Opie, *The Lore and Language of Schoolchildren* (Oxford: Oxford University Press, 1959).

p. 163 Otto Isakower, 'On the exceptional position of the auditory sphere', *International Journal of Psychoanalysis*, 20 (1939), pp. 340–48.

p. 164 Papin sisters, see Francis Dupré, *La 'Solution' du passage à l'acte: le double crime des soeurs Papin* (Toulouse: Érès, 1984).

p. 164 Blow, see Schreber, *Memoirs*, op. cit., p. 89.

p. 165 Lacan on verbal hallucination, see François Sauvagnat, 'La "Desensorialisation" des hallucinations acoustico-verbales: quelques résultats actuels d'un débat centenaire', in *Polyphonie pour Ivan Fonagy* (Paris: L'Harmattan, 1997), pp. 391–404. See also André Ceillier, 'Du rôle des hallucinations psychiques dans l'exploration de l'inconscient', op. cit., pp. 142–54; and 'Étude sur les variétés du langage automatique', *Annales Médico-Psychologiques*, 12 (1924), pp. 161–74 and 25–6; Bleuler, *Dementia Praecox*, op. cit., pp. 110–11; Henri Grivois, 'Les hallucinations verbales psychomotrices', *L'Évolution Psychiatrique*, 51 (1986), pp. 609–23; the articles collected in *Quarto*; *Les Psychoses*, 28–9 (1987); and Georges Lantéri-Laura, 'Histoire de la clinique des hallucinations', in *Hallucinations, regards croisés* (Paris: Masson, 2002), pp. 15–20.

p. 167 Field of perception, Lacan, *Le Seminaire Livre 5. Les Formations de l'inconscient* (1957–8), ed. J.-A. Miller (Paris: Seuil, 1998), p. 480. This would suggest that Lacan's famous remark in his seminar of 8 April 1975 that in paranoia 'the voice sonorizes the look' is the wrong way round. Against this inversion one could evoke the claim that paranoia is exceedingly rare in the blind, but not uncommon in the deaf. As a counter-example, this is too literal, as a blind person can certainly have the sense that they are being looked at, just as a deaf person can feel that someone's voice singles them out.

p. 167 Glass of milk, Bleuler, *Dementia Praecox*, op. cit., p. 100.

p. 168 Karl Kleist 'Cycloid, Paranoid and Epileptoid Psychoses and the Problem of Degenerative Psychoses' (1928), in Steven Hirsch and Michael Shepherd, *Themes and Variations*, op. cit., pp. 297–331. Gods, see Schreber, *Memoirs*, op. cit., p. 168. For examples in autism, see Leo Kanner, 'Autistic disturbances of affective contact', *Nervous Child*, 2 (1942), pp. 217–50.

Chapter 7

p. 170 Parachute, Marcel Czermak, *Passions de l'objet* (Paris: Éditions de l'Association Freudienne Internationale, 2001), p. 87. Bleuler's critique of

course of psychosis, *Dementia Praecox*, op. cit., footnote to p. 245. For
Lacanian accounts of triggering, see Christian Hoffman, 'Quelques réflexions à propos du déclenchement de la psychose et de ses suppléances dans
le monde contemporain', *Figures de la Psychanalyse*, 9 (2004), pp. 49–61;
François Leguil, 'Le déclenchement d'une psychose', *Ornicar?*, 41 (1987),
pp. 71–5; Pierre Naveau, 'Sur le déclenchement de la psychose', *Ornicar?*,
44 (1988), pp. 77–87; and Alexandre Stevens, 'Déclenchement de la psychose', *Travaux*, 3 (1988), pp. 21–40. On perplexity, see Gustav Störring,
*Wesen und Bedeutung des Symptoms der Ratlosigkeit bei psychischen Erkrankun-
gen* (Leipzig: Thieme, 1939); the papers in 'L'énigme et la psychose', *La
Cause Freudienne*, 23 (1993); and F. Fuentenebro and G. E. Berrios, 'The
predelusional state: a conceptual history', *Comprehensive Psychiatry*, 36
(1995), pp. 251–9. Personal signification, see C. Neisser, 'Erörterungen
über die Paranoia vom klinischen Standpunkte', *Centralblatt für Nerven-
heilkunde und Psychiatrie*, 60 (1892), pp. 1–20.

p. 172 On meaningfulness, see Karl Jaspers, *General Psychopathology*, op. cit.
Bed linen, ibid., p. 601. MacDonald, see Bert Kaplan (ed.), *The Inner
World of Mental Illness*, op. cit., p. 175. Pillow, see John Custance, *Wisdom,
Madness and Folly*, op. cit., p. 72.

p. 172 Renée, *Autobiography of a Schizophrenic Girl*, op. cit., p. 29.

p. 174 Lacan, *De la psychose paranoïaque dans ses rapports avec la personnalité* (1932)
(Paris: Seuil, 1975), pp. 270–71.

p. 175 Hole, see Lacan, *The Seminar of Jacques Lacan, Book* 3, op. cit. Gregory Zilboorg, 'The dynamics of schizophrenic reactions related to
pregnancy and childbirth', *American Journal of Psychiatry*, 85 (1929),
pp. 733–67.

p. 175–6 Sign language, see E. Stanley Abbot, 'What is paranoia?', *American
Journal of Insanity*, 71 (1914), pp. 29–40.

p. 177 Hélène case, see Geneviève Morel, *Sexual Ambiguities*, op. cit., p. 263.

p. 180–81 Freud, *Introductory Lectures on Psychoanalysis* (1916–17), *Standard
Edition*, vol. 16, p. 425. Gregory Bateson, 'A theory of play and phantasy',
Psychiatric Research Reports, 2 (1955), pp. 39–51.

p. 181 Glass tubes, see Paula Elkisch, 'On infantile precursors of the "influ-
encing machine" (Tausk)', op. cit., pp. 219–35. Marguerite Valentine,
'The last resort: some notes on the suicide of a patient', *British Journal of
Psychotherapy*, 20 (2004), pp. 295–306.

p. 185 Marcel Czermak, *Passions de l'objet*, op. cit., p. 99.

p. 186 Denise Sainte Fare Garnot, 'À propos de l'impression d'être immortel', in Marcel Czermak, ibid., pp. 231–45.

p. 187 End of the world, see Freud, *Psychoanalytic Notes on an Autobiographical Account of a Case of Paranoia (Dementia Paranoides)*, op. cit.; and A. Wetzel, 'Das Weltuntergangserlebnis in der Schizophrenie', *Zeitschrift für die gesamte Neurologie und Psychiatrie*, 78 (1922), pp. 403–17.

p. 189 Nathalie Charraud, *Infini et inconscient. Essai sur Georg Cantor* (Paris: Anthropos, 1994), p. 197.

p. 190 Isabelle Robert, 'L'épure d'une vie', *Carnets de Lille*, 5 (2000), pp. 61–3. Brigitte Lemonnier, 'Un enfant maltraité', ibid., pp. 73–7.

p. 193 Cotton, see Robert Whitaker, *Mad in America,* op. cit., pp. 81–2.

Chapter 8

p. 195 Devil, see J. Lévy-Valensi and Boudon, 'Deux cas de délire de persécution à forme demonomaniaque développes chez des débiles à la suite de pratiques magiques', *L'Encéphale*, 3 (1908), pp. 115–19.

p. 197 Taken from the world of the mother, see Lacan, 'On a Question', op. cit., p. 472. Note that Lacan refers here to how the subject 'assumes' rather than 'interprets' the desire of the mother. Ludwig Binswanger, *Schizophrenie* (Pfullingen: Neske, 1957). Louis Wolfson, *Le Schizo et les Langues*, op. cit., p. 75.

p. 197 William Niederland, *The Schreber Case* (New York: Analytic Press, 1984), p. 31.

p. 198 Helene Deutsch, 'Some forms of emotional disturbance and their relationship to schizophrenia', *Psychoanalytic Quarterly*, 11 (1942), pp. 301–21; and Nathaniel Ross, 'The "as if" concept', *Journal of the American Psychoanalytic Association*, 15 (1967), pp. 59–82. See also Paul Hoch and Phillip Polatin, 'Pseudoneurotic forms of schizophrenia', *Psychiatric Quarterly*, 23 (1949), pp. 248–76; and Paul Federn, 'Principles of psychotherapy in latent schizophrenia', *American Journal of Psychotherapy*, 2 (1947), pp. 129–44. Mixture of many shadows, see Hilde Bruch and Stanley Palombo, 'Conceptual problems in schizophrenia', *Journal of Nervous and Mental Disease*, 132 (1961), pp. 114–17.

p. 200 Friend closes door, see Marcel Czermak, *Passions de l'objet*, op. cit., p. 99.

p. 200 Body boundary and Stanley, see Paula Elkisch, 'On infantile precursors of the "influencing machine" (Tausk)', op. cit., pp. 219–35; and 'The Struggle for Ego Boundaries', *American Journal of Psychotherapy*, 5 (1956), pp. 578–602.

p. 201 *Tabula rasa*, see Kurt Eissler, 'Notes upon the emotionality of a schizophrenic patient', op. cit., pp. 199–251.

p. 201 Functional formula, see Geneviève Morel, *Sexual Ambiguities*, op. cit.

p. 202 Esthela Solano-Suarez, 'La clinique des noeuds', *La Cause Freudienne*, 51 (2002), pp. 102–6.

p. 205 Harold Searles, *The Nonhuman Environment*, op. cit.

p. 206 Louis Sass, *Madness and Modernity*, op. cit., p. 395. Bruno Bettelheim, *The Empty Fortress*, op. cit.

p. 207–8 Colette Soler on order and Rousseau, *L'inconscient à ciel ouvert de la psychose*, op. cit.; and *L'Aventure littéraire, ou la psychose inspirée: Rousseau, Joyce, Pessoa* (Paris: Éditions du Champ Lacanien, 2001). Robert Howard, 'James Tilly Matthews in London and Paris 1793: his first peace mission – in his own words', *History of Psychiatry*, 2 (1991), pp. 53–69. Creation, see Fabienne Hulak (ed.), *Pensée psychotique et création de systèmes* (Ramonville: Érès, 2003); and Luis Izcovich, *Les Paranoïaques et la psychanalyse*, op. cit., pp. 290–333.

p. 208 Guy Trobas, 'Le Symbolique alteré', *Ornicar?*, 47 (1988), pp. 80–87.

p. 209 Gérard Pommier, *Le Dénouement d'une analyse*, op. cit., pp. 275–6.

p. 209 Suicidal after eating, Louis Wolfson, *Le Schizo et les langues*, op. cit.

p. 210 Thinner, see M. L. Hayward and J. E. Taylor, 'A schizophrenic patient describes the action of intensive psychotherapy', op. cit., p. 228.

p. 211 Geneviève Morel, *La Loi de la mère* (Paris: Anthropos, 2008). See also Catherine Millot, 'Epiphanies', in Jacques Aubert (ed.), *Joyce avec Lacan* (Paris: Navarin, 1987), pp. 87–95.

p. 213 Marguerite Sechehaye, *Symbolic Realization* (New York: International Universities Press, 1951). On Sechehaye, see Charles Odier, 'Réflexions sur la guérison d'une schizophréne par la "réalisation symbolique"', *L'Évolution Psychiatrique*, 14 (1949), pp. 407–16.

p. 216–17 Manfred Bleuler, *The Schizophrenic Disorders*, op. cit., p. 490. Augustin Ménard, *Voyage au pays des psychoses* (Nîmes: Champ Social Éditions, 2008), pp. 15–17.

p. 221 Éric Laurent, 'Pour la vérité', 'L'expérience psychanalytique des psychoses', *Actes de l'École de la Cause Freudienne* (Paris: 1987), pp. 169–71.

p. 222 Ellen Corin, 'The "Other" of Culture in Psychosis', in Joao Biehl et al., *Subjectivity: Ethnographic Investigations* (Berkeley: University of California Press, 2007), pp. 273–314.

p. 224 Weiss and Freud, see Paul Roazen, *The Historiography of Psychoanalysis* (New Brunswick: Transaction, 2001), p. 182.

Chapter 9

p. 226 Lacan, *De la psychose paranoïaque*, op. cit. Jean Allouch, *Marguerite ou l'Aimée de Lacan* (Paris: EPEL, 1990). See also Marie-Magdeleine Chatel, 'Faute de ravage, une folie de la publication', *Littoral*, 37 (1993), pp. 9–44; and the documents published by Jean Allouch and Danielle Arnoux, 'Historique du cas de Marguerite: suppléments, corrections, lecture', ibid., pp. 173–91. See also Thierry Vincent, 'Le problème du sens dans la psychose: la controverse Lacan–De Clérambault sur la paranoïa', *L'Évolution Psychiatrique*, 56 (1991), pp. 875–85.

p. 227–8 Recently discovered, see Jacques Chazaud, 'Vestiges du passage à Ville-Evrard d'une aliénée devenue illustre', *L'Évolution Psychiatrique*, 55 (1990), pp. 633–5. 'Garçonnière', see Lacan, *De la psychose paranoïaque*, op. cit., p. 221. 'Poétereau', ibid., p. 224.

p. 229–30 Love to hate, ibid., p. 225. C de la N, ibid., pp. 225–6. Secret garden, ibid., p. 227. Mute struggle, ibid., p. 232.

p. 231 Leaves uncured, ibid., p. 161.

p. 232 Her mission, see Lacan, *De la psychose paranoïaque*, op. cit., pp. 166–7.

p. 233–4 Think of the children, see Bert Kaplan (ed.), *The Inner World of Mental Illness*, op. cit., p. 99. Why Duflos, see Lacan, *De la psychose paranoïaque*, op. cit., p. 162. Link of Duflos to Benoît, see Jean Allouch, *Marguerite*, op. cit., pp. 292–306.

p. 234 Helpers, see Henri Maurel, *Le Thème de protection et la pensée morbide* (Paris: Presses Universitaires de France, 1954); and Jules Séglas and P. Bezançon, 'De l'antagonisme des idées délirantes chez les aliénés', *Annales Médico-Psychologiques* (1889), pp. 5–33.

p. 234 Maurice Dide, *Les Idéalistes passionnés* (Paris: Alcan, 1913).

p. 235 Criminal mother, see Lacan, *De la psychose paranoïaque*, op. cit., p. 163.

p. 236 A year or so, see Lacan, 'Motifs du crime paranoïaque: le crime des soeurs Papin', *Le Minotaure*, 3/4 (1933), pp. 26–7.

p. 237–8 Too far, 'Conférences et entretiens dans des univérsities nord-américaines' (1975), in *Scilicet*, 6/7 (Paris: Seuil, 1976), p. 10. Definitive loss, Lacan, *De la psychose paranoïaque*, op. cit., p. 265. Divorce, ibid., p.158.

p. 239 Accounts of the death, see Allouch, *Marguerite*, op. cit., pp. 222–6; and Didier Anzieu, *Une peau pour les pensées* (Paris: Clancier-Génaud, 1986), pp. 15–16. Grief, Lacan, *De la psychose paranoïaque*, op. cit., pp. 222 and 240–41.

p. 239 Fire in wood, ibid., p. 182.

p. 240 Court record, see Allouch, *Marguerite*, op. cit., p. 169.

p. 240 'Je l'ai frappé', see Allouch, *Marguerite*, op. cit., pp. 356 and 169.

p. 242 Dating, see ibid., p. 146. Joan of Arc, Lacan, *De la psychose paranoïaque*, op. cit., p. 176. 'Amoureuse des mots', ibid., p. 191.

p. 245 'L'élue de Dieu', see Didier Anzieu, 'Postface', in Allouch, *Marguerite*, op. cit., p. 553.

Chapter 10

p. 246 Freud, *From the History of an Infantile Neurosis* (1917–19), *Standard Edition*, vol. 17, pp. 1–124; 'The Memoirs of the Wolf-Man', in Muriel Gardiner (ed.), *The Wolf-Man and Sigmund Freud* (London: Hogarth, 1972), pp. 3–132; 'My Recollections of Sigmund Freud', in ibid., pp. 135–52; Ruth Mack Brunswick, 'A Supplement to Freud's "History of an Infantile Neurosis" ', in ibid., pp. 263–307; Muriel Gardiner, 'The Wolf-Man in Later Life', in ibid., pp. 311–66. Karin Obholzer, *The Wolf-Man: Conversations with Freud's Patient – Sixty Years Later* (New York: Continuum, 1982). Patrick Mahoney, *Cries of the Wolf-Man* (New York: International Universities Press, 1984).

p. 247 Diagnosis, see Muriel Gardiner, 'The Wolf-Man in Later Life', op. cit., pp. 358–66.

p. 247 Candid enough, see Freud's letter to Sándor Ferenczi (13 February 1910) in Eva Brabant et al., *Letters to Ferenczi*, vol. 1, p. 138.

p. 249 Went to pieces, Freud, *From the History of an Infantile Neurosis*, op. cit., p. 99. Merciless display, ibid., p. 22. Intense interest, Pankejeff, 'The Memoirs of the Wolf-Man', op. cit., p. 25.

p. 250–51 A woman with whom, ibid., p. 75. In this moment, ibid., p. 86. At the same time, Freud, *From the History of an Infantile Neurosis*, op. cit., p. 20.

p. 252–3 Dread, ibid., p. 25. Anus–vagina, ibid., p. 79. No judgement, ibid., p. 84

p. 254 Calmed down, ibid. p. 85. Fifty years, see Serge Viderman, *La Construction de l'espace analytique* (Paris: Denoël, 1970). Gesticulating, 'The Memoirs of the Wolf-Man', op. cit., p. 5.

p. 255–6 Curious habit, Ruth Mack Brunswick, 'A Supplement to Freud's "History of an Infantile Neurosis"', op. cit., p. 268. Nothing visible, ibid., p. 264. Normal course, 'The Memoirs of the Wolf-Man', op. cit., p. 115.

p. 257 With every person, Muriel Gardiner, 'The Wolf-Man in Later Life', op. cit., p. 324. Nightmare, Gardiner (ed.), *L'Homme aux loups par ses psychanalystes et par lui-même* (Paris: Gallimard, 1981), pp. 375–402 and 381. On the presence of obsessional symptoms in psychosis, see the review by E. Stengel, 'A study of some clinical aspects of the relationship between obsessional neurosis and psychotic reaction types', *Journal of Mental Science*, 91 (1945), pp. 166–87.

p. 258–9 End a letter, see 'The Memoirs of the Wolf-Man', op. cit., p. 78. No reaction, Freud, *From the History of an Infantile Neurosis*, op. cit., p. 23. Mood change, 'The Memoirs of the Wolf-Man', op. cit., p. 46. Contact, ibid., p. 50.

p. 259–61 Trying to understand, Gardiner, 'The Wolf-Man in Later Life', op. cit., p. 359. Appeal, Karin Obholzer, *The Wolf-Man*, op. cit., pp. 28–9. Seek advice, ibid., p. 6. Desperate appeals, ibid., p. 247. Teeth, ibid., p. 80.

p. 261–3 Carefully dressed, Gardiner, 'The Wolf-Man in Later Life', op. cit., p. 358. Contraindicated, ibid., p. 364. No such thing, Karin Obholzer, *The Wolf-Man*, op. cit., p. 51. Discovered land, see Gardiner, 'My Recollections of Sigmund Freud', op. cit., p. 140.

p. 263–4 Alexis, see Brunswick, 'A Supplement to Freud's "History of an Infantile Neurosis"', op. cit., p. 302. Gathered strength, see Obholzer, *The Wolf-Man*, op. cit., p. 56. Incorrect diagnosis, ibid., p. 59. Rank's critique, see Otto Rank, *Technik der Psychoanalyse*, vol. 1 (Vienna: Deuticke, 1926), pp. 142ff. Rank's interpretation of the wolf dream becomes more tenuous when we realize that it recapitulates almost exactly a case he describes earlier in his book, in which a patient has a dream featuring a tree, based, he argues, on the pictures of Freud and his disciples that were on display in his office. Where Rank had a picture of Freud, Freud, he tells us, had a picture of Rank, and it is difficult not to discern in this symmetry the matrix of Rank's own conflict with his master.

p. 265–6 Professor Freud's questions, see Brunswick, 'A Supplement to Freud's "History of an Infantile Neurosis"', op. cit., p. 278. Favourite son, ibid., p. 284. In the first dream, ibid., p. 291. Why do you stare, ibid., p. 289. See the exchange here between Brunswick and Harnik in *Internationale Zeitschrift fur Psychoanalyse*, 16 (1930), pp. 123–9 and 17 (1931), pp. 400–402. Interestingly, the film *The White Sister* contains a scene in which a painting is destroyed.

p. 266–7 He was well, ibid., p. 296. No trace, ibid., p. 263. Terrible nightmare, Gardiner, 'The Wolf-Man in Later Life', op. cit., p. 327. There are discrepancies in the accounts here: see ibid., p. 333.

p. 268 Make Pankejeff psychotic, ibid., p. 364.

p. 269 Well suited, see Gardiner (ed.), *L'Homme aux loups par ses psychanalystes et par lui-même*, op. cit., p. 381.

p. 270 Fixed point, Obholzer, *The Wolf-Man*, op. cit., p. 243. A robber, ibid., p. 101. Father and son, ibid., p. 162.

p. 271 Measure of recovery, see 'The Memoirs of the Wolf-Man', op. cit., p. 129. As soon as possible, Gardiner, 'The Wolf-Man in Later Life', op. cit., p. 348. Mediate between them, Obholzer, *The Wolf-Man*, op. cit., p. 121. Through wall, see Brunswick, 'A Supplement to Freud's "History of an Infantile Neurosis"', op. cit., p. 289.

p. 272 Dying words, see *L'Homme aux loups par ses psychanalystes et par lui-même*, op. cit., p. 385.

Chapter 11

For this chapter, I have used the following sources: Dame Janet Smith's Shipman Inquiry, at www.the-shipman-inquiry.org.uk; 'Harold Shipman's Clinical Practice 1974–1998', Chief Medical Officer's Report (Department of Health, 2001); Mikaela Sitford, *Addicted to Murder: The True Story of*

Dr Harold Shipman (London: Virgin, 2000); Wensley Clarkson, *Evil Beyond Belief* (London: John Blake, 2005); Carole Peters, *Harold Shipman: Mind Set on Murder* (London: Carlton, 2005); and Brian Whittle and Jean Ritchie, *Harold Shipman: Prescription for Murder*, 2nd edn (London: Time Warner, 2005).

p. 274 Badcock, see Whittle and Ritchie, *Harold Shipman: Prescription for Murder*, op. cit.; and 'Shipman hooked on death', *Sun* (14 January 2004) and *The New York Times* (2 February 2000).

p. 274 He could be psychotic, see Shipman Inquiry, p. 188.

p. 274 Not psychotic, see Jeremy Laurance, 'Shipman "may be sent to Broadmoor"', *Independent* (2 February 2000), and Whittle and Ritchie, *Harold Shipman: Prescription for Murder*, op. cit., p. 399.

p. 276 He was a saint, see Clarkson, *Evil Beyond Belief*, op. cit., p. 50.

p. 277 Catastrophic, ibid., p. 73.

p. 284 Dictated by his fear, see Shipman Inquiry, p. 191.

p. 285 Poison his body, see Whittle and Ritchie, *Harold Shipman: Prescription for Murder*, op. cit., p. 270.

p. 286 Best doctor in Hyde, ibid., p. 185. Underperforming, see Shipman Inquiry, p. 184.

p. 286 Most expensive, see Whittle and Ritchie, *Harold Shipman: Prescription for Murder*, op. cit., p. 312.

p. 288 Too many patients, Clarkson, *Evil Beyond Belief*, op. cit., p. 125.

p. 292 Trial letter (13 January 1999), retrieved from www.criminalprofiling.com.

p. 293 Cellmate letter (26 February 1999) to David and Mavis Stott.

p. 293 My normality, see Whittle and Ritchie, *Harold Shipman: Prescription for Murder*, op. cit., p. 341.

Chapter 12

p. 294–5 On communities, see John Gale et al., *Therapeutic Communities for Psychosis, Philosophy, History and Clinical Practice* (London: Routledge, 2008). Piera Aulagnier, *The Violence of Interpretation*, op. cit., p. 168. On variety of therapies, see Yrjö Alanen et al. (eds), *Psychotherapeutic Approaches to Schizophrenic Psychoses*, op. cit.

p. 296 Existential wager, see Marguerite Sechehaye, 'Introduction', in Arthur Burton (ed.), *Psychotherapy of the Psychoses*, op. cit., p. 7. Frieda Fromm-Reichmann, 'Notes on the development of treatment of schizophrenics by psychoanalytic psychotherapy', *Psychiatry*, 11 (1948), pp. 263–73.

p. 297 Arthur Burton (ed.), *Psychotherapy of the Psychoses*, op. cit. Helm Stierlin, 'The adaptation to the "stronger" person's reality: some aspects of the symbiotic relationship of the schizophrenic', *Psychiatry*, 22 (1959), pp. 143–53. Lewis Hill, *Psychotherapeutic Intervention in Schizophrenia*, op. cit.; and Gregory Zilboorg, 'Affective reintegration in the schizophrenias', *Archives of Neurology and Psychiatry*, 24 (1930), pp. 335–47. On ideals, see Lewis Hill, *Psychotherapeutic Intervention in Schizophrenia*, op. cit., p. 57.

p. 297 Idea of future, see Gérard Pommier, *Le Dénouement d'une analyse* (1987) (Paris: Flammarion, 1996). Colette Soler, *L'Inconscient à ciel ouvert de la psychose*, op. cit.

p. 298 Kurt Eissler, 'Limitations to the psychotherapy of schizophrenia', op. cit., p. 390.

p. 298 Lewis Hill, *Psychotherapeutic Intervention in Schizophrenia*, op. cit., p. 4.

p. 298 Falsification, see Jacob Arlow, 'Discussion of Dr Fromm-Reichmann's Paper', in Eugene Brody and Frederick Redlich (eds), *Psychotherapy with Schizophrenics*, op. cit., pp. 112–20.

p. 301 Alfredo Zenoni, 'The Psychoanalytic Clinic in Institution: Psychosis', available at www.ch-freudien-be.org/Papers/index.html.

p. 301 Ellen Corin and Gilles Lauzon, 'Positive withdrawal and the quest for meaning', *Psychiatry*, 55 (1992), pp. 266–78.

p. 301 Lacan, *De la psychose paranoïaque*, op. cit., p. 288.

p. 305 See Harry Stack Sullivan, 'The modified psychoanalytic treatment of schizophrenia', *American Journal of Psychiatry*, 11 (1931), pp. 519–36; *Schizophrenia as a Human Process* (New York: Norton, 1962); and François Sauvagnat, 'Secrétaire de l'aliéné aujourd'hui', *Ornicar?* digital, 76 (1999).

p. 306 Joey's machines, Bruno Bettelheim, *The Empty Fortress*, op. cit., p. 260.

p. 307 Content interpretations, see Frieda Fromm-Reichmann, 'Some aspects of psychoanalytic psychotherapy with schizophrenics', in Eugene Brody and Frederick Redlich (eds), *Psychotherapy with Schizophrenics*, op. cit., pp. 89–111.

p. 308 Alaska, reported in Alphonse De Waehlens and Wilfried Ver Eecke, *Phenomenology and Lacan on Schizophrenia, after the Decade of the Brain*, op. cit., p. 83.

p. 308 Historicity, see Werner Mendel, 'A Phenomenological Theory of Schizophrenia', op. cit., pp. 106–55 and 149.

p. 310 Harold Searles, *The Nonhuman Environment*, op. cit., pp. 302–3.

p. 311 Weigert 'The psychotherapy of the affective psychoses', pp. 349–76, in Arthur Burton (ed.), *Psychotherapy of the Psychoses*, op. cit., p. 374.

p. 311 Alfredo Zenoni, 'La mesure de la psychose', *Quarto*, 80/1, 2004, pp. 17–24.

p. 311 Hating, see M. L. Hayward and J. E. Taylor, 'A schizophrenic patient describes the action of intensive psychotherapy', op. cit., p. 218.

p. 312 Yrjö Alanen, *Schizophrenia*, op. cit., pp. 6–7.

p. 313 I and You, Renée, *Autobiography of a Schizophrenic Girl*, op. cit., p. 52.

p. 314 Whatever the therapist does, see Herman Nunberg, 'The course of the libidinal conflict in a case of schizophrenia' (1921), in *Practice and Theory of Psychoanalysis* (New York: International Universities Press, 1948), pp. 24–59.

p. 315 Knight's list, see Eugene Brody and Frederick Redlich (eds), *Psychotherapy with Schizophrenics*, op. cit., pp. 15–16.

p. 316 Helm Stierlin, 'The adaptation to the "stronger" person's reality', op. cit., pp. 143–52 and 149. Escape, see Silvano Arieti, *Interpretation of Schizophrenia*, op. cit., p. 560.

p. 316–17 Gertrud Schwing, *A Way to the Soul of the Mentally Ill* (1940) (New York: International Universities Press, 1954). Narrow path, see Arthur Burton, 'Paradox and Choice on Schizophrenia', in Burton (ed.), *Case Studies in Counseling and Psychotherapy* (New Jersey: Prentice-Hall, 1959), pp. 257–81. Gérard Pommier, 'Du langage d'organe à l'amour du Nom: le point noeud du transfert dans les psychoses', *La Clinique Lacanienne*, 15 (2009), pp. 115–34.

p. 318–19 Mortifying erotomania, see Lacan, 'Présentation des *Mémoires d'un névropathe*' (1966) in *Autres Écrits* (Paris: Seuil, 2001), pp. 213–17. Yjrö Alanen, *Schizophrenia*, op. cit., p. 212. Witness, see Colette Soler, 'Quelle place pour l'analyste?', *Actes de l'École de la Cause Freudienne*, 13 (1987), pp. 29–31; and Joseph Attié, 'Le psychanalyste à l'école de la psychose', *Pas Tant*, 13 (1986), pp. 5–13.

p. 320 Arthur Burton, 'The Quest for the Golden Mean: A Study in Schizophrenia', in *Psychotherapy of the Psychoses*, op. cit., pp. 172–207, p. 185.

p. 321 Marriage, see Arthur Burton, 'The Alchemy of Schizophrenia', in *Schizophrenia as a Life Style*, op. cit., pp. 36–105 and 89.

p. 321–2 Françoise Davoine, Confer seminar, Tavistock Centre (5 June 2010). Beginnings and endings, see Arthur Burton, 'The Alchemy of Schizophrenia', op. cit., p. 81.

Afterword

p. 324 Recent review, see John Read et al., 'Prejudice and schizophrenia: a review of the "mental illness is like any other" approach', *Acta Psychiatrica Scandinavica*, 114 (2006), pp. 235–54; M. C. Angermeyer and H. Matschinger, 'Causal beliefs and attitudes to people with schizophrenia: trend analysis based on data from two population surveys in Germany', *British Journal of Psychiatry*, 186 (2005), pp. 331–4. WHO study, Liz Sayce and Claire Curran, 'Tackling Social Exclusion across Europe', in Martin Knapp et al., *Mental Health Policy and Practice across Europe*, op. cit., pp. 34–59.

p. 325 First eugenic country, see Robert Whitaker, *Mad in America*, op. cit., p. 60; Ian Robert Dowbiggin, *Keeping America Sane* (Ithaca: Cornell University Press, 1997); Stefan Kuhl, *The Nazi Connection: Eugenics, American Racism and German National Socialism* (Oxford and New York: Oxford University Press, 1994); and Allan Chase, *The Legacy of Malthus* (New York: Knopf, 1975).

p. 326 Us and them, see Helm Stierlin, 'Contrasting attitudes towards the psychoses in Europe and the United States', *Psychiatry*, 21 (1958), pp. 141–7.

p. 327 Mary Loudon, *Relative Stranger* (London, Canongate, 2006), p. 334. Waste of time, Diane Lefevre, Confer seminar, Tavistock Centre (5 June 2010). More mature, see Peter Fonagy and Anthony Bateman, *Psychotherapy for Borderline Personality Disorder* (Oxford: Oxford University Press, 2004), pp. 123, 145 and 220.

p. 328–9 Jacques Hochmann, *Histoire de la Psychiatrie* (Paris: Presses Universitaires de France, 2004). Anna Freud Centre, as reported in *The Times*

(12 May 2007). Peter Fonagy, 'Psychotherapy meets neuroscience', *Psychiatric Bulletin*, 28 (2004), pp. 357–9.

p. 329–30 Letting the drug be enough, see Don Jackson, *Myths of Madness*, op. cit., p. 74. Prophecy, see Nathaniel Lehrman, 'Rethinking Schizophrenia', *Ethical Human Psychology and Psychiatry*, 8 (2006), pp. 69–76. Container, see Yrjö Alanen, *Schizophrenia*, op. cit., p. 188.